1941

The America that Went to War

WILLIAM M. CHRISTIE

Carrel Books

Library of Congress Cataloging-in-Publication Data is available on file.

Cover design by Rain Saukas
Cover photo credits: Library of Congress

ISBN: 978-1-63144-055-7
Ebook ISBN: 978-1-63144-054-0

Printed in the United States of America

CONTENTS

INTRODUCTION v

CHAPTER 1   January: Politics   1

CHAPTER 2   February: Popular Entertainment   31

CHAPTER 3   March: Art, Education, and Literature   56

CHAPTER 4   April: Social Change   76

CHAPTER 5   May: The War Over There   91

CHAPTER 6   June: The Great Debate   116

CHAPTER 7   July: Sports   150

CHAPTER 8   August: Leisure Time and Travel   177

CHAPTER 9   September: Preparedness   207

CHAPTER 10   October: Labor and Business   235

CHAPTER 11   November: Home Life   260

CHAPTER 12   December: The End of Peace   289

NOTES 311

BIBLIOGRAPHY 322

ACKNOWLEDGMENTS 338

INDEX 340

Introduction

On the evening of December 2, 1941, the Columbia Broadcasting System hosted a dinner at the Waldorf Astoria in New York honoring Edward R. Murrow and his wife, Janet. The couple had just returned from London, where Murrow had been broadcasting for CBS since before the beginning of the war. In that time he had become far and away the overseas radio correspondent most widely heard throughout the United States. After listening to the various tributes given him this evening, Murrow responded with a short talk describing Britain and the war as he saw them. In his talk he offered three questions the British were constantly asking themselves: "If America comes in, will she stay in? Does she have any appetite for the greatness that is being thrust upon her? Does she realize that this world or what is left of it will be run from either Berlin or Washington?"

As Murrow posed these questions to his American audience, a Japanese fleet was already approaching Pearl Harbor with the airplanes, bombs, and torpedoes that would force the answers on a somewhat unwilling and thoroughly unprepared country. Yet the very fact that these questions could still be asked in the late fall of that year is itself an indication of how different America was from the country that less than two years later invaded the continent of Europe, not to mention the America that dropped the atomic bomb, drew the line in Korea, and produced transistors, microwaves, rock and roll, the civil rights movement, untold prosperity, and untold anxiety over the next quarter century. It is simply not possible to understand what we became without first understanding what we were.

For America, the year 1941 marked the most decisive turning point in the twentieth century. On December 7 the nation was thrust into a position of world leadership from which it would never escape. Isolation from the rest of the world and an inward-looking concern with our own affairs without reference to what happened elsewhere were no longer options. During this year we were consumed by a debate over our place in the world. Finally, at the beginning of December, Japan, Germany, and Italy resolved the debate for us.

Even internally 1941 was a year of great changes. As the nation emerged from the Depression and reveled in the prosperity brought on by defense spending, the competing interests of business, labor, and government jostled with one another to define their new power relationships. Social institutions, too, began to change as African Americans demanded their fair share of the American promise. New forms of communication, especially radio, began to pull together the disparate parts of the country.

Nineteen forty-one was also a year of excitement that engaged the attention of the public. Newspapers and radio kept people up-to-date while the Royal Navy chased the German battleship *Bismarck* across the North Atlantic. The nation—and the world—gasped when Hitler audaciously invaded Russia. At home racing fans thrilled as a remarkable colt won the Triple Crown, baseball fans watched a young outfielder hit safely in 56 consecutive games, and boxing fans saw Joe Louis nearly give away his World Championship before finally knocking out Billy Conn.

Perhaps the hardest thing for people to grasp today is how different America was in 1941. We could afford to isolate ourselves from the rest of the world in part because we were economically self-sufficient. Not only did we produce enough food to feed ourselves and still have plenty left for export, we also produced 61 percent of the world's oil, meeting all of our own needs and making a good profit from what we exported (including our exports to Japan). Domestically, the nuclear family, with a working husband and a wife at home, was the unchallenged foundation of social order. Our vision was circumscribed by the limits of the regions in which we lived. Most people never visited other parts of the country, and foreign lands existed only as photographs in *LIFE* or *National Geographic*.

In this book I have tried to present a picture of the United States as we were and as we saw ourselves in the last year of isolation and the last year of peace. I have tried to present the history of that year as we experienced it, allowing readers to think themselves back three-quarters of a century to understand the country that would be completely transformed by World War II. To this end I have made some decisions that deserve a bit of explanation. In the first place, whenever money is discussed, it will be in terms of 1941 dollars. An average worker supported his family on about $2,500 a year. A loaf of bread cost 8¢ and a quart of milk cost 13¢. Salaries and prices have not increased evenly over the years, but readers can make comparisons by using the Consumer Price Index. On average, items costing $1.00 in January of 1941 would cost $16.80 in January of 2016. In addition, some of my terminology may seem out of date. I have tried to write in language that reflects the usage of 1941. Modern terminology, and especially modern slang, has been avoided wherever possible. Some readers may be struck by references to African Americans as Negroes. Negro was the normal respectful term used in 1941 and appears in quotations from the period. In deference to more modern sensibilities, the term African American is used in the main text. References to ethnicity in general were much more common, and seldom were they resented. Finally, I have tried wherever possible to avoid writing prospective history. Harry Truman was a Senator from Missouri who spent the year investigating defense contractors. Thurgood Marshall was an N.A.A.C.P. attorney who was arguing an important discrimination case in the federal courts. Lieutenant Colonel Dwight Eisenhower was Chief of Staff of the Third Army. Their subsequent careers are not a part of this story. I have tried to avoid the temptation to stand in 1941 and peer into the future.

To this principle I offer here one exception. In Chapter 11 I discuss the pending increases in income tax rates and how they affected average Americans. It is worthwhile to add a few points of comparison between 1941 and 2016 so readers can see just how different the overall tax structure was before World War II. In 1941 federal excise taxes, corporate taxes, and personal income taxes brought in about 88 percent of all federal revenue, with the relatively new Social Security tax bringing in only about 12 percent. Excise taxes (liquor, tobacco, gasoline) brought in the largest amount, about one third of the total. Today personal income taxes and payroll taxes (Social Security and Medicare) together account for 81 percent of federal tax revenue. Excise taxes and corporate taxes bring in only about 9 percent each. Even more, the personal income tax structure is much more level today than it was in 1941. With adjustments for inflation, a person with a taxable income of $425,000 today pays a marginal tax rate of 39.6 percent, the top marginal rate. The tax rate on an equivalent income in 1941 was 51 percent, and the top marginal rate was 81 percent. This difference in the distribution of the tax burden should be borne in mind when thinking about the impact of the tax increases discussed in Chapter 11.

It is worth noting that this book is not arranged as a sequential narrative of the events of 1941. Others have undertaken that task, and you will find their works cited in the bibliography. Rather, the present work should be seen as a series of vignettes, arranged around twelve broad themes. It is my hope that through these vignettes, readers can think themselves back into the year 1941 and begin to imagine what it was like to live in the America of that time. As an organizing device for these themes, I have chosen for each month of the year an event or activity that occurred during that month and used it to introduce the thematic chapter to which it relates. So, for example, the story of American politics in 1941 begins with January 20, the date of President Roosevelt's third inaugural. The story of popular entertainment begins with the February 27 Academy Awards ceremony in Los Angeles. So the year continues, concluding, of course, with the December attack on Pearl Harbor and the immediate effects of that attack on all other aspects of American life. It should also be noted that in some cases it has been necessary to extend the narrative back into 1940 or even earlier. We do not live exclusively in the present. Our vision of the world right now is conditioned by our memories of recent events, and the same need for context applies to the story of 1941.

A final note is needed on the cultural unity of America (or lack thereof). Communication was much weaker then than now. Newspapers carried some national and international news, and many people subscribed to one or more national magazines. Radio reached most homes, bringing popular entertainment and a good measure of educational programming. But to an extent almost unimaginable today, people's views were shaped by the regions where they lived, regions where they spent their whole lives and which they seldom left, even on vacation. In many ways America in 1941 was four different countries. Boundaries were fuzzy and shifting, but the regional differences were clear.

To mark the (rough) boundaries of the North, draw a line from Chicago to St. Louis and thence to Washington. This region was further subdivided into the East (east of the Appalachians) and the Midwest. Despite certain differences between the two subregions, the North was the unified economic and cultural center of the country. It contained fourteen of the nation's seventeen major symphony orchestras, most of its radio stations, all of its television stations, and all of its major league baseball teams. The nation's political power was concentrated in Washington, and economic power was concentrated in New York.

South of this region and stretching west to the middle of Texas was the South, an area almost the exact opposite of the North. By virtually every measure imaginable, the South was the poorest, weakest, most backward region in the country. An insistence on maintaining a rigid system of racial segregation consumed energy and resources that the South could ill afford. While the rest of the country took its first halting steps toward racial justice and equality, the South clung tenaciously to the ways of the nineteenth century. And those ways were anything but moonlight and magnolias.

Between these regions and the Rocky Mountains lay the West, a vast area rich in natural resources and short in people and rainfall. The few inhabitants were sturdy, independent folk, tending to be very conservative in their outlook. They spent their energy wresting a living from the land, and they wanted no part of troubles overseas.

The Pacific Coast was almost like a detached part of the North, with the remaining orchestras, several fine universities, good newspapers and radio stations, strong cultural links across the Pacific, and first-class baseball in the Pacific Coast League. The principal difficulty was communication with the rest of the country. Train travel to the East took days, air travel was terribly expensive, and even telephone calls cost enough to remain a rare indulgence.

Although each of these regions had developed and retained its own distinctive characteristics, the country as a whole was sufficiently unified that it is possible to paint a general picture of America just before it was finally and fully thrust onto the world stage. That picture, with its nuances and shadings of money and race and region, is the purpose of this book.

CHAPTER 1

January: Politics

ARMED SECRET SERVICE agents sat in the gallery of the church when the president arrived for prayers. Heavily armed federal agents kept watch on rooftops. Cars with armed Secret Service agents flanked the presidential limousine on the way to the Capitol. Armed Secret Service agents stood on the roof of the Capitol, where for the first time ever visitors were not permitted.

Americans had never seen anything like it. The level of security for Franklin Roosevelt's third inaugural was completely unprecedented.

War was raging across the world. America's possible role in that conflict was being hotly debated in the halls of Congress and across the country. For the first (and only) time in history, an American president was being inaugurated for a third term. And this particular president was both widely admired and widely hated.

In a year filled with passions and uncertainties, many people could remember the day forty years earlier when President William McKinley had fallen to an assassin's bullet. On this Inauguration Day the Secret Service was taking no chances. Monday, January 20, 1941, was a bitterly cold day in Washington. The high temperature that afternoon was only 33°; and it was closer to 28° at 10:30 in the morning when President Franklin D. Roosevelt left the White House for the brief trip to St. John's Church on H Street, just on the other side of Lafayette Park. The sky was clear, and a sharp wind blowing off the Potomac River made the air feel even colder. As on previous Inauguration Days, President Roosevelt attended a brief prayer service before going to the Capitol to be sworn in for a new term. The mood this day, however, was different from the hopeful atmosphere that had surrounded his first inaugural in the Depression year of 1933. It was even more different from the triumphal atmosphere following his landslide re-election in 1936. The chill in the air matched the subdued, cautious feelings in the crowds that gathered for this unprecedented occasion.

At noon the inaugural party appeared on the freshly painted platform on the East Front of the Capitol. As the Marine Band played "Hail to the Chief," Roosevelt entered, leaning on the arm of his son James, a captain in the Marines. The Capitol Plaza was filled, but not crowded. *Newsweek*'s estimate of a million spectators was surely much too high. Vice President Henry A. Wallace was sworn in by his predecessor, "Cactus Jack" Garner. Then Chief Justice Charles Evans Hughes, white-haired, seventy-eight years old, himself once a candidate for president (losing narrowly to Wilson in 1916), now only five months from retirement, stepped forward to administer the oath to Roosevelt. It took less than a minute, and the president turned to address the crowd:

> On each national day of inauguration since 1789, the people have renewed their sense of dedication to the United States. In Washington's day the task of the people was to create and weld together a nation. In Lincoln's day the task of the people was to preserve that Nation from disruption from within. In this day the task of the people is to save that Nation and its institutions from disruption from without.

The speech, a little under 1,400 words, was not one of Roosevelt's better efforts. It was full of generalities, mainly a paean to democracy and the spirit of America. He was interrupted five times by muffled applause, muffled by the gloves and mittens everyone was wearing. At the end he waved his top hat to the crowed, turned, and left the Capitol. At the White House he reviewed an inaugural parade that was also different from the cheerful events of the past. There were the usual contingents of West Point cadets and Annapolis midshipmen, the usual cars loaded with dignitaries. But the bulk of the parade was a demonstration of America's military might, such as it was. Tanks and armored cars were mixed with light and heavy field artillery. They drove by fast, as if eager to get back to business. The president, too, was eager. As soon as the parade was over, he returned to the White House and got back to work.

Politics in the America of 1941, as has been true for most of the past century, was a bafflingly complex array of parties and alliances, interest groups and personalities. To be understood properly, it must be considered separately on the national, state, and local levels, where party affiliations and personal alliances had very different meanings. Sometimes these interests and affiliations aligned; but more often they crossed in complex ways, making it difficult to construct one unified picture of the American political scene.

On the national level there were three principal political viewpoints represented in the two main political parties. The contrast between the mainstream Democratic and Republican parties had for many years been largely economic. Throughout the twentieth century, the center of American political and economic opinion shifted back and forth. In periods of great prosperity, like the 1920s, when millions dreamed of gaining riches from speculation in the stock market (though only 1 percent of Americans were active in the market), corporate America was held in something like reverence. During the Great Depression opinion shifted strongly toward government action to help the working class. Wherever the center lay, however, the Republican Party by and large supported corporate interests, while the Democratic Party generally supported the workers. Of course, such a sweeping generalization had many exceptions. There were Democrats whose economic beliefs were as conservative as those of any Republican. And the Republican

Party had a progressive wing, in the tradition of Teddy Roosevelt, that sought to restrain the corporations and benefit the workers.

Yet there was still a third tradition, strongly populist in character, that distrusted all government intervention and regulation. Big business and organized labor were equally regarded with suspicion if not outright hostility. The stronghold of this sentiment was in the South, and members of Congress who held this viewpoint constituted the Southern wing of the Democratic Party. For cultural reasons associated with this region, the Southern Democrats showed two additional characteristics that distinguished them. First, they strongly supported the American military establishment. During all the debates on intervention and rearmament, only one Southern Democrat, Senator Robert Reynolds of North Carolina, consistently opposed the president. All the rest backed the defense buildup and the president's interventionist actions. In the second place, Southern culture and Southern politics were solidly grounded in racial segregation. Any proposed legislation, economic or social, would be measured against the Southern racial standard. As a result, Roosevelt often could not move as far or as fast as he and other Northern Democrats would have liked. The Southern faction in the party was strong enough to block any congressional action that was perceived as a threat to Southern institutions.

Apart from their racial views and their dislike of organized labor, the Southern populists found themselves more in agreement with the mainstream Democratic Party than with the Republicans on both domestic and foreign affairs. Their affiliation with the Democrats was also strengthened by memories of the Civil War and Reconstruction, when the Republicans had been the party of the abolitionists. With few exceptions, then, the Republican Party was not a factor in Southern politics.

Despite the persistent economic division between the two major parties, presidential elections could and did turn on non-economic issues; and in 1940 the economy was not the dominant issue that it had been in 1932. Of course, Democrats could point to a strong economic record that was only slightly compromised by the recession of 1937. In fact, the employment picture was improving to such a degree that Republicans were unable to make the economy a direct issue in the campaign. Instead they used the proxy issue of big government intruding into people's private lives, a reflection of the constitutional tradition of weak federal government. New Deal programs could not be attacked as having no benefit to ordinary people. They clearly had. But they could be attacked as an improper and perhaps unconstitutional extension of federal power at the expense of the states and of private interests.

Prominent in the campaign was an issue that was highly emotional for many people. Franklin Roosevelt was running for a third term, and there was a strong feeling that George Washington's two-term tradition should be respected. All over the country, and especially in the Republican Midwest, one could see political campaign buttons saying, "NO THIRD TERMITES." Democrats responded with their own buttons saying, "BETTER A THIRD TERMER THAN A THIRD RATER." But resistance to a third term was muted by the international situation and the threat that war could come to this country. The Republicans had limited themselves on this issue by nominating their most strongly interventionist figure, Wendell Willkie. New York District Attorney Tom Dewey, who had built his reputation as a corruption fighter, had gone into the 1940 Republican convention with a lead in delegates and an air of invincibility. But a carefully orchestrated "spontaneous" demonstration for Willkie had stampeded the convention and taken the nomination away from Dewey. As a Wall Street lawyer, Willkie appealed to the conservative economic interests in the G.O.P., but the economic planks of the Republican platform sounded like little more than some uninspired tinkering with the Democratic agenda. As an interventionist, Willkie also had difficulty making defense preparedness a significant issue. He strongly supported rearmament as the best way to keep America out of the European war, and his interventionism limited his ability to attack the president. The best he could manage was the assertion that Roosevelt was moving recklessly toward confrontation with Germany and that the re-election of Roosevelt would guarantee our involvement in the war. Weak as the charge sounded, it had enough of an effect that Roosevelt had to respond. In Boston on October 30 he came out with a categorical statement that his critics enthusiastically repeated after Pearl Harbor:

> And while I am talking to you mothers and fathers, I give you one more assurance. I have said this before, but I shall say it again and again and again: Your boys are not going to be sent into any foreign wars.

As Americans began to feel the dangers of war coming ever nearer, they voted by a rather narrow margin not to change leadership in a time of uncertainty.

The election of 1940 and Roosevelt's third inaugural thus marked a significant turning point in American politics. Until then, most Americans had held a view of the federal government in general and of the presidency itself that was very much like that of the authors of the Constitution a hundred and fifty years earlier. In this view government was a necessary evil that should be kept as small and weak as possible. Within the governmental structure that the Constitution created, the president was far from the central figure. The very structure of the government emphasized the power of Congress to limit the power of the presidency. Yet as Harold Laski pointed out in *The American Presidency*, "the Congress is not a body capable of constructive leadership; the functions it performs most effectively are those of criticism and investigation rather than responsibility for the direction of affairs." In the minds of most Americans, the Great Depression was a crisis that called for powerful presidential leadership; and the acquiescence of Congress in Roosevelt's legislative program during the first one hundred days of his presidency supported Laski's viewpoint.

Initially the difficulties of Roosevelt's second term seemed like a renewal of the old pattern. Congress began to reassert its power and the president had more and more difficulty advancing his program. But the storm clouds over Europe and the ensuing debate over America's role in the world (Chapter 6) caused people to start to rethink the nature of government and the presidency. Gradually they perceived a need for continuing strength in the White House, not just strength in time of acute crisis. They also perceived a need for presidential strength in the face of congressional opposition. In Laski's words, they came to understand that "no democracy in the modern world can afford a scheme of government the basis of which is the inherent right of the legislature to paralyze the executive power." The need for consistent leadership from a strong president was, as much as anything else, at the heart of Roosevelt's election victory. The American people knew what they had in F.D.R. What they did not know was what continuity of strong leadership for another four years might mean to the American political system. In many ways the political life of 1941 was an attempt to figure out the answer to that question.

The sense of threat from without was perhaps inevitably matched by concern with threats from within. Martin Dies was a young congressman representing Texas's Second Congressional District. He was an ambitious man whom the *New Republic* described as "in a great hurry to make a national reputation." With the rise of the Nazis in Germany and the admiration some Americans were expressing for Hitler and Mussolini, Dies thought he had found his cause. Beginning in 1932 he steadily introduced bills, which just as steadily died, to establish a House committee to look into un-American activities being carried on in this country by outside agitators. In 1938, with tensions increasing in Europe, his persistence paid off; and the Special House Committee for the Investigation of Un-American Activities was established for a period of two years. Dies was made chairman, and he asked for a budget of $100,000 to carry out his investigation. The House allowed him a quarter of that. He began hearings in August to ferret out subversives and expose their activities. Although he repeatedly said he would not allow the committee "to become a three ring circus," he soon established a pattern of receiving all manner of unsubstantiated allegations, no matter how ridiculous they might seem. People would be named and their reputations tarnished, but they seldom had a chance to respond.

Although Dies began by looking into the activities of Fritz Kuhn's German American Bund, he soon found he could get more public attention by concentrating on Communists. At this point others began using Dies for their own purposes. The American Federation of Labor, which claimed to represent the whole American labor movement, was engaged in a bitter dispute with John L. Lewis and his breakaway Congress of Industrial Organizations (Chapter 10). A number of open or covert members of the Communist Party were involved with the C.I.O., although they never came close to controlling the organization. But their mere presence offered an opportunity for representatives of the A.F. of L. to go before the Dies Committee and use it as a forum for attacking the C.I.O. Dies's methods were sloppy in the extreme, and he overreached badly when his chief investigator, J. B. Matthews, released a list of Hollywood stars who allegedly supported Communist organizations. The inclusion of twelve-year-old Shirley Temple on the list caused no little hilarity and led Dies to be more circumspect thereafter.

By 1941 the public was beginning to lose interest in the Dies Committee, and Dies himself was diverted by a new opportunity to advance his political career. In April Texas senator Morris Sheppard died, and a special election was scheduled to fill his seat. Dies was one of sixteen candidates on the ballot, and he campaigned vigorously. But Governor Lee "Pappy" O'Daniel was extremely popular in the rural areas of East Texas that were Dies's home base. The more progressive urban votes were captured by Congressman Lyndon Johnson, who ran on a platform of support for the New Deal. O'Daniel won the election, and Dies finished a distant fourth.

As the nation entered 1941, national politics centered on one overarching issue, defense preparedness and intervention in the European war (Chapter 6). In its January 13 issue, *Newsweek* noted that the new Congress would have to deal with few important issues unrelated to defense. Martin Dies would ask for his committee extension and a $1,000,000 budget, the administration would ask for an increase in Social Security benefits, and a new antilynching bill was expected to be introduced. But overshadowing all these would be the debate on the Lend-Lease bill early in the year, followed by appropriations for a tremendous growth in defense expenditures. The latter would in turn lead to the largest increase in personal income taxes that Americans had seen.

The president noted the overmastering importance of the international crisis in his annual State of the Union message to Congress on January 6. After reviewing the progress of Nazi aggression in Europe and the importance of British naval power in securing American defense, Roosevelt asserted that the American republics, not just the United States, were in grave danger.

> That is why this Annual Message to the Congress is unique in our history. That is why every member of the Executive Branch of the Government and every member of the Congress face great responsibility and great accountability. The need of the moment is that our actions and our policy should be devoted primarily—almost exclusively—to meeting this foreign peril. For all our domestic problems are now a part of the great emergency.

Then, after noting that the election had not turned on any substantial difference over international policy, Roosevelt called for ever increasing efforts to shore up the country's defense. He explicitly referred to the role of Britain in keeping the war away from American shores and endorsed the Lend-Lease bill that would be introduced four days later. Then, after a brief mention of some domestic social programs he would like to see strengthened, the president ended with the part of the speech that is most remembered.

> In the future days, which we seek to make secure, we look forward to a world founded upon four essential human freedoms.
>
> The first is freedom of speech and expression—everywhere in the world.
>
> The second is freedom of every person to worship God in his own way—everywhere in the world.

The third is freedom from want—which, translated into world terms, means economic understandings which will secure to every nation a healthy peacetime life for its inhabitants— everywhere in the world.

The fourth is freedom from fear—which, translated into world terms, means a world-wide reduction of armaments to such a point and in such a thorough fashion that no nation will be in a position to commit an act of physical aggression against any neighbor—anywhere in the world.

With this the national political agenda for the year was set.

When one turns to politics on the state level, a very different pattern of alignments emerges. In the South, always a special case, the dominance of the Democratic Party meant, in effect, that there were no true political parties. There were merely shifting rivalries and alliances that had to be worked out within the ostensible framework of a single party. Memories are long in the South, and "The War" referred not to World War I, nor to the Spanish-American War or the Indian Wars. The War, capitalized, was the Civil War, often referred to as the War of Northern Aggression or, more politely, the Late Unpleasantness. After The War the victorious North had imposed a military occupation government on the conquered South and extended the franchise to recently emancipated Negroes. The Republican Party, the party of Lincoln, of emancipation, and of reconstruction, was anathema in the South for almost a century thereafter. In 1941 the United Confederate Veterans was still an active organization. Except in a few areas like the Southern Appalachians, which had been Unionist during The War, it was not politically (or sometimes socially) respectable to be a Republican.

The dominance of a single party throughout the region had several consequences. In the first place, all political contests were decided in the Democratic primary. The winner of the primary was guaranteed victory in the general election, often running unopposed in November. This arrangement put great power in the hands of the party leadership.

In most Southern states the conduct of primaries was regarded as a function of the party, not of the government. The party could decide by its own rules who could and who could not vote in the primary. In practice this generally meant that not only African Americans but also poor whites were shut out of the political process. In some places a token number of African Americans were allowed to vote, but this privilege was extended only to those who could be relied upon to vote as they were told. However, the exclusion of African Americans was coming under pressure. In Texas in 1940, an African American, Lonnie Smith, was denied the right to vote in the July 27 Democratic primary. Supported by the N.A.A.C.P., whose attorney, Thurgood Marshall, argued the case, Smith brought suit in federal court, arguing that the Texas statute, which let the Democratic Party deny him the vote, was unconstitutional. Texas argued that the Democratic Party was a private organization and that the federal government had no right under the Constitution to regulate a party's primary election. The case was still winding its way through the federal court system in 1941 and would not finally be resolved (in Smith's favor) for three more years. But in May the Supreme Court gave a clear indication of how it might turn out. In *U.S. vs. Classic,* a somewhat similar case from Louisiana that did not explicitly involve racial issues, the court held unanimously that where the primary was an integral part of the election process, the federal government had the right to intervene. Until the Smith case was formally decided, however, exclusion of African Americans continued.

The dominance of a single party in the South also meant that personal alliances carried more weight than formal party structures. Sometimes personal rivalries brought a special edge to the political process. In 1940 U.S. Senator Matthew Neely of West Virginia successfully ran for governor of his state, succeeding the outgoing Governor Homer A. Holt. As a courtesy, Neely resigned his Senate seat early to allow his appointed successor some seniority in the new Senate. Governor Holt moved quickly and appointed Clarence E. Martin, a conservative Martinsburg attorney and former American Bar Association president, to the seat. Neely was not consulted, did not approve, and had his own candidate in mind. On January 13, just after taking the oath of office as governor, Neely voided Martin's appointment. In his place he named Dr. Joseph Rosier, President of Fairmont State Teachers College. Martin contested the change, and the public was treated to a private spat being argued out on the floor of the Senate. The fight was all the more embarrassing because Neely, who had been chair of the Senate Rules Committee, had neglected to clean his personal materials out of the committee's files. He left there a copy of a private letter he had written nastily criticizing some of his Senate colleagues. The letter was promptly copied and circulated among the offended senators. Not enough damage was done to stop Rosier's confirmation, but he was not able to take his seat until May. The final vote was 40-38.

Statewide networks of political relationships were in kind not greatly different from the urban political machines that had once flourished widely and were still sometimes found in Northern cities. But while urban machines were limited in their reach and only occasionally and inconsistently exerted statewide influence, political alliances in the one-party South could reach well beyond the cities. It is probably no accident that the three political organizations that were able to control entire states in 1941 were all in the South: the Harry F. Byrd organization in Virginia; the Max Gardner organization (the so-called Shelby Dynasty) in North Carolina; and the Ed Crump machine in Tennessee.

Even in 1941 Harry F. Byrd was an anachronism. Born in 1887, he never lost the mind-set of the small-town Southern newspaper owner, farmer, and political operator. Having left school at 15 to take over the operation of his father's failing newspaper in Winchester, Virginia, Byrd never could understand why anyone needed more education than he had. During his years in power, Virginia schools remained badly underfunded. In just about every way, Byrd's own experience limited his vision of what Virginia needed.

As the largest apple grower in the state, Byrd knew the importance of good roads for getting his crop to market. But the roads he wanted were the ones his orchards needed. His home territory in the

Shenandoah Valley had long had a good arterial highway, the Valley Turnpike. So when highway construction projects started in the 1920s, he pressured the Highway Commission to put its emphasis on building secondary, farm-to-market roads. Byrd seemed unable to look past his own parochial interests to see the desperate need for arterial highways in the rest of the state. Further, Byrd's aversion to debt made him reject bonding to finance the much-needed road construction. As a member of the legislature in 1922, he had led the fight against bonds. He insisted that a gasoline tax of 3¢ a gallon would let the state complete its projected highway system on a pay-as-you-go basis within seven years and save millions in interest payments. (A decade later the gasoline tax was up to 5¢ a gallon and the system was still far from complete.)

Byrd's personal honesty did not prevent him from closing his eyes to the questionable maneuvers of some of his lieutenants in getting out the vote. The vote, of course, was primarily the white vote. Virginia was a poll-tax state, and Byrd had a lifelong interest in keeping African Americans and most poor whites from voting. Negroes were technically allowed to vote in the Democratic primary, but their participation was not encouraged. The organization assumed paternalistically that it could look after their interests well enough without their involvement. Virginia in fact had a reputation for racial harmony, supported by one of the strongest antilynching laws in the country. But it was a paternalistic harmony, and the strength of the caste system was beyond doubt.

Byrd's power base was the Courthouse Ring, the network of local officials, sheriffs, county clerks, and others, mostly appointed by the governor in Richmond, who administered justice and supervised local affairs. Byrd knew them all and shaped his policies to keep them happy. While governor he maintained the fee system, by which local officials received most of their income (sometimes more than the governor's salary) not from their salaries but from fees generated by their offices. Byrd recognized the risk of corruption inherent in the system, but he kept it in order to keep the Courthouse Ring happy. When pressure for civil service reform became irresistible, Byrd managed to keep some offices, most notably the sheriff's offices, within the scope of political patronage. In return for his support, the Courthouse Ring gave Byrd absolute loyalty and thus almost unlimited power in statewide matters.

Byrd's mode of operation is well illustrated by his handling of the 1941 gubernatorial election. By this time Byrd had been in the U.S. Senate for almost a decade, but he still maintained control of Virginia politics. Governor James Price, elected with Byrd's support in 1937, was coming to the end of his term. Price had made moves to assert his independence of the Byrd Organization and even contemplated challenging Byrd in the senatorial election of 1940. Byrd got his lieutenants to sabotage Price's plans so thoroughly that the challenge never developed. Still, Byrd wanted a more loyal governor in 1941. Although he protested that he never hand picked a governor, Republican Benjamin Muse had a point when he said, "Governors of Virginia are appointed by Harry Byrd, subject to confirmation by the electorate." Leading contenders would emerge by consensus from within the organization. They would meet with Byrd, who would discuss them with his advisors and sound out local opinion. Then he would make his decision and give a subtle indication of his preference.

In 1941 State Senator William Tuck, a longtime friend and loyal organization supporter advanced a strong claim for consideration. So did Congressman Colgate Darden, who projected a somewhat more dignified and reassuring image than the unpolished Tuck. Both had several meetings with Byrd. In November of 1940, Tuck came away from one meeting with the feeling that Byrd had been very cold toward him. He also noticed that some of Byrd's closest associates were helping Darden with his campaign. Tuck took the hint and graciously withdrew from the race. Byrd's warmth returned and Tuck was rewarded with the nomination for lieutenant governor. Nothing overt was ever said. Darden easily defeated two antimachine candidates in the Democratic primary and Benjamin Muse in the general election. Virginia's restrictive electoral laws helped. In the November election only 7.8 percent of adult Virginians cast votes. Virginia regularly ranked close to last among the states in its voting rate.

Just across the state line, the North Carolina political organization of former Governor O. Max Gardner exercised a level of control only slightly less effective than that of the Byrd Organization. Called the Shelby Dynasty after Gardner's home town, the machine was largely his creation. Governor from 1929 to 1933, Gardner in 1941 was a well-to-do lawyer and lobbyist as well as a textile manufacturer.

In 1920 Gardner had run for governor, challenging the political machine of race-baiting Senator Furnifold Simmons. He lost what was probably a stolen election, and, biding his time, built up his law practice, his personal fortune, and his control over the local political machine in Cleveland County. When he ran again in 1928, this time with the approval of the dying Simmons machine, he faced no trouble in the primary or general election. Two years later he asserted his political dominance by backing Josiah Bailey, who defeated the aging Simmons for the U.S. Senate. Then in December of 1930 Senator Lee Overman, a power in Washington since 1903, died in office. Gardner used this vacancy as an opportunity to bring the remnants of the Simmons machine under his sway. He gave the interim appointment to Cameron Morrison, a former Simmons ally who had beaten him in the questionable gubernatorial election of 1920. Leaving the governorship, he moved to Washington where he set up office as a lawyer and lobbyist. But he worked hand-in-hand with Bailey to dispense patronage and control politics back home. In this he was greatly helped by his friendship with Franklin Roosevelt, who had been governor of New York while Gardner was governor of North Carolina.

Gardner's power base was traditional, supported by local courthouse officials and political patronage. In the mountainous western part of the state, the slow counting of absentee ballots let local officials adjust the returns as needed, a practice Gardner did not officially approve but tolerated as a necessity. It was said that control of the election machinery was worth 20 percent of the vote. Likewise the beneficiaries of state patronage followed the common custom of rebating to the party a percentage of their salaries. Individual pressure was not usually brought to extract the contributions, but department heads were given quotas to fill. The Gardner machine could also count on the financial support of the wealthiest businessmen and industrialists in the state. In cases of dire necessity, like the 1937 gubernatorial primary that saw a strong challenge to the power of the machine, Federal W.P.A. and C.C.C. supervisors could be asked to have their employees get out and campaign. Since these two agencies employed 225,000 North Carolinians in the '30s and '40s, their impact was considerable.

During Gardner's time as head of the machine, only one major election went against him. In 1932 Cameron Morrison, having been appointed to Lee Overman's Senate seat, was running for a full term in Washington. Opposing him in the primary was Asheville lawyer Robert R. Reynolds, a playboy populist who had already gone through four marriages and three unsuccessful runs for public office. In the Depression people were prepared to listen to demagogues, and they readily listened to Reynolds. Although he was financially well off because of an inheritance from his first wife, he portrayed himself as a poor country lawyer, Buncombe Bob, running against the plutocrat Morrison. (Cam Morrison had also come into his money through his wife, the widow of a Durham financier.) By the time Morrison and Gardner realized that Reynolds had to be taken seriously, the challenger had built up substantial popularity and succeeded in painting Morrison as a Wall Street tool. Reynolds won the primary decisively and went to Washington, where he soon made a reputation as a demagogue even more entertaining than Huey Long.

As soon as he got to the Senate, Reynolds proposed to Josiah Bailey that between them they demand a 10 percent salary kickback from all federal patronage appointees in North Carolina. Bailey, the straitlaced son and grandson of Baptist ministers, was appalled and refused to cooperate. Without Bailey's help or Gardner's access to the White House, Reynolds used his own methods to promote the interests of his friends, generally with little effect. When he approached the president about appointing his good friend Marcus Erwin as U.S. Attorney, Roosevelt refused. In a face-to-face meeting he told Reynolds it was well known that Erwin kept a "fat whore" in Charlotte. Reynolds smiled and answered, "Well, Mr. President, she's not so fat." Roosevelt was amused but still would not appointment Erwin. Months later, after other Democrats persuaded Roosevelt that Reynolds had been taught his lesson, the appointment went through.

By 1941 Reynolds's demagoguery and lack of interest in serious work had become more alarming than amusing. By patiently rising through the seniority system, he became chairman of the Senate Military Affairs Committee upon the death in April of Senator Morris Sheppard. Fortunately for the country, Reynolds at the time was more interested in matrimony than in politics. At a Washington party he had met Evalyn Washington McLean, daughter of *Washington Post* heir Edward McLean and mining heiress Evalyn Walsh McLean, owner of the Hope Diamond (Chapter 11). Although he was fifty-seven and she was nineteen when they met, the two were immediately attracted to each other and married in October. Thereafter he concentrated his attention on his young wife and left committee affairs in the hands of others. Reynolds later decided not to run for a third term, and the Shelby Dynasty was able to reclaim the lost Senate seat.

In many ways Tennessee had the most interesting of all the state-wide organizations. Despite popular impressions, not all urban political machines were corrupt. One of the most powerful urban bosses was Ed Crump of Memphis, whose reputation for personal integrity and whose opposition to graft equaled the reputations of Byrd and Gardner. Crump was also the only urban political boss who could extend his control effectively and consistently across his entire state. Crump was a well-to-do investment banker, real estate broker, and insurance agent. His firm had a reputation for absolute integrity, and Crump was never known to solicit any form of graft or allow his lieutenants to do so. Crump served three brief terms as mayor beginning in 1910, and thereafter he stayed away from public office (with one exception noted below), preferring to control Memphis and most of Tennessee from behind the scenes. But his control was no less effective for that. A teetotaler himself, he was lax in the enforcement of prohibition laws; but he managed to keep organized crime out of the city with a strong police force and vigorous action against prostitution and gambling.

A large part of Crump's strength came from the black vote. Although Tennessee was a poll-tax state, it was not a white-primary state. Enforcement of voting laws was evenhanded in Memphis, whose population was 41 percent black. African Americans voted in large numbers, and they knew whom to vote for because Crump saw to it that black neighborhoods received good public services. Added to this was the great number of white voters who benefitted from honest government and a neat, clean, quiet city. But the benefits came at a significant price. As John Gunther pointed out, "a whole generation has grown up without fulfilling the first and simplest duty of citizenship, that of exercising political choice."

Crump's power base in Memphis allowed him to extend his influence statewide except for the Republican enclaves in the mountains of East Tennessee. It was said that a statewide election would generally produce about 400,000 votes, of which 260,000 would be Democratic. As in most Southern states, the Democratic primary was where elections were really decided, so a little over 130,000 votes in the primary were all that were required for election. The Crump organization reliably controlled 100,000 votes in the Memphis area. A Crump opponent for statewide office would need to win 80 percent of the remaining votes, an almost insurmountable task.

Crump could exercise his influence in ways that were far from subtle. When one politician dared to run against the Crump organization, he found there were no places in Memphis that he could rent for political rallies, nor would any Memphis printer make campaign posters for him. On the other hand, the Memphis *Press-Scimitar* waged a running battle against the Crump machine for years and was never threatened in any way. Crump was known to buy advertising in any newspaper in the state, friendly or otherwise, to publish vitriolic attacks on his political enemies. In person, however, he could be charming and entertaining.

Crump provided the country with a measure of political amusement following the 1940 election. His chosen candidate for mayor that year was Walter Chandler, the congressman representing the Ninth District, which included Memphis. But Crump also wanted Chandler in Washington during the early part of 1941 to vote on the Lend-Lease bill. If Chandler had run for mayor, he would have had to give up his seat in Congress. Crump's solution was simple. Chandler ran for re-election to Congress. Crump ran for mayor. Crump's ally Joseph Boyle ran for vice-mayor. All, of course, were elected, along with a city commission loyal to Crump. Chandler returned to Washington to complete his work there. Crump's term of office was to begin on January 1, 1941, but he felt he had better things to do with his time than keep the mayor's chair warm for Chandler. He wanted very much to attend the Sugar Bowl game between Tennessee and Boston College in New Orleans on New Year's Day. So on New Year's Eve Crump went to the railroad station to catch the midnight train to New Orleans. Just after midnight on January 1, Crump, standing on the station platform, took the oath of office as mayor. He immediately handed over his resignation as mayor and boarded the train for New Orleans in company with U.S. Senator Kenneth McKellar, a long-time friend and ally. Joseph Boyle took the oath of office as vice mayor, automatically became acting mayor, and the next morning convened the City Commission, which dutifully elected Chandler as mayor, effective upon his resignation from Congress.

The only thing Crump could not control was the Sugar Bowl score: Boston College 19, Tennessee 13.

The dominance of a state by a special interest group took an unusual form in Montana. The economy and government of the state were controlled in 1941, as they had been for many years, by Anaconda Copper Mining Company, working in alliance with Montana Power Company. The companies held a vise-like grip on the legislature. Since Anaconda owned or controlled six of the eight daily newspapers in the five principal cities, it was hard for liberal legislative candidates to gain public attention. If a liberal did manage to be elected, the pressure on him was almost irresistible. One lobbyist was heard to boast, "Give me a case of Scotch, a case of gin, one blonde, and one brunette, and I can take any liberal!" In the case of Burton K. Wheeler, a liberal reformer best known as an isolationist foe of Roosevelt, Anaconda resorted to an extreme measure. Wheeler was such a persistent gadfly in the legislature that Anaconda worked behind the scenes to get him elected to the U.S. Senate and so out of state politics completely.

Legislators who gave in to company pressure were said to wear the copper collar. The companies took immense riches from Montana but gave virtually nothing in return. They made sure the legislature discouraged new industry from moving in to compete for labor. That way wage rates could be kept low. Taxes were kept so low that public services were absolutely minimal. Parks and playgrounds were scarce and ill maintained, and 37 percent of the population had no access to public libraries. There was constant tension between the companies and labor, but the unions were powerless. A worker who caused trouble for Anaconda would find that he had also been blacklisted by the railroads, the state's only other major employers. While most political machines stayed in power by providing stability and a basic level of public services, Anaconda maintained power by sheer economic force, treating the state like a colony to be exploited.

It should not be thought, however, that state politics in the rest of the country was fully representative and democratic. While the franchise might be extended more widely or not manipulated so corruptly, state legislatures were often apportioned in ways that gave added strength to particular interests, notably agricultural interests, rather than equally to all voters. Perhaps the most extreme example of skewed apportionment was in Vermont, which followed the New England pattern of dividing the entire state into townships. The state constitution gave each township one representative in the lower house. Therefore the town of Stratton, with a population of 8, sent one legislative representative to Montpelier. So did the city of Burlington, with a population of 27,686. This pattern of unbalanced representation was common throughout New England. In the Connecticut House, the city of New Haven (population 160,605) had two representatives while Tolland County (population 31,866) had twenty-two. The justification offered was that the rural population had to be alert so "none of that crazy stuff" from the urban areas could be enacted. While the situations were seldom so extreme in the rest of the country, most other states did have unbalanced representation in at least one house of the legislature. Typically, as, for example, in Maryland, a bicameral legislature might have a State Senate with two senators from each county and a House of Delegates with proportional representation. Since 1934 Nebraska had stood apart from all the other states in having a single legislative chamber. In 1941 the people of the state still regarded their unicameral system as something of an experiment. The single house had only forty-three members, elections to the legislature were required to be nonpartisan, and all debates (including all committee meetings) had to be open to the public, a remarkable innovation for the time.

On the local level America was gradually emerging from the days of the corrupt big-city political machine and was starting to elect local officials who were generally honest and reasonably efficient. The country was also seeing the slow but steady growth of merit-based civil service on state and local levels. Since 1883 the lower-level employees of the federal government had been supervised by the Civil Service Commission and were appointed, retained, and promoted on the basis of merit. But many officials, such as a local postmaster or United States Attorney, remained outside the system. On state and local levels the merit system was much less common. In some locales even policemen on the beat were political appointees who could be replaced at will—and very likely might be replaced if a different party took office. Patronage was the lifeblood of every political machine, and supporters of the winning party could be assured of jobs for themselves and their family members. Naturally, the most important patronage appointments were to the local election commissions, which could manufacture or lose votes as needed in close elections. In the worst machines, generally on the municipal level, political appointments meant not only employment, but also prosperity, as the better jobs offered ample opportunity to solicit bribes. Even in the less corrupt machines, it was generally understood that political appointees would "voluntarily" contribute a percentage of their salaries to the party campaign fund. Most regarded this contribution as a prudent investment in job security.

By the 1910s and 1920s voters were tiring of the most abusively corrupt machines, and reform movements sprang up to oust them. The object of these movements was not to end patronage. That was too deeply ingrained to be eradicated quickly. Rather, the goal for most reformers was to put an end to graft, or at least excessive graft, and see that citizens got reasonably efficient services for their tax dollars and reasonable justice from the courts. Only a few reformers aimed to do away with patronage altogether and base all civil service appointments on merit alone. One of these radical reformers was New York City's Fiorello La Guardia, who had ousted Mayor John P. O'Brien in 1933. La Guardia made the corruption of the Democrats' Tammany Hall organization his main campaign theme, even though O'Brien himself was not known to be corrupt. It was common for political organizations, no matter how venal the leaders, to have a number of honest members who could be put forward in visible positions. O'Brien had become mayor in a special election after the surprise resignation and flight to Europe of the notorious Mayor Jimmy Walker. O'Brien promised to be a thousand percent different and to take neither advice nor direction from Tammany Hall. But when asked who his new police commissioner would be, he reportedly answered, "I don't know. I haven't had the word yet."

La Guardia ran on what was known as the Fusion Ticket, a combination of Republicans and Reform Democrats. Thanks to extensive vote stealing by the Tammany organization, including some intervention by mobsters on behalf of the Democrats, the election was much closer than it otherwise would have been. But La Guardia still won a convincing victory by something like 250,000 votes and embarked on a determined, frenetic, and largely successful campaign to clean up New York City government.

To his inexhaustible energy and absolute incorruptibility, La Guardia added other advantages. The son of an Italian father and a Jewish mother, neither of whom practiced the religions they were reared in, Fiorello was an Episcopalian as a result of his early education in Episcopal schools. He had grown up in the west, where his father had been an Army bandmaster; but his wife Marie was a native New Yorker and a Lutheran. A sensitivity to New York's rich ethnic and religious complexity was bred into him.

La Guardia's frenetic pace of work kept him in the public eye and provided both effective government for the city and colorful copy for journalists. He worked 16-hour days, opened everything from book fairs to baseball games, and gave standing orders that he was to be notified of every fire in which a fireman's life might be in jeopardy. Whenever possible he showed up at those fires himself, believing that when firemen were putting their lives on the line, their mayor should be there with them. His colorful style brought him national and even international prominence, and he was bitterly disappointed when Roosevelt passed over him for secretary of war in 1940. Roosevelt was looking for some Republicans for the cabinet in order to create a more bipartisan administration (and, not incidentally, to weaken partisan Republican attacks in an election year). But La Guardia had been such a strong supporter of the New Deal that his Republican credentials had long been in doubt, and he would have done Roosevelt little good. La Guardia even hoped Roosevelt might choose him for the vice presidency to create a bipartisan ticket; but those hopes, too, came to nothing.

Early in 1941 Roosevelt asked La Guardia to assume the unpaid directorship of the Office of Civilian Defense. La Guardia accepted readily and, without resigning as mayor, spent the next year trying to figure out what the Office of Civilian Defense was supposed to do. He persuaded Eleanor Roosevelt to be his assistant, and together they traveled the country giving encouragement and assessing civil defense needs. Given their other commitments, the demands were too much for either of them. After Pearl Harbor they both resigned their O.C.D. positions.

Although the urban machine was in its declining years, a few notoriously corrupt organizations survived. Chicago still had clear memories of corrupt Republican Mayor William H. Thompson, whose right-hand man, Fred Lundin, had been responsible for the widely quoted remark, "To hell with the public, we're at the feed box now." Thompson had been defeated in 1931 by Anton Cermak, a Democrat whose ethical standards were not known to be significantly higher, but who at least represented a change of face. Cermak was assassinated in May of 1933 and was succeeded by Edward J. Kelly, who, together with Cook County Democratic Chairman Patrick Nash, built up a notably corrupt and long-lived machine. Prior to being tapped as mayor, Kelly had been chief engineer of the Chicago Sanitary District, long a major source of patronage and profits for politicians. Nash owned the company that did most of the contracting work for the district, and both men profited handsomely from the relationship. Kelly twice barely escaped conviction and imprisonment. In 1928 the district attorney got a grand jury to bring indictments against a number of Sanitary District officials, Kelly included. A politically reliable judge quashed the indictments on a technicality. The district attorney tried again, and this time Kelly escaped indictment. No official reason could be given, but the jury foreman worked for a company that sold materials to the Sanitary District. A few years later Kelly was again in trouble, this time for not paying taxes on the huge amount of money he had received in his years with the district. For reasons unreported, the federal government was willing to negotiate a reduced payment of back taxes and refrain from pressing criminal charges.

Kelly profited, as Thompson had not, from two important relationships. First, Kelly was a long-time friend of Robert McCormick, publisher of the Chicago *Tribune*, whose editorial pages were notably easier on Kelly than they had been on Thompson. Kelly's relationship with McCormick, strange in itself, dated to the days when McCormick was president of the Sanitary District and Kelly was a rambunctious foreman. They forged a long-lasting friendship that stood Kelly in good stead. Second, the Cook County machine was able to deliver a consistently large Democratic vote for presidential candidates, and the mayor soon became a personal favorite of the president's. That Kelly could maintain good relations with both McCormick and Roosevelt, who cordially detested each other, says much about his political skills—and also about the strange alliances often created in American politics. Roosevelt's influence seems to have had a moderating influence on Kelly. Although Chicago remained one of the most corrupt cities in the country, Kelly, having had his two brushes with the law, kept himself personally separate from the graft that was common among his lieutenants. After all, he had already made his pile back in the twenties. There was no need to be greedy.

Kelly also forged an especially strong relationship with Roosevelt's close friend and aide Harry Hopkins. At various times Hopkins was director of the Federal Emergency Relief Administration, director of the Civil Works Administration, and director of the Works Progress Administration. In these roles he was in a position to influence the distribution of a tremendous amount of federal relief money to the states, and Kelly saw to it that a good share of that money came to Chicago. The federal assistance was of great importance to Depression-era Chicago, and Kelly took full credit for securing the aid. It was natural, then, that the mayor of Chicago was one of Roosevelt's staunchest supporters.

As mayor of the largest city in a state with twenty-nine electoral votes, Kelly had a powerful voice in national Democratic circles even before the 1940 Chicago convention that nominated Roosevelt for his third term. Chicago's population was very nearly equal to that of the rest of the state. With downstate Illinois being heavily Republican, the national Democratic Party needed a strong showing in Chicago to capture those electoral votes. Despite some up and downs over the years, Kelly had consistently shown that he could deliver Democratic votes when they were needed. The 1940 Democratic National Convention, held in Chicago, showed that Kelly could also deliver support in a highly unconventional way.

Roosevelt had not let his third-term intentions be known until shortly before the convention, and he was determined not to accept the nomination if even 150 delegates voted against him on the first ballot. Enough people were opposed to Roosevelt, opposed to a third term, or both, that the president needed an overwhelming endorsement, even a stampeded convention. Harry Hopkins arranged it, as he arranged so many other things. Working with Kelly, Hopkins had Convention Chairman Alben Barkley read a letter from Roosevelt saying he really did not want the nomination. Suddenly voices coming from all the loudspeakers in the building shouted, "We want Roosevelt!" Political bosses, following careful instructions, joined with the echoing sounds and started a demonstration that lasted almost a full hour. Kelly had wired the convention hall and had arranged for those initial shouts to come from a microphone located, of all places, in the sanitary sewer under the building. The next day Roosevelt was nominated on the first ballot, getting 946 votes against a combined 147 for his opponents. Without Kelly's help it would not have been possible; and Kelly had reinforced his standing, as well as his personal security, with the administration in Washington.

The story of protected corruption was similar in Jersey City, New Jersey, where Mayor Frank Hague maintained power by means fair and foul. He built the city one of the finest hospitals in the country and provided free medical care to the indigent—or even to those who claimed to be indigent—and this in a day when the American Medical Association still opposed group health plans that might keep doctors' fees down. On the other hand, Hague received a kickback of 3 percent of every city employee's salary and half of any raise. It was said that a contractor who wanted to do business with the city would have to visit the Mayor's office. Sitting across the desk from the Mayor, the contractor would see a secret drawer emerge from under the top of the desk. Into that desk the contractor was expected to place a sealed envelope containing the cash bribe necessary to secure the contract. The drawer would unobtrusively withdraw, and shortly thereafter the contract would be awarded. Of course, the contractor would have inflated his bid sufficiently to cover the bribe and any other incidental payments. Everybody profited except the taxpayer. Hague's multiple ways of raising money—always in cash—were so profitable that shortly before his death in 1956, he confided to his attorney that he was worth about $8,000,000, a figure the attorney estimated was low by a factor of ten. His message to potential opponents was simple: "Play ball with me and I'll make you rich."

Hague took advantage of the New Jersey law that provided for permanent voter registration. His hand-picked election board was none too careful in keeping track of voters who had died. Although he could never capture control of the legislature, Hague's ability to generate votes, legal or otherwise, for Democrats was a crucial advantage in a swing state with 16 electoral votes. Before 1932 New Jersey had been reliably Republican, and it was not a state the Democrats could afford to take for granted. Consequently the federal government was never aggressive in looking into corruption in Jersey City. The city police routinely read every telegram sent from Jersey City. Hague operatives in the post office regularly opened and read people's letters. The city defied federal court orders enforcing freedom of speech and assembly. None of it mattered. The Democratic National Committee needed Frank Hague. Instead of being indicted, Hague was able to ensure that all federal political patronage for New Jersey was placed in his hands. It would be years before New Jersey could shake off the Hague machine.

Even though the machines were in decline, on occasion they provided the nation with some diverting entertainment. Missouri had long been notable for its two Democratic machines, the Pendergast organization in Kansas City and the Dickman organization in St. Louis. Tom Pendergast controlled Jackson County and had wide influence throughout the state. In 1934 he had selected an obscure local politician, Harry Truman, to be the next United States Senator. Two years later Pendergast had backed Lloyd Stark for governor and had seen Stark elected in an exceptionally corrupt campaign. Like John P. O'Brien in New York, both Truman and Stark were personally honest politicians who served to divert attention from the corrupt machines behind them. When U.S. Attorney Maurice Milligan began a corruption probe into the Pendergast organization, Stark turned on Pendergast and assisted the investigators. In 1939 Pendergast was convicted of income tax evasion (he had failed to report a bribe he received) and served fifteen months in Leavenworth.

The stage was set for the 1940 election campaign when both Truman and Stark would have to defend their seats. Truman had never publicly separated himself from the Jackson County Democratic organization, and Stark declared himself a candidate for Truman's Senate seat, running on an antimachine platform. Unfortunately for Stark, District Attorney Milligan thought Stark was claiming too much credit for an investigation that Milligan had led, and Milligan also filed for the Senate. The two men split the antimachine vote, and Truman won re-election.

Meanwhile the governorship was open; and the Democrats nominated Lawrence McDaniel, excise commissioner in St. Louis. McDaniel was backed by the St. Louis Democratic machine of Mayor Bernard F. Dickman. Dickman had taken the trouble to consult with Jim Pendergast, now running what was left of his father's machine, and gained the support of that organization as well. With both major cities supporting McDaniel, his election seemed assured.

But the publicity surrounding the Milligan probe had damaged the Democratic Party and alienated many voters, especially in rural parts of the state. Republican Forrest C. Donnell, a political novice, ran a vigorous anticorruption campaign and won by the narrow margin of 3,613 votes. The campaign itself was not especially bitter. Despite clear personality differences, McDaniel and Donnell had much in common. They had known each other for years. They lived in the same part of St. Louis. They attended the same Methodist church. McDaniel had even been a member of the men's Sunday school class taught by Donnell. They belonged to the same Masonic lodge. Their wives and children were friends and members of the same clubs. It was the work of the Dickman machine after the election that ended their long friendship.

In Missouri, as in a number of other states, municipal elections were held in April following the November general election. Dickman was running for re-election as mayor of St. Louis, and he counted on the politically appointed election board to resolve any voting questions in his favor. Consequently he was more than a little upset by Donnell's intention as governor to appoint nonpartisan election and police boards. Within hours after the election results were announced, the Democratic leaders in St. Louis were meeting to plot strategy. Dickman approved their plan, and the bosses went to work.

The Missouri Constitution provided that the Speaker of the State House of Representatives would tally the vote and certify the winner of the gubernatorial election. When the legislature convened for that purpose in the middle of January, the Speaker refused to carry out the constitutionally prescribed duty. After an all-night session ending at 4:55 A.M. on Saturday, the House, controlled by a 114-70 Democratic majority, voted along party lines to refuse certification and to set up a committee "to investigate unmistakable evidence of fraud and irregularity." Inaugural preparations had to be called off, and the governor's ceremonial honor guard took off their blue dress uniforms and went home.

The Democratic leaders knew they could not hope to prevent Donnell's eventual inauguration, but they hoped to delay it until after the municipal elections in April. They expected that Governor Stark, continuing in office until his successor could be inaugurated, would leave in place the election boards that might be needed by the Dickman machine. Newspapers and magazines reported the contests in detail, and the whole country watched in fascination.

Donnell and the Republicans immediately appealed to the State Supreme Court. Public opinion was heavily on their side, and they hoped the court would move quickly to enforce the election result, even though all the members of the court were Democrats. Even Governor Stark denounced the machine strategy. Late in February the court unanimously ordered the Speaker to certify the result, and Donnell was finally inaugurated on February 26.

The last act of the drama was now to be played. In the mayor's race the Republicans nominated Judge William D. Becker, who the previous fall had been defeated for re-election to a third twelve-year term on the court of Appeals. Mayor Dickman scrambled to distance himself from the gubernatorial fiasco and tried to run on his generally progressive record. But the political damage had been done. Judge Becker won convincingly, 183,112 to 147,428. Not only did he win, he brought in with him a G.O.P. majority on the St. Louis Board of Aldermen.

Becker immediately pushed through an amendment to the city's charter instituting a merit system for hiring city employees, seriously limiting the possibility of re-establishing a strong political machine in the city. It was the spread of the merit system in states and cities across the country that was bringing an end to the era of the political machine. It should be remembered, however, that in 1941 the great objection to machine politics was not autocratic control *per se*.

Most citizens simply did not expect a fully representative process for selecting public officials. It was generally assumed that government functioned by balancing the views of various interests and lobbies, not by ensuring an equal voice for all individual voters. What people asked of their government was efficiency and honesty. Reform movements were aimed at graft and corruption, not at the electoral process itself. The whole system was beginning to change, but in 1941 that change had not gone very far, nor were most voters insisting that it do so.

CHAPTER 2

February: Popular Entertainment

ON THE EVENING of February 27, the luminaries of Hollywood gathered in the Biltmore Bowl of the Los Angeles Biltmore Hotel for the annual banquet and awards ceremony of the American Academy of Motion Picture Arts and Sciences. This year's meeting was a special one. For the first time the President of the United States was giving formal recognition to the work of the Academy. On a direct radio link from Washington, President Roosevelt addressed those in attendance for six minutes, praising their creative work.

The awards ceremony itself also had a new feature. In prior years, the Academy had counted the votes for the various awards and distributed the results to the press under a publication embargo. Newspapers were prohibited from printing the results until after the ceremony. But 1940's ceremony had been a special one. David O. Selznick's *Gone With the Wind* was nominated and favored for so many awards that there was considerable speculation as to just how many it would take. Seizing an opportunity for a major scoop, the *Los Angeles Times* broke the embargo and printed the list of Oscar winners in its 8:45 P.M.

edition. Bob Hope was hosting his first Oscar ceremony and could not resist opening with a quip, "What a wonderful thing, this benefit for David Selznick."

The mortified Academy immediately changed procedures. In 1941 the accounting firm of Price Waterhouse & Co. was given the job of counting the votes and determining the winners. Along with the celebrity guests on February 27, there arrived a representative from Price Waterhouse carrying a locked briefcase. In the briefcase were sealed and labeled envelopes containing the names of the award winners, names known only to Price Waterhouse. Alfred Lunt and Lynne Fontanne presented the acting awards, each preceded by the soon-to-be-familiar phrase, "The envelope, please."

The year 1940 had not produced quite so notable a list of movies as had some other years, and the award winners were sometimes less memorable than some of their competition. David Selznick won Best Picture with *Rebecca*, his second award in a row, beating out *The Grapes of Wrath*, *The Philadelphia Story*, and seven other nominees. In most years the movie that wins Best Picture will also win Best Director. But this year John Ford (*The Grapes of Wrath*) won that category over Alfred Hitchcock (*Rebecca*) and three others. Jimmy Stewart (*The Philadelphia Story*) and Ginger Rogers (*Kitty Foyle*) won Best Actor and Best Actress.

Perhaps it was inevitable that current events would intrude even into the Oscar ceremony. Charlie Chaplin's *The Great Dictator*, a satirical look at Hitler and Mussolini, was nominated for five awards, though it did not manage to win any. A special Oscar went to Colonel Nathan Levinson, Director of Sound at Warner Brothers, "For his outstanding service to the Industry and the Army during the past nine years, which has made possible the present efficient mobilization of the motion picture industry facilities for the production of Army training films." Bob Hope, hosting his second Oscar ceremony, also received a special plaque, presented by his co-host, producer Walter Wanger, honoring his "achievements in humanity." Hope was already known for the many benefit shows he put on, having given 258 free performances in 1940 alone. For just a moment Hope was speechless. Then he asked plaintively, "But how can I get this into my scrapbook?"

The Academy Awards did produce one bit of controversy. Walt Disney had felt that *Fantasia* had been unduly slighted by the Academy. Although it had won several critical awards, it was not nominated for an Oscar. In a pique, Disney withdrew all of his short cartoons from consideration. As a result, M-G-M's *The Milky Way* won the Oscar for Best Short Subject, Cartoon. This was the first time in seven years that a Disney production had not won this category. Disney did not, however, withdraw all his work. *Pinocchio* won two awards, one for Best Musical Score and one for Best Song, "When You Wish Upon a Star."

Hollywood returned to its best 1930s form with the movies that were released in 1941. *How Green Was My Valley* from 20th-Century-Fox would win the Oscar for Best Picture, but it had strong competition from other classics like *The Little Foxes, The Maltese Falcon,* and *Sergeant York.* Walt Disney returned to the short competition, winning yet again with *Lend a Paw.* Disney's *Dumbo* would also take an Oscar for Best Score for a musical. *Dumbo*, released in late October, was made on a tight budget to try to recoup some of the earlier losses from *Pinocchio* and *Fantasia.* The latter two had been artistic successes but financial failures. *Dumbo* was the least expensive of all Disney's animated features, but it grossed more than *Pinocchio* and *Fantasia* together.

One of the greatest movies of 1941 almost did not get released at all. As Orson Welles was filming *Citizen Kane* late in 1940, word spread in Hollywood that the film was modeled very closely on the life of newspaper publisher William Randolph Hearst. Hearst was none too pleased at the prospect. At a mid-January preview screening, Louella Parsons, movie critic for the Hearst papers, attended in the company of two Hearst lawyers. What they saw confirmed their worst fears. From the general theme of the millionaire publisher who tries to build a successful political career, to the disruption of his marriage by an affair with a show girl, to the acquisition of ostentatious wealth and the relocation of a European castle to his private estate, the parallels were too clear to miss. There was enough fiction in the film to make it unlikely that a lawsuit for defamation could succeed, and R.K.O. pictures ignored the dark hints that were circulated. Hearst turned to more direct forms of pressure. It was announced that unless R.K.O. agreed not to release the picture, R.K.O. and its films would not be so much as mentioned in any Hearst paper. When a favorable review of R.K.O.'s *Kitty Foyle* appeared in an early edition of the *Los Angeles Examiner*, a Hearst paper, the lapse was quickly spotted. The review disappeared from later editions. Even these efforts failed to stop Welles and R.K.O., and the completed film received strongly favorable reviews at its early screenings. One critic, Joshua O'Hara, called it the greatest film ever made. Hearst got little support from his fellow publishers, as other newspapers and magazines happily accepted full-page advertising for the forthcoming film. But Hearst's efforts probably did have a slight effect on the box office. Early attendance figures were not what the producers had hoped for. His opposition may also have had another delayed effect, for *Citizen Kane* lost out on the Best Picture Oscar. Nominated for nine awards, the film won only the Oscar for Best Original Screenplay.

The preview screening of *Citizen Kane* was a common practice for the movie industry. Members of the press would be invited to a showing prior to the release date so the newspapers and magazines could prepare their advance publicity. But the recent crop of mediocre movies led to a number of bad early reviews, which hurt the early box office revenues. So in July the Hays Office (officially the Motion Picture Producers and Distributors of America) announced that there would be no more preview showings for the general press. Henceforth only trade publications and magazines that needed long lead times for their reviews would be invited, and they would have to sign agreements not to publish before the release date. The only studio that continued the former practice was United Artists, who were not a part of the Hays organization. Just after the edict came out, they celebrated their independence with a preview showing of *New Wine* (a biography of Franz Schubert), followed by a party at which the wine flowed freely.

The Hays Office was a trade group headed by William H. Hays, former U.S. Postmaster General and the first director of M.P.P.D.A. The organization had been created in 1922 to clean up the image of the industry after a series of scandals. Will Hays, a conservative Indiana Republican and a Presbyterian deacon, was the studios' choice for the directorship; and his name became the informal designation for the organization. Then during the early 1930s movies started to become more daring in their subject matter and presentation. *I Am a Fugitive from a Chain Gang* was graphic in its portrayal of brutality in Southern prisons. Fay Wray briefly appeared topless in a famous scene from *King Kong*. In the Czech film *Ecstasy*, Hedwig Kiesler (who later changed her name to Hedy Lamarr) even had a long scene in which she appeared totally nude. Numerous groups, but most especially the Roman Catholic hierarchy, clamored for restrictions on what could be shown on screen. Will Hays and several studio heads, fearing the possibility of government intervention and censorship, felt it would be better to censor themselves. So in 1934 the M.P.P.D.A. established the Production Code Authority to establish standards of morality that would keep the movie industry free from external control. In order to be released for distribution in theaters, a movie had to have a P.C.A. seal of approval. Even United Artists had to conform to the code in order to get theaters to show their films.

To administer the P.C.A., Hays hired Joseph I. Breen, a conservative Catholic journalist with close ties to the church hierarchy. The code he enforced was essentially the same code that had been written several years earlier by a Catholic priest and that had been agreed to but ignored by the studios. Now Breen began to interpret the code narrowly and enforce it strictly. Coarse language and sexual innuendo were strictly forbidden. There was a minor crisis in 1939 when David Selznick was filming *Gone with the Wind*. The code prohibited any form of profanity, effectively banning Rhett Butler's famous exit line, "Frankly, my dear, I don't give a damn." Eventually Selznick convinced Breen that the industry would become a laughing stock if he had to change a line that had already become a classic. Breen, ever sensitive to ridicule, gave in and the line was kept.

In 1940 the political climate in Hollywood began to shift in an important way. Heretofore Breen had barred all political controversy, and especially liberal political views, from the movies. But that year

Samuel Goldwyn wanted to distribute the British film *Pastor Hall*, a strongly anti-Nazi dramatization of the life of German Lutheran pastor Martin Niemöller. Breen was adamantly opposed to the film's release, regarding it as outright propaganda. He persuaded all the major studios to reject it. But James Roosevelt, the president's son, headed a company called Globe Productions. He announced that he would distribute the movie and would include an introduction to be read by his mother, First Lady Eleanor Roosevelt. This clear signal from the White House not only secured the certification and release of *Pastor Hall*; it also applied a sudden and sharp constraint on the right-wing leanings of Joseph Breen. The studios now felt themselves empowered to produce films much more in line with the growing interventionist temper of the American people. This was especially the case after September, when Germany banned the distribution of all American made films. Heretofore the studios had earned anywhere from 30 percent to 40 percent of their revenue from foreign distribution. With foreign markets other than Britain and the Western Hemisphere gradually being cut off, the studios no longer had financial motives to appease the Fascists.

Although Breen now could not impose his political censorship on the movie industry, he was still able to impose his conservative views regarding sexual matters. In the spring of 1941 his office decided that women's sweaters were becoming too tight and suggestive, sometimes even showing the outlines of nipples. So he issued a decree threatening to ban pullover sweaters from the movies. The first victim was the veteran actress Bette Davis, who had prepared a whole wardrobe of sweaters for the film version of *The Man Who Came to Dinner*. Every sweater was rejected by Breen. But this time the P.C.A. had overstepped. Pullover sweaters were a highly popular fashion that spring, and *Newsweek* observed that the movies were banning what most women wore every day. Already sensitive to criticism and ridicule, Breen now became increasingly touchy. The sniggering over the sweater issue was the last straw for him. In addition to the ridicule, Breen was burning out in his job. He had always refused to delegate any of his censorship authority, and his immense workload was breaking him down. In April he resigned as P.C.A. director and took a job with R.K.O. The sweater issue was quietly dropped.

In addition to the production of training films for the Army, Hollywood got involved in the defense effort in more personal ways. When Jimmy Stewart was drafted in February, he failed his physical. At 6'3" and 138 pounds, he was five pounds underweight for the army. Going home and eating everything in sight, he gained enough weight to pass the physical (by one ounce) in March and enlist in the Air Corps. He already had a private pilot's license, but he needed 100 more hours of flying time to qualify for his proficiency board exam. After getting those hours at his own expense, he passed his exam and received his commission in January of '42.

For some in Hollywood, the war in Europe had a very personal meaning. Word of the Fascist persecution of Jews had spread widely, and most of the leading figures in the movie industry, men like Louis B. Mayer, Samuel Goldwyn, and David O. Selznick, were themselves Jewish. They were well aware that anti-Semitism was widespread in the United States, and they did not want to do anything to inflame it. While the executives themselves did not try to hide their ethnicity, they regularly had Jewish movie stars change their names to conceal their ethnic identity. The very essence of Hollywood was the creation of an illusion, an image of a happy, unified America populated mainly by characters representative of old-stock Protestants (Chapter 11). The names of Hollywood's stars should be consonant with that image. So when the Austrian Jewish actress Hedwig Kiesler came to America, Mayer had her change her name to Hedy Lamarr. Likewise Meshilem Meier Weisenfreund became Paul Muni. Issur Danielovitch legally changed his name to Kirk Douglas, and Marion Pauline Levy adopted her mother's maiden name, performing as Paulette Goddard. For these and other Jews in Hollywood, the change of name did not lessen their sense of Jewish identity. But in the minds of the American people, the non-Jewish names reinforced the fiction of national unity and, to some degree, uniformity.

In 1941 the movies were also exploring another entertainment area, the music of the Big Bands. Musical movies had been around for a long time, ever since Al Jolson's groundbreaking *The Jazz Singer* of 1927. Since Gene Autry's *In Old Santa Fe* in 1934, the singing cowboy movie had been the most prominent variety of musical film. Autry himself had already made 41 such films through 1940, and he had written songs for several others. Roy Rogers already had 33 movie credits to his name, or more properly to his names. Several of his early movies with his singing group, the Sons of the Pioneers, were made using his birth name, Leonard Slye. There had also been numerous dance movies, the best of them featuring Fred Astaire. Although the music merely provided background and rhythm for the dancing, several of the films had produced notable popular tunes, such as "Cheek to Cheek" (*Top Hat*, 1935), "Pick Yourself Up" (*Swing Time*, 1936), and "They Can't Take That Away from Me" (*Shall We Dance?*, 1937). Now the producers were extending their range to include well known Big Bands, and the band leaders themselves were looking for new opportunities to perform. Perhaps the most successful venture in this area was *Sun Valley Serenade*, released by Twentieth Century Fox on August 29. With a rather thin plot, the movie was principally a vehicle for the music of Glenn Miller and the skating of Sonja Henie. No one would ever claim it was one of the great classic movies, but *Sun Valley Serenade* was good enough to get three Oscar nominations. Both Henie, the star of the show, and Milton Berle (as the band's press agent) received strong reviews for their acting. Other bands followed Miller in pursuing movie roles. In July Woody Herman and his Herd began filming *Wake Up and Live*, which was released about six months later as *What's Cookin'?* Singers, too, were appearing in movies, with or without the well-known bands behind them. One of the most popular singing groups in the country, the Andrews Sisters, made three films in 1941, all of them with Bud Abbott and Lou Costello: *Buck Privates*, *In the Navy*, and *Hold That Ghost*. Even the veteran crooner Rudy Vallee made two films that year, *Time Out for Rhythm* and *Too Many Blondes*.

One of the reasons the band leaders were happy to work with the studios was the sudden elimination of most of their opportunities to be heard on radio. Big Band music was easily the most popular type of music in the country, and radio provided the principal opportunity for most people to hear it. Martin Block's "Make Believe Ballroom," now in its seventh year, attracted a huge audience. Block, whose success was now earning him a salary of $100,000 a year, had over 23 sponsors for the program with more on a waiting list hoping to get air time. A survey taken at the end of 1940 had Glenn Miller's orchestra as the nation's most popular dance band and Guy Lombardo and his Royal Canadians as the number one "sweet music" ensemble. But on January 1, the successful and profitable radio broadcasts were shut down by a copyright dispute.

For over 25 years, A.S.C.A.P., the American Society of Composers, Authors, and Publishers, had been the principal organization representing the compositional and publishing side of the music business. Organized in 1914 by composer Victor Herbert and eight other music writers and publishers, A.S.C.A.P. managed copyrights and collected fees for composers and publishers. Among the fees collected were the performance fees that radio stations paid for playing the popular music of the big bands. Fees were generally based on a stations' gross receipts and provided a "blanket license" that allowed the station to broadcast as much A.S.C.A.P. music as it wanted. During the fee negotiations in 1940, A.S.C.A.P. pressed for substantial increases in the broadcasting fees, demanding that the networks pay 7½ percent of their total broadcast revenue. But radio executives had seen this move coming for some time. The previous year they had established their own competing organization, Broadcast Music, Inc. Ostensibly created to cover genres that A.S.C.A.P. had neglected, B.M.I. in fact represented an attempt to introduce competition into the industry as a way of keeping broadcast fees down. Now the two organizations were thrown against each other. A.S.C.A.P. responded with the musical equivalent of a strike, banning all A.S.C.A.P. music from the airwaves as of January 1, 1941, unless stations signed on and paid the fees demanded. Glenn Miller's orchestra, the nation's favorite, was the first one taken off the air. Woody Herman was caught in a serious bind because his band's theme song, "Blue Prelude," was covered under the A.S.C.A.P. ban. He moved quickly to record a new tune, "Blue Flame," which then became his theme.

A.S.C.A.P. representatives pursued their goal aggressively, monitoring stations across the country, recording broadcasts, and filing a lawsuit whenever a station played a banned song. At the same time the organization tried to present a front of reasonableness, offering to allow stations to pay on a per-use basis if they wished. But they also introduced a policy change, prohibiting their members from allowing B.M.I. to represent them also. This last move triggered federal intervention. On February 26 the U.S. Department of Justice entered the fray by filing an antitrust lawsuit against A.S.C.A.P. The broadcasters also found themselves with certain other advantages in the dispute. A.S.C.A.P. had always been dominated by publishers and had neglected many new composers, as well as performers of blues, swing, and Latin music. Black composers and performers had been almost completely excluded. Consequently B.M.I. took in far more new members than expected, and the stations started playing a variety of music in styles new to the public. During the first half of the year, B.M.I. music dominated the charts, and A.S.C.A.P. disappeared from the Top 20. Popular opinion was also strongly against A.S.C.A.P., and sales sagged, hurting the A.S.C.A.P. members. A.S.C.A.P. tried recording its own program, "A.S.C.A.P. on Parade," offering it to any stations that would sign up and pay the fee. The variety show was produced by Billy Rose and featured popular classics by such composers as Irving Berlin and George M. Cohan. It was not a success.

Early in May the Mutual network announced that it had reached an agreement with A.S.C.A.P. for a fee of 3 percent of broadcast revenue. NBC and CBS held out, hoping for a better deal. Those two networks had a special advantage: Their parent companies also controlled RCA Victor and Columbia Records, respectively. These two, together with Decca, produced almost all the records issued in America. Their hostility generated enormous pressure on A.S.C.A.P., pressure that eventually proved too much to resist. In August NBC signed an agreement for 2¾ percent of broadcast revenues, with an additional 2¼ percent coming from affiliate stations to cover their non-network programming. CBS soon followed suit. The whole matter was finally closed when A.S.C.A.P. signed a consent agreement with the Justice

Department, ending all the lawsuits. To even things out, B.M.I. signed a similar consent decree; and the pattern of music broadcasting finally stabilized. A.S.C.A.P. emerged from the fight much weaker and much poorer. While their 1940 radio revenues had been $4,750,000, in 1941 they were only $3,500,000.

In addition to radio, the Big Bands derived a great portion of their income from live performances. Even the biggest names did not limit themselves to the major urban centers like New York and Los Angeles. Their tours took them all across the country, anywhere local organizers could pay their fee. Different parts of the country, however, tended to prefer different kinds of music, and the bands gravitated to those areas where their individual styles were most popular. The Northeast, for example, preferred the swinging style pioneered by Benny Goodman; and Glen Gray, Duke Ellington, and the Dorsey Brothers were especially popular there. In the Midwest, on the other hand, the ballrooms preferred a softer sound and attracted bands like those of Guy Lombardo, Kay Keyser, and Lawrence Welk. The West Coast was more eclectic in its musical taste. Bob Crosby's Orchestra played fine, lively, high quality swing music. Bob also took eight members of the orchestra and created a smaller ensemble, the Bobcats, who specialized in Dixieland.

It would be easy, however, to overstate the differences among the various dance orchestras. While each one did have its own distinctive sound and its own stylistic preferences, they all played a very great deal of sweet music. In their live performances the bands made most of their money playing for dances. Since there were many dancers but few experts, all the orchestras made sure that for most of the evening they would be playing songs to which the audience could do a gentle foxtrot. When the bands became more venturesome and interspersed some "hot" music, the crowds often stopped dancing and stood around the bandstand to listen. Dance hall managers sometimes interpreted this as a lack of interest. They expected to see people dancing, so bandleaders had to limit the amount of hot music they played. Managers also took the view that while men might attend a dance alone in order to hear the music, a woman would always be accompanied by one or more men. It was therefore important to offer music that would attract women to their dance halls; and this, to the managers, required a great preponderance of sweet music.

The increased number of teenagers in the audience during this period gave some encouragement to bandleaders who preferred swinging rhythms. The wild enthusiasms of adolescent fans encouraged many musicians to program more of the music they liked. Yet for all the headlines they grabbed, young people actually had rather little impact on the range of music that was played. While their enthusiasm was appreciated, not least for the publicity it gave, they would notoriously arrive early, leave early, and spend very little money while in attendance.

In contrast to the dance halls, the recording studio gave ensembles greater freedom to express their distinctive styles. As a result, the variety of music preserved on records does not necessarily reflect what one would have heard at a live event. Recordings were an important source of income for many bands, producing some $3,000,000 in earnings for band musicians during 1941. Yet many band leaders, and their sponsors, were ambivalent at best about the financial impact of recordings. Apart from the A.S.C.A.P. dispute, small local radio stations could save the cost of network fees by playing music from records and pocketing the local advertising dollars. As a result of this tension, some band leaders, including Fred Waring and Paul Whiteman, had long since stopped recording altogether. Even those bands that did make recordings sometimes found them a hindrance to their live performances. Many pieces included solo passages that were largely improvisatory, and performers would play them differently each time. But once a recording was made, the version of the solo that just happened to be on the record was regarded as definitive by the public. The next time the band played the piece live, the audience might express its disappointment at hearing something different from what they expected. Yet despite the ambivalence, recording continued steadily during 1941. Especially during the A.S.C.A.P. boycott, one of the principal means of getting music to a wide audience was through jukeboxes. There were some 400,000 of the devices in use throughout the country, and industry estimates suggested that 50-60 percent of all records sold were intended for use in jukeboxes.

New music was also being written in spite of the boycott, some of it of topical interest. Irving Berlin wrote two new songs reflecting interest in the war, "A Little Old Church in England" and "When That Man is Dead and Gone," the latter a satire on Hitler. The songs were published in February and immediately sold at a rate of 1,000 copies a day. Glenn Miller recorded the two pieces together for Bluebird, even though it would be months before they could be widely heard on the radio. This was also the year when Miller first recorded his enduring hit, "The White Cliffs of Dover," with Ray Eberle doing the vocal. That song was a notable success for Kate Smith, who also recorded it this year. Smith's rendition of "God Bless America," the Irving Berlin song she had first performed in 1938, had already become a classic. It was as closely identified with her as her official theme song, "When the Moon Comes over the Mountain."

Most band leaders were very careful to protect the interests of their radio sponsors, who were more often than not cigarette companies. Camels sponsored Benny Goodman and Bob Crosby, Chesterfield sponsored Glenn Miller and Harry James, and Raleigh sponsored Tommy Dorsey. Miller was known to castigate any member of his crew who smoked anything other than a Chesterfield. Old Gold boasted the longest list of sponsorships, including Whiteman, Artie Shaw, Larry Clinton, Frankie Carle, and Woody Herman. Lucky Strike's "Your Hit Parade" featured its own orchestra, led by Mark Warnow. The show purported to conduct surveys to identify the country's top tune at the moment, but the producers never revealed how the tunes were actually selected. Before and after the A.S.C.A.P. boycott, the airwaves were positively filled with Big Band music. NBC and CBS together broadcast some seventy bands, while Mutual featured a large number of lesser-known bands from their regional affiliates. These national and regional programs were almost always presented live. The broadcasting of recorded music was generally the preserve of local stations.

One of the most remarkable features of the Big Bands in 1941 was their relaxed attitude to race relations. Black bandleaders like

Duke Ellington, Jimmie Lunceford, Lionel Hampton, Fletcher Henderson, Earl Hines, Count Basie, and Cab Calloway mixed easily with their white counterparts. The artistic interchange among the bands was also important. Some critics believe that it was the combination of Goodman's precise musicianship with the liveliness of Fletcher Henderson's arrangements that kicked off the great era of swing music. Similarly Sy Oliver worked as an arranger for Tommy Dorsey, just as William Grant Still had done arrangements for Paul Whiteman back in the '20s. Ellington, especially, was creating stylistically rich and complex music in 1940 and '41, reflected in recordings of standards like "Passion Flower" and "Blue Serge." A number of the white bandleaders even had black musicians in their ensembles. Benny Goodman was the leader in this area, employing at one time or another Lionel Hampton, Teddy Wilson, and Cootie Williams. Roy Eldridge played trumpet for Gene Krupa, and Lena Horne sang for Charlie Barnet. On one occasion, Krupa found himself in jail in York, Pennsylvania, after starting a fight with a restaurant manager who refused to serve Eldridge with the rest of the band. The band leader had to be bailed out and pay a $10.00 fine. In September, notwithstanding his need for money, Artie Shaw cancelled a planned tour of the South when he found that he would not be able to bring trumpeter Hot Lips Page with him. Even in cosmopolitan New York the reception of black orchestras could be uneven. Duke Ellington performed at Loew's State Theater on Broadway but was excluded from the Paramount and the Strand. Relations were somewhat easier on the West Coast, where Hampton's orchestra was based for most of this period.

As the Big Band era progressed, this musical style largely absorbed and superseded the jazz tradition of the 1920s. Yet especially in the cities, jazz clubs kept alive the tradition of small-ensemble, improvisatory jazz. The center of this tradition seemed to be along 52nd Street in New York City, but good jazz could be heard in cities from Boston to San Francisco. The Benny Goodman Sextet (which, despite the name, usually had seven players) was also making jazz available to the rest of the country through its numerous recordings. On the West

Coast Woody Herman formed a septet from his band and recorded with them under the name Woody Herman and His Woodchoppers. Woody described their first record, "South" backed with "Fan It," as pure Dixieland. Herman's attitude was typical of most musicians. They enjoyed playing in a variety of different styles, and they saw no strict divisions among them. Indeed, differences among musical genres were seen primarily as a marketing device by which record companies could more effectively target the interests of their customers. Such distinctions were of much more importance to critics than to musicians. Musicians regularly listened to one another and fed off one another's interpretations. Stylistic boundaries were constantly shifting, and the chemistry among performers was producing some exciting music.

Leadership of the bands during this period was almost exclusively male. A rare exception occurred in 1939 when Chick Webb died in surgery in Baltimore. Ella Fitzgerald, who was Chick's lead singer, immediately took charge of the band and renamed it Ella and Her Famous Orchestra. She led it successfully for the next three years, making numerous appearances and cutting over a hundred recordings, until the group broke up at the beginning of the war. Even more unusual was Billie Rogers, whom Woody Herman hired in the fall of '41 as a trumpeter. There had been many female vocalists (and Rogers, with a good voice and perfect pitch, also sang for Herman), but Billie was the first female instrumentalist hired by a major band.

For all these performers, except occasionally those at the very top, life was financially uncertain and precarious. The Ink Spots, the top black quartet, might command up to $20,000 a week. But a performer like Billie Holiday was in many ways more typical. Her engagements at various night clubs seldom lasted more than a few weeks, and she was constantly on the lookout for new work. For most of the winter and spring of 1941 she sang at Kelly's Stables on 52nd Street, where she made $300 a week. Later in the year she went to Los Angeles to help open a new night club called Café Society. Unfortunately, the club failed quickly and she was left unpaid, without even enough money in her purse for a bus ticket home to New York. Stan Kenton encountered yet another financial problem, the rapacious agent. When Kenton signed his first contract, the agent wanted a 50 percent commission. Stan held out and got the figure down to a standard 10 percent. But the agent, recognizing a potential gold mine in this band leader, tried all kinds of devious tactics to get the contract changed. When Kenton needed to borrow money to get his band to a distant engagement, the agent offered to lend him $300—if he would renegotiate the contract. Kenton also learned later that the agent was turning down many booking requests for his band, hoping the financial pressure would cause him to give in. Finally the struggling young band opened at the Hollywood Palladium in November, and Kenton's career took off.

Despite the avowed intention of the founders of B.M.I. to feature musical genres neglected by A.S.C.A.P., for the most part the networks did not become venturesome and explore different musical styles during the boycott. Generally they broadcast unimaginative arrangements of old standards that were out of copyright. In February the NBC Blue network did experiment with a Monday night program, the Chamber Music Society of Lower Basin Street. The show was largely a jazz jam session with fourteen current or former players from the NBC Symphony. But such ventures into diversity were rare. Folk and country music were generally regarded as too old fashioned. On a national level they were restricted to special interest programs like the "National Barn Dance," broadcast from WLS in Chicago over the NBC Blue network, or the venerable Grand Ole Opry, hosted by Roy Acuff and broadcast from WSM in Nashville over NBC Red. (Although NBC tried to run Red and Blue as separate networks, the company was careful not to broadcast those two programs at the same time.) Like so many other music programs, Opry had a tobacco sponsor, in this case Prince Albert pipe tobacco. But country music was in fact more widely popular than the major networks realized. Ernest Tubb made a breakthrough in 1941 with his recording of "Walking the Floor Over You," which became a million seller.

In addition to the regional variations within country music, there were also stylistic differences. During the late '30s, Bill Monroe and the Bluegrass Boys on the *Opry* had started to develop the distinctive bluegrass sound. Regarded as the father of bluegrass music, Monroe fostered the development of a number of younger musicians. The style was still limited mainly to the Southern Appalachians, but it was growing in popularity. One of the most notable proponents of bluegrass during this period was Lester Flatt, whose program was broadcast over WDBJ in Roanoke, Virginia.

Folk music occupied a special niche in American life in 1941. On the one hand there was increasing academic interest in recording and preserving traditional folk tunes, much as there had been in England half a century earlier. Notable collectors were John Lomax, archivist at the Library of Congress, assisted by his son Alan, and Jimmy Morris (later known as the performer Jimmy Driftwood) in Arkansas. There had been a period in the late '30s when the folk tradition seemed to be in danger of dying out, as well known performers like Son House and Mississippi John Hurt dropped from view during the hard times of the Depression. But in 1941 folk music was beginning a comeback. Perhaps the best known performing group was the Almanac Singers, based in New York. The somewhat elastic membership of the group included Woody Guthrie, Bess Lomax (daughter of John Lomax), Millard Lampell, Pete Seeger, and Sis Cunningham. Their work was promoted by Bess's brother Alan at CBS. In addition to making numerous recordings of folk musicians like Vera Hall, Horton Barker, and Huddie Ledbetter (Leadbelly), Lomax also produced *Wellsprings of America* on the CBS School of the Air. It was this vehicle that first made folk music widely known to the general population. By 1941 the genre had attracted sufficient attention that one of its best known practitioners, Josh White, was asked by the government to make a goodwill tour of Mexico in company with the Golden Gate Quartet. White was a versatile performer, who was also known for his many recordings of blues, gospel, ballads, and work songs.

One special feature of the folk music tradition was its identification with liberal and left wing causes. Lee Hays, who sometimes sang with the Almanacs, was a union organizer who became interested in folk music through its frequent use at union rallies. The best known supporter of union causes was Woody Guthrie, who actively sought out union rallies and strikes at which he could perform in support of the workers. He and Pete Seeger had also spent time the previous summer at the Highlander Folk School in Tennessee (see Chapter 3), performing, teaching, and encouraging. Paul Robeson, whose enthusiasm for the Soviet Union helped his popularity during the second half of the year, also included artistic arrangements of folk songs in his broadly diverse repertoire.

Then as now, musicians and fans were divided on just how to classify the blues. Most of the great blues performers, like Leadbelly, moved seamlessly from blues to folk to jazz to swing. But apart from formal musical characteristics (12-bar harmonic pattern, three-line stanza, common use of the keys of F and B-flat), one great feature of blues was its association with black performers. While some white bands, particularly Goodman's, included blues in their repertoire, it was almost always with the addition of black soloists. One of the greatest was Charlie Christian, who began playing with Goodman in 1939. Christian has been described as not the first electric guitarist, but the first electric guitarist who mattered; and his use of amplification allowed the guitar to stand out as a solo instrument in a larger band. Still the blues were generally associated with smaller ensembles, and Christian's 1941 recording of "Profoundly Blue" with Edmond Hall and Meade Lux Lewis remains a classic of the genre.

The master of mixed genres was, of course, Benny Goodman. The previous December he had made his classical debut at Carnegie Hall performing the Mozart *Clarinet Concerto*. In April he returned to perform Prokofiev's *Overture on Yiddish Themes*. And in October he performed the Mozart with the Philadelphia Orchestra and then returned to the podium to conduct a tango by Stravinsky. The December concert was not Goodman's first appearance in Carnegie Hall. Back in 1938 he had performed there under the auspices of Sol Hurok, who announced that the Goodman Orchestra would be "replacing Jack Barbirolli and his Philharmonic Cats, the regular band in that spot," a reference to John Barbirolli, conductor of the New York Philharmonic.

In 1941 America was still largely unfamiliar with classical music. Certainly live performances were not readily accessible. There were only seventeen professional symphony orchestras, all clustered in the northeastern quarter of the country and along the Pacific coast. Apart from Seattle, San Francisco, and Los Angeles, there were no professional symphonies west of Minneapolis and St. Louis or south of Cincinnati and Washington. All such orchestras were located in major cities, and they served only about 24 percent of the country's total population. For three quarters of the American people, symphony concerts were effectively out of reach.

Some attempt was made to extend the reach of classical music to wider audiences. A number of orchestras offered a series of outdoor concerts in the summer, making the music accessible to people who might not be able to afford tickets during the winter season. Such venues were found across the country, from Robin Hood Dell in Philadelphia and Ravinia Park in Chicago to Red Rock in Denver and the Hollywood Bowl in Los Angeles. The best known and most prestigious of these was certainly the Berkshire Symphonic Festival, held on the Tanglewood Estate in the Berkshire Hills of Massachusetts. The festival had been going since 1934, and since 1936 it had featured the Boston Symphony under Serge Koussevitzky. In 1940 Koussevitzky had realized his dream of offering a summer music school in conjunction with the festival, and in its second year the Berkshire Music Center enrolled 340 students. A little more than a third of these were known as advanced students, serious musicians who aspired to musical careers. The rest were serious amateurs, more interested in music as a part of culture than in musical careers. The new music shed, designed by Finnish architect Eliel Saarinen, could seat an audience of 6,000; but the summer concerts attracted as many as 13,000, with the majority sitting on the grass just outside.

Some people were also able to enjoy recordings of classical music, but this access was limited in a way that access to popular tunes was not. All styles of music were recorded on standard 10-inch or 12-inch discs made of a shellac compound and played at 78 RPM. At that speed it was not possible to get more than about three or four minutes of music on one side of a record. A recording of a longer work, perhaps twenty or forty minutes, required a whole album of discs, recorded on both sides. In February a recording of Tchaikovsky's *6th Symphony* by Wilhelm Furtwängler and the Berlin Philharmonic was released in the United States. Selling for $6.50, this 46-minute piece was recorded on six 12-inch records. The listener had to stay near the record player and change the records every few minutes. Works like operas were generally available only as excerpts. Certainly few families could afford a record player like the Capehart Radio-Phonograph, advertised as "the radio-phonograph with the time-proved record changer that *turns the records over*—playing 20 records (40 selections) *continuously* on both sides or either side." Even at that, the player's limit was about an hour of music. There was also something of an elitist appeal to classical music in America, as reflected in the price of recordings. The $6.50 price tag on the recording of Tchaikowsky's *6th Symphony* represented a substantial investment. It can be contrasted with another six-record set released at the same time. Decca charged only $2.60 for Bing Crosby's album, which included such standards as "Deep Purple," "My Melancholy Baby," and "I Cried for You." Faced with these conditions, popular interest in and support for classical music was barely beginning to develop, and only in a limited number of urban areas.

As radio came of age in America, the networks took seriously their educational obligations. Radio broadcasts, usually from New York, provided what little exposure most people got to classical music. In 1937 David Sarnoff, President of the Radio Corporation of America, parent company of both Victor Records and NBC, had launched the NBC Symphony Orchestra and hired Arturo Toscanini as its conductor. The relationship was not always harmonious. Toscanini regarded the orchestra as his own possession, while Sarnoff regarded the musicians as employees of RCA, available for use elsewhere when they were not rehearsing or performing with the orchestra. The two men feuded over this issue, with the result that in March of 1941 Toscanini declined to sign a new contract. The network immediately signed Leopold Stokowski to a three-year agreement. Until the previous year Stokowski had been conductor of the Philadelphia Orchestra, and in 1939 he had carried out the amazing collaboration with Walt Disney that resulted in the movie *Fantasia*. Stokowski was replaced at

Philadelphia by Eugene Ormandy, who had already been doing most of the conducting there for several years. The Philadelphia Orchestra and the Boston Symphony were both regulars on the CBS network.

One long-running program of classical and light classical music was the *Voice of Firestone*, broadcast Monday nights at 8:30 on the NBC Red network. The Firestone family, founders and principal owners of Firestone Tire and Rubber, took a very personal interest in the show they sponsored. For many years the song "In My Garden," composed by Mrs. Harvey Firestone, introduced the program. In January "In My Garden" fell afoul of the A.S.C.A.P. dispute, and Mrs. Firestone quickly composed another song, "If I Could Tell You," to take its place. When the A.S.C.A.P. dispute was ended in the fall, "In My Garden" returned to the program. But by then "If I Could Tell You" had become so firmly established as the program's theme song that "In My Garden" was used to close the show. The *Voice of Firestone* featured many well-known singers whose performances of operatic arias were interspersed among classical and light classical orchestral works.

Sometimes attempts were made to make live classical music available to larger audiences. For several years the Metropolitan Opera had maintained a spring travel program, bringing live opera to those who could not otherwise come to New York to hear it. Their biggest draw in April of 1941 was, as always, Cleveland. Over six days in the Cleveland Municipal Auditorium, they offered a repertoire ranging from the *Barber of Seville* to *Tristan und Isolde*. Half of the 68,000 people who came to hear them were from out of town, traveling from as far away as Pittsburgh and Buffalo. These tours were in addition to the regular Saturday afternoon Met broadcasts live from New York on the NBC Blue network, sponsored by Texaco and introduced by long-time announcer Milton Cross. Washington's National Symphony Orchestra, under its conductor Hans Kindler, toured more widely than any other orchestra. In 1941 they offered 261 concerts in 87 different cities. Clearly there was an appetite in America for classical music, but few communities had the resources to provide performances of top quality. Many had amateur bands and orchestras that introduced people to classical and light classical music, but their quality was uneven, certainly not at the level that could be found in the major cities.

Far more familiar to most Americans in 1941 were the products of the Broadway stage, both musicals and straight drama. Then, as now, the center of musical theater was New York, where the extremely popular *Pal Joey* ("Bewitched, Bothered and Bewildered") had been running since December 25 of the previous year and would keep going until August 16, a solid run of 270 performances. An even longer run was enjoyed by the musical revue *Hellzapoppin'* from 1938, which closed on December 14 of '41 after 1,404 performances. The fine crop of new musicals for this year included *Lady in the Dark*, *Panama Hattie*, *Let's Face It!*, and *Cabin in the Sky* ("Taking a Chance on Love"), which was notable for its all-black cast, including Ethel Waters and Rex Ingram. George Jessel and Sophie Tucker had a successful run of 171 performances in the generally forgettable *High Kickers*, but the show flopped when it went on the road. Musicals were often dependent for their success on the star quality of their performers. Eddie Cantor returned to the Broadway stage in December with *Banjo Eyes*, a musical adaptation of the Abbott and Holm hit play, *Three Men on a Horse*. The musical had a good run of 126 performances, but closed when Cantor strained his back and had to go into the hospital. Live musical performances were available on the other side of the continent, too. Duke Ellington opened a musical revue that summer at the Mayan Theater in Los Angeles. *Jump for Joy* ran successfully for ten weeks.

Apart from musicals, theater critics generally regarded the 1940-41 season as one of the best in New York theater history and the 1941-42 season as the very worst. Of course, the opinion of critics was not always the best guide to the popularity of plays. William Saroyan's *The Time of Your Life* had won both the New York Drama Critics' Plaque and a Pulitzer Prize in the fall of 1940, but it lasted for just thirty-two performances. Nor was modest popularity enough to attract investors. Theater production was a risky business. Fully 80 percent of the straight plays produced on Broadway lost money. Musicals did somewhat better: Because of their higher cost, investors were much more careful and selective in deciding which shows to back, and about half of the musicals showed a profit.

January saw the opening of Moss Hart's *Lady in the Dark* and Joseph Kesselring's ever-popular *Arsenic and Old Lace*; while the powerful *Native Son* by Richard Wright and Paul Green opened in March at the St. James Theater, with Orson Welles directing. The highlight of the fall was the New York opening of Noël Coward's *Blithe Spirit*. While the war in Europe prevented most British artistic creations from crossing the Atlantic, Coward's play, which had enjoyed great success in the West End in London, was eagerly awaited when it opened in New York in November. Off Broadway the Savoy Opera Guild leased the Cherry Lane Theater in Greenwich Village and put on a well-received series of Gilbert and Sullivan classics. They opened with *The Mikado* on June 14 and continued through the season with three performances a week. Shakespeare, too, was almost always available in New York. The highlight of the 1940-41 season was a production of *Twelfth Night* starring Maurice Evans and Helen Hayes. Evans returned for the 1941-42 season with *Macbeth*, featuring Judith Anderson as Lady Macbeth. Their production enjoyed huge success and became an enduring classic when they starred in the film version.

While Broadway was the capital of the theatrical world, good theater was widely available across the country, though opportunities were somewhat more limited in number. Chicagoans were constantly complaining that America's Second City never saw the number of productions they felt it deserved. In fact, during 1941 there were never more than six plays in production in Chicago at any one time. Chicago was heavily dependent on Broadway for its fare. Plays that were successful in New York would sometimes be sent out in new productions even before the New York run had closed. Unfortunately, the New York producers would not always pay close attention to what was happening with the new venture. *Blithe Spirit*, such a success in New York, was poorly cast and poorly produced in Chicago, where it was a resounding flop.

San Francisco had an even more difficult time. The Bay Area generally received few new plays and had to settle for established hits from previous seasons, such as *Tobacco Road*, *Anna Christie*, and (yet again) *Hellzapoppin'*. Even these came under threat in the 1941-42 season as nighttime blackouts were ordered in the whole city after the attack on Pearl Harbor. Somehow the theater district coped. Down the coast in Southern California the theatrical opportunities were likewise limited. But 1941 did see one attempt to increase the availability of live theater in the land of the movie studios. During the summer producer David O. Selznick secured theater space in nearby Santa Barbara and opened two original plays. *Lottie Dundass* by Enid Bagnold was a full-length drama starring Geraldine Fitzgerald. Selznick paired it with a short curtain-raiser, *Hello Out There*, by William Saroyan. He also produced a revival of Eugene O'Neill's *Anna Christie* with Ingrid Bergman and a revival of George Bernard Shaw's *The Devil's Disciple* with Sir Cedric Hardwicke.

Elsewhere in the country, regional theater companies, commonly known as straw hat theaters, were flourishing; and there were at least 80 of them away from the East Coast. While most of their business was done in the summer, some were so successful that they kept their seasons going through September or even later. Most presented a steady stream of established Broadway hits, the 1941 favorite being *George Washington Slept Here*. The quality of production was also generally high, especially in the shows that took part in what was known as the visiting star system. Hollywood stars who wanted the prestige or experience of a Broadway résumé would take leading roles in summer productions as they toured the country. The arrangement allowed the movie actors and actresses to test their ability in live theater while giving audiences of their fans the opportunity to see Hollywood stars in person. The arrangement was also financially beneficial to the stars, who were generally well compensated for their work. Few could command the $1,500 a week that Tallulah Bankhead got, but performers like Harpo Marx and Alex Woollcott could get $400 a week each for their work in *The Yellow Jacket*. Others like Faye Wray, Clarence Derwent, and Alfred Drake were also regulars on the circuit.

The summer theater circuit also provided playwrights and producers an opportunity to try out new material before assuming the cost and risk of a New York opening. Around 75 new plays were introduced each year in the straw hat theaters, of which perhaps four might make it to Broadway. For those with potential but needing some revision, well known and well compensated "play doctors" would be brought out from New York to determine whether a play could be salvaged and what revisions might be needed.

In some areas a new theatrical experience was offered during the summer months, the outdoor theater. Most featured productions by local companies of established classics. The Sylvan Theater, for example, on the grounds of the Washington Monument in the Nation's Capital, put on some high quality Shakespeare productions for an audience that brought blankets and picnic suppers to enjoy as they sat on the ground in front of the stage. One outdoor theater was pioneering a different kind of drama. Since 1937 Paul Green's play *The Lost Colony* had been performed every summer in the outdoor amphitheater in Manteo, North Carolina. The play chronicled the founding and subsequent disappearance of the first English colony in North America. Green, a North Carolina native, had written it specifically for this location and this kind of theater. This one play was performed there nightly for the entire summer season, the prototype for other local outdoor dramas that began to be produced after the war.

CHAPTER 3

March: Art, Education, and Literature

ON THE EVENING of March 17, a glittering assembly of dignitaries gathered in Washington, D. C., for the formal opening of the National Gallery of Art. The new white marble building, erected on the site of the old Baltimore and Potomac Railroad station, was already being referred to as the American Louvre. With four acres of exhibit space, the structure cost $15,000,000 to build and housed art collections valued at over $100,000,000. The opening of the Gallery represented the culmination of a dream of the late Andrew W. Mellon, who wanted America to have a national art gallery to rival the great collections of Europe. Mellon himself had built a distinguished personal collection, having bought many of his paintings from the cash-strapped galleries of a Europe devastated by the World War and subsequent revolutions. A number of his purchases had come from such notable collections as the Hermitage in Leningrad, the Alte Pinakotek in Munich, and the Kaiser Friedrich in Berlin. Now the whole Mellon collection, housed in a building mostly paid for by Mellon, belonged to the United States. They were joined there by 376 paintings, almost 100 sculptures, and more than 1,300 Renaissance bronzes from the collection of Samuel H. Kress. Another collection, belonging to Joseph E. Widener of Philadelphia, was promised to the nation as a future gift. Andrew Mellon had died in 1937, but he had lived long enough to see his gift accepted by Congress, which authorized the construction of the Gallery.

The opening ceremonies were the highlight of the late winter social season in Washington. Brilliant dinner parties preceded the opening. Gallery Director David Finley and his wife hosted a dinner at the Sulgrave Club, with ambassadors, high government officials, and the perennial Alice Roosevelt Longworth in attendance. Mr. and Mrs. David K. E. Bruce hosted their dinner at the 1925 F Street Club. Mr. Bruce was a Gallery trustee, and his wife was the daughter of Andrew Mellon. After the dinners the 8,000 invited guests gathered in the great central hall of the Gallery for the official ceremonies. So large was the crowd that loudspeakers had to be set up so that guests could hear the speeches coming from the platform at the east end of the hall. At least six ladies fainted and had to be revived at first aid stations staffed by the Red Cross. Some guests, including Vice President and Mrs. Wallace, arrived for the ceremony, stayed a decent length of time, and then made an early exit. Others lingered late into the evening.

Paul Mellon officially presented the Gallery to the nation on behalf of his late father. The gift was accepted by President Roosevelt, who saw the Gallery as an affirmation that the "freedom of the human spirit and human mind which has produced the world's great art and all its science shall not be utterly destroyed." There was irony in the acceptance of this gift by Roosevelt, who had regarded Andrew Mellon as the embodiment of all that was wrong with American business practices in the 1920s. But on this evening the political differences were forgotten. The Rev. Z. T. Phillips, Chaplain of the Senate, offered the invocation, and was joined on the platform by Mrs. Roosevelt, Dr. Charles Abbott, Secretary of the Smithsonian Institution, and other trustees of the Gallery. The following morning the Gallery opened to the general public for the first time. In accordance with Mellon's wishes, there was no admission charge.

The opening of the National Gallery of Art was but the latest and most notable event in a trend that had been gaining strength for some time. As the nation emerged from the Depression, it was widely believed that improvements in the economic welfare of the general public should be accompanied by improvements in cultural opportunities. Efforts by orchestras and opera companies to take their productions out to smaller cities (Chapter 2) were only a part of this trend. Samuel Kress, who donated such a large part of his art collection to the new National Gallery, was also making smaller, but still significant gifts to art museums in cities across the country. Kress had built his S. H. Kress & Co. chain of five-and-dime stores by locating them in smaller cities which were not otherwise served by such variety stores, and his gifts of art rewarded the kinds of places that had given him his success. A number of cities took advantage of the fact that British museums and galleries were closed for the duration of the war. Much British art could be seen on touring exhibitions throughout the United States.

To bring art and art news to people all across the country, publisher Henry Luce's *Life* magazine included in most issues an article on the life and work of some contemporary American artist, often with color reproductions of representative works. The series had been going on for some time, and the previous year the magazine had even arranged for the publication of a large-format book on modern American painting. The book, containing high-quality color reproductions, proved quite popular. During the current year the series continued. One feature on portrait painters gave representative prices they charged for their works. Another showed a number of the murals commissioned for government buildings under the New Deal programs. Even amateur artists could sometimes find their works reproduced in these articles. On occasion the scope of coverage could be broadened, as when the work of British war artists was shown. Foreign artists active in the United States were also featured. They included the controversial Mexican muralist Diego Rivera, the Cuban painter Mario Carreño, and the Brazilian sculptor Maria Martins, who also happened to be the wife of the Brazilian ambassador to the United States. Especially notable was the feature on Salvador Dali, one of the many European refugees who spent the war years in the United States.

The large expatriate art community helped to create a vibrant cultural environment in New York, but one native-born painter created special excitement that fall. The young black artist Jacob Lawrence had spent most of 1941 creating a series of 60 paintings depicting the great migration of African Americans from the rural South to Northern cities in the late teens and early twenties. The vibrant paintings, noted for their "harsh primary colors and extreme simplicity of artistic statement," went on display at the Downtown Gallery in November. That same month *Fortune,* also a Luce publication, published a portfolio of 26 of the works, together with an interpretive essay in which the magazine took the opportunity to remind its readers (mostly wealthy whites) that "the 13 million U.S. Negroes are citizens of a shadowy subnation that is terra incognita to most whites. . . . In every country in the world Hitler has used the American Negro as prime propaganda to convince people that U.S. democracy is a mockery. . . . While carrying the 'four freedoms' to the earth's ends American democracy might well bestow them on its Negroes, who are woefully in need of them." Lawrence's powerful paintings gave mighty reinforcement to the message of the essay.

Not content with simply publishing the work of others, *Life* also commissioned several series of paintings on its own initiative. Those featured were generally significant but less well known incidents from more recent American history. For example, Alexander Hogue portrayed the oil gusher that came in at Spindletop, south of Beaumont, Texas, in 1901, ushering in the Texas oil boom. Another series, commissioned in line with Henry Luce's strong views on internationalism and defense preparedness, depicted scenes from modern military life. Never content with the second rate, Luce included such artists as Peter Hurd and Henry Billings in his commissions. In addition to these paintings, *Life* also pursued its self-appointed educational mission by commissioning an essay by the British writer Somerset Maugham, who described several of his favorite paintings and what he found so attractive in them.

For people interested in art, magazines and visits to galleries were not the only available outlets. Some people wanted to try their hands themselves. For them, institutions like the Federal Schools and the Washington Art Institute offered correspondence courses in painting and drawing. These schools advertised widely in popular national magazines, appealing to the desire of Americans for educational self-improvement.

In a nation founded upon the ideal of equal opportunity, few areas of life exhibited greater inequality, both of opportunity and of achievement, than education. The form of the educational ladder was a familiar one, starting with elementary school and progressing through high school and college to graduate and professional schools. Kindergartens were rare, as were separate middle schools or junior high schools. The junior college was a development of the 1920s that as yet had not spread very far. Yet the number of Americans who had taken full advantage of the educational system was quite small. Across the nation, the average adult had completed just 8½ years of school. Only one adult in seven had completed four years of high school. Not even one in twenty had completed four years of college. A person needed a special reason to go to college. Even then, well over half of those who started college did not complete four years. If one wanted to go into a profession such as law or medicine, if one wanted to go into science or become a secondary school teacher, if one's family were prosperous and wanted to polish a son's education for a few more years before he entered the family business, then college was a realistic goal. If one wanted to be an elementary teacher, one would attend normal school. If one wanted to become a military officer, one might join a college R.O.T.C. program. If one wanted to become an Army or Navy pilot, one needed at least two years of college or junior college. Whatever one's ambition, there had to be a very specific reason for continuing past high school. Lacking such a reason, a high school graduate was considered adequately prepared for a business career.

Overall America made a substantial investment in education. The public school systems of the country spent over $2 billion and employed a million people to educate our 25 million pupils. Yet the expenditure for each pupil had hardly changed—had actually declined slightly—in the last decade. Even more, the distribution of these resources varied widely across the country. America's tradition of local control of schools meant that expenditures reflected a state's wealth and priorities rather than nationwide policies. New York spent $146.40 for each pupil in 1940. Mississippi spent $24.89. In New York the average school teacher earned over $2,600 a year, a reasonable middle-class salary. In Mississippi the average school teacher earned less than $560 a year, a figure that was actually 10 percent less than it had been ten years earlier. Many schools, especially in prosperous urban areas, had modern buildings and up-to-date facilities. Many rural areas had little money to spend maintaining their buildings.

The federal government was beginning to make some small efforts to alleviate these inequalities. In areas where defense plants were expanding and Army bases were being established, the growth in population had put a severe strain on school systems. Using the defense buildup as a pretext, the government started to involve itself in an area traditionally reserved to the states and counties. There was no objection, however, since the federal government limited its involvement to providing extra funds to the local authorities, funds that amounted to $150,000,000 a year. The large number of training camps in the South meant that region got a larger share of the money, a share that it very badly needed. But not all the money for impacted areas went to the South. There were pressing needs all over the country. Even the relatively prosperous Pacific Northwest felt the strain. In Seattle, for example, nearby Ft. Lewis, McChord Field, Puget Sound Navy Yard, and Sand Point Naval Air Station were themselves expanding. But the greatest growth was in the local defense industries like Boeing and Seattle-Tacoma Shipbuilding. Because of the pressure on facilities, in September the state and federal governments together provided the city with $2,000,000 for new school construction.

Despite the construction of new school buildings, in isolated areas there were still remnants of an earlier time. Especially in the sparsely populated West, the one-room school house of popular lore could still be found. A one-room school in Montana, for example, might educate upwards of twenty children of area ranchers in first through eighth grades. The young teacher would be a graduate of the state normal school, well trained for her job. She would also probably be paid slightly better than her counterparts in town since some incentive would be needed to attract her to an isolated area. While such schools seldom had electricity or running water, the teacher would likely be given a small house to live in and coal for the stove. A battery-powered radio would keep her connected with the wider world.

The one-room school was not limited to isolated areas in the West. This form of school was also the norm for rural black schools in the segregated South. There the teacher, almost always a young black woman, was usually a recent high school graduate with no further training. Since both black and white schools were controlled by local all-white school boards, the authorities had little interest in what happened in black schools, so long as they did not become inciters of social change. Resources were poor to nonexistent. Swedish sociologist Gunnar Myrdal, researching race relations in America, reported on one black school in Georgia, not far from Atlanta, where no one knew who or what the President of the United States was. None of the pupils even knew who Booker T. Washington was, nor did they know anything about Europe. Only one pupil had a vague idea that Europe was beyond the ocean. Certainly the local white school board would have been pleased to know that no one at the school could identify W. E. B. DuBois or the N.A.A.C.P.

Despite the low percentages of adults who had completed high school or college, the American commitment to education was increasing in 1941. The end of the depression meant that fewer young people felt it was necessary to drop out of school to help support their families. Although only one adult in seven had finished high school, among young people aged 14 to 17 fully two thirds were enrolled in school. But the increasing number of high school students, coupled with the increasing needs of industry for a technically trained work force, brought again to the fore some old debates that for twenty years had divided the educational profession.

Ever since World War I there had been a deepening split over the purpose of education and the best ways of achieving that purpose. At the one end were the traditionalists who valued knowledge for its own sake, who emphasized structure and mental discipline, and who held to a curriculum of English, foreign language (with Latin often preferred to the modern languages), mathematics, history, and science. At the other end were the progressives who saw pure knowledge as a tool for solving applied problems, who wanted to adapt teaching methods to children's different learning styles, and who wanted to enrich the curriculum with activity- and experience-based classes in the arts and applied skills. Between the two were a wide variety of different beliefs and approaches, and each side tended to characterize the other in terms of its most extreme proponents. Progressives characterized traditionalists as grim killjoys who believed education should be difficult, demanding, and even painful. Traditionalists accused progressives of coddling students and not preparing them for the real world.

One of the deep divisions between the two sides was over preparation for higher education. Traditionalists argued that the more liberal progressive curriculum would not prepare students adequately for the rigors of college. Progressives responded that only one high school graduate in six went on to college anyway. Even more, over a quarter of those who started college did not return for the sophomore year. Since the traditional system was not always giving good preparation even to that small minority who started college, more attention should be paid to the needs of the great majority who entered directly into the workforce. This argument spoke to another of the great debates in American education, the conflict between those who would limit education, especially advanced education, to a small elite, and those who would make advanced education as widely available as possible.

To bring some rationality to what had become a highly emotional debate, in 1932 the Commission on the Relation of School and College, a part of the Progressive Education Association, began what was to be known as the Eight-Year Study. Funded by the Carnegie Foundation and the General Education Board of the Rockefeller Foundation, the study tracked 1,475 students from thirty secondary schools that agreed to reform their curricula in ways that would emphasize the relevance of education to the needs of contemporary students. The nature of instructional reform varied widely from school to school, with some being rather conservative in the changes they introduced and others trying to adopt as many progressive curricular ideas as possible. The 1,475 students in the study were all college bound. For each of them, the college he or she attended identified another student who was as similar as possible in all academic and nonacademic characteristics, except that the student in the comparison group had attended a traditional high school or preparatory school. The participating colleges compared the academic performance and extracurricular activities of the students being studied, and the data were compared and analyzed by the Commission.

The tracking ended in 1940, and in 1941 the first reports were published. On virtually every quantifiable measure the students from progressive schools did slightly better than the students in the control groups. In fact, the more innovative and progressive the high school, the better its graduates performed in college. Differences were particularly notable when results other than grades and academic honors were considered. Students from progressive schools proved more resourceful and adaptable, showed more intellectual curiosity and drive, possessed more precise and objective analytic skills, and evinced more interest in national and international affairs. Yet these reports from the study did nothing to quell the disagreements. As is normal in American public debates, the presentation of clear facts had no effect whatsoever on ingrained opinions.

For young people who had a reason for wanting a college education, progress from high school to the college campus followed a familiar pattern. Certain admissions requirements had to be met, including completion of a traditional high school curriculum (except, of course, for those participating in the Eight Year Study). Money for college was seldom a serious obstacle. Most public colleges and universities charged nothing or next to nothing in the way of tuition. Even at more prestigious public institutions that did charge student fees, the amount was small. At the College of William and Mary in Virginia, for example, student fees were only $75 for a semester. If a student had the academic ability to succeed in college, family, friends, or college donors would usually be able to cover the small amounts needed. Students could frequently find part-time jobs to pay the modest costs for room and board. Indeed, the most serious obstacle college freshmen faced was inadequate preparation. Many found that their education to that point had not equipped them for college, even when they had successfully completed all the classes required for admission. With few students seeking to continue past twelfth grade, schools had little motivation to maintain the rigorous standards needed to prepare their students for higher education. Many a young person started college, lasted a semester, and used family finances as a pretext for not continuing further.

Because so few people had attended college and even fewer had finished, a college degree was held in high esteem; and students would sometimes resort to devious means to complete their degrees successfully. Even in 1941 the ghostwriting of student papers was a flourishing business, with prices ranging from $3 to $25. Theses and dissertations could also be purchased, though at substantially higher prices. One professional writer in New York charged $55 for a master's thesis entitled "Experience as a Factor in the Success of Business Teachers." Unfortunately for the writer, his "client" was an undercover investigator for the State Department of Education; and the result was a criminal charge for helping someone to obtain a degree by fraudulent means.

Even higher was the esteem accorded to professors. To be a college professor was to be a respected leader in one's community. Academic salaries reflected this high regard, with college faculty regularly earning as much as doctors and dentists. To preserve and enhance this status, most colleges and universities observed the fundamental principles of academic freedom; and many offered their senior faculty job protection in the form of tenure. In 1940 a series of meetings between the Association of American Colleges (A.A.C.) and the American Association of University Professors (A.A.U.P.) culminated in the publication of what became known as the 1940 Statement of Principles on Academic Freedom and Tenure. The 1940 Statement was a revision of earlier statements, and it commanded widespread and immediate support. The A.A.C., the A.A.U.P., and the American Association of Teacher Colleges all formally endorsed the statement in 1941. The key provisions protected the freedom of teachers in their research and publications and in the teaching of their subject matter. They also endorsed the granting of tenure after a probationary period. In the spring of 1941, events began to unfold in Georgia that revealed just how fragile academic freedom was, and how easily a political leader could take control of a public university.

In his early years, Eugene Talmadge was not man whom one would have expected to try to destroy the academic reputation of the University of Georgia. A Phi Beta Kappa graduate of that institution, Talmadge had taught school for a few years and then returned to his alma mater to complete his law degree. But years of hard farming and an unremunerative law practice had left him restless and longing for some path to fame and prosperity. He found it in politics, and especially in the kind of demagogic Southern populism that appealed to poor, uneducated dirt farmers. Talmadge was a product of the Old South, the poor, rural, undereducated South, the South for whom the defeat of the Civil War still rankled. Above all he was a product of the racist South. Poor whites, like the marginalized in all eras, needed a scapegoat, someone to look down on, someone to blame for their troubles, someone to be kept in subservience so that they themselves could stay one step above the bottom of the ladder. For Talmadge and the people he appealed to, that person was the Negro, who had to be kept in his place. Elected governor in 1940, Talmadge, like all demagogues, was always looking for a new issue with which to arouse his base of support. In 1941 he found that issue in the most emotionally charged of subjects for white Southerners, segregation.

The story actually began back in 1937 when Dr. Walter D. Cocking, newly appointed Dean of the College of Education at the University of Georgia, began working to improve standards, institute new programs, and transfer or fire unproductive personnel. One of the teachers removed by Dean Cocking was a Mrs. Sylla Hamilton, who, abetted by others who shared her disaffection, began corresponding with Governor Talmadge about Cocking's alleged plans to educate Negroes and whites together.

At the same time, another tempest was building over in Statesboro at the Georgia State Teachers College, where the progressive president, Dr. Marvin Pittman, was trying to remove faculty deadwood and improve teaching standards. A jealous senior professor, R. J. H. DeLoach, who apparently had been shuffled into teaching economics to minimize the harm he could do, began his own correspondence with the governor, accusing Pittman of improper involvement in local politics and other misbehavior, all charges that were completely unfounded. But Pittman had placed himself in jeopardy by forging close relationships with the Negro faculty at Tuskegee Institute in Alabama. Talmadge had his issue.

As governor, Talmadge was an *ex officio* member of the Georgia Board of Regents. At the May meeting of the Board, Talmadge objected to the reappointment of Pittman, accusing him in vague terms of partisan political involvement. The Board, accustomed to giving the governor what he wanted, agreed. Talmadge then opened up his tirade against Cocking and offered a motion to dismiss "any person in the university system advocating communism or racial equality." The Board again acquiesced. But university President Harmon Caldwell heard of the votes and went public with an angry letter of resignation. The Board quickly reconvened and voted to give the accused men a hearing before dismissing them.

The hearing was scheduled for July 14, and Talmadge blatantly manipulated the Board to get the result he wanted. All of the governor's most trusted advisors, including his wife, tried to get him to back off; but he would have none of it. The hearing in the capitol turned into a circus, the galleries packed with Talmadge's red-neck supporters. All of the evidence exonerated Cocking and Pittman of the charges against them. None of it mattered. By separate 10-5 votes the Board fired both of them. Then the storm broke.

The first move came from the Commission on Institutions of Higher Education of the Southern Association of Colleges and Secondary Schools, which announced that it was forming a committee to investigate the firings. The Southern Association was the regional accrediting body for schools in the Southeast and had the authority to suspend or revoke the accreditation of the University of Georgia. Talmadge held firm: "We credit our own schools down here," he responded. On September 1 the Commission suspended the ten white schools in the university system for "unprecedented and unjustifiable political interference." On October 14 the university was expelled from the Southern University Conference. Across the nation Georgia was held up to ridicule, and Georgians increased pressure on the governor to compromise. On November 1 the regents met and appointed a committee to meet with the Accrediting Commission and determine what action they needed to take in order to regain their accreditation. They also voted to be "honor bound" to abide by whatever arrangements the committee agreed to with the Commission. The two committees quickly reached an agreement, which included the rehiring of Cocking and Pittman. But when the Board of Regents met again on November 19 to ratify the agreement, Talmadge manipulated the meeting so as to block the rehiring. Again his advisors urged moderation, and again Talmadge refused to budge. The result was predictable. On December 4 the Accrediting Commission revoked the accreditation of the university system's ten white schools.

The damage done to governor's reputation was severe, but the damage done to Eugene Talmadge was even worse. The *Atlanta Constitution*, no friend of the governor's in the best of times, commented that "There was no racial issue in Georgia until the Governor created it. That is one of the most horrible things a man can do." *Life* magazine held him up for ridicule before the entire country: "Georgia is one of the poorest and most illiterate of the 48 states. Talmadge is the red-suspendered darling of thousands of voters who can barely read or write, and who spend about $100 a year for food per family. He is counting on their ignorance and racial prejudice to keep his little dictatorship going." Although Talmadge professed not to care about the actions of the Accrediting Commission, he soon came to realize the mistake he had made. Being ridiculed and humiliated in front of the rest of the country was too much for Georgia's voters. Ten months later Talmadge lost the gubernatorial primary to Ellis Arnall. The sole substantive issue in the race was higher education.

Apart from the schools and colleges, formal opportunities for adult education were limited in 1941. In Eastern cities there were the language and citizenship classes of the sort immortalized by Leonard Q. Ross (Leo Rosten) in his H*Y*M*A*N K*A*P*L*A*N stories. There were also numerous organizations like DeForest's Training, Sprayberry Academy of Radio, and International Correspondence Schools, which offered mail-order instruction in technical trades. Other schools offered correspondence classes in accounting and even in law, all aimed at men hoping to advance in their careers. But per-haps the most innovative and controversial effort in adult education came from the Highlander Folk School in Summerfield, Tennessee, a small community near the eastern edge of the Cumberland Plateau.

Highlander was founded in 1932 by Myles Horton and was loosely modeled on Danish folk high schools. Horton's intent was to take edu-cation to people where they were, to educate them in subjects that met their real-life needs, and to empower them to find within themselves and within their social groups the answers to the problems that faced them. With this mission, the school inevitably became involved in the labor movement, and quite early on it became well known as a training center for labor organizers. Just as inevitably the school became a center of controversy, especially as Horton insisted on full racial equality in all its educational programs. A local white-supremacist group, the Grundy County Crusaders, persuaded Martin Dies that his House Committee for the Investigation of Un-American Activities should look into Highlander as a center of Communist activity. Federal investigators made numerous inquiries into the school's relationship with Communist organizations (there were none) and with Negroes, always linking the two together. Nothing came of the Dies investigation, but the message to the school was clear: Stay away from racial issues. Equally clear was Horton's reaction. He looked for even more creative ways to help African Americans help themselves. Highlander remained uncompromisingly committed to racial equality, a stance that accounted for a very large part of the opposition to the school. In the spring and summer of 1941 the attacks on Highlander were finally beginning to die down and support was rising.

The curriculum at Highlander was thoroughly practical. Terms generally lasted six weeks, with shorter workshops in the summer. Classes in labor history, economics, union problems, and labor journalism formed the core of the offerings. Classes in public speaking, parliamentary procedure, and drama were oriented toward ways of delivering the labor message and toward the management of union affairs. The very success of the school gave another cause for opposition from leaders of business and industry. By 1941 over 50 percent of the school's alumni held or had held office in labor unions.

While the educational programs at the Highlander Folk School were all oriented toward meeting the practical needs of the students, that mission was not narrowly construed. Horton himself had been an English major in college. Literature classes figured in the curriculum at Highlander, and literacy projects were an important part of the school's outreach. Even more prominent were the music classes taught and supervised by Horton's wife Zilphia. The school played an important role in the encouragement and preservation of the folk music tradition in the United States; and musicians like Pete Seeger, Woody Guthrie, and Huddie Ledbetter were regular visitors.

The Hortons saw clearly the power of music in labor organizing, both as a means of sustaining worker morale and as a way to keep strikes and demonstrations from becoming violent under provocation.

Although few Americans took advantage of formal advanced education, there remained nevertheless a strong national interest in continuing personal education and self-improvement. Much of this interest, of course, was mere dabbling. Literary critic Douglas Bush, himself a Harvard professor, spoke of America's "thirst for literary cocktails," observing that "for the last twenty years or so, America, as Sherwood Anderson once remarked, has been on a culture jag, and the itch for self-improvement inspires or affects all classes of society."

Literary appetites were satisfied by a variety of magazines that offered poetry, short stories, essays, and sometimes serialized novels. At the one end were the campus-based magazines like the *Yale Review* and the *South Atlantic Quarterly* (at Duke University). Also appealing to a more intellectual audience was the *New Yorker*, which had a well established reputation for publishing some of the best authors. At the other end of the spectrum were special-interest publications like *Popular Science* or *Railroad Magazine*, which usually included in each issue a short story that would appeal to the interests of its readers. In the middle of the range, seeking to appeal to a wide audience, was the *Saturday Evening Post*, with a large national circulation. While many of its authors were regular contributors who cranked out rather unremarkable fiction, the *Post* was able to attract a number of well-known writers like James Thurber, Ben Ames Williams, MacKinlay Kantor, *New Yorker* columnist Brendan Gill, Booth Tarkington, Erle Stanley Gardner, Stephen Vincent Benét, and others of their rank. C. S. Forester departed from his Hornblower novels to write *The Captain from Connecticut*, a serialized novel about an American naval officer in the days of sail. Agatha Christie's mystery novel *The Body in the Library* was serialized in May and June.

For many readers, a popular way of buying books was through the Book-of-the-Month Club. New subscribers would receive the current book dividend for free, and thereafter they would receive a book dividend for every two regular books purchased. The dividends were generally special club editions of well-known, popular, or important works. Typical was a special two-volume boxed edition of Marcel Proust's *Remembrance of Things Past*. One special nonfiction volume from 1940, Harold J. Laski's *The American Presidency*, was still popular in 1941, made all the more relevant by Roosevelt's third election and inauguration. Laski, Professor of Political Science at the University of London, probably knew more about American politics than most Americans.

Inevitably, the nonfiction bestsellers of 1941 clearly reflected the interests of the times. Topping the list was William L. Shirer's *Berlin Diary*, an engrossing narrative of his time as a radio and newspaper correspondent in wartime Berlin. Shirer was posted to Berlin as a correspondent for Universal Services in 1934, just after Hitler had purged the *SA*. He remained there until December of 1940, when increasingly tight censorship made it clear to him that he could no longer report the news accurately. During all his time there he kept diaries, which he managed to smuggle out past the Gestapo inspectors when he left. Back in America he turned these diaries into a narrative describing the changes in Germany during the last years of peace and the first years of war. It was an instant bestseller and highly influential. Shirer's conclusions are perhaps best encapsulated in a brief passage near the end of the book:

> There is one final question to be tackled in these rambling conclusions: does Hitler contemplate war with the United States? I have argued this question many hours with many Germans and not a few Americans here and have pondered it long and carefully. I am firmly convinced that he does contemplate it and that if he wins in Europe and Africa he will in the end launch it unless we are prepared to give up our way of life and adapt ourselves to a subservient place in his totalitarian scheme of things.
>
> For to Hitler there will not be room in this small world for two great systems of life, government, and trade. For this reason I think he also will attack Russia, probably before he tackles the Americas.

Popular sympathy for Britain made a best seller of *Blood, Sweat and Tears*, a collection of British Prime Minister Winston Churchill's major speeches. Some of the early speeches, such as that on the Eire Bill, were of little interest to Americans. But the latter part of the book contained speeches of the very greatest interest, concluding with one of his best known, the radio broadcast of February 9, with its closing line, "Give us the tools, and we will finish the job."

Yet another influential bestseller was *Out of the Night* by Jan Valtin, the autobiography of a Soviet double agent who barely escaped occupied Europe with his life. The book was especially effective because its Kafkaesque world of *agents provocateurs*, constant treachery, double agents, and political infighting within the communist hierarchy are described in simple, direct, unadorned language as if this world were a perfectly normal and natural one. The book appeared early in 1941, and excerpts were serialized in *Life*.

For several years John Gunther's *Inside* books had been a popular way for Americans to learn about lands they had never visited and, for the most part, never expected to visit. *Inside Europe* had already gone through several editions, the latest in 1940. Each had been thoroughly revised to keep up with Hitler's most recent antics. In 1939 *Inside Asia* had appeared, giving most Americans their first overview of the varied cultures and their history over the whole continent, including the war in East Asia, the nationalist movement in India, and the problem of Jewish-Arab coexistence in Palestine. Now in 1941 came Gunther's latest contribution, *Inside Latin America*, a rich portrait of a highly complex region.

Other books published during the year were direct in urging greater involvement in the European conflict. In the fall a young John Kennedy, son of the American ambassador to Great Britain, turned his Harvard senior thesis into a book, *Why England Slept*. The title was obviously derivative from Winston Churchill's 1938 book, *While England Slept*, which attacked the appeasement policies of the Chamberlain government. The obvious message was that America was endangering its own security by ignoring the threat posed by Nazi Germany.

It was perhaps inevitable that many of the novels published in 1941 would also be heavily influenced by world events. Ranking near the top of the list was Eric Knight's *This above All*, a long and dull novel about a working-class soldier who is evacuated from Dunkerque, is hospitalized for a time, becomes thoroughly disenchanted with the war and decides not to go back to the army, meets an upper-class young woman in the W.A.A.F., begins an affair with her, and dies after being injured in an air raid in London. Such a sluggish novel as this could scarcely rise to near the top of the bestseller list were it not for the author's prior success with *Lassie Come Home*, coupled, of course, with widespread public interest in stories related to the war in England.

Very different and far more despairing was Arthur Koestler's *Darkness at Noon*, a novel that gave many people in the West their first intimate sense of what existence was like in Stalin's Russia. It is the story of an old Bolshevik, Rubashov, caught up in the madness of Stalin's great purge. Finally crushed by the ceaseless pressures of interrogation and torture, Rubashov confesses to false charges of treason and, at the end of the book, is executed.

Not all the year's novels, however, were so heavily influenced by current events. At the top of the bestseller lists was A. J. Cronin's *The Keys of the Kingdom*, which traces the life of Father Chisholm, a simple Scottish priest, and his struggle to serve God in the face of prejudice, bureaucracy, political manipulation, and military conflict. The one constant through the novel is the ability of a simple priest to touch individual lives. John P. Marquand's *H. M. Pulham, Esq.*, is even further removed from the contemporary international conflict. Harry Pulham is a well-bred, conventional Harvard graduate and investment consultant who moves through life in a way that is totally predictable for his class but that leaves him strangely unsatisfied. He finds it impossible to communicate with anyone on a really deep level because his perceptions and self-reflections will not take him to that level in himself. With none of Father Chisholm's redeeming grace, Pulham is a superbly drawn character that the reader is finally only too happy to leave behind.

Gertrude Stein was perhaps one of the most famous American writers never to make the bestseller list. Her tortured and often incomprehensible writing appealed to only a small group of devotees. In February Stein published her latest novel, *Ida*. As was the case with all her novels, Random House ordered a press run of 2,500 copies. They had the market well analyzed. Fewer than fifty copies were left unsold, but there was no need for a second printing. The protagonist of

Ida was based in part on the Duchess of Windsor, to whom the publisher, Bennett Cerf, sent a complimentary copy. The Duchess replied gratefully, but confessed that she did not understand a word of the book. Neither did the reviewers. And, by his own admission, neither did Bennett Cerf.

CHAPTER 4

April: Social Change

ON APRIL 28, the United States Supreme Court handed down a decision that was little noted at the time, but that marked an important step forward on the path toward equal rights for African Americans. Four years earlier, in April of 1937, Rep. Arthur W. Mitchell of Chicago, the only black member of the U.S. House of Representatives, traveled by train from Chicago to Hot Springs, Arkansas, for a short vacation. Mitchell traveled in a Pullman car from Chicago to Memphis and then transferred to another Pullman car for the trip to Hot Springs. But as soon as the train crossed the Mississippi River into Arkansas, the train conductor forced Mitchell to leave the Pullman and ride in a separate car provided for black passengers. In this the railroad was complying with Arkansas law, which required segregated passenger car facilities for whites and blacks.

The descriptions of the two passenger cars are worth quoting directly from the Supreme Court's opinion:

> The Pullman car was of modern design and had all the usual facilities and conveniences found in standard sleeping cars.

It was air-conditioned, had hot and cold running water and separate flushable toilets for men and women. It was in excellent condition throughout. First-class white passengers had, in addition to the Pullman sleeper, the exclusive use of the train's only dining-car and only observation-parlor car, the latter having somewhat the same accommodations for day use as the Pullman car.

The coach for colored passengers, though of standard size and steel construction, was 'an old combination affair', not air-conditioned, divided by partitions into three main parts, one for colored smokers, one for white smokers and one in the center for colored men and women, known as the women's section, in which appellant sat. There was a toilet in each section but only the one in the women's section was equipped for flushing and it was for the exclusive use of colored women. The car was without wash basins, soap, towels or running water, except in the women's section.

Mitchell filed a complaint with the Interstate Commerce Commission, which ruled in favor of the railroad, finding that the Rock Island had provided Mitchell with transportation as required by Arkansas law. Mitchell then took his case to the U.S. District Court, which found that it did not have jurisdiction. From there Mitchell took his appeal directly to the Supreme Court.

The court's unanimous opinion (*Mitchell v. U.S.*, 313 U.S. 80 (1941)) was clear and emphatic. Referring to "a fundamental right of equality of treatment," the court found that the railroad had denied Mitchell equal accommodation solely because of his race. Arkansas law could not overrule the U.S. Constitution. No excuse availed. The judgment was reversed and the case was sent back to the I.C.C. for action in Mitchell's favor. It was a stunning result. The case was the first crack in the armor of segregation that had been maintained for forty-five years by the separate-but-equal doctrine. Back in 1896, also in a transportation case, the Supreme Court had held in *Plessy v. Ferguson* that segregated facilities were permissible so long as equal facilities were provided to both races. The country then turned away further efforts by African Americans to secure equal rights. In case after case the courts refused to examine closely whether facilities provided were, in fact, equal. As long as separate facilities were provided, regardless of actual quality, they were presumed to be equal. In 1941 the Supreme Court was not quite willing to go so far as to overturn the doctrine set out in *Plessy*. But it was prepared, as it had not been before, to look closely into the condition of the facilities that were alleged to be equal and make an impartial judgment concerning them. It was a small step, but it was a step. It was also a step that the Roosevelt administration was prepared to support. Solicitor General Francis Biddle filed a brief supporting the plaintiff. Social conditions were beginning to change.

Racial consciousness was still strong in the America of 1941, and it was not limited to African Americans. The social and political establishment still thought of this country not just as a white man's country, but as one in which the white Anglo-Saxon Protestant heritage was the one to which all others should adapt. Anyone not of this heritage was somehow different, suspect. Even heroes were not immune. Before Joe DiMaggio acquired the nickname Joltin' Joe, sportswriters commonly referred to him as the Big Dago. Even his teammates regularly called him Daig. He reportedly disliked the name but said little about it. Likewise, Ted Williams found it expedient not to publicize the fact that his mother was half Mexican. He felt he might not get the breaks that every young ballplayer needed if his racial background were known. African Americans, however, still experienced the most pronounced forms of racial labeling. In the fall the public health authorities in Memphis decided to take steps to promote good child-rearing practices among African Americans. At the Tri-State Negro Fair they offered free medical examinations for babies by sponsoring a Healthiest Baby Contest. *Life* magazine, with its nationwide circulation, ran a picture article on the fair under the headline, "Doctors Pick Prize Pickaninnies at Memphis Tri-State Negro Fair." No one complained.

Yet the times were slowly changing, and awareness was growing of significant social problems facing the country. In the South the incidence of lynchings had dropped off sharply in recent years. From time to time bills had been introduced in Congress to make lynching a federal crime. While these bills sometimes passed the House, as had been the case in 1938, they regularly died in the Senate. But Southern leaders, recognizing the steadily increasing pressure for various kinds of civil rights reforms, had undertaken to reduce the incidence of lynching in order to prove that the states could handle the matter without federal intervention. Their efforts had met with a good deal of success, and with the sharp drop-off in lynchings had come an accompanying reduction in congressional pressure for an antilynching bill. One such bill was introduced in 1940 and another in 1941. Both remained tied up in committee and never came up for a formal vote.

Despite the apparent inactivity in Congress, other efforts were going on behind the scenes. In 1939 Roosevelt had appointed former Michigan governor Frank Murphy as attorney general. Murphy immediately established a Civil Liberties Unit within the Criminal Division of the Justice Department. Recognizing that getting an anti-lynching law through Congress would be an uphill battle, Murphy charged the Civil Liberties Unit with finding a way to bring lynching with the scope of activities prohibited by existing federal law. The work was still underway when Murphy was named to the Supreme Court the following year, but the outline of the strategy was clear: The government threatened to use the Enforcement Act of 1871, origi-nally aimed at the Ku Klux Klan, as a device to bring lynching within the scope of federal law enforcement. No one was quite sure whether it would work, although the presence of Murphy on the Supreme Court was encouraging.

Outsiders were also starting to look closely at the race question in America. In March the Swedish economist and sociologist Gunnar Myrdal returned to the United States to complete his research and begin the writing of what would be one of the most important books of its time, *An American Dilemma: The Negro Problem and Modern Democracy*. With funding from the Carnegie Corporation of New York, Myrdal had already paid one visit to this country and begun the research, especially in the South, on racial discrimination and its impact on American society. Now he returned to complete the project. Myrdal found that outside the South, people were dimly aware of racial discrimination but avoided thinking about it. In the South people were fully aware of it and sought rationalizations for it in terms of their distinctive social system. But everywhere he found people sensitive to the sharp contrast between racial discrimination and the American ideal of equality of opportunity. He also found some hope in the growing employment opportunities brought by increasing prosperity, and he placed great faith in the power of education, not just for African Americans but for whites as well.

The buildup of national defense preparedness presented other opportunities for small but significant social changes. The draft was taking so many young men out of the work force that more and more employers were recruiting women to fill in. In Philadelphia the Sun Oil Company lost so many service station attendants that it actively recruited and trained young women to fill gas tanks, wash windshields, and check oil levels. The draft was also putting pressure on defense industries, and in August Consolidated Aircraft in San Diego announced immediate openings for 400 women. At the same time, when Frye Aircraft School in Long Beach enrolled its fall class, half the students were women. The aircraft industry was regarded as ideal employment for women. Many airplane parts were made of lightweight aluminum and so were easier to handle. And the wiring and instruments in the airplanes required considerable skill and manual dexterity to assemble, qualities that women could provide extremely well. In Baltimore the Glenn L. Martin Company began actively recruiting young women for technical, clerical, and even some production line jobs. Many of these women came from relatively impoverished parts of Appalachia. The jobs they found in the city not only provided them with much needed money to help their families, but also opened their eyes to cultural opportunities of which they had scarcely been aware.

Somewhat surprisingly, the government still lagged in the employment of women, so much so that in July Mrs. John L. Whitehurst of Baltimore, influential President of the General Federation of Women's Clubs and the first woman to serve on the Board of Regents of the

University of Maryland, blasted the government for not employing more women, especially in policy-making positions. She noted that of all the policy-making positions in the federal government, only seven were filled by women. She also noted that the government had brought 262 business leaders to Washington to serve the country for a nominal $1.00 a year. Amid all these dollar-a-year men, there was only one dollar-a-year woman. Her attack so stung Sidney Hillman, Associate Director of the Office of Production Management, that he immediately started putting pressure on defense industries to increase the hiring of women.

Social change progressed by another small step that spring when A. Philip Randolph, President of the Brotherhood of Sleeping Car Porters, faced down President Roosevelt over unequal job opportunities for African Americans. Back in June of 1925, Randolph, a young activist and publisher of a Socialist periodical, *The Messenger*, was approached about leading an effort to organize Pullman porters into a union. There was already a union, organized and controlled by the Pullman Company, as was permitted by the laws at that time. The union never conducted any serious negotiations with Pullman. The carefully chosen union representatives merely met with company officials every few years, listened to speeches about how good the company had always been to the porters (all of whom were African American), and received the company's latest "offer" of a new pay rate. There was never anything to do but nod and accept the new rate.

By 1925 the low pay and poor working conditions caused many porters to want to form an independent union. But since Pullman automatically fired anyone who showed signs of independence in such matters, it was important to find a leader who was not beholden to the company in any way. Randolph was finally persuaded to take up the challenge, a task that consumed him for the next twelve years. In 1937 he finally succeeded in forcing Pullman to sign a contract calling for substantially increased pay, reduced working hours, and the elimination of a number of oppressive working conditions. It was the first time in history that a company had signed a contract with an independent union with black membership, and it marked Randolph's emergence as the most important and powerful black labor leader in the country.

Three years later, a new challenge confronted Randolph. America had emerged from the Depression and the increased defense activity in late 1940 and early 1941 had provided abundant jobs and a developing labor shortage that pushed up wages. Yet African Americans were generally left out of the new prosperity. It was estimated that defense needs would require at least 250,000 new workers, yet 75,000 skilled and experienced black construction workers were still unemployed. Some major defense contractors, like North American Aviation, announced that they would continue to maintain their company policy prohibiting the employment of African Americans regardless of the labor shortage. Against this backdrop Randolph lobbied the administration for greater efforts to end discrimination in defense work. All he got were vague promises that were quickly forgotten after the November election returned Roosevelt for his third term. It was clearer than ever to Randolph that if African Americans were to receive fair treatment, they would have to exert a kind of pressure that the government could not ignore. And so he approached the leaders of major civil rights organizations and asked them to help him organize a 10,000 person march on Washington to demand equal treatment. Although some leaders were hesitant, the overall response was so enthusiastic that Randolph increased his target to 100,000 marchers.

The march on Washington was scheduled for July 1, and it soon became clear to Roosevelt that there was, indeed, a groundswell of support for this demonstration. He asked his wife Eleanor, well known as a supporter of equal rights, to persuade Randolph to call off what promised to be a huge embarrassment for the administration. She traveled to New York to meet with Randolph, Walter White of the N.A.A.C.P., and Mayor LaGuardia, but Randolph was unmoved. He wanted an executive order ending racial discrimination in defense employment, and he would not cancel the march for anything less. The First Lady reported back to the president that the march was still on, and LaGuardia told him that only a face-to-face meeting with Randolph would have a chance of averting what could be a violent clash with the Washington police, who were predominantly southern and largely unsympathetic to African Americans.

Roosevelt agreed to the meeting and saw Randolph on June 18, less than two weeks before the date for the march. Roosevelt called in all the pressure he could. In addition to Randolph and Walter White, Roosevelt invited Henry Stimson, Secretary of War; Robert Patterson, Undersecretary of War; Frank Knox, Secretary of the Navy; William Knudsen and Sidney Hillman, Co-Directors of the Office of Production Management (which oversaw defense contracts); Anna Rosenberg, Regional Director of the Social Security Board and Roosevelt's trusted liaison with La Guardia; Aubrey Williams, Director of the National Youth Administration; and Mayor La Guardia. Randolph would not bend. Roosevelt offered to call the managers of defense plants and urge them to hire African Americans. Randolph found that unsatisfactory. Roosevelt offered to talk further if the march was called off. Randolph refused. Roosevelt offered to have his aides work things out with defense contractors. Randolph replied that the government itself was one of the worst offenders. La Guardia suggested that since Randolph was not going to call off the march, they seek a formula for agreement. Finally Roosevelt yielded and a committee was named to draw up the executive order. Joseph Rauh, an O.E.M. lawyer, prepared draft after draft, each tougher than the last and each vetoed by Randolph. Finally a draft was prepared that Randolph could accept, and on June 25 Roosevelt signed Executive Order 8802, providing that "there shall be no discrimination in the employment of workers in defense industries or government because of race, creed, color, or national origin." Interestingly, the phrase, "or government," is inserted in handwriting in the original typed document. The order also established in O.P.M. a Committee on Fair Employment Practice to enforce the terms of the order.

If the enforcement of Executive Order 8802 sometimes fell short of the hopes of its originators, it nevertheless represented a major step forward toward racial equality in the country. The goal might seem distant, but a process of radical change had been set in motion. Randolph had long believed that change would come about only through the efforts of African Americans pushing forward themselves. Now it had been initiated by the president of the union representing some of the lowliest of the workers on the railroads.

Despite these small signs of progress, there was still massive resistance to changes in race relations, especially in the South. Indeed, apart from Executive Order 8802 and *Mitchell v. U.S.*, 1941 marked a pause in civil rights progress in the United States. Activists, however, were exploring some subtle shifts in strategy. One such shift involved an attempt to outlaw the poll tax.

For a number of years eight Southern states had charged a fee, typically $1.00 or $2.00, for the right to vote. This poll tax was a tempting target for civil rights supporters because it did not apply exclusively to African Americans. In fact, it was estimated that 60 percent of those kept from voting by this tax were poor whites. The poll tax was primarily a means by which the Southern upper classes, all white, could hold onto power. In many areas political bosses would actually pay the poll tax for their loyal supporters, white or black, whom they could count on to vote as instructed. The first bill to outlaw the poll tax was introduced by Rep. Lee Geyer of California during the 1939 session. The bill was referred to the House Judiciary Committee, where it died. In January of 1941, Rep. Geyer introduced his bill once again, and once again it was referred to the Judiciary Committee. This time, however, Geyer also introduced a bill making his poll tax bill a special order of business. This procedural move eventually allowed discharge votes that brought the original bill to the floor for debate. To look a bit into the future, the poll tax bill passed the House by a substantial majority but, like antilynching bills in the past, died in the Senate of an acute case of Southern filibuster.

This period also saw the beginnings of another kind of social change that would ultimately have wide implications. In 1941 only about twelve million Americans had any form of medical insurance to help cover hospital costs. Even fewer, about three million, had insurance for doctors' bills. The vast majority of these insurance plans were provided through employers, unions, or fraternal organizations, with a very small number provided by commercial insurance companies.

Virtually all paid their benefits directly to the insured, who in turn was responsible for paying the hospitals and doctors. But in 1937 employees of the Home Owners Loan Corporation used a $40,000 government grant to establish the Group Health Organization to provide medical care directly to its members in return for a monthly membership fee. The organization employed its doctors directly, and the members did not have to worry about paying their bills so long as they went to doctors in the group. This was not the first such organization. Small health maintenance groups had been established on the West Coast around the turn of the century. But those were highly local in their nature and were a form of employer-sponsored insurance. This new organization was an independent entity with strength and potential size to change the character of health care. Other such groups soon followed. Against this new development the American Medical Association, fearing that such schemes might diminish the incomes of its members, fought back vigorously. Claiming that such groups were illegal, the A.M.A. tried to prevent doctors who worked in such groups from having staff privileges at hospitals in the areas they served. The Medical Society of the District of Columbia even threatened to expel any doctors who participated in the G.H.O. In 1938 the Justice Department stepped in and charged the A.M.A. in general and the Medical Society of the District in particular with violating the Sherman Anti-Trust Act. The case wound through the courts, and in April of 1941 the two medical associations were found guilty. Although their opposition to group health plans continued, they were forced to stop their active measures against participating doctors and hospitals.

While these social changes were being pressed forward at the highest levels in Washington and New York, another kind of social change was sweeping across all of rural America. In 1933, at the beginning of the New Deal, only about one American farm in ten was served by an electric power company. There were also about 150,000 that had their own electric generating plants, expensive to run and limited in their power output. The vast majority, about 87 percent, had no electricity whatsoever. Despite romantic Jeffersonian images of the sturdy yeoman farmer and the peacefulness of rural life, for those without power, farming had changed little since the time of Jefferson.

For farmers who could afford a tractor, the crop work was a great deal easier. But most farmers could not afford tractors. In 1940 there were 1,567,000 tractors at work on American farms, but there were also 13,932,000 horses and mules, still doing the great majority of the work of cultivation. For the rest, it was all hand labor. A dairy farmer was limited in the number of cows he could milk by hand each day. After milking he had to store the milk in cans in a cool place, often an ice house or ice cellar, and keep the temperature under fifty degrees until the truck from the dairy arrived to pick it up. If the temperature rose above fifty degrees, the day's work was lost. If the farmer did not have a good, functional windmill to power his well pump, every drop of water had to be pumped by hand and carried to the house or to the watering trough. By 1941 the situation had become even more dire because of a severe labor shortage. More and more young men were being called up by the draft, and many others were moving to the cities to find jobs in the rapidly growing defense industries. The difficulty in hiring farm help meant that fewer people were having to do more of the back-breaking work. Most farm women developed a stooped posture and rounded shoulders, not from disease, but from years of carrying 80 pounds of water each trip from the well to the house.

In 1935 90 percent of farm cooking was done on wood stoves, difficult to start, impossible to regulate, dirty and hard to clean. The stove burned all day, heating water for cooking and cleaning, cooking meals, boiling water for canning the produce from the garden. On laundry day the clothes were washed and rinsed in separate tubs, each kept filled with hot water from the stove. A few of the more prosperous farmers managed to buy their wives modern wringer washing machines powered by small gasoline engines. These had to be kept outside on the porch because of the exhaust. If the machine was placed in an enclosed laundry room, an elaborate system of ducts was needed to carry the fumes outside. In either case the water still had to be carried by hand and heated on the wood stove. On ironing day the irons, literally made of cast iron and weighing six or seven pounds each, had to be heated on the stove, wiped clean of soot from the wood fire, and applied to the clothes before they cooled. It generally took two irons to do a man's shirt.

In 1935, when streamlined trains were roaring across the country and streamlined air liners were flying across the Atlantic, 90 percent of American farms had no indoor plumbing. Without electric pumps to move the water, it was impossible to bring the necessary facilities indoors. The outhouse was still the normal place for bodily relief; many farms, especially in the South, lacked even that convenience. Washing up was done in cold water in a tub or trough. For the Saturday night bath, a tub might be brought into the kitchen in cold weather, but the back porch or back yard was not an uncommon location. Evenings were quiet times, illuminated by kerosene lamps. Each lamp produced about the amount of light generated by a 25-watt incandescent light bulb. Lamps were hard to keep trimmed properly, and there was a constant risk of fire if one were knocked over. In wintertime many farmers did their morning and evening milking in the dark. The risk of fire was too great to allow a kerosene lantern in the barn. In the evening many families would gather around the radio for news and entertainment— if they could afford to buy the radio and the replacement batteries that powered it.

This primitive state of affairs did more than make life immensely difficult for a farm family. It also limited the farm's productivity and hence the family's income. In the South, where agriculture was still unbalanced by an overreliance on cotton and tobacco, the low farm productivity was a major factor contributing to the malnutrition that plagued the region. The situation was exacerbated by the refusal of power companies to extend their lines into less profitable rural areas. When Roosevelt established the Tennessee Valley Authority in 1933, some of the most vocal opposition came from power company interests. They were not prepared themselves to extend service to rural parts of the Tennessee River Valley, but they most certainly did not want the government going in and providing service to customers that they might want to take for themselves in the future. When the T.V.A. became established and started producing substantial amounts of electricity, the power companies put pressure on the government to have the T.V.A. sell power to them so they could resell it at a profit. But the T.V.A. held to its statutory mandate to give priority to "States, counties, municipalities and cooperative organizations of citizens or farmers, not organized or doing business for profit, but primarily for the purpose of supplying electricity to its own citizens or members."

The almost immediate success of the T.V.A. in improving economic conditions in its service area provided a model for the Rural Electrification Administration when it was established by Executive Order 7037 in May of 1935. Originally conceived of as a relief agency, the R.E.A. quickly evolved into a lending agency. It provided low-interest loans, together with administrative guidance and technical expertise, to local nonprofit agencies, almost always local electrical cooperatives, so they could supply electric power in rural areas. Opposition from power companies was fierce. In many cases, when a co-op was planning a power grid for a local area, the nearest power company would quickly put up a power line serving the part of the region with the highest density of customers. These so-called spite lines were intended solely to rob the co-op of its most profitable customer base, thereby rendering the whole co-op project economically unfeasible. About 200 of these spite lines were known to have been put in place across the country, and a number of them did kill or cripple the co-ops that were their targets.

In spite of all the opposition, once the R.E.A. established itself, clarified its mission, and began making loans, the response was tremendous. By the end of 1941, 800 co-ops were providing power to a million farms, nearly 35 percent of the total number in the country. In just over four years of full operation, the R.E.A. had seen almost a quarter of all American farms electrified. Further, the agency's technical advice and assistance had enabled the co-ops to carry out the work with remarkable efficiency. Whereas the typical cost to build one mile of rural power line had been $1,500 to $2,000, the co-ops were able to do the job for an average of $824. Farmers across the country signed up readily, eager to pay the $5.00 membership fee. One farmer was told that he could not join at present because even at its reduced rates, the co-op could not economically extend its line to his isolated house. A few days later he came back to pay his fee and join up. He had moved his house close enough for the line to reach.

The impact of rural electrification was immediate and profound. Most obvious was the improvement in the quality of life. The first item purchased after power was connected was almost always an electric iron. Just after that came a new radio. About two-thirds of the families bought new washing machines and almost half bought vacuum cleaners within a year of getting electric power. Equally important were the water pumps to bring water from the well to the house and electric motors to power equipment that had previously been run by gasoline engine or by hand. Electrification also meant the family no longer had to go to town to buy wet-cell batteries to power the family radio. Their link to the outside world, the evening radio, was no longer threatened by battery failure. Typical of the reaction of farm families to this new luxury was the statement of the Tennessee farmer who stood up in church one Sunday to give his testimony. "Brothers and sisters, I want to tell you this," he said. "The greatest thing on earth is to have the love of God in your heart, and the next greatest thing is to have electricity in your house."

In addition to the improved quality of life, electrification brought benefits that were less anticipated. Many expected that the availability of electricity would improve farm productivity, but few realized how dramatic the improvement would be. Electric brooders increased survival rates for piglets and, for some farmers, doubled pork production. The purchase of electric milking machines allowed farmers to increase the size of their herds by 50 percent, and electric coolers eliminated wastage from warming. One farmer reported that he had previously spent $45.00 a month on ice to cool his milk. After investing in an electric cooler, he was able to maintain better temperature control; and his total electric bill was only $10.00 a month. The cows, on the other hand, were not quite so happy as the farmers. After being milked by hand all their lives, most cows took a dim view of the newfangled milking machines. Consequently there was great demand for experienced farm hands who could manage the cows gently and get them accustomed to a new way of doing things.

There were also secondary benefits. Once the power poles were in place, it was a simple matter to add telephone lines so farms could communicate with other farms and with the outside world. The rural electrification intended for farms also benefitted many small villages. General stores installed lights so they could remain open late. Coolers held cold drinks for local residents who stopped by to chat of a summer evening. Tourists who had previously driven through the area without stopping would now see the illuminated gasoline sign and stop at night to buy gas. New demand and new farm prosperity greatly benefitted local appliance dealers who had trouble meeting the pent-up demand. Up until December of 1941, the R.E.A. sent a traveling Farm Equipment Tour through twenty-eight midwestern states. Setting up a large circus tent at each stop, the R.E.A. representatives would demonstrate new electrically powered farm equipment and explain its benefits. Appliance manufacturers quickly caught on to the marketing potential of these tours and started sending their own agents tagging along with the R.E.A. representatives to demonstrate their products and take orders.

The R.E.A. was so proud of its accomplishments that in 1939 it commissioned a short documentary, *Power in the Land*, which made its debut in August of 1940. Although not a prize winner, it was a competently made and interesting 38-minute film featuring veteran actor William Adams as narrator and poet and writer Stephen Vincent Benét as commentator. The film chronicled the changes that occurred in the lives of an Ohio family when electric power reached their farm. It was well received, especially in farming communities that could appreciate its message. Yet for all these success stories, and despite the speed of progress, rural electrification was still very much a work in progress as 1941 drew to a close. When Pearl Harbor brought the formation of new co-ops to a virtual halt, there were still almost four million American farms left waiting for electricity.

CHAPTER 5

May: The War Over There

ON THE MORNING of Tuesday, May 13, Americans opened their newspapers to find a strange story on the front page. The previous Saturday night a solitary German Messerschmitt 110 fighter had crashed in Scotland. The pilot had bailed out and broken his ankle on landing. When a local farmer arrived with a pitchfork to take him prisoner, the pilot behaved very strangely. Taken to the farmhouse, he chatted cordially with the family in fluent English until soldiers arrived to take him away for questioning. He was unarmed, and his plane had been unarmed also. Very calmly he submitted to a search, which revealed nothing but some personal effects. But as the soldiers took him away to the military hospital in Glasgow, he asked to speak personally with Wing Commander the Duke of Hamilton, who commanded the R.A.F. fighter sector in the east of Scotland. This strange request was forwarded to Hamilton, who visited the prisoner the next morning. It was only then that the pilot identified himself as Rudolf Hess, Deputy Führer and the third most powerful man in Nazi Germany.

Hess knew something of the Duke, although the two had never met. He knew that the Duke, like Hess, was an enthusiastic pioneer aviator. He also believed that the Duke would be sympathetic to proposals for a negotiated peace between Germany and Britain. He said he had brought just such proposals with him, and he knew Hitler would be favorably disposed toward a negotiated peace along these lines. He hoped Hamilton would assist him in contacting the British government authorities and presenting his proposals. Hamilton was able to excuse himself and telephone London. Hesitant to tell too much over what might be an unsecured phone line, he gave just enough information to prompt Churchill to have him fly down with complete details.

The incident proved highly embarrassing to both sides. The bombshell astonished Hitler, who feared that secret plans, including the impending attack on Russia, might be compromised. Goebbels promptly declared that Hess had gone insane, and that nothing he said could be relied upon. But the apparent defection of the third-ranking man in the Reich profoundly shocked the Nazi hierarchy. On the other side, Churchill was trying valiantly to convince the American people that Britain was determined to fight the war through to the finish. All chances for increased American aid would vanish if America thought the British were about to negotiate peace with Germany. The situation had to be handled with great delicacy.

While the British interrogated Hess (and had him examined by a battery of psychiatrists), the government released virtually no information to the press. This official silence led to all manner of wild speculations, including the dreaded speculation that Britain was, indeed, prepared to contemplate a peace offer. Churchill felt obliged to send a special message to Roosevelt, assuring the president that Britain did, indeed, intend to fight on. Very gradually the incident faded from public attention, and Hess sat out the war in the Tower of London.

Despite America's determination to stay out of the shooting war, there remained a strong fascination with events overseas and a desire to keep up with the latest war news. Dramatic and exciting stories especially gripped the attention of the public; and in the spring of 1941, there was no story more exciting than the pursuit and sinking

of the German battleship *Bismarck*. *Bismarck* was Germany's ultimate weapon in the attempt to starve England into submission. At
the beginning of the conflict Great Britain needed to import over
60,000,000 tons of supplies every year. This amount included all of
its oil, without which it was impossible to fight a modern war. It also
included half of the food consumed by the British people. German
leaders believed, with good reason, that if they could cut off Britain's
ocean commerce, the country could not survive and would have to
sue for peace. Britain, at the same time, realized that protection of the
merchant fleet had to be the country's top priority.

Memories of the submarine menace in World War I caused many
people to focus on German submarines as the greatest threat to merchant shipping. But the British Admiralty realized that the German
surface fleet posed a far greater danger. A submarine captain was
regarded as an ace if he sank more than 50,000 tons of shipping. A
surface ship could sink that much in a month. In early 1941 the prospects for British supply convoys changed markedly for the worse. The
battleship *Bismarck*, launched two years earlier, completed her sea trials
and prepared for her first combat cruise. *Bismarck* was the largest ship
in the German navy, and at 41,700 tons one of the largest in the world.
Her main battery of eight 15-inch guns could throw 1,800-pound
projectiles up to 22 miles. Even more, her top speed of 30 knots made
her the fastest battleship then in service. Accompanied by the cruiser
Prinz Eugen, she was capable of destroying any convoy at sea. Sinking
her quickly became the top priority of the Royal Navy.

Thanks to agents in Scandinavia, the British were aware that
Bismarck was ready to begin her cruise, and they were also informed
shortly after she left Norwegian waters for the North Atlantic on May
21. But there were several possible routes from the North Sea to the
North Atlantic; and the Royal Navy's thinly stretched Home Fleet,
under the command of Admiral John Tovey, would have to try to cover
them all. It was unlikely that the Germans would try to pass through the
English Channel and even less likely that they would try the Pentland
Firth on the north tip of Scotland, within sight of the great British
naval base at Scapa Flow in the Orkney Islands. But they could easily

try to break out either north or south of the Færoe Islands, or they could head farther west and enter the Atlantic through the Denmark Strait between Iceland and Greenland, from there to descend on the North Atlantic convoy routes from the north. The heavy cruisers *Norfolk* and *Suffolk* were already patrolling the Denmark Strait, and Tovey dispatched the battlecruiser *Hood* and the new battleship *Prince of Wales* to support them. The area around the Færoes was patrolled by the light cruisers *Manchester* and *Birmingham*, assisted by the RAF Coastal Command. These waters were close enough to Scapa Flow to be reinforced quickly if needed.

H.M.S. *Hood* was the largest ship in the Royal Navy. At just over 47,000 tons she was second in size only to the French navy's *Richelieu*, then at Dakar being repaired. Her armament was equal to that of the *Bismarck*, although British gunnery skills were generally inferior to those of the Germans. But *Hood* had been designed in the middle of the First World War, when many naval theorists preferred the battlecruiser to the battleship. In size and armament the two types were similar. But the battlecruiser carried considerably less armor and was therefore able to achieve significantly higher speeds, the speed advantage being considered more important than the armor protection. This theory was exploded, literally, at the Battle of Jutland, where three British battlecruisers blew up when they were hit by German fire. Consequently, battlecruisers still under construction had their armor increased, although it was still thin by battleship standards. *Hood*'s deck armor was three inches or less, while *Bismarck* carried almost five inches. Further, design improvements in the 21 years since *Hood* was commissioned had taken away the battlecruiser's speed advantage. *Bismarck* was actually two knots faster than *Hood*.

At 10:22 on the evening of May 23, when it was still quite light at that northern latitude, the contact came that the British had been waiting for. A lookout on *Suffolk* spotted the *Bismarck* and *Prinz Eugen* in the Denmark Strait. The Germans were approaching the convoy routes from the north. Signals were immediately radioed to the Admiralty in London and to the Home Fleet. The British cruisers began shadowing the Germans until forces could be assembled that would be strong enough to deal with so powerful an enemy. Vice Admiral Lancelot Holland on the *Hood* adjusted his course and speed slightly so he would intercept the German ships about dawn on the 24th. Holland was concerned about his thin deck armor and intended to charge directly at the Germans at top speed. The deck was more vulnerable to high arcing fire from long range than it was to the relatively flat trajectory of short-range fire.

Shortly after 5:30 on the morning of May 24, the two forces first made visual contact. A few minutes before 6:00 *Hood* and *Prince of Wales* opened fire. *Bismarck* and *Prinz Eugen* hesitated until *Hood* had fired her sixth salvo. Then they responded. As had been the case at Jutland, German gunnery was extremely accurate. At 6:00 a German shell struck the *Hood*, penetrated to the magazine and ignited almost fifty tons of high explosive. *Hood* was practically blown in half and sank quickly. From her crew of 1,300, only three men survived. The Germans then turned their guns on *Prince of Wales*, which was soon so badly damaged that she had to break off action and withdraw. But before withdrawing, *Prince of Wales* had managed to score three hits on *Bismarck*. One struck the forecastle, ruptured oil tanks, and weakened a bulkhead. The damage reduced *Bismarck's* cruising range and forced her to cut her speed slightly. Admiral Günther Lütjens decided to shake off the British cruisers that had shadowed him and sail to the occupied French port of Brest, where he could make repairs before resuming his mission. That night he managed to slip away from his pursuers and turn southeast toward the French coast.

Until now the news of *Bismarck's* sortie and the British pursuit had been kept from the world, a military secret to both combatants. But the sinking of *Hood* changed the picture completely. This was a propaganda opportunity that was simply too good to pass up. The Propaganda Ministry in Berlin soon had the story of the battle spread round the world, and the British were forced to admit the ignominious loss of their largest ship. Americans, now alerted to the drama unfolding in the Atlantic, became eager for news of the chase. Speculation was rife, yet for several days there was little news to report. Lütjens had given the British the slip, and no one outside the German *Kriegsmarine* had any idea where *Bismarck* was.

British Coastal Command tried to assist the Navy in finding *Bismarck*, detailing some of their new Catalina seaplanes to the task. These American aircraft had an enormous range, with a fuel capacity that allowed them to stay aloft for up to twenty-eight hours. But they were new and unfamiliar to British pilots; and often American instructors, clandestinely assigned to help the British adjust to the Catalinas, would go along on their search and rescue missions. On the morning of the 26th, Liuetenant Dennis Briggs was flying his long-range Catalina over the eastern Atlantic. On board the plane, officially as an instructor but actually as an extra observer and pilot, was Lieutenant Tuck Smith, USN. Smith was at the controls at 10:30 that cloudy morning when, through a break in the clouds, he spotted a large, solitary ship making for France. Suspecting it might be *Bismarck*, he used the extensive cloud cover to get closer so he could confirm his suspicion. Misjudging the distance, he got too close and emerged from the clouds right over the ship. Smith managed to evade the heavy anti-aircraft fire that was sent up at him, and he got off a message to the Admiralty that their target had been located.

Signals went out to the Home Fleet and to the aircraft carrier *Ark Royal*, which had been dispatched from its usual duties in the Mediterranean to help with the search. There seemed little chance that the Home Fleet could catch *Bismarck*, so *Ark Royal* launched air strikes to try to slow her down. Fairey Swordfish torpedo planes took off to look for *Bismarck* and try to do some damage to her. The first strike almost ended in disaster when the planes attacked the cruiser *Sheffield* by mistake. The second strike found the target, but most of the torpedoes missed. Two, however, hit home. One, striking amidships, did little serious harm. But the other, launched near the end of the attack, struck the stern and jammed the rudder, forcing the ship to turn back toward her pursuers. The damage could not be repaired, and the Home Fleet closed in for the kill.

First to attack, shortly after 1:00 in the morning, was a squadron of destroyers. Their torpedoes did no damage, but they kept the Germans awake and alert all night. As dawn broke, Tovey approached in his flagship, H.M.S. *King George V*. With him was the battleship *Rodney*, detached from convoy duty to help with the chase. *Rodney* was one of the strangest looking battleships ever built. Her three great turrets, each mounting three 16-inch guns, were all mounted forward of the bridge. That meant she could bring all her firepower to bear while coming straight at the enemy. Her captain used this configuration to full advantage, opening fire at 8:45 as he closed with *Bismarck*. This time it was the British gunnery that proved superior. Maneuvering skillfully and firing accurately, *Rodney* and *King George V* put *Bismarck*'s main gun turrets out of action by 9:30. They then continued pounding her until Tovey broke off the action and ordered H.M.S. *Dorsetshire* to finish her off with torpedoes. With the sinking of *Bismarck* it was the turn of the British Admiralty to announce that the Royal Navy had sunk the world's most powerful battleship.

The victory at sea was a powerful encouragement to the British people, one that they especially needed that month. Londoners had been enduring the Blitz, the nightly German bombing, for nine months; and they had managed to persevere through everything the Germans had thrown at them. Although the worst of the night bombing raids were over by the end of October 1940, periodic attacks continued through the winter and early spring, inflicting heavy damage but causing fewer and fewer civilian casualties. In one final supreme effort, the Germans launched their last major attack on London on the night of May 10. Flying almost 600 sorties, the *Luftwaffe* dropped 800 tons of bombs on the British capital. Over 2,000 fires were started and over 1,400 people were killed. Westminster Abbey was damaged and the chamber of the House of Commons destroyed by bombs. Americans were deeply moved by the news photograph of Winston Churchill standing somberly in the ruins.

News from London reached most Americans through the regular radio broadcasts from correspondents like John MacVane and Fred Bates of NBC, Arthur Mann of Mutual, and especially Edward R. Murrow and Larry LeSeur of CBS. Even the *Chicago Tribune* sponsored occasional broadcasts from its London correspondent John

Steele. Among these, Ed Murrow was clearly the leader. He had lived in London for five years and knew the city and its people intimately. His twice-daily broadcasts commanded by far the largest audience in America, and his views contributed to the shaping of American opinion and the gradual abandonment of neutrality. Murrow tried to maintain objectivity and avoid advocacy, but he often came close to crossing the line between the two. The British government regarded him as a friend and, partly through his influence, developed a somewhat relaxed censorship policy. They believed that the more information the American public received about British resistance, the more likely America would be to increase material aid and eventually come into the fighting war. Murrow and the other correspondents were free to describe the Blitz and how the British were holding up under it. The personal character of these narratives, emphasizing both the horrors of the bombings and the resilience of the British people, made a profound impression on American audiences.

All the radio broadcasts were sent live from London in the middle of the night and in early afternoon so they could be heard in the morning and evening across America. Alone among the correspondents, Murrow was allowed to go up on top of the broadcast building so their listeners could hear the sounds of air raid sirens, fire engines, and sometimes actual bombs falling. In November Murrow finally got an opportunity to be openly supportive of Britain when CBS brought him and his wife Janet back from London for three months of speaking tours, him on behalf of CBS, her on behalf of Bundles for Britain.

News from Africa was encouraging to the British during 1941. The previous summer Mussolini had decided he needed some conquests of his own to keep up with his Axis partner. In September he ordered Marshal Rodolpho Graziani, governor of the Italian colony of Libya, to invade Egypt and drive out the British forces there. Graziani prepared methodically for the invasion, securing supplies, laying his plans, and organizing a mobile bordello. On September 13 he ordered the assault to begin. After a massive artillery bombardment, the 10th Army under General Italo Gariboldi moved forward to seize and occupy the British frontier posts, which the British had already abandoned several weeks earlier. Advancing unopposed at the rate of twelve miles a day, the army halted at the desert outpost of Sidi Barrani, 60 miles inside Egypt and 80 miles from the main British defensive line. There Graziani set up defensive positions, paved the road in his rear, brought up supplies, established a forward base, and erected a monument to his achievements before departing for his headquarters in Tripoli. Gariboldi and the army were still in place on December 9 when the British Western Desert Force under Lieutenant General Richard O'Connor launched an attack that sent the Italians scurrying back across the frontier to their fortress base at Bardia, where they dug in and waited to see what O'Connor would do next.

Back in Europe, Mussolini was hungry for more glorious triumphs even closer to home. In 1939 he had pressured the Albanian government to accept Italian suzerainty and become a kingdom within the new Italian Empire. Now the Duce wanted even more to prove his worth as Hitler's ally and to extend the empire to Greece as well. During the latter part of 1940 he exerted pressure on the Greek government to accept the same arrangement he had forced upon the Albanians. The Greeks, however, proved resistant to his pressure; and so on October 30 the Italian army based in Albania launched an invasion of Greece. Within two weeks the Greeks drove the Italians completely out of the country and launched an offensive of their own that gained them control of much of southern Albania.

As if the defeat at the hands of the Greek army were not sufficient humiliation for the Italian armed forces, on the night of November 11-12, the British Royal Navy launched an attack on the Italian navy's anchorage at Taranto on the instep of the Italian boot. Twenty obsolescent Fairey Swordfish torpedo planes, launched from H.M.S. *Illustrious*, severely damaged three of the Italian navy's six battleships as well as one destroyer. Only two planes were lost in the action. The attack was especially important since the harbor at Taranto was less than forty feet deep, a depth that was previously regarded as too shallow for an effective aerial torpedo attack. The British had attached special fins to their torpedoes to make them run at a shallower depth, and it is likely that their success at Taranto inspired the Japanese navy to develop a similar device for use in the shallow waters of Pearl Harbor a year later.

Thus the year 1941 dawned with the Italian armies thrown back on their heels in both Libya and Albania. Only in East Africa did they still hold captured territory and the initiative for attack. Italian East Africa had been created in 1936 following the Second Italo-Ethiopian War, in which Mussolini had used a manufactured border incident as an excuse to invade and conquer Ethiopia. The Duce regarded the acquisition of colonies by conquest as indispensable for a nation seeking to be recognized as a great power. From the Italian colonies of Eritrea and Italian Somaliland the invading troops had crushed the small and ill-equipped Ethiopian army, forced the Emperor Haile Selassie into exile, and unified the three territories into a single colony. The war was strongly condemned by the western democracies; but their inability to create an effective, unified response glaringly exposed the utter helplessness of the League of Nations.

If Mussolini wondered what the British were going to do in East Africa in 1941, he did not have long to wait. At the end of the first week in January the British forces in Sudan crossed the frontier and, for the first time since 1936, raised the Ethiopian flag over Ethiopian soil at the little village of Gubba. Two weeks later the general British offensive began all around the borders of Italian East Africa, and Americans turned to their atlases to find out where these strangely named places were located. Kassala, Agordat, Asmara, Cheren, Neghelle, and Chisimaio provided a geography lesson to anyone who could manage to locate them on the map. By April 2 the British were in full control of Eritrea, and on May 5 Emperor Haile Selassie returned to his capital, Addis Ababa, and slept in his own palace for the first time in five years. It took the British a little more time to finish the campaign. Late in May the Duke of Aosta, Italian Viceroy in East Africa, surrendered in his mountain stronghold. It was not until November 28, however, that Lieutenant General Guglielmo Nasi surrendered the last Italian troops in the country. By that time the majority of British and Empire soldiers in Ethiopia had been transferred to the Libyan dessert, where their services were badly needed against the Germans.

The several Italian debacles were deeply disturbing to Hitler, who wanted to secure his southern flank through diplomatic means rather than by military force. Successful diplomatic efforts had to be supported by a perception of military might, and Italian ineptitude could undermine Nazi efforts. Late in November Yugoslavia refused outright to join the other Balkan countries in allying themselves with Germany. Prince Paul, Regent for the young King Peter II, was trying to maintain a balance among the various ethnic groups that made up his country. The two most important were the Serbs, the dominant group in Yugoslavia and strongly pro-British, and the Croats in the north, restive under Serb dominance and strongly pro-German. Yugoslavia's resistance to German blandishments substantially raised the tension in the region as 1940 came to an end.

Greek success against the Italians was of concern to Hitler, but it also bothered the British. The British were anxious to add whatever allies they could recruit in their fight against Germany. They wanted to become involved in the fighting in Greece as a way of diverting Hitler from any plans to invade England. The Greeks, on the other hand, wanted to secure their frontiers against Italian aggression, but they wanted to do it in such a way that they gave Hitler no cause for alarm nor any excuse to intervene in the Mediterranean. So long as they could handle the Italians on their own, they were content to do so without British help. Churchill exerted substantial pressure on Greek Premier Ioannis Metaxas to accept British involvement, and Metaxas adamantly refused. But on January 29 Metaxas died of blood poison and was succeeded by the much weaker Alexandros Koryzis, Governor of the Bank of Greece and a mere political functionary. Real political power was held by King George of the Hellenes, the long-time ally of Metaxas. Churchill, still pressing for British involvement, sent Foreign Secretary Anthony Eden to Athens to talk to the King. Eden promised the King 100,000 men, 250 pieces of field artillery, and other munitions far beyond the resources Britain had available. With such promises, and in the face of continuing German troop buildups in Rumania and Bulgaria, King George finally agreed to accept British aid. The consequences were disastrous.

In Libya the British forces had opened 1941 in an aggressive fashion. On January 1 the Western Desert Force was officially redesignated XIII Corps. On January 3 they began their assault on Bardia. On January 4 the Italian fortress fell. On January 5 the mopping up was complete and the Italian survivors were in full flight back to Tobruch. It is a rule of thumb that in a direct assault, the attacker wants to have a numerical superiority of three to one. Counting only his assault troops, O'Connor's forces were *inferior* to the Italians by almost that same ratio. Yet with his outstanding planning and the superb fighting qualities of his men, he was able to defeat the Italian army with surprising ease. In six weeks he had destroyed eight Italian divisions, taken 70,000 prisoners, captured an important fortress, and seized hundreds of enemy tanks, artillery pieces, and trucks. These last were of the greatest importance. The harsh desert climate was damaging to all kinds of machines, and transport was always in short supply.

Now General Sir Archibald Wavell, British Commander in Chief in the Middle East, saw the fortress of Tobruch as an important prize, a major base with port facilities that could sustain a British advance further west. With the recently captured transports and supplies, he authorized O'Connor, who was already halfway from Bardia, to continue his advance to Tobruch. On January 21 the British assault on the Italian fortress began with an artillery barrage. By nightfall the superior British gunnery had knocked out all of the Italian artillery; and Australian infantry had captured General Petassi Manella, the garrison commander. The next afternoon it was all over. In addition to the 25,000 prisoners, 23 tanks, 208 artillery pieces, 200 trucks, and two months' worth of food, XIII Corps had captured the port with so little damage that three days later British ships were unloading food and supplies. Equally important in the desert, Tobruch's functioning water plant was capable of producing 40,000 gallons of fresh water every day. And with or without permission, O'Connor was already moving west in pursuit of the remnants of the 10th Army.

The Italian forces fell back to a defensive line on the eastern side of the Cyrenaican peninsula. Anticipating a British advance, Graziani on February 1 ordered Gariboldi to turn over command of the army to

Lieutenant General Giuseppe Tellera, who was to abandon Cyrenaica and withdraw the army to Syrte, where Gariboldi would organize new defensive positions. When O'Connor discovered the Italian withdrawal, he moved at once, notwithstanding a severe shortage of fuel and ammunition. The Australians pressed the 10th Army from the rear as it withdrew westward along the coast road. O'Connor and the British armored force raced across the desert, hoping to beat the Italians to the Gulf of Syrte near the village of Beda Fomm.

Early on the morning of February 6, the British won the race, beating the Italians to the coast by the space of half an hour. Trapped between the two forces, the 10th Army launched a series of desperate attacks, trying to break out to the west. They all failed, and Tellera was mortally wounded in the fighting. By 9:00 the next morning the fighting had ended. The 10th Army had ceased to exist and 20,000 Italian soldiers had gone into captivity. Captured equipment included hundreds of trucks and enough fuel to allow O'Connor to continue his advance into Tripolitania and so drive the Italians completely out of North Africa. He promptly requested permission from Wavell and was equally promptly turned down. Events in Greece had overtaken him.

Feeling the Italians could safely be ignored, Churchill ordered Wavell to begin withdrawing troops from the Libyan front and transfer them to Greece in support of the pledge made by Eden. O'Connor went over to the defensive and returned to Egypt to take command of British forces there, leaving Lieutenant General Philip Neame in command of the small forces left at the front in Tripolitania. Churchill's views appeared to receive support on March 28 when the Mediterranean Fleet intercepted an Italian fleet that was sailing to attack the British convoys bound for Greece. The Italians lacked effective air cover, they had no radar, and their gunnery was poor. In action off Cape Matapan at the southwest tip of Greece, the Mediterranean Fleet first damaged the Italian battleship *Vittorio Veneto* in an aerial torpedo attack. Then that night the British battleships caught an Italian cruiser division unawares. In what was Italy's worst naval defeat, the British sank all three Italian heavy cruisers and two of the four destroyers and severely damaged a third destroyer. The victory was well publicized in both Britain and the United States and gave an important boost to British morale.

Back in Greece, the arrival of British troops made Hitler realize that he would have to intervene militarily in order to secure his southern flank. As the German army developed its plans to attack Greece and relieve the Italians, it became clear that the only practical invasion route led through Yugoslavia. Consequently Hitler stepped up the pressure on Prince Paul, even promising that Yugoslavia would not be used as a base for military operations. Britain and the United States tried to keep the country neutral, but German pressure and threats became too great. On March 25 Yugoslavia signed the Tripartite Pact with Germany. The next night, however, Yugoslav air force officers seized Belgrade, repudiated the treaty, and forced Prince Paul to resign as regent. They installed the young King Peter on the throne and set up a provisional government under the air force chief of staff, General Dušan Simović.

German reaction was swift. Early on the morning of April 6, German planes appeared over Belgrade and began a bombing campaign designed to paralyze the government. German, Italian, and Hungarian armies poured across the border and sped through the country. Croatian troops, hostile to the Serbs and in any case pro-German, deserted in large numbers. Even the Croatian chief of staff of the First Army Group began immediate negotiations with the Germans for the establishment of an independent Croatia. The whole invasion was so quick and easy that the entire German army suffered just 558 casualties, only 151 of them killed, during the entire campaign. An armistice was signed on April 17 and King Peter fled the country.

On the same day that the Germans and their allies invaded Yugoslavia, other German forces cut across the southern part of that country to attack Greece. The suddenness of the invasion and the direction from which it came made the defense of Greece almost impossible. The Greek First Army was easily handling the Italians in Albania. In the east, the Greek Second Army occupied the mountainous Metaxas Line, a string of fortifications defending the country against their traditional enemies, the Bulgarians. But between the two the border with Yugoslavia had been left unfortified. The Yugoslavians themselves had posed no threat to the Greeks, and friendly relations had obtained between the two countries. Now the only army protecting central Greece from the Germans in that sector was made up of 52,000 Australian and New Zealand troops under Major General Sir Henry Wilson, reinforced by two inexperienced Greek divisions. Even worse, significant gaps existed between the defending armies, and these gaps provided the Germans with ready pathways into the defenders' rear areas.

Despite the defenders' weaknesses, the Greek campaign was far different from that to the north. The Germans lost more men just attacking the Metaxas Line than they had lost in all of Yugoslavia. Yet penetration of the gaps between the defending armies proceeded swiftly. Wilson, seeing that his position was untenable, began a hard-fought withdrawal southward. With determined resistance from the Australians and New Zealanders, and with strong covering support from the remaining Greek divisions, Wilson was able to evacuate almost 40,000 of his 52,000 men. Prime Minister Koryzis committed suicide on April 18, and Athens fell to the Germans on the 27th.

After the conquest of Greece, the subsequent invasion of Crete was by no means a certainty. There was, in fact, no necessity for it from the German point of view. But the German parachute force was the one element of the German armed forces that had never been tested in a major combat operation, and Hitler was persuaded to employ it here to round off the defense of his Mediterranean flank. On May 20 the 7th Air Division dropped from the skies over the three airfields on the northern coast of Crete, at Maleme, Retimo, and Heraklion. Waiting for them were 40,000 troops recently evacuated from Greece. The Commonwealth troops were ready, and the numbers should have favored them. Indeed, hundreds of paratroopers were killed during the drop itself. But the Commonwealth forces had lost a great deal of equipment during the evacuation of Greece, and the shortage of radios especially hindered any attempt at a coordinated defense. Positions were held too long when reinforcements were expected but not actually forthcoming. Positions were abandoned when they should have been held at all costs. A quarter of the troops were without arms, having abandoned them during the retreat. Slowly and at great cost the Germans gained control of the airfields and brought in the additional forces that decided the battle. Major General Bernard Freyberg, commanding the Commonwealth troops, finally had no choice but to order the evacuation of the island. Those who could make it to the coast were taken aboard Royal Navy vessels during the nights of May 28–31.

Freyberg's losses were heavy, with almost 5,500 killed and wounded and over 12,000 captured. Almost half of the 11,000 Greek soldiers, many without weapons, were forced to surrender. The Royal Navy, too, suffered heavily in the fighting around Crete, with four cruisers and four destroyers sunk and four cruisers, a battleship, an aircraft carrier, and four destroyers seriously damaged. Yet the Navy succeeded in bringing off more than 18,000 men and returning them safely to Egypt. The Germans, too, suffered heavily, with over 6,600 killed, wounded, and missing out of the 29,000 engaged, an extremely high casualty rate. For a time rumors circulated that former World Heavyweight Champion Max Schmeling was among the dead. It soon emerged, however, that he was alive though seriously wounded.

The Battle of Crete captured America's attention as reports arrived in late May and early June. Soldiers on both sides had taken numerous photographs, and both sides released them in large numbers to illustrate the heroism of their troops. The drama of the world's first large-scale airborne invasion also captured the imagination, and both British and American commanders carefully studied the battle reports for lessons to be learned. British claims of German losses were of course exaggerated, but nothing could hide the fact that Commonwealth forces had suffered a serious defeat. The loss was the more embarrassing because back in the Libyan desert where the soldiers were badly missed, German intervention in relief of the Italians had already started to turn the tide of battle.

Just as Hitler had decided that he had to do something to rescue his incompetent ally in Greece, so also in North Africa he sent German reinforcements to stabilize the deteriorating situation. In February a German force of two divisions began landing in Tripoli under the command of *Generalleutnant* Erwin Rommel. On March 24, just over a month after his arrival, Rommel launched probing attacks followed by a full-scale assault on the British in Cyrenaica, following in reverse the same strategy O'Connor had followed the previous year. In just over a week he drove the British out of western Cyrenaica, in the process capturing both O'Connor and Neame.

Rommel's drive finally came to a halt at Tobruch, the fortress O'Connor had so easily captured in January. Now the garrison was commanded by the Australian Major General Leslie Morshead, whose defensive tactics were to become standard textbook material for war colleges. Rommel cut off Tobruch from the east, where his men reached the Egyptian border on April 28. He then launched an extended series of attacks that succeeded only in depleting his supplies and increasing his casualties. The British tried to relieve Tobruch but failed so miserably that Wavell was replaced by General Sir Claude Auchinleck, Commander-in-Chief, India. Wavell was sent to India, in effect swapping jobs with Auchinleck.

Auchinleck knew that inadequate preparation was a major cause of the failure of the relief effort, and he wanted to spend all the time necessary in preparation for his next offensive. The next few months were devoted to the creation of a new force, the 8th Army. To command it he requested and was given General Alan Cunningham, the victorious commander in East Africa. In July he sent the British 6th Division by sea to Tobruch to relieve Morshead and his exhausted Australians. The rest of his time he spent building up his forces, training them for desert warfare, and preparing the major offensive he was to launch in November. Operation *Crusader*, as it was called, was to be a massive armored attack aimed at destroying the German army in North Africa and raising the siege of Tobruch. Launched on November 18 after several weeks of delays, *Crusader* achieved the latter goal but not the former. After bitter fighting, Rommel stopped the British advance. But he was almost out of supplies and had lost most of his tanks. On the night of December 4, Rommel began a systematic withdrawal from eastern Cyrenaica, and the siege of Tobruch was lifted.

If there was one thing in all the war news that puzzled Americans the most, it was the role of the French. Whose side were they on, anyway? Were they really neutral? Why, on the one hand, was Admiral François Darlan so cooperative with the Germans. Or why, on the other hand, was General Charles de Gaulle continuing to fight the Germans? Perhaps nothing puzzled American readers more than the stories of the French campaign in Syria. At the close of the First World War, the remnants of the old Ottoman Empire were parceled out to the various Allied powers for administration until they were deemed ready for self-government. The United Kingdom was assigned the mandate for Palestine (including Transjordan) and Mesopotamia, while France received the mandate for Syria (including Lebanon). When the Franco-German armistice was signed in 1940, Vichy France retained control of the various French colonies and mandates. In some cases Germany effectively told the French what actions they should take. But for the most part Hitler was content to let the French have the trouble and expense of administering territories in which he had no great interest.

The British, however, had no way of knowing about Hitler's lack of interest in Syria. Britain was always sensitive to possible threats to its oil sources in Mesopotamia, so when de Gaulle offered a plan for a Free French takeover in Syria, Churchill was more than willing to listen. De Gaulle proposed that his commander in the Middle East, General Georges Catroux, send an Anglo-French expedition into Syria from Palestine and Mesopotamia. The field commander, General Paul LeGentilhomme, was to capture Damascus and take control of Syria for the Allies. Churchill was receptive to the proposal. On June 8 the Anglo-French forces crossed the border from Palestine into Syria, initiating a campaign that mixed fratricidal tragedy with high comedy. In several sharp clashes both the Free French and the Vichy French sustained around a thousand casualties. But most of the time the French simply refused to fight one another. In one "battle" a Free French unit stormed and captured a hill with their rifles slung over their shoulders. The Vichy French defenders refused to open fire and allowed themselves to be captured. When the Free French took Damascus, the

Vichy government had already left. The conquerors tried to enter along the main street, but found that it was blocked by workmen repairing the streetcar line. So they diverted their triumphal entry to another part of town, which turned out to be the red-light district. There they received a tumultuous reception from the inhabitants.

For the first half of 1941, the ambiguity in the identity of the French was matched by the ambiguities in German-Russian relations. The signing of the Nazi-Soviet pact in 1939 had caught the whole world by surprise. Everyone had assumed that the Nazis and the Communists were mortal enemies, yet here they were professing friendship for one another. It was widely believed that cynicism and significant ulterior motives underlay the treaty, but the secretive nature of both regimes precluded any clear analysis or understanding of the relationship. Nevertheless, for almost two years the two countries had developed strong trade relations that had brought Germany much needed foodstuffs, industrial raw materials, and most especially oil. Now during the first months of 1941 there were growing signs of a change in Germany's attitude. Rumors were circulating throughout Europe of a planned German attack on the Soviet Union. By early March the accumulating evidence was even appearing publicly in newspapers and magazines. On March 17 *Newsweek* reported on rumors of a Nazi-Soviet breach, though the general sense was that it would not come in the immediate future. The magazine stated that the Western powers were trying to convince Soviet dictator Joseph Stalin of Hitler's aggressive intentions, but that Stalin was not interested in listening. Indeed, it was widely known that the paranoid Stalin regarded all such reports as British disinformation, designed to separate him from his alliance with Hitler and bring a new ally into the war for Britain.

Consequently, when Americans heard on June 22 that the German invasion of the Soviet Union had been launched that morning, the surprise was more at the timing than at the invasion itself. Nevertheless, the scope of the attack did cause the world to hold its breath, as Hitler had said. Massed for the assault were more than 3,000,000 men, 7,000 artillery pieces, 3,000 tanks, and 2,700 airplanes. The forces were arranged in three great army groups. In the north, an army group under Field Marshal Wilhelm Ritter von Leeb aimed at the encirclement and capture of Leningrad. In this effort it anticipated the cooperation of the Finnish army under Field Marshal Carl Mannerheim. In the center, an army group under Field Marshal Fedor von Bock was to drive on Moscow, gobbling up on the way as much Russian territory and as many Russian soldiers as possible. To the south, an army group under Field Marshal Gerd von Rundstedt had as its objective the Black Sea coast, including the Crimea, and the rich agricultural, industrial, and mineral resources of Ukraine. Despite the warnings, these forces caught the Russians completely by surprise. On the first day of battle alone, the Luftwaffe destroyed a quarter of the entire Soviet Air Force.

Perhaps the most amazing feature of the invasion, apart from the suddenness of its launch, was the speed with which the Germans advanced. By July 19, less than a month after the start, the Germans had covered as much as 300 miles, captured over 600,000 prisoners, captured or destroyed 5,700 tanks and 4,500 guns, and destroyed over half the divisions in the Soviet Army. By September 1 they were closing the ring around Leningrad in the north and nearing Crimea in the south. But in the center the advance had slowed down some 200 miles short of Moscow. The two regimes revealed none of their internal debates about continuing strategy. Instead, their respective propaganda machines produced thousands of words and photographs, extolling on the one side the victories of the invincible German military machine, and on the other side the unconquerable heroism of Russians defending their motherland.

Despite all the propaganda, by the end of September the Germans could proclaim to the world the verifiable facts that they had almost completely encircled Leningrad and cut Crimea off from the rest of the Soviet Union. To the knowledgeable observer, however, certain disquieting signs were appearing. In the north, Hitler had counted on the Finns to complete the encirclement of Leningrad on the north and east. Finland had a long-standing grudge against Russia, dating back to the days of the Tsar. Hitler now counted on the small but powerful Finnish army to take a major role in the capture of Leningrad. But

Mannerheim, the Finnish Commander-in-Chief, refused to do any more than occupy Finnish territory that Russia had seized a few years earlier. This refusal left open a supply route across Lake Ladoga that would serve to keep Leningrad alive.

In the center, the slowing of the German advance raised a serious question as to whether the Germans would be able to reach and hold Moscow before the winter weather stopped all activity. Russian roads were often no more than dirt tracks, and the fall rains regularly turned the hard, dry earth into a sticky morass. The rainy season was then followed by the onset of the winter cold. The ground would freeze, and for a short time operations could be resumed. But when the deep freeze of winter set in, temperatures would drop to more than -20° C. Even motor oil would freeze, military movement would become impossible, and soldiers without adequate shelter or winter clothing would likely lose limbs to frostbite, if indeed they survived the bitter nights at all. In the event, that is exactly what happened. Army Group Center got to within 18 miles of Moscow, but no closer. Stiffening Russian resistance and defensive positions dug by hand by thousands of Muscovites kept the invaders just that far away. By the first week of December, all maneuvering had come to a halt; and the Germans, who had counted on spending the winter in the safe shelter of Moscow, were starting to experience the first of what would be over 100,000 cases of frostbite. The invasion had stalled. Leningrad and Moscow were still uncaptured, and everyone expected the Russian front to become inactive until the spring thaws.

Growing awareness of what was happening in Europe brought about some small symbolic changes in America. The swastika, long recognized as a traditional American Indian symbol, was being abandoned because of its Nazi associations. The original shoulder patch of the 45th Infantry Division was a gold swastika on a square red diamond. In 1939 the Nazi associations had caused the patch to be replaced. The new design featured a stylized gold thunderbird, another American Indian symbol, on the same red background. Until 1941 Catawba College in North Carolina had called its yearbook the *Swastika*, presuming an association with the nearby Catawba Indian tribe. By 1941, however, the Nazi association had grown too strong; and the yearbook was renamed the *Sayakini*, purportedly a Catawba word meaning "friendship."

Another symbolic change involved the Pledge of Allegiance, recited daily in most schools and at many public events. The Pledge was always accompanied by a salute, but the form of the salute was quite variable. The most common form in 1941 was still the Bellamy Salute, named for Francis Bellamy, author of the original Pledge. In the Bellamy Salute the right arm was raised, either straight upward or toward the flag, with the palm open and facing forward. Because this salute was so close to that used by the German Nazis and Italian Fascists, there was strong and growing pressure to devise some alternative expression of American patriotism. In 1941 the most common alternative was a military-style salute. Another version had the right hand placed across the chest with the open palm facing downward. The form with hand over the heart was also widely used and was growing in popularity.

To most Americans, the war overseas meant the war in Europe and the Mediterranean area. In 1937, however, the Japanese Kwangtung Army, which already in 1931 had invaded Manchuria and created the puppet state of Manchukuo, launched a full-scale invasion of China. The Japanese advanced rapidly, but the Chinese had the advantage of vast territory and a poor transportation network. The defenders withdrew into the interior of the country, trading space for time. By late 1938, the conflict had settled down to a war of attrition. The Japanese had reached the limit of their logistical capability, and the Chinese were content to let the Japanese exhaust themselves in occupying a territory that could never be completely pacified.

Unable to advance with their armies, the Japanese adopted a strategy of bombing the Chinese into submission. The Chinese air force was practically useless against the attack. In October of 1940 Chiang Kai-shek sent his air force advisor, a retired U.S. Army Air Corps captain named Claire Chennault, to Washington to secure planes and, if possible, personnel to blunt the Japanese air offensive. On Chennault's recommendation, Chiang asked especially for fighter planes to defend against the bombers and their fighter escorts. The abrasive and persistent Chennault arrived in Washington that fall to present his plan for the transfer of fighters to the Chinese air force. Knowing the extremely poor quality of Chinese pilots, Chennault also asked for American pilots and maintenance personnel to be sent to China with the planes. Over the strenuous objections of both the Army and the Navy, Chennault worked his way through the bureaucracy until he finally secured Roosevelt's approval for the project. One hundred older model P-40 fighters, originally destined for Britain, were diverted to China with the promise that the British would receive a newer model as replacements. Roosevelt also allowed American pilots to resign their military commissions and fly as "contractors" for the Chinese air force. Arriving in China late that summer, the first pilots formed the nucleus of the American Volunteer Group, informally known as the Flying Tigers from the insignia painted on their planes. Although formed in secrecy, the Flying Tigers quickly gained wide recognition, both in China and in the United States. They were rushed into combat right after Pearl Harbor and inflicted such severe casualties on the Japanese that the bomber offensive was effectively blunted.

Except for the very late entry of the Flying Tigers, the stalemate in China produced little news in America. In so far as this country was conscious of China, its attention was on the people and their sufferings. For many decades American Christian missionaries had worked in China and had developed close contacts there. A number of prominent Americans had been born in China to missionary parents. Perhaps the most notable, and certainly the most influential, was Henry Luce, son of Presbyterian missionaries and editor and publisher of *Time, Life,* and *Fortune.* Through his magazines Luce tried to keep the Chinese struggle before the American people. In this he was aided by his wife, the writer Clare Boothe Luce, who published under her maiden name.

The previous fall Clare Boothe had published a book, *Europe in the Spring,* which chronicled her visit to western Europe in the spring of the year, just before the German invasion of France. In it she emphasized the complaisance of the French and British in the face of the clearly aggressive intentions of Germany and Italy. In the spring of this year, Henry Luce decided to make a tour of the land of his birth to see just how the war was progressing and how the people were coping. His wife accompanied him, hoping to produce a book on China to match her portrait of Europe. Despite the prominent people she met and the vast amount of information she gathered, the book never quite came together. Instead Boothe settled for a series of articles published in *Life*.

In addition to touring and publishing, Henry Luce tried to help China in more concrete ways, principally by joining the Board of Directors of United China Relief. This organization was founded in March in New York City to raise funds to aid the Chinese people. With the help of such board members as Pearl Buck, Eleanor Roosevelt, and John D. Rockefeller III, within three months the Board had raised over half a million dollars.

United China Relief was not the only organization concerned with helping civilians affected by the war. In January of 1940, Mrs. Natalie Wales Latham, a young, twice-divorced New York socialite with a substantial excess of energy and a passionate love of England, had founded Bundles for Britain, a charity whose stated purpose was "to provide comforts and necessities for Great Britain at war." Wanting to do something to help the people of the country she loved, Mrs. Wales Latham approached the British Consul in New York and asked if there were anything she and her friends could do for the British people. He gave her an encouraging reply, and she promptly wired Mrs. Winston Churchill to ask what Britain needed. Mrs. Churchill, whom Mrs. Wales Latham had never met, took the request seriously enough to send a reply, but apparently thought that a New York socialite would not be able to accomplish anything important. She suggested knitting wool stockings for seamen on minesweepers, and mailed the official Admiralty specifications for those items. Undeterred, Mrs. Wales Latham organized her socialite friends, persuaded the Chairman of the Board of Metropolitan Life Insurance to let her have a rent-free storefront in a building the company owned, and set about organizing new chapters of her organization.

The first six months of Bundles for Britain were a period of relatively slow growth, with about a hundred chapters opening in various parts of the country. But as word spread, so did the interest in the project. By 1941 new chapters were being organized at the rate of about twenty a week. Mrs. Wales Latham kept close control over the organization. It was, after all, officially registered with the State Department as a foreign agent, and all legal requirements were scrupulously observed. As interest grew, so did the range of assistance provided to the British. From the beginning Mrs. Wales Latham kept in touch with Mrs. Churchill, who provided an ever-growing list of needed items. Woolen stockings were still on the list, but so were warm clothing for the soldiers after Dunkerque, good used clothing for civilians, blankets, surgical equipment, ambulances, hospital beds, sleeping bags, blood transfusion kits, children's cots, X-ray machines, and scores of other badly needed items. The value of their in-kind assistance was well over a million dollars already and was growing rapidly. But Bundles also sent badly needed cash to help with reconstruction, sometimes as much as $150,000 in a month, to provide emergency relief for bombed-out Coventry or help rebuild destroyed hospitals or fund other urgently needed projects.

CHAPTER 6

June: The Great Debate

ON THE AFTERNOON of Sunday, June 22, the playwright Robert Sherwood was in New York to attend a rally of Fight For Freedom, an interventionist organization that urged support for the British in their struggle against Germany and Italy. As Sherwood entered the Golden Gate Ballroom in Harlem on that very hot day, he passed a line of pickets whose signs and literature revealed them to be members of the Communist Party. The signs attacked the "Fight For Freedom warmongers, tools of Britain and Wall Street." Appealing to the majority of residents of Harlem, they handed out pamphlets calling for African Americans to march on Washington and demand equality and peace. Sherwood walked into the ballroom for the rally, where the featured speakers were the journalist Herbert Agar and the writer Dorothy Parker. The rally lasted an hour and a half. When Sherwood walked out, the pickets were gone and the calls for the march had been cancelled. In that short space of time, orders had come from Moscow to party headquarters and been passed on to the pickets that they should immediately stop all isolationist activity and support American

intervention in the war. The next day the Communist Party newspaper, the *Daily Worker*, changed its editorial policy, advocated support
for Britain and for Lend-Lease, was thoroughly interventionist and,
most remarkable, thoroughly pro-Roosevelt. The reason for the abrupt
change, of course, was what happened in Eastern Europe that Sunday
morning when the German armies began their invasion of Russia,
suddenly transforming the Soviet Union into an ally of Great Britain.

The German invasion threw into turmoil a debate whose lines had
settled into a predictable pattern leading to a nearly predictable result.
Not since the Nazi-Soviet pact of August 1939 had alignments been
so shaken. Ever since the end of World War I, America had regarded
events in Europe with a reserve bordering on hostility. We were told
we had fought to make the world safe for democracy. But instead of
democracy, all we saw was a continuation of the same old power politics. American businesses had profited during the war, but their profits
were subsidized by loans from our government to the warring Allies.
After the war only Finland repaid its loans. There was even a lingering
hostility toward Great Britain in many parts of this country. Some of
the hostility was an inheritance from Revolutionary times, some arose
in immigrant communities that had no reason to love Britain, and
some arose from a sense that we had rescued Britain at great expense
with no benefit to ourselves. The British failure to pay their World
War debts certainly did not help.

The Neutrality Act of 1935 marked a significant shift in American
foreign policy, forbidding the shipment of war matériel to any nation
engaged in war with another. In order to limit the risk of involvement in a foreign war, we were for the first time willing to limit our
own right to trade. This was followed by the Neutrality Act of 1936,
which extended the embargo for another fourteen months and also
prohibited all loans to warring countries. The Neutrality Act of 1937
extended the embargo to all trade with belligerents, including parties
to a civil war. Remembering the uproar over the loss of American
life when the *Lusitania* was sunk in 1915, Congress also prohibited
travel by Americans on ships of warring nations. But in a concession
to American industry, the Act included a cash-and-carry provision,

allowing belligerents to buy war supplies in the United States so long as they paid for them before shipment and transported the matériel under their own national flags.

In a speech in Chicago in October of 1937, Roosevelt adumbrated a new approach to American foreign policy. Noting that 90 percent of the people in the world desired peace, he said that a way needed to be found to carry out their will. Then, in a famous phrase, the president said, "When an epidemic of physical disease starts to spread, the community approves and joins in a quarantine of the patients in order to protect the health of the community against the spread of the disease." He made his point clear by observing that "war is a contagion." He insisted that he was determined to keep out of war but that it was impossible to escape its dangers. The immediate public reaction to the speech was strongly negative. Many people felt the president was leading the country down a path to war, and Roosevelt had to backtrack quickly.

In 1938 the people's fears were aroused again when Europe appeared to be on the brink of war over the intended German annexation of the Sudetenland in Czechoslovakia. Although war was finally averted by the Munich agreement, Americans recognized that the Western democracies had yielded to totalitarian threats and had suffered a humiliating defeat. Despite popular indignation, polls revealed that fully 95 percent of the American people were adamantly opposed to becoming involved in a foreign war. On the other hand concern for the advance of the dictators did enable the president to ask for an increase of $300,000,000 in defense spending. Roosevelt cast the request in terms of the need for national and hemispheric defense, appealing to American sentiments that dated back to the time of the Monroe Doctrine. Tensions in Europe further increased American anxieties when the Germans and Italians signed their "Pact of Steel" in May of 1939 and, to everyone's surprise, the Germans and Russians signed their nonaggression treaty in August. The latter event was particularly disconcerting to the tiny but noisy Communist Party in the United States of America (C.P.U.S.A.). Heretofore supporters of a more aggressive American line toward Germany, they suddenly became vocal isolationists, wanting to keep America out of any European conflict.

The outbreak of war in September 1939 raised the stakes in the debate over American isolation. American hostility toward the Germans (and the Russians after they rushed in to share in the spoils) was almost universal. President Roosevelt moved promptly to declare American neutrality, which cut off the shipment of arms to any of the belligerents. In practice this meant a cutoff to England and France, since Germany did not need any outside source of arms. Therefore the administration's first order of business was to try to change the existing neutrality legislation so arms shipments to the Allies could resume. Accordingly, the president called for a special session of Congress to convene on September 21.

There was strong congressional support for ending the embargo, even as everyone wanted to stay out of the war. The real issue to be negotiated was how much discretion Congress would allow the president in providing that support. Roosevelt, desiring maximum flexibility in handling war aid, wanted to have the Neutrality Act repealed entirely. But with distrust for the administration running high, Congress was unwilling to go that far. In the event, the Neutrality Act was amended to restore the lapsed cash-and-carry provision, but restrictions on American shipping and American travel in the war zone were tightened.

Despite revulsion at the fate of Poland and general Nazi policies, Americans still regarded the war as an internal European affair that would soon be resolved, one way or another, without our participation. Nevertheless, after the German conquest of Denmark and Norway, and especially after the fall of France and the Low Countries in the spring of 1940, the issue became more grave. Only Britain stood between us and total German control of the eastern Atlantic, including major American trade routes. If Britain were defeated and Hitler gained control of the British colonies in the West Indies, the threat to American security would be severe.

As 1940 progressed, more and more people came to understand that American security depended greatly on British survival. In May

William Allen White, the widely known and respected editor of the *Emporia Gazette*, became so concerned that he contacted other newspaper editors and other prominent citizens, urging the founding of local groups to mobilize and channel public opinion. He wanted to urge Congress to make America "a nonbelligerent ally of France and England." "I stand aghast," he wrote, "at what will happen if the English either scuttle their ships or turn them over to Germany." The response was so positive that by the end of the month, White could write to Roosevelt asking for "sailing orders" for the newly formed Committee to Defend America by Aiding the Allies.

The fall of France in June gave new urgency to the question of America's involvement. To interventionists like those on the White committee, American aid for Britain was now more important than ever. England could not be allowed to succumb. She had to be supported so America would not be put in the position of having to face Germany alone. To the isolationists, however, the fall of France was merely the prelude to the imminent fall of England. Support for the British meant backing a losing cause, and America should pressure Britain to seek a negotiated peace with Germany and thereby end the threat of war. The fierce and growing opposition between the two groups sometimes obscured the fact that both had the goal of keeping America out of the war. They differed sharply over the best ways to achieve that end.

Even the largely isolationist Republican Party was affected by the developments in Europe. The Republican National Convention opened in Philadelphia just two days after France signed the armistice with Germany. So shaken were the delegates that they even included in their platform a mild statement of support for Britain. After repeating their opposition to involvement in foreign wars and calling "for the prompt, orderly, and realistic building of our national defense," they added a brief statement of support for the allies:

Our sympathies have been profoundly stirred by invasion of unoffending countries and by disaster to nations whole ideals most closely resemble our own. We favor the extension to all peoples fighting for liberty, or whose liberty is threatened, of such aid as shall not be in violation of international law or inconsistent with the requirements of our own national defense.

This statement is strikingly similar to the clause adopted by the Democrats a month later:

In self-defense and in good conscience, the world's greatest democracy cannot afford heartlessly or in a spirit of appeasement to ignore the peace-loving and liberty-loving peoples wantonly attacked by ruthless aggressors. We pledge to extend to these peoples all the material aid at our command, consistent with law and not inconsistent with the interests of our own national self-defense—all to the end that peace and international good faith may yet emerge triumphant.

More important than any platform is the selection of a presidential candidate. Here, too, international events had their effect. Going into the convention, the principal Republican contenders were Tom Dewey, Robert Taft, and Arthur Vandenberg, all isolationist to one degree or another. Although many factors went into the ultimate victory of Wendell Willkie (including a carefully planned "spontaneous" demonstration), the trauma of the French defeat did nothing to harm the cause of the one prominent Republican who was an outspoken internationalist. The selection of Wendell Willkie, coupled with the words of the platform, guaranteed that the debate over assistance to the Allies would not be a factor in the presidential campaign.

Because the great majority of Americans strongly supported strengthening American defenses, Congress readily approved increased military and naval appropriations. In July 1940 the Two-Ocean Navy Act was passed, authorizing an expansion of the Navy with over 1.3 million tons of new warships. In September Congress voted over $5 billion for expanding and equipping the Army. Special attention was paid to the Air Corps, which was to receive 19,000 new planes. Americans also recognized the need to increase the size of the Army beyond the numbers that could be recruited voluntarily. By August polls were showing as many as 86 percent of the country supporting a peacetime draft as a regrettable necessity. With both Willkie and Roosevelt supporting the move, Congress in September authorized the first peacetime draft in American history. In spite of the fulminations of such arch-isolationists as Senator Gerald Nye and Representative Hamilton Fish, Congress permitted the call-up of the National Guard for up to twelve months of training and deployment within the Western Hemisphere. At the same time it provided for the registration of men from 18 to 35 and for their induction and training. Like the Guard, draftees could be called up for up to twelve months, and their deployment was limited to the Western Hemisphere.

At the same time the president was looking for ways to provide aid to Britain without getting America involved in the fighting. Even isolationist Republicans, with few exceptions, wanted the United States to find ways to strengthen the defenses of the Western Hemisphere. A shortage of offshore bases in the Atlantic rendered the eastern seaboard vulnerable to attack, and there were British bases in their Caribbean territories. At the same time the U.S. Navy had over 150 destroyers left over from World War I, which it did not need and which were destined for scrapping. A trade seemed to be in order. America could transfer 50 of those destroyers to the Royal Navy in exchange for leases on naval bases in Newfoundland and the Caribbean.

Negotiations on the bases-for-destroyers deal dragged out over several months in the late summer of 1940. The isolationists might grumble that the country was violating the spirit if not the letter of neutrality. But there was no way they could object to the basic outlines of the deal. Nevertheless, the exchange agreement, finalized in September, effectively marked the end of America's true neutrality and the beginning of a new phase in our foreign policy, a state of non-belligerency that was nevertheless officially sympathetic to the Allies.

Despite the strong public feeling of support for the Allies, some people were worried that continued American assistance would inexorably lead us into the European war. During the summer a young student at the Yale Law School, R. Douglas Stuart, Jr., was worried enough that he decided to take some kind of formal action. Accompanied by Kingman Brewster, Jr., editor of the *Yale Daily News*, Stuart attended the Republican Convention in Philadelphia, where he sought out Ohio senator Robert A. Taft and other delegates who were likely to be sympathetic to his cause. Following these meetings he went to Washington to see Burton Wheeler of Montana, Bennett C. Clark of Missouri, Robert LaFollette of Wisconsin, and others who were known to oppose Roosevelt's foreign policy. Word of Stuart's activities came to the attention of General Robert E. Wood of Chicago, president of Sears Roebuck and Company. Wood was an acquaintance of Stuart's father, who was vice president of Quaker Oats. Impressed by the young man's energy and sympathetic to his vision, Wood wrote to Stuart, commending him for his work.

Stuart's response was to travel to Chicago to meet with Wood and others regarding his vision for a new organization, initially called the Emergency Committee to Defend America First. With promises of financial support from Wood and his friends, Stuart set up offices in the same building that housed the headquarters of Quaker Oats. When the Democratic Convention came to town, Stuart met again with Wheeler and other potential supporters. By the end of August, a steering group had been established and had held the first formal meeting of what was now known as the America First Committee. The members of the national committee included prominent business executives and industrialists, civic leaders, clergymen, and even President Roosevelt's cousin Alice Roosevelt Longworth, daughter of former President Theodore Roosevelt.

On September 4 the new committee published an announcement of its formation and a statement of its guiding principles:

1. The United States must build an impregnable defense for America.
2. No foreign power, or group of powers, can successfully attack a *prepared* America.
3. American democracy can be preserved only by keeping out of the European war.

4. "Aid short of war" weakens national defense at home and threatens to involve America in war abroad.

It was surely no coincidence that the announcement was first reported in the *Chicago Tribune*, published by Roosevelt's archenemy Colonel Robert R. McCormick.

By the time America First was organized and publicized, the destroyers-for-bases exchange had already been announced. Public support for the measure was so extensive that the national committee realized it would be futile to oppose or try to reverse the agreement. They also realized that, given their concern for the defense of the Western Hemisphere, they could scarcely object to the acquisition of new naval bases to enhance that defense. But a new crisis was developing that would force the president to ask Congress for a change in the existing laws. That request would give America First its first chance to affect the fundamental direction of American foreign policy.

Existing neutrality legislation permitted Britain to acquire war matériel in the United States. But the purchases had to be paid for in cash, and the transportation had to be provided by the British. Britain was rapidly running out of cash. During the fall word leaked out that British assets would last only through the late summer of 1941. After that they would have no more cash to spend. Even worse, the supplies they were purchasing were only minimally adequate for the basic defense of the home islands. New and larger purchases were needed if Britain were to pursue a more aggressive fight against Hitler. For those purchases there was no money available.

At a press conference on December 17, Roosevelt almost casually announced that he would be proposing legislation to remedy this problem. He would ask Congress for authority to take over the current British orders that had been placed with American factories and then, from the war matériel so produced, lend or lease to the British the supplies they needed to pursue the war. All America would ask was that when the fighting was over, they would repair and return the matériel, replacing in kind any that was lost. He said he wanted to get "rid of the silly, foolish old dollar sign" and replace it with "a gentleman's obligation to repay in kind." The president then produced the analogy that would stick in people's minds.

Well, let me give you an illustration: Suppose my neighbor's home catches fire, and I have a length of garden hose four or five hundred feet away. If he can take my garden hose and connect it up with his hydrant, I may help him to put out his fire. Now, what do I do? I don't say to him before that operation, "Neighbor, my garden hose cost me $15; you have to pay me $15 for it." What is the transaction that goes on? I don't want $15—I want my garden hose back after the fire is over. All right. If it goes through the fire all right, intact, without any damage to it, he gives it back to me and thanks me very much for the use of it. But suppose it gets smashed up—holes in it—during the fire; we don't have to have too much formality about it, but I say to him, "I was glad to lend you that hose; I see I can't use it any more, it's all smashed up." He says, "How many feet of it were there?" I tell him, "There were 150 feet of it." He says, "All right, I will replace it." Now, if I get a nice garden hose back, I am in pretty good shape.

In other words, if you lend certain munitions and get the munitions back at the end of the war, if they are intact haven't been hurt—you are all right; if they have been damaged or have deteriorated or have been lost completely, it seems to me you come out pretty well if you have them replaced by the fellow to whom you have lent them.

Somewhat disingenuously Roosevelt told the reporters he could not give them any more details because he was still working on them. He would not be able to present a formal proposal until the new Congress convened on January 3.

Twelve days later, Roosevelt gave one his most important speeches. In a fireside chat on December 29, the president presented the outline of his proposed legislation. He began directly by affirming his desire to keep the country out of war:

This is not a fireside chat on war. It is a talk on national security; because the nub of the whole purpose of your President is
to keep you now, and your children later, and your grandchildren much later, out of a last-ditch war for the preservation
of American independence and all the things that American
independence means to you and to me and to ours.

After an extended discussion of the importance of British survival
and the threat to America if the Axis prevailed, he exhorted manufacturers not to carry on business as usual, but to exert every effort to
increase arms production as much as possible. Then came the stirring
passage:

As planes and ships and guns and shells are produced, your
Government, with its defense experts, can then determine how
best to use them to defend this hemisphere. The decision as to
how much shall be sent abroad and how much shall remain
at home must be made on the basis of our over-all military
necessities.

We must be the great arsenal of democracy. For us this is
an emergency as serious as war itself. We must apply ourselves
to our task with the same resolution, the same sense of urgency,
the same spirit of patriotism and sacrifice as we would show
were we at war.

We have furnished the British great material support and
we will furnish far more in the future.

There will be no "bottlenecks" in our determination to aid
Great Britain. No dictator, no combination of dictators, will
weaken that determination by threats of how they will con-
strue that determination.

On January 10, House Majority Leader John McCormack and Senate
Majority Leader Alben Barkley rose in their respective houses to
introduce the bill. The president had asked the leaders to sponsor the
bill in order to emphasize its importance. Normally such duties were

assigned to the chairmen of the committees to which the bills would be sent. The bill was introduced under the official designation H. R. 1776, more commonly known as the Lend-Lease Act of 1941. The choice of 1776 was not accidental, but the reason was not what people surmised. McCormack represented a district heavily populated by Irish Americans, who would resent anything done to help England. House Parliamentarian Lewis Deschler suggested the number as a patriotic designation that would help McCormack defuse the anti-British sentiment in his district.

Once the bill was introduced in each house, it was referred to the two foreign affairs committees, which scheduled hearings. Now the struggle between isolationists and interventionists was fully joined. Testimony for the administration was led by Secretary of State Cordell Hull, followed by Treasury Secretary Henry Morgenthau, Secretary of the Navy Frank Knox, Secretary of War Henry Stimson, and William Knudsen, Co-Director of the Office of Production Management. In opposition were Joseph Kennedy, former ambassador to Great Britain and a well-known defeatist; Norman Thomas, perennial Socialist Party candidate for president; General Robert Wood of the America First Committee, and aviation hero Charles Lindbergh.

The critical sections of H. R. 1776 read as follow:

SEC. 3. (a) Notwithstanding the provisions of any other law, the President may, from time to time, when he deems it in the interest of national defense, authorize the Secretary Of War, the Secretary of the Navy, or the head of any other department or agency of the Government—

(1) To manufacture in arsenals, factories, and shipyards under their jurisdiction, or otherwise procure, to the extent to which funds are made available therefor, or contracts are authorized from time to time by the Congress, or both, any defense article for the government of any country whose defense the President deems vital to the defense of the United States.

(2) To sell, transfer title to, exchange, lease, lend, or otherwise dispose of, to any such government any defense article, but no defense article not manufactured or procured under paragraph (1) shall in any way be disposed of under this paragraph, except after consultation with the Chief of Staff of the Army or the Chief of Naval Operations of the Navy, or both.

Isolationists, with America First taking the lead, argued that this step would inevitably lead the country into war. For many of them, the tremendous power given to the president was an equally important issue. Congressman Hamilton Fish, who represented Roosevelt's home district, urged people to speak out against "the President's dictator bill." Interventionists, following the president's line, countered that arming Britain was the best way to keep America out of war. While conceding that the president was asking for extraordinary powers, they argued that the need was so urgent that no other course would suffice. Roosevelt himself pointed out to reporters that the bill would require a separate appropriations bill to provide funds to carry out its provisions. Consequently there was no usurpation of congressional authority. Congress still had the power to block implementation where it saw fit.

The rhetorical battle intensified when Burton Wheeler attacked Lend-Lease as "the New Deal's triple 'A' foreign policy—it will plow under every fourth American boy." Roosevelt responded with a rare personal retort, telling reporters he regarded Wheeler's statement "as the most untruthful, as the most dastardly, unpatriotic thing that has ever been said. Quote me on that. That really is the rottenest thing that has been said in public life in my generation." Public reaction was sharply divided. America First published Wheeler's remarks in a pamphlet, but many Americans were outraged by them and agreed strongly with the president.

The threat of war was the main theme of the debate in the Senate. Opponents of the bill, realizing that many administration supporters favored an even greater measure of intervention than the bill provided for, asked point blank why, if Hitler was so great a threat and Britain needed our help to defeat him, the administration did not openly ask for a declaration of war. The administration, not wanting to admit to the woeful state of American preparedness and our own need for munitions and supplies, skirted carefully around the issue. Sensing a need for some support from Britain on this point, Harry Hopkins in London spoke to Churchill about including in an upcoming radio broadcast (February 9, 1941) a statement of Britain's determination to persist and prevail. The result was one of the most memorable of Churchill's addresses, with its moving peroration:

> We shall not fail or falter; and we shall not weaken or tire. Neither the sudden shock of battle, nor the long-drawn trials of vigilance and exertion will wear us down. Give us the tools, and we will finish the job.

Both America First and the Committee to Defend America by Aiding the Allies (the White committee) were intensely active during the whole course of the debate. All during the congressional hearings, public opinion polls showed that the American public favored passage of the bill, sometimes by a bare 50 percent, sometimes by a more substantial margin. But the White committee concentrated its most intense publicity in the midwestern heartland, home base for the isolationists. And in this area during the course of the debate, the polls showed a small but perceptible shift of opinion toward support for Lend-Lease.

From the beginning it was clear to everyone that Roosevelt had the votes in Congress to pass the bill any time he wanted. But F.D.R. was a canny politician. By allowing the whole debate to be played out in public, he gave Americans time to accustom themselves to the idea of greater intervention. People were also able to feel that a variety of voices had been heard and a shared conclusion had been reached. The developing of a public consensus was as important to the president as the passage of the bill itself. In his desire to attract the widest possible body of support, the president also allowed a number of amendments to be attached to the bill. He agreed to a time limit on Lend-Lease, allowing the act to expire at the end of 1942. He also agreed to consult with the leaders of the Army and Navy before transferring any war matériel, and he agreed to report to Congress every ninety days on transfers made under the act. On one proposed amendment he made a clever compromise. Some opponents objected to the use of American naval vessels to escort supply convoys into the waters of the war zone. They feared that escort activities would inevitably involve us in the shooting war, and they tried to attach an amendment prohibiting the use of American ships for convoy duty. Roosevelt had argued all along that the president has the power to order convoying without congressional approval. The language proposed would have seriously limited this power. So he allowed an amendment saying that nothing in the bill permitted the use of American vessels to be used in convoys. Each side could interpret this language as it chose.

Several proposed amendments were summarily blocked by administration supporters. One would have eliminated the Lend-Lease provision and substituted a simple loan to Britain. Another would have prohibited any aid to Soviet Russia if that country became involved in the war. Yet another would have prohibited the use of American shipyards to repair the vessels of belligerent states. All were rejected by Roosevelt and his advisers. Some proposed amendments were offered with their sponsors' tongues planted firmly in their cheeks. New York Representative Vito Marcantonio (American Labor Party) introduced an amendment that read,

It is the declared policy of the United States that the original Thirteen Colonies are not obsolete or surplus. Any opinion of the Attorney General to the contrary notwithstanding, nothing in this act shall be construed to authorize or to permit the President of the United States to lease, lend, or transfer the original Thirteen Colonies to King George of England.

Despite the president's desire to build a broad coalition in Congress, when the bill was reported out of committee and came to the floor, the vote was generally along party lines. In the House only 24 out of 159 Republicans supported the bill and only 25 out of 261 Democrats voted against the administration. The Senate vote showed 10 out of 28 Republicans supporting Lend-Lease and 14 out of 65 Democrats in opposition. From the South, solidly Democratic, proud of its British heritage, and respectful of its military traditions, came but a single senatorial Nay, that of Buncombe Bob Reynolds of North Carolina. The Midwest, home of Anglophobia, Republicanism, and the *Chicago Tribune*, was almost as solidly opposed. One fifth of all the House votes against the bill came from Ohio and Illinois. The slight differences between the House and Senate versions of the bill were quickly reconciled, and the president signed Lend-Lease into law on March 11.

After the passage of Lend-Lease, the debate turned to the question of how American supplies were to be delivered to Britain. It had become clear to the Royal Navy that the best protection for shipping was to group the transports into convoys and have them cross the ocean under the protection of small, fast destroyers and corvettes. These vessels, equipped with Asdic (the British name for Sonar), could often detect German submarines that threatened the convoys. When enemy boats were discovered, the escorts were fast enough to pursue them and attack with depth charges. Since combat between a submarine and a destroyer could not be avoided, many Americans insisted that no American naval vessels should be engaged in convoy duty. It was feared that if an American warship were sunk or damaged by a German submarine, the result would be full and immediate American involvement in the war.

Yet full American involvement was getting closer. On May 7 Secretary of the Navy Frank Knox announced that the oceanic functions of the Coast Guard were being taken over by the Navy, a move that made a large number of Coast Guard cutters available for potential escort duty. But Roosevelt remained cautious. He was unwilling to get too far ahead of popular opinion. So in a move typical of the man, he chose to make a strong speech laying out the case for action but in fact containing no concrete proposals.

On the evening of May 27, Roosevelt brought together the ambassadors and ministers of all the American states in the East

Room of the White House. In their presence he broadcast one of the most famous of his fireside chats to the nation. His 45-minute speech was eagerly anticipated by a country anxious to know where its president was leading. Even a baseball game was suspended so the speech could be broadcast to the crowd. The president carefully structured his speech in terms of the defense of the Western Hemisphere. Nothing was said about any kind of direct American involvement in Europe. But he made it clear that the defeat of Britain would give Germany control of the North Atlantic and bring German naval power within sight of our shores. The threat to French West Africa and the Suez Canal were merely preludes to Germany's desire for world domination, including a stranglehold on the Americas.

Then, after describing the American naval tradition of maintaining peace and protecting commerce, he became specific.

> The blunt truth is this—and I reveal this with the full knowledge of the British government: the present rate of Nazi sinkings of merchant ships is more than three times as high as the capacity of British shipyards to replace them; it is more than twice the combined British and American output of merchant ships today.
>
> We can answer this peril by two simultaneous measures: first, by speeding up and increasing our own great shipbuilding program; and second, by helping to cut down the losses on the high seas.

After detailing the progress of German aggression, Roosevelt observed that the initial threat to America could begin almost anywhere in Western Europe or Africa, and it was imperative for America both to protect the Americas and to keep supplying Britain, our main defender in the Atlantic. Finally, after a stirring peroration appealing to Magna Carta, the Declaration of Independence, the Constitution, and the Emancipation Proclamation, he announced, "I have tonight issued a proclamation that an unlimited national emergency exists and requires the strengthening of our defense to the extreme limit of our national power and authority."

Roosevelt expected that his speech might have an approval rate of about 50 percent. Consequently he was delighted that initial reaction was 90 percent favorable. Perhaps this reaction was a result of the general confusion, especially in Congress, about what it actually meant in concrete terms. Obviously we would be stepping up our support for Britain, but that was old news. People could read into the message whatever meaning they chose, and even isolationists were generally glad the speech was not any stronger than it was. Roosevelt was still treading carefully. Even after he received reports of the *Robin Moor* sinking, he sent a restrained message to Congress recommending no concrete action.

The *Robin Moor* was a merchant ship sailing under the American flag for the Seas Shipping Company of New York. On May 21 she was stopped in mid-Atlantic on her way to Mozambique via Cape Town by the German submarine U-69. The submarine captain, Lieutenant Jost Metzler, informed the captain of the *Robin Moor* that the ship was carrying contraband of war and was to be sunk. The captain and crew were given thirty minutes to get into their lifeboats. Metzler promised he would radio their position to rescuers. He never did, and the lifeboats drifted for up to eighteen days before the passengers and crew were rescued. Senator Burton Wheeler tried to claim that 70 percent of the cargo was contraband and the ship had been legally sunk, but public opinion was against him. Although Roosevelt stopped short of direct retaliation, he did order the closing of all German and Italian consulates except at their embassies in Washington.

Meanwhile the American armed forces were moving ever closer to direct involvement in the shooting war. Following the German occupation of Denmark in April of 1940, the British government had become concerned about the possibility of German occupation and use of Danish overseas territories. The Færoe Islands, less than 200 miles from the north coast of Scotland, were quickly occupied by British troops, but concern remained about Greenland and Iceland. Greenland was clearly in the Western Hemisphere, and the

Monroe Doctrine was emphatic on the matter of European colonialism. Not only would the United States resist any effort to establish new European colonies in this hemisphere, but it would also oppose the transfer of any existing colony from one European power to another. The Danish ambassador to the United States, Henrik de Kauffmann, worked closely with Assistant Secretary of State A. A. Berle to arrange for the United States to take over the protection of Greenland and hold it in trust until full Danish sovereignty could be restored. The agreement was signed on April 9, the first anniversary of the German occupation of Denmark. The German authorities in Copenhagen were naturally furious, but there was little they could do. American troops moved in and established bases in Greenland. Even more important, they shut down the German weather stations that were operating on Greenland's east coast. While those weather stations were technically civilian operations, the weather reports they sent to Berlin had been of material assistance to the German naval forces operating in the North Atlantic.

Iceland was a different matter. The country had achieved home rule in 1918 and anticipated full independence from Denmark in 1944. When German troops occupied Denmark, the Icelandic *Alþingi* (Parliament) announced that the King was unable to carry out his constitutional duties; and Iceland effectively declared independence. When Britain invited Iceland to join the war as a belligerent, the country refused, preferring to remain neutral. With Iceland practically defenseless against a possible German invasion, the British government decided they could not afford the risk of a German base so close to their shipping lifeline across the Atlantic. On May 10, 1940, the 2nd Royal Marine Battalion landed at Reykjavik and effected a quick and bloodless occupation of the country. Protests were muted after the British promised not to interfere with internal affairs and to leave as soon as the war was over. Both promises were kept.

By the spring of 1941, the Royal Marines in Iceland were badly needed for combat duties elsewhere. After careful negotiations, the Icelandic government, which had declared official full independence on May 17, was persuaded to invite the United States to take over the occupation of the country and protect its independence and neutrality. Agreement on the invitation was reached on July 1, and the 1st Marine Provisional Brigade began landing there on the 7th. Reaction in the United States was surprisingly muted. Most people accepted the president's statement that Iceland was well within the Western Hemisphere, and there was widespread agreement that hemispheric protection was an essential obligation of the United States. The occupation also created an excellent cover for the use of American Naval vessels to escort convoys across the ocean as far as Iceland. Of course it was necessary for merchant ships to travel to Iceland to keep the Marines supplied. And of course convoys were the safest way for them to travel. And if other ships chose to travel in those convoys, well that was only natural. Isolationists fumed at an act that brought the country even closer to war, but on this issue they enjoyed little popular support.

The German invasion of the Soviet Union on June 22 completely changed the trend of the debate. The Communist Party, small but noisy, had been isolationist ever since the signing of the Russo-German nonaggression pact in August of 1939. Prior to that, of course, they had followed the Kremlin line in their total hostility to Nazism. Since then they had been cautiously pro-German and strongly anti-British. Their support had often been something of an embarrassment to other isolationists, especially those with fascist leanings. But the German attack caused another change of face, as the C.P.U.S.A. took its directives from Moscow. Now they advocated full American involvement in supplying aid to Russia. The switch was widely ridiculed in the press and destroyed what little credibility the party still had.

But even as the invasion eliminated the Communists as a force for isolation, it also breathed new life into the efforts of America First. The national committee met and quickly issued a statement emphatically reaffirming their opposition to any kind of American involvement:

> The entry of Communist Russia into the war certainly should settle once and for all the intervention issue here at home. The war party can hardly ask the people of America to take up arms behind the red flag of Stalin. With the ruthless forces of

dictatorship and aggression now clearly aligned on both sides
the proper course for the United States becomes even clearer.
We must continue to build our own defenses and take no part
in this incongruous European conflict.

The emphasis on the militant atheism of Stalinist Russia was a theme
that ran through many of the isolationist statements at this period.
Bennett C. Clark asked if anyone "could conceive of American boys
being sent to their deaths singing 'Onward Christian Soldiers' under
the bloody emblem of the Hammer and Sickle." On July 2 Charles
Lindbergh was quoted in the *Chicago Tribune* as saying, "I would a
hundred times rather see my country ally herself with England, or
even with Germany with all her faults, than with the cruelty, the god-
lessness, and the barbarism that exist in Soviet Russia."

Even as Lindbergh was making this statement, a movie première
in New York had set off a reaction far beyond what anyone could have
expected. *Sergeant York* was a reasonably accurate (for Hollywood)
biography of Sergeant Alvin York, the World War I hero who won the
Medal of Honor for his exploits in France. An unlettered Tennessee
mountain boy, York was originally a pacifist. But when he was drafted,
he persuaded himself that serving in the Army was what was required
of him if he were to render unto Caesar the things that are Caesar's.
His marksmanship, honed by hunting small game to support the
family, served him well when he attacked a German machine gun
emplacement that had pinned down his company. He single-hand-
edly picked off more than 30 Germans and took the surrender of 132
others, marching them back to the American lines. After the war he
became a celebrity when the *Saturday Evening Post* publicized his
exploits. Attempts were made to have York star in a film about his
Army service, but he turned the offers down.

Finally in 1940 Warner Brothers managed to secure York's approval
of a film about his life, subject to his approval of the script and the studio's donation of $50,000 to a Bible school York wanted to found. They
also agreed to the hero's request that Gary Cooper be cast in the starring role. When the film opened at New York's Astor Theater, Warner

Brothers mounted a huge publicity campaign, including a Broadway parade with York marching along with other World War veterans. The first showing was attended by Eleanor Roosevelt, General John J. Pershing (who had presented the Medal of Honor to York), Wendell Willkie, and Henry Luce. Luce even aided in the publicity for the movie by making it *Life* magazine's Movie of the Week in the July 14 issue. The feature included three pages of stills from the film plus production shots of the studio and set. The public loved the movie, which grossed $4,000,000.

The rabid isolationists, however, were already hostile to Hollywood because of its shift toward interventionism (Chapter 2). Now they were incensed at what they saw at this movie's glorification of war. To them the film industry had gone too far in support of the administration's foreign policy. Montana Senator Burton Wheeler, Chairman of the Interstate Commerce Committee, saw an opportunity. Alleging that the movie industry operated as a monopoly in restraint of trade, dictating what the American public could and could not see, Wheeler empaneled a select subcommittee, with Senator D. Worth Clark of Idaho as chairman, to investigate the industry. The ostensible object, clearly within the jurisdiction of his committee, was to inquire into monopolistic practices. The true object, however, was to persuade the public that the administration was using Hollywood as a propaganda tool to lead America toward war. Wheeler stacked the committee with isolationists and ruled that only committee members could question witnesses. But he did appoint one token interventionist, Democrat Ernest McFarland of Arizona. Since McFarland was a freshman senator, Wheeler assumed that he would be restrained and innocuous. He could not have been more wrong. McFarland proved to be the undoing of the isolationists.

When the hearings opened on September 9, the first witness was Gerald Nye, who read a 41-page statement into the record. Nye was especially vicious in his attack on the Jewish leadership of the film industry, and he accused them of producing films that created an indelible impression on innocent Americans. When Nye finished, McFarland began questioning him on the films he found objectionable.

Probing relentlessly, McFarland got Nye to admit that he had not even seen many of the films he criticized and he was relying on the reports of others. Of the films Nye had seen, he could remember few if any of the specific features that had made the purported indelible impression. McFarland's intense questioning left Nye's credibility in shambles. Meanwhile, Wendell Willkie, legal counsel for the film industry, was producing reams of press releases as he prepared industry leaders for their testimony. Following his advice, they went on the attack. Nye had accused Warner Brothers of producing more propaganda films than any other studio. Harry Warner responded that Nazism was evil and America should be fighting with England on the side of freedom. By the time the sessions were recessed on September 26, Wheeler's forces had been thoroughly routed. The meetings were not reconvened.

Meanwhile, another element had entered the Great Debate, the state of preparedness of the U.S. Armed Forces. When the Selective Service Act was passed in 1940, it had provided for a term of service of twelve months for draftees and National Guardsmen. That year was almost up, and discharges would begin in September. In his biennial report to Congress in July, Chief of Staff General George C. Marshall pointed out that training was not yet complete and the Army was far from ready to carry out its task of national defense. Discharging these almost but not completely trained soldiers would require the process to start all over again and significantly impair the preparedness effort. At the same time he spoke of the difficulties in meeting all our commitments when Guardsmen and draftees still by law could not be sent to serve outside the Western Hemisphere. General Marshall proposed that the service restriction be removed and draftees and Guardsmen be retained on active duty for the duration of the National Emergency.

American desire to avoid foreign military involvement was still strong, and the call for lifting the service restriction never had a chance of approval. But even the isolationists, calling as they did for strengthening America's own home defenses, recognized the validity of Marshall's manpower concerns. Extending the term of service for the duration of the Emergency was too much, and Senator Taft proposed an extension of two to four months. That was too short, and the administration's supporters countered with a proposal for an eighteen-month extension and no change in the restrictions on deployment. The compromise was accepted and the bill easily passed the Senate.

The House was a different matter. Draft extension ran into serious opposition in the lower chamber. In truth, the opposition was less rigid than it appeared. Everyone assumed that the bill would pass and the president would get what he wanted. Consequently a number of congressmen decided it would be safe to vote against the bill in order to curry favor with voters back home. There had been a good deal of grumbling about the inequality of the draft and the inconvenience to families whose sons were away at camp. A number of representatives therefore saw a nay vote as a safe way to tell their constituents they were mindful of their interests without actually threatening to derail the process. The problem was that too many representatives thought that way. When the final vote was tallied, the draft extension passed by a single vote, 203-202. Sixty-five Democrats joined with 133 Republicans in voting nay. More predictably, only twenty-one Republicans joined their 185 Democratic colleagues in voting aye. The closeness of the vote actually unnerved Congress. The House, especially, realized now that it was no longer possible to play political games with military preparedness. They would have to take their role seriously and provide the support the Army needed to carry out its role. The close vote thus had the somewhat ironic effect of strengthening the president's hand in dealing with Congress.

While Congress was scaring itself over the draft extension bill, President Roosevelt was not even in Washington. On August 3 the president embarked from New London, Conn., on the presidential yacht U.S.S. *Potomac* for what was reported to be a fishing trip along the New England coast. But once he was out of sight of land, the president transferred to the cruiser U.S.S. *Augusta*, flagship of the Atlantic Fleet. The *Augusta* sailed directly to Placentia Bay off the village of Argentia, Newfoundland, where the United States had just begun construction of a naval base as a part of the bases-for-destroyers deal. While he was there Roosevelt inspected the base construction and actually did a little bit of fishing as he was said to be doing. On

August 9, another ship arrived, the new battleship H.M.S. *Prince of Wales*, the same ship that with *Hood* had fought *Bismarck* and *Prinz Eugen* in the Denmark Strait three months earlier. On board *Prince of Wales* was Prime Minister Winston Churchill, come to meet his American counterpart for the first time. Both leaders were accompanied by senior officers of the armed forces and the foreign service.

For four days the American and British leaders conferred almost continuously about the state of the war, the military condition of each country, and the broad outlines of strategy should the United States become actively engaged as a belligerent. Because of uncertainties about America's status, very little of a formal nature could be decided. But the parties did produce a memorable communiqué, essentially just a press release, which has gone down in history as the Atlantic Charter. Framing the discussions as a conference about the details of Lend-Lease, the communiqué included a statement of eight principles which the president and the prime minister had agreed upon. Foremost among these were a disavowal of any desire for territorial aggrandizement and an affirmation of the right of people to choose the form of government under which they live. There was also a commitment to freedom of the seas, to free commerce and economic cooperation, and to the abandonment of force as a means of settling international disputes.

With so many major figures gone from Washington, rumors began to fly. The president was accompanied by Chief of Staff Marshall, Chief of the Air Forces General H. H. Arnold, Chief of Naval Operations Admiral Harold Stark, Under Secretary of State Sumner Welles, and a supporting cast of high-ranking officers. But no word of what actually happened was allowed to leak out until all were safely back in Washington. When the press was finally told and the text of the Atlantic Charter was released, the reaction was predictable. The isolationist press was particularly vitriolic, with the *Chicago Tribune* taking the lead in a scathing editorial. But popular reaction was generally favorable. The American people are fond of noble ideals, and the eight principles of the charter provided them in good measure. There was some carping that the document contained no reference to freedom of religion, but Roosevelt tried to cover over that omission in his report to Congress. The American people were especially pleased with assurances that the British were not seeking, by secret treaties, to expand the reach of their empire.

The following month another event further weakened the isolationist cause, shook the America First Committee, and almost led to that organization's demise. Back in April Charles Lindbergh had decided to lend his support to America First in a formal way. Lindbergh had long been known as a staunch opponent of American involvement in the war. At a speech on the 17th of that month he was introduced by General Wood as an official member of the Committee. Another speech followed in Madison Square Garden on the 23rd. Lindbergh attracted enough attention that supporters of the administration began aiming attacks at him.

Lindbergh was able to ignore most of his critics, but he could not ignore the president. At a press conference on April 25, Roosevelt was asked why a distinguished flyer like Lindbergh, a colonel in the Army Air Corps Reserve, was not called back to active duty when the Army needed trained pilots. Roosevelt launched into a lengthy history lesson, comparing Lindbergh to the Copperheads, the Northern politicians who, during the Civil War, had argued for a peaceful separation from the Confederacy. Finally, in response to a direct question, he affirmed that he was talking about Lindbergh as an appeaser. Lindbergh felt his honor as an officer had been called into question, and he promptly sent the president a letter resigning his commission. The letter was accepted without comment.

Over the next few months Lindbergh intensified his speaking schedule, attracting both prolonged applause from his isolationist supporters and vituperative attacks from his opponents. His fame and prestige ensured that many people would listen to what he had to say. His acknowledged expertise in aviation also meant people would respect his opinion when he described the power and effectiveness of the *Luftwaffe*. But his political naiveté and ability to say the wrong thing in a very public manner made him a natural target for interventionists. Lindbergh regularly made embarrassing remarks and then wondered what all the fuss was about when the storms of protest arose. His greatest blunder came in a speech at an America First rally in Des Moines, Iowa, on September 11. Lindbergh was beginning to feel as if he were fighting a losing battle in trying to keep the country out of war. He decided that he had to throw aside all caution and tell the exact truth as he saw it.

Just a week before the Des Moines rally, the subdued conflict at sea almost erupted into all-out war. On September 4 a German submarine, *U-652*, was patrolling off the coast of Iceland in search of convoys to attack. In the same area was the U.S.S. *Greer*, an old destroyer launched right at the end of World War I. The *Greer* was on a scheduled run, carrying U.S. mail to Iceland. Overhead a British patrol plane on the lookout for German submarines spotted the German lying just below the surface and directly in the path of the *Greer*. The pilot immediately radioed contact information to the destroyer, and Commander J. J. Mahoney, in command of the *Greer*, altered course to track the submarine. As he followed it, he relayed its position to the British so their planes could drop depth charges on it. After three hours of this harassment, the German turned on the *Greer* and fired several torpedoes, all of which missed. Mahoney responded by dropping a pattern of depth charges, which likewise had no effect. After a few more hours of cat and mouse, contact was broken off. The *Greer* proceeded to Iceland, and the *U-652* resumed its war patrol.

Word of the action spread quickly, with each side accusing the other of initiating hostilities. The president held off making a response until the very evening of the Des Moines rally. Consequently the president's fireside chat was piped into the auditorium for the audience to hear before the America First speakers. After describing the attack on the *Greer* and announcing the sinking of the U.S. merchant ship *Steel Seafarer* in the Red Sea, Roosevelt assured his listeners that "we are keeping our feet on the ground" and not rushing precipitously to war. But a strong response was still called for in order to protect the freedom of the seas, especially in the waters near the coast of the Americas. "If submarines or raiders attack in distant waters, they can attack equally well within sight of our own shores. Their very presence in any waters which America deems vital to its defense constitutes an attack." Warning that "when you see a rattlesnake poised to strike, you do not wait until he has struck before you crush him," the president announced a new policy. "From now on, if German or Italian vessels of war enter the waters, the protection of which is necessary for American defense, they do so at their own peril." Nevertheless, Roosevelt reassured Americans that he was not seeking war. "The sole responsibility rests upon Germany. There will be no shooting unless Germany continues to seek it."

Immediately after the president finished, Lindbergh and his hosts walked onto the stage. The audience was generally receptive to their message, though there were hecklers in the crowd. After the introductions, Lindbergh began what he expected would be the hardest-hitting speech of the isolationist campaign. Warming to his subject, he came to this critical passage:

> When this war started in Europe, it was clear that the American people were solidly opposed to entering it. Why shouldn't we be? We had the best defensive position in the world; we had a tradition of independence from Europe; and the one time we did take part in a European war left European problems unsolved, and debts to America unpaid.
>
> National polls showed that when England and France declared war on Germany, in 1939, less than 10 percent of our population favored a similar course for America. But there were various groups of people, here and abroad, whose interests and beliefs necessitated the involvement of the United States in the war. I shall point out some of these groups tonight, and outline their methods of procedure. In doing this, I must speak with the utmost frankness, for in order to counteract their efforts, we must know exactly who they are.
>
> The three most important groups who have been pressing this country toward war are the British, the Jewish and the Roosevelt administration.

The crowd was attentive as he began to discuss these groups one by one. When he came to the Jews, he spoke what he thought were words of sympathy and understanding:

The second major group I mentioned is the Jewish.

It is not difficult to understand why Jewish people desire the overthrow of Nazi Germany. The persecution they suffered in Germany would be sufficient to make bitter enemies of any race.

No person with a sense of the dignity of mankind can condone the persecution of the Jewish race in Germany. But no person of honesty and vision can look on their pro-war policy here today without seeing the dangers involved in such a policy both for us and for them. Instead of agitating for war, the Jewish groups in this country should be opposing it in every possible way for they will be among the first to feel its consequences.

Tolerance is a virtue that depends upon peace and strength. History shows that it cannot survive war and devastations. A few far-sighted Jewish people realize this and stand opposed to intervention. But the majority still do not.

Their greatest danger to this country lies in their large ownership and influence in our motion pictures, our press, our radio and our government.

I am not attacking either the Jewish or the British people. Both races, I admire. But I am saying that the leaders of both the British and the Jewish races, for reasons which are as understandable from their viewpoint as they are inadvisable from ours, for reasons which are not American, wish to involve us in the war.

We cannot blame them for looking out for what they believe to be their own interests, but we also must look out for ours. We cannot allow the natural passions and prejudices of other peoples to lead our country to destruction.

Throughout the speech the sympathetic audience drowned out the hecklers, and the next day Lindbergh took the train home to

New York. It was only upon his arrival there that he learned of the furious reaction his speech had provoked. The vituperation heaped on him was intense. Roosevelt, recognizing that the reaction against Lindbergh could only help his own policies, showed great restraint. Press secretary Steve Early said simply that Lindbergh's speech sounded like something coming out of Berlin. He let the Republicans tear Lindbergh apart, and they did so with a vengeance. Governor Dewey of New York offered one of the milder reproofs when he called the speech "an inexcusable abuse of the right of freedom of speech." Posters appeared in New York saying, "ADOLF LOVES LINDY."

Lindbergh's few supporters were those most closely aligned with him on the America First Committee. But even General Wood recognized the damage that had been done, and he called an emergency meeting of the Committee in Chicago to discuss the speech. Lindbergh had breakfast with Wood and explained that he was not anti-Semitic. He said he had intended merely to explain that he understood why Jews hated Hitler. He did not attend the luncheon meeting at which the speech was discussed, though he met with the committee later in the afternoon when it approved a statement denying that it was anti-Semitic. Although General Wood had a policy against prior censorship of members' speeches, he came to an understanding with Lindbergh that the Committee would be given a chance in the future to see advance copies of his texts.

The damage done by the speech, however, could not be undone. General Wood had already contemplated the possibility of disbanding America First. Congress was feeling increasing pressure to repeal the Neutrality Act; and Wood felt that if it did so, war would be inevitable and the Committee would no longer serve any useful purpose. Already prospects were discouraging. A number of prominent Committee supporters were now sending in their resignations. The character of America First was changing as the committee found it more and more difficult to recruit and retain liberals in its cause. The change was more pronounced in local chapters than in the national committee, which tried to keep to its simple message and mission.

America's mood was also changing. The majority, who had long favored increased aid to England, were expressing their views more openly. On October 2, Burton Wheeler was badly heckled at an America First rally in Los Angeles. On October 5 Madison Square Garden hosted a large preparedness rally with the title "Fun to be Free." Entertainers included Jack Benny, Carman Miranda, Ethel Merman, and Bill "Bojangles" Robinson. *Life* magazine, whose editor Henry Luce was himself a strong interventionist, kept pressing its internationalist message, sometimes with sharp but subtle cuts. In the October 27 issue *Life* opened its regular article on national defense with a prominent photograph of an infantryman of the 1st Division. This photograph was bound to annoy Colonel McCormick of the *Chicago Tribune*, who was a World War veteran of the 1st Division and inordinately proud of that association.

With the change in America's mood, President Roosevelt on October 9 asked Congress to repeal the "crippling provisions" of the neutrality act and allow American merchant ships to be armed. He also asked that American merchant ships be permitted to enter the ocean combat zones. He argued that the proposed changes would not make the United States any less neutral, but they would enable America to provide better assistance to the British in their fight against Nazi Germany. Speaking for the America First Committee, General Wood again raised the level of rhetoric, asserting that the president was "asking Congress to issue an engraved drowning license to American seamen." The Committee pulled out all stops in its last major campaign to alter America's foreign policy. Advertisements and a letter writing campaign to Congress asserted that the proposed repeal was a war measure. But despite the Committee's strongest efforts, Congress again gave Roosevelt what he wanted. The repeal measure was passed on November 13.

While the vote on repeal was not really in doubt, Roosevelt's hand had been strengthened by two incidents that occurred in October. On the 17th the U.S.S. *Kearny*, a new destroyer commissioned just thirteen months earlier, was called to the aid of a convoy that was being attacked by a German wolf pack south of Iceland. The *Kearny* and four other destroyers plunged into the action, and *U-568* promptly put a torpedo into her starboard side. The *Kearny* was able to limp back to Iceland, escorted by the *Greer*, but America had suffered her first casualties of the war. Eleven men were killed and twenty-two wounded in the attack. Because the *Kearny* had actively involved herself in the fight, American response was muted. But on October 31 an even more deadly attack brought the United States and Germany to the brink of war. The U.S.S. *Reuben James* was one of five destroyers escorting convoy HX 156 when it was attacked unexpectedly by *U-552*. A single torpedo struck the destroyer and ignited the forward magazine, blowing the bow completely off. The rear section remained afloat for five minutes. Only 46 of her 161-man crew were rescued. This time the reaction was more pronounced, with many calling for a declaration of war. Still Roosevelt held back from that step, asking only that the neutrality repeal be passed as quickly as possible.

The reaction to the sinking of the *Reuben James* was not all one-sided. America First blamed Roosevelt for sending American ships on convoy duty. Had he not put the Navy in this position, they said, the *Reuben James* would never have been involved in combat and would never have been sunk. By this time it was becoming clear to the isolationists that only a change of leadership would change America's direction. On December 1 America First announced that it would play an active role in the 1942 congressional campaigns, working to elect senators and representatives who were committed to keeping America out of war. The National Committee had always been predominantly Republican, and many America First supporters opposed Roosevelt in general, not just his foreign policy. Nevertheless, the Committee always made a studied effort to portray its efforts as non-partisan. In this announcement, the Committee made it clear that it would offer its support to any candidate, regardless of party, who would oppose an interventionist foreign policy.

Three days later an incident occurred that almost led to espionage charges being filed against leading isolationists. In July the president had asked the War and Navy Departments for a report on the services' needs that would allow them to "defeat our potential enemies."

The response was a confidential "Army and Navy Estimate of United States Overall Production Requirements," code named Rainbow Five. The planning assumptions used were that Hitler could not be defeated without American help, and the United States would become involved in the war by July 1, 1943. It envisioned an Army of 10,000,000 men, half of whom would be deployed abroad, and 80,000 planes. Some Air Corps officers grumbled that the planners were not giving them enough planes, and sometime in the fall a copy of Rainbow Five was leaked by an Air Corps officer (whose identity is still officially unknown) to isolationist Senator Burton Wheeler. Wheeler promptly shared the information with Chesly Manly, Washington political correspondent for McCormick's *Chicago Tribune*. On the morning of December 4, Chicago readers were treated to banner headlines:

F.D.R.'S WAR PLAN!
GOAL IS 10 MILLION ARMED MEN;
HALF TO FIGHT IN AEF

In Washington the *Herald-Tribune*, published by McCormick's cousin Cissy Patterson, was only a bit more modest:

F.D.'S SECRET WAR PLAN REVEALED

Both papers revealed full details of the military's plans for what they would need in the event of all-out war. Interestingly, Cissy's brother Joe Patterson, publisher of the *New York Daily News*, declined to print the report, although he did run an indirect story about the scoop the other papers had obtained.

Predictably there was a firestorm of reaction. Republican congressman George Tinkham of Massachusetts had the whole of Rainbow Five published in the *Congressional Record*. At the same time, several cabinet officers pressed Roosevelt to have McCormick and Patterson indicted under the Espionage Act of 1917. Oddly, the president seemed uninterested in pursuing the matter. He refused to discuss it at his December 5 press conference, and he chose not to press criminal charges against the papers. The F.B.I. did investigate the matter and soon discovered who was responsible, but the name was never revealed. It was widely assumed that Roosevelt felt the matter would blow over quickly (as it did). It was also widely assumed that the president was told who the culprit was and chose to deal with him privately. Just three days after the publication of the plans, the entire debate came to a sudden halt.

CHAPTER 7

July: Sports

JULY 17TH WAS a mild day in Cleveland. It rained early in the day, but by evening the weather had cleared and a gentle breeze was blowing in off Lake Erie. That evening there were 67,463 people in the city whose minds were not on the weather. Hours before game time they had started arriving at Cleveland Municipal Stadium for the second of a three-game series between the Indians and the New York Yankees. The previous afternoon the teams had played over in League Park, a much smaller stadium where the Indians played their home games when large crowds were not expected. The Yankees had dominated that game, winning 10-3. The loss was painful for the Indians. Coming into the series at 50 and 33, five games behind the league-leading Yankees, they had hoped to use this home stand to close the gap. Now they had fallen another game behind. But few people outside Cleveland were paying much attention to the standings. What mattered more was that Yankee center fielder Joe DiMaggio had gotten three hits in five trips to the plate. He also had drawn a walk, but the hits were what counted. The Streak, now reported in capital letters on the sports pages of the nation, was at 56 games.

Back on May 15, DiMaggio had gotten a first-inning hit at Yankee Stadium, driving in leadoff batter Phil Rizzuto. Unfortunately for the Yankees, that was their only run in a 13-1 loss to the White Sox. But for DiMaggio it was the start of a streak that still has baseball fans talking. DiMaggio got a hit in the next game and then the next and then the next. He kept on getting at least one hit in every game until on June 17 he went one for four against the White Sox, breaking the old Yankee team record of 29 straight games set in 1919 by Roger Peckinpaugh (now in 1941 the Cleveland manager). DiMaggio kept on hitting, extending his streak game after game. The longer it went on, the greater became the publicity and the pressure. The next target was 41 games. Back in 1922 George Sisler of the St. Louis Browns had hit safely in 41 consecutive games, a record for the modern era (20th Century). On June 29, a steamy hot day in Washington, DiMaggio tied Sisler's record in the first game of a double header and broke the record in the second game. Only one record remained.

Way back in 1897, Wee Willie Keeler had hit safely in 44 straight games, playing for the old Baltimore Orioles. Now DiMaggio had his sights set on Keeler's record. On July 1 he tied Keeler in the second game of a double header against Boston. Then on Wednesday, July 2, a scorching hot day in New York, DiMaggio came up against Dick Newsome of the Red Sox. In his first at bat he flied out to right center, where Stan Spence made a great catch. In his second at bat he grounded out to Jim Tabor at third. When he came up again in the fifth, he drove a 2-0 pitch over the wall in left. Ted Williams, playing left field for Boston, just turned around and watched. DiMaggio had the record all to himself, and now every game extended it. The season paused for the All-Star Game in Detroit's Briggs Stadium on July 7. Joe collected a hit there, too, but that didn't count in the streak. Ten days later the Yankees were in Cleveland.

The games on July 16 had run DiMaggio's streak to 56 games, a number that was all but unbelievable. For the night game on the 17th, the teams moved over to Municipal Stadium, with a seating capacity of

78,811. Al Smith was on the mound for the Indians, Lefty Gomez for the Yankees. When DiMaggio came to bat in the first inning, he took the first pitch for a ball and then pulled a curve hard to third. Back on June 1 Cleveland third baseman Ken Keltner had been burned on just such a hit. He had reached for it, but the ball had tipped the fingers of his glove as it shot down the line. This time Keltner, remembering the earlier hit, was playing almost in left field and hugging the line, determined that DiMaggio would not get one past him the same way again. The move paid off. Keltner was just able to get to the ball, plant himself in foul ground, and throw DiMaggio out by a whisker.

In the fourth inning DiMaggio came up for the second time and worked the count full, fouled off a change, and then took an inside curve for ball four. Two trips to the plate, no hit. In the top of the seventh DiMaggio's at-bat was a replay of the first inning. He drove an inside breaking ball down the line; Keltner backhanded it and threw him out. In the top of the eighth, with the bases loaded and one out, DiMaggio got on top of a fastball and bounced it to Lou Boudreau at short. Boudreau handled a bad hop and flipped to Ray Mack at second, who turned and fired to Oscar Grimes at first. Double play, inning over.

The Indians came back with two runs in the bottom of the ninth, raising the possibility that DiMaggio might get a fifth at bat in extra innings. But their rally fell short, and the game and the streak were over. Joe was both disappointed and relieved. The competitor in him wanted to keep hitting, but the human being welcomed the relief from the pressure. Phil Rizzuto later reported that as he and DiMaggio walked out of the clubhouse that night, Joe told him the Heinz 57 people had been following the streak. According to Rizzuto, DiMaggio said a hit in the 57th game would have meant a $10,000 deal with Heinz.

In the middle of DiMaggio's streak, the whole country paused for a moment to grieve over the loss of one of the greats. Early in the 1925 season, Yankees manager Miller Huggins was trying to maneuver his team out of seventh place in the American League. His first baseman Wally Pipp, although coming off the best year of his career, was hitting just .244. On June 2, Huggins decided to sit Pipp and start a promising youngster, Lou Gehrig, playing his first full season in the majors. Gehrig had played the day before, coming in as a pinch hitter in the eighth. But this was his first start, and he made the most of it, going 3 for 5 with a double. Huggins decided to stay with Gehrig at first, and at the end of the season Pipp was sold to the Cincinnati Reds for $7,500. Gehrig's play wasn't enough to get the Yankees out of the second division that year, but it stayed good enough to keep him in the lineup for 2,130 straight games. But in 1938 Gehrig's performance unaccountably began to slip. A lifetime .344 hitter to that point, he saw his season average plunge to .295. During spring training in 1939, everyone on the team noticed that something was wrong. Gehrig tried to start the season just as he had before, but his performance was weak. After only eight games, in which he hit just .143, Gehrig took himself out of the lineup, temporarily as he thought. A visit to the Mayo Clinic changed the outlook entirely. Gehrig announced to his teammates and the rest of the world that he was suffering from amyotrophic lateral sclerosis and would have to take time off from baseball. The temporary absence became permanent as he got weaker and weaker. His official retirement was announced in June of '39, and in October Mayor Fiorello La Guardia appointed him to a ten-year term as a parole commissioner. Gehrig kept up his work as long as he could; but in May of '41, the illness reached an acute stage, leaving him in great pain and forcing him to resign from his job. On the evening of June 2, he died at his home in New York. La Guardia ordered all the flags in the city lowered to half staff, and all major-league ballparks followed suit.

Six weeks later, after DiMaggio's streak ended, baseball attention shifted to Boston, where a cocky youngster and an aging veteran added more excitement to the season. Ted Williams had gained a certain amount of attention even during DiMaggio's streak because his batting average had been holding up above the magic plateau of .400. At the All-Star break the average stood at .405, and Williams traveled to Detroit to play left field for the American League on July 8. He was one for three when he came to bat in the bottom of the 9th, with runners on the corners and two out. The American League was trailing 5-4. On the mound was right hander Claude Passeau of the Cubs, who had struck Williams out in the 8th. Passeau had a tailing fastball that he liked to throw inside to left-handed hitters like Williams. His first pitch was low, the second was fouled off, and the third was high. With the count 2-1, the fourth pitch was the inside fastball that Williams was expecting. He swung; and the moment the ball left the bat, the whole park knew the game was over. The towering home run hit the facing on the right field roof, and Williams rounded the bases, clapping his hands all the way.

Ted returned to Boston and resumed his pursuit of a full-season .400 batting average. Before the end of the month, he figured prominently in yet another landmark game. Veteran Red Sox pitcher Lefty Grove was nearing the end of his career. He had amassed 299 victories over 17 seasons with the Athletics and the Red Sox, and he wanted that 300th win. But Grove was struggling. He was well past his prime in 1941 and was no longer the pitcher that sportswriter Bugs Baer once said was able to "throw a lamb chop past a wolf." He would compile a 7-7 record this year, with an ERA of 4.37, the second worst of his career. Ten years earlier, pitching for the Athletics, he had been 31-4 with an ERA of 2.06, both numbers the best in the league and the best of his career. Philadelphia fans remembered with delight the day he had struck out Babe Ruth, Lou Gehrig, and Bob Meusel on nine pitches. Now he was trying to reach the coveted 300 mark. On July 25 Grove started against the Cleveland Indians and did not pitch well at all, giving up six runs. But Ted Williams came through with a two-run homer in the eighth to put Boston ahead 8-6, and Grove held on for a 10-6 victory, his 300th. He started a few more games but never won another. His arm had given out, and he retired at the end of the season to await induction into the Hall of Fame.

Williams kept hitting well as the season wore on. He was not just hitting. He was hammering the ball. His 185 hits that year included thirty-three doubles, three triples, and thirty-seven home runs, with only twenty-seven strikeouts. Pitchers became so reluctant to pitch to him that he also accumulated 147 walks. But in September his batting average started slipping somewhat. He managed to keep it just over .400 going into the last series of the season, three games against the Athletics at Shibe Park in Philadelphia. But on Saturday, September 27, Williams went 1 for 4, with a double off Roger Wolff. At the end of the day the batting average stood at .39955. By baseball rules, that would have rounded off to .400. With the pennant race already decided, manager Joe Cronin asked Williams if he wanted to sit out the last two games. Williams refused. His refusal had elements of both principle and practicality. As a matter of principle, Williams felt that a record should not count if he did not play out the whole season. As a matter of practicality, he knew people would always consider a rounded-off .400 to be a tainted record. He had to get the average cleanly above .400 or let it lapse clearly below. To him there was no choice. He had to play in both games of Sunday's double header.

Ted came up to bat for the first time on Sunday leading off the top of the second inning. As he stepped up to the plate, umpire Bill McGowan called time and pulled out his pocket whisk to brush off home plate. Williams later recalled that as McGowan turned "his big rear end" toward center field, he said to no one in particular, "If a man's going to hit .400, he's got to be loose." As McGowan stepped behind the plate and adjusted his big mattress of a chest protector, Athletics catcher Frankie Hayes had his own word for Williams: "Mr. Mack [Philadelphia owner/manager Connie Mack] says we're going to pitch to you today, but we're not going to give you anything." Many of Ted's walks had come against the A's, who feared the damage done by his bat. Williams was thus assured that he would receive fair treatment but no gifts. Fair treatment was all he needed.

In his first at bat, he singled to right, raising his average to .40089. In his second at bat he homered to right, raising his average to .402. In his third at bat he singled again to right, raising his average to .4035. In his fourth at bat he singled again to right, raising his average to .404867. In the ninth he reached base on an error by second baseman Crash Davis, dropping his average to .40397. It was now virtually certain that he would finish the season cleanly above .400, and in the second game he kept on hitting. He singled to right in his first at bat (.405), doubled in his second at bat (.40659), and flied out to left in his final at bat of the season, giving him a season batting average of .4057, rounded off to .406. No one has hit .400 since then.

Fans expected New York and Boston to do well, but the surprise team of 1941 was the Brooklyn Dodgers. Brooklyn had not won a pennant since 1920, when the team was known as the Robins. For most of the intervening years they had languished in the second division, usually just ahead of the Boston Braves and the Philadelphia Phillies. In 1937 they finished sixth, trailing the Giants by 33½ games. In 1938 their record was better, finishing 18½ behind the Cubs; but they dropped into seventh place, ahead of only the hapless Phillies. In March of 1938 the Dodgers' principal owner, Stephen McKeever, who had also served as president and general manager, died at the age of 84. The team promptly hired Larry MacPhail from the Cincinnati Reds to take over as president.

MacPhail proceeded to restock his roster with talent from wherever he could find it. When Commissioner Kenesaw Mountain Landis, in one of his periodic attacks on the farm system, declared seventy-three of the Cardinals' minor-league players free agents, MacPhail took shortstop Pete Reiser from Newport in the class D Northeast Arkansas League. When the Boston Red Sox placed Pee Wee Reese of their AA Louisville Colonels farm team on the trading block, MacPhail gave up four players and $35,000 to gain his services. In 1939 Dixie Walker of Detroit tore a cartilage in a knee. The Tigers feared that his playing days were ending and placed him on waivers. MacPhail, needing hitters, promptly signed him. When in 1938 the Indians became concerned that injuries might curtail the career of pitcher Whitlow Wyatt, they sent him down to the AA Milwaukee Brewers of the American Association. After Wyatt was named MVP in the Association that year, Brooklyn purchased his contract. Sensing a need for new leadership on the field, at the end of the 1938 season MacPhail fired manager Burleigh Grimes and named hot-tempered shortstop Leo Durocher player-manager. The hard-drinking MacPhail and the fiery Durocher made an unlikely pair, but they turned the team around. In 1939 the Dodgers finished third behind the Reds and the Cards. In 1940 they passed the Cards and finished second, though still twelve games back of the Reds. In 1941 they were ready to contend for the pennant.

At the beginning of the season, contention was all that fans thought the Dodgers were capable of. Most sportswriters favored the Reds, behind the pitching of Paul Derringer and Bucky Walters, to win their third pennant in a row. The Dodgers were expected to finish second, the Cards third. But the Reds opened the season by losing three in a row to the Cards and one to the Pirates before winning seven of their next eight games (including a split with St. Louis). The Dodgers, too, opened the season by getting swept by their hated New York rivals, the Giants. But the Dodgers righted the ship quickly and won twenty-two of their next twenty-five games. By the middle of May it was clearly a two-team race. Brooklyn was 22-6 and St. Louis was 18-7. Of the other six teams, only the Giants had a winning record at 13-11-1. Over the next two weeks the Cardinals started winning more and the Dodgers hit a losing streak. By Memorial Day the Cards had moved into first place, and at the end of June the two teams were tied at 47-23. The whole season continued that way. Entering the last week of the season, Brooklyn was clinging to the thinnest of leads, 96-53-3 to the Cards' 94-53-2. Both teams started the week on the road, the Dodgers with one at Philadelphia and two in Boston before returning home to meet the Phillies twice. St. Louis had a tougher schedule, going to Pittsburgh for four games and Chicago for two. The Cardinals split both series while the Dodgers took one from the Phillies and swept the Braves, clinching the pennant. The final split with Philadelphia did not really matter. Over the course of the grueling season, the Dodgers and the Cardinals evenly split the twenty-two games they played against each other.

Over in the American League, the race stayed close for a while. At the end of May the Indians were leading the league behind the tremendous pitching of 22-year-old Bob Feller, on his way to a twenty-five-win season (his third in a row with more than twenty wins). Chicago was in second place, while the Yankees in third were just half a game ahead of Detroit. The Tigers were not given much of a chance in the race, even though they had won the pennant in 1940. Their star power hitter, Hank Greenberg, had been called up in the draft and inducted into the Army on May 7. Without his bat, the Tigers stayed right where they were and finished fourth, tied with the Indians, who faded despite Feller's best efforts. After the All Star break DiMaggio and the Yankees played so well they clinched the pennant on September 4, the earliest it had even been done. Boston and Ted Williams tried to make a race of it, finishing second, seven games ahead of the White Sox but seventeen games behind New York.

The stage was now set for a so-called Subway Series. It would be the sixth time two teams from New York had played each other in the Series, but on the other five occasions the National League had been represented by the Giants. This would be Brooklyn's first series appearance since 1920, and the team had never won. Dodger fans were eager for victory. The Series went five games, but it was the ninth inning of the fourth game that was burned into Brooklyn's memory. On October 1 the Yankees won the first game 3-2 at Yankee Stadium, but the Dodgers evened the series the next day with the same score. After a rain out on the 3rd, the Series resumed in Brooklyn, where the Yankees eked out a 2-1 win. The next day broke the Dodgers' hearts. After scoring two runs in the fourth and two runs in the fifth, the Dodgers took a 4-3 lead into the ninth inning. Hugh Casey had come on in relief in the fourth and had pitched superbly. In the top of the ninth he got Johnny Sturm and Red Rolfe to ground out. Then Tommy Henrich came up and took a ball and two called strikes. Casey and the Dodgers were one strike away from evening the Series at two games each. Henrich fouled off the next pitch and then took two balls to fill the count. The next pitch was a sharp curve ball that came in like a fast ball and suddenly broke down out of the strike zone. Henrich swung over it for strike three. But Mickey Owen, arguably the best catcher in the league, couldn't handle the pitch. The ball got away and Henrich raced to first base. As had happened in the past, under stress Hugh Casey lost his composure. What followed was the Dodger fan's worst nightmare. DiMaggio singled. Charlie Keller doubled, putting the Yankees ahead when both Henrich and DiMaggio scored. Bill Dickey walked. Joe Gordon doubled in two more runs. Phil Rizzuto walked. Finally pitcher Johnny Murphy grounded out to end the half inning. When Murphy took the mound in the bottom of the ninth with a 7-4 lead, the Dodgers had no heart left in them. They went quietly in order and the Yankees had a 3-1 Series lead. The final game was almost an afterthought. Whitlow Wyatt pitched a complete game for the Dodgers, giving up two runs in the second and one in the fifth. But Brooklyn could not give him any run support, scoring only once in the third. The Yankees took the Series four games to one. As the saying goes, they're still talking about it.

While baseball was enjoying arguably its greatest season ever, world events were beginning to have an effect. Driving home to New York after the 1940 World Series, Detroit first baseman Hank Greenberg and his brother Joe decided they should stop in some out-of-the-way town and register for the draft. That way they could avoid the reporters who constantly followed Hank. They stopped in Geneva, New York, to complete the process. Joe listed his address as the family home in New York, but Hank, for some unknown reason, listed his address as the Leland Hotel in Detroit, where he lived during the season. The brothers then continued home and thought little more about the matter.

After the first of the year, Greenberg took some time for a vacation in Hawaii. Upon his return to New York, he was met by a crowd of reporters wanting to know what he was going to do about the draft. He learned there were very few draft-eligible men living in the vicinity of the Leland Hotel, and his draft number had come up much earlier than expected. Several major league players were seeking deferments so they could play the 1942 season; and rumors began to circulate that Greenberg, too, had asked for one. When questioned, the chairman of Greenberg's draft board confirmed that he had not asked for one, but the press stayed on Hank's back and kept hounding him with questions about his status. The attention derived, of course, from Greenberg's prominence as a four-time All Star and also from the fact that he was known to be the highest paid player in baseball, with a $55,000 contract for 1941. Hank went to Detroit for his draft physical and failed it, the doctors deciding that his flat feet made him exempt. The press immediately jumped on the story, and there were hints of favoritism or, given Hank's salary, even outright bribery. Greenberg decided that the only thing he could do to clear his reputation was to ask for another examination, and this time he passed. He was inducted on May 7, only the second big league player drafted (after pitcher Hugh Mulcahy of the Phillies), giving up his baseball salary for the $21 a month of an Army private.

Greenberg was assigned to an infantry anti-tank company and rose to sergeant. In the fall, the draft law was amended to exempt men over 28, and Greenberg, 30, applied for and received an early release from active duty. His release came on December 5. After the attack on Pearl Harbor two days later, Hank realized he had no chance of remaining a civilian. He also knew that when he was recalled to duty, he would be reassigned to his old outfit. So he took advantage of the opportunity to enlist voluntarily, joining the Army Air Forces to avoid infantry service. He thus became the first but by no means the last major leaguer to enlist voluntarily for the war.

Baseball was America's National Pastime in 1941, and no other sport had nearly the same number of fans. Its place in the minds of the American people is well illustrated by the headlines in the Cleveland *Plain Dealer* on November 25. On that day the Germans announced they had broken through on the main road to Moscow. On that day the American consulate advised all Americans in Japan to leave for their own safety. But the top headline in Cleveland that day was BOUDREAU SIGNS TO MANAGE INDIANS. Cleveland had signed shortstop Lou Boudreau as player-manager to replace Roger Peckinpaugh. At 24 Boudreau was the youngest manager in major-league history, and his signing was by far the most important event in Cleveland on November 25.

For most Americans living south or west of St. Louis, however, there was little opportunity to see a major league game. For them major league baseball lived only on radio and in the newspapers. Major league teams could be found in Boston (Braves and Red Sox), New York (Yankees, Giants, and Dodgers, though no true Brooklyn fan would acknowledge that the borough had been a part of the

City of New York since 1898), Philadelphia (Athletics and Phillies), Washington (Senators: "Washington: First in war, first in peace, and last in the American League"), Pittsburgh (Pirates), Cincinnati (Reds), Cleveland (Indians), Detroit (Tigers), Chicago (White Sox and Cubs), and St. Louis (Browns and Cardinals). The South was too poor to support a franchise, the West too thinly populated. The Pacific Coast was too far away unless a team's schedule was worked out with great care. And for most of the summer of 1941, that kind of care was being given to an extraordinary proposal.

For years the hapless St. Louis Browns had been the doormats of the American League. Playing in the same city as the powerful and popular Cardinals, the Browns lost money as freely as they lost games; and team president Donald Barnes knew he had to do something to save the franchise. All that summer he negotiated the details for a daring and visionary plan to move the Brownies to Los Angeles. He got Sam Breadon, owner of the Cards, to agree to pay him $350,000 to leave town. He persuaded Phil Wrigley of the Cubs to sell him Wrigley Field in Los Angeles, home of the Cubs' PCL farm team. He worked out travel details with American League president Will Harridge, who got the other owners to agree. Everything was in place for rubber-stamp approval by the league at the winter meetings in Chicago. The meetings opened on December 8, the day after the attack on Pearl Harbor; and all the plans had to be scrapped. Likewise scrapped were Wrigley's plans to install lights at Chicago's Wrigley Field so the Cubs could play night games in 1942. The electrical equipment, ready for installation, was instead donated to the war effort; and the Cubs continued to play their home games in the afternoon.

For those Americans who could not watch a major-league game, and even for many who could, there were three principal vehicles for savoring baseball. In the Far West the Pacific Coast League, while technically a minor league, played baseball of a quality only slightly below that of the majors. For African Americans, segregated baseball provided the Negro National League on the East Coast and the Negro American League in the Midwest. These teams provided an exciting brand of baseball played by athletes who, but for the color of their skin, could have played and starred in the major leagues. Finally, throughout America were scattered the minor league teams, stocked with promising young players who hoped to make it to the majors.

For most of the country, the only live professional baseball people got to see was minor-league ball. But there was plenty of it, and much of the play was of a very high quality. Forty-one leagues with over 280 teams competed in cities large and small. Attendance in 1941 was down to about 16,000,000 from a high of almost 20,000,000 the previous year. The drop was attributed to the increasing pressure of defense production, which limited people's leisure time. At the top of the minors were the three AA leagues, each with eight teams. The teams of the American Association in the Midwest and the International League in the Northeast had, by 1941, all developed relationships with major league clubs. Although baseball Commissioner Kennesaw Mountain Landis had vigorously opposed the development of the farm system, by this year he had bowed to the inevitable and permitted player-development agreements that eased the path of many players into the major leagues.

In some ways the minor leagues were more advanced than the majors. Realizing that most of their fans were working people whose free time was at night, the minors starting playing night baseball as early as 1930, five years before the first major-league night game. The teams discovered, as the majors would do later, that attendance, and therefore revenue, was better at night. The minor leagues also pioneered the first playoff system, known as the Shaughnessy Plan. In the '20s and '30s it was common for fan interest to wane late in the season when it became clear that one team had a strong enough record to cruise to the league championship. To sustain fan interest throughout the season, Frank Shaughnessy of the International League introduced a playoff system in 1933. The team with the best record in the league would play a best-of-five or best-of-seven series against the team with the fourth best record. Likewise, the team with the second best record would play the team with the third best record. The winners of these two series would then meet in a best-of-seven championship series. This playoff system meant that at the end of the season,

The M-3 medium tank was the most modern armor the Army possessed.

The P-40 Warhawk was the Army's standard fighter.

The U.S.S. *Enterprise*, shown here in June 1941, was commissioned in 1938.

The U.S.S. *North Carolina* was the Navy's newest battleship, May 1941.

Planting time in Connecticut. America was still largely agricultural.

Housing for migratory farm workers in Florida.

A quiet afternoon in Cascade, Idaho.

A tenement in Brockton, Massachusetts.

A homestead with a dirt floor in Pie Town, New Mexico.

A quiet afternoon in Washington, D.C.

The 1941 Chevy Club Coupe was a classy way to get around.

Going to town on Saturday afternoon in Greene County, Georgia.

Most long-distance travel was by train.

The Lockheed Super Electra was the main competitor of the DC-3.

Defense work provided a tremendous boost to American industry.

Defense work also provided new employment opportunities for thousands of women.

half of the teams in the league would still have a shot at the championship. The Shaughnessy Plan spread rapidly through the minor leagues. During the Depression the sustained fan interest and the extra revenue from the post-season games was often the difference between profit and loss for the teams. For a time the American Association and the International League also held a Junior World Series between their respective champions. In 1941 the Columbus Redbirds of the American Association beat the Montreal Royals of the International League four games to two in the Series.

On the West Coast, the AA Pacific Coast League was almost like a third major league. The PCL was able to attract and retain high-quality talent in large part because of the balmy coastal weather. In contrast to the other minor leagues, and even to the major leagues, the PCL was able to play long seasons, well into November, and the extra pay that the players received for those long seasons was a strong incentive to stay in the PCL until they could command good salaries from the majors. In the 1930s the PCL season had sometimes been as long as 225 games, but in 1941 the schedule had dropped back to around 175 games, about twenty more than a major-league schedule. The PCL championship was decided by the winning percentage during the regular season. There was a playoff, but it was something of an afterthought. The championship trophy went to the team with the best overall season average. In 1941 it belonged to the Seattle Rainiers and their 104-70 record.

At the A level, the Texas League and the Southern Association were designated A1, placing them midway between the Class A Eastern league and the three AA leagues. Nonetheless the quality of play was still high, and Class A sent some excellent players to the majors. One of the most notable was Tommy Henrich, who reached first on Mickey Owens' passed ball in the World Series.

The four Class B leagues and eleven Class C leagues also produced some fine baseball and served a useful function in developing talent for the majors. Nearly all major-league players had spent several years learning their trade in the minors. The Middle Atlantic League (Class C) was notable for the number of players promoted to the big leagues.

The nineteen Class D leagues were highly variable in their financial stability and quality of play. Some, like the Northeast Arkansas League, hung together with just four teams. Others, like the Kitty League (covering Kentucky, Illinois, and Tennessee) fielded as many as nine. Many leagues were barely hanging on as the military draft sapped their manpower. Yet the Class D clubs constituted almost half of all professional baseball teams in the country, and they brought the sport to smaller cities from Cheyenne, Wyoming, to Valdosta, Georgia.

Like most of the rest of America in 1941, the National Pastime was still the segregated National Pastime. White baseball owners were perfectly willing to accept the cost of admission from black fans, although some parks, like Griffith Stadium in Washington, had special segregated seating sections. But the white owners were in no way willing to allow black players on their teams. Some managers, most vocally the always vocal Leo Durocher, felt the best black players could make a valuable contribution to white baseball. But the owners were unified in their opposition. Many white players, too, opposed integration of the major leagues. For some it was nothing more than the simple realization that the addition of black talent would mean that some white players would lose their jobs. In this they were backed by Commissioner Kennesaw Mountain Landis. Although Landis publicly denied that there was any bar to hiring black players in the major leagues, behind the scenes he worked quietly and steadily to ensure that it did not happen.

With the color bar in place, the black community was left to its own devices to provide baseball opportunities for its young men. Ever since the 1880s there had been black professional baseball teams, and in 1920 the National Association of Colored Professional Base Ball Clubs was organized under the leadership of Rube Foster, Chicago entrepreneur, sometime pitcher, and manager of the Chicago American Giants. The Association, generally known as the Negro National League, survived for twelve years. But it became increasingly shaky after Foster's death in 1930 and could not survive the onset of the Depression, ceasing operations in 1932. The following year Gus Greenlee of Pittsburgh put together the second Negro National League, which was joined by a Negro American League in 1937. Although the Negro leagues suffered from a lack of central leadership, the six teams in each circuit enjoyed a certain measure of financial and geographic stability during this period. Their greatest problem was the independence of the owners, who all placed their individual financial interests ahead of the game as a whole. Their attitude encouraged contract jumping, a practice whereby top players would move freely from team to team, regardless of contractual obligations, whenever an owner made them a better offer. Contract jumping extended across the border into Mexico, where players could make good money and be free from the racial discrimination they experienced in the States.

Although the two Negro leagues did not play a World Series until 1942, they did meet in an annual East-West All Star game, an enormously popular event that drew fans of both races and that often meant the difference between profit and loss for the weaker teams. With the owners concentrating on profits and the players regularly jumping contracts, black fans placed less emphasis on team loyalty than fans of the white leagues. Individual players were the great attraction, and an appearance by Satchel Paige, for example, was sure to draw a large crowd. On July 27 over 50,000 fans crowded into Comiskey Park in Chicago to watch the East team defeat the West 8-3. Paige, representing the Kansas City Monarchs, pitched two innings and gave up one hit. In the off season both black and white players would organize into barnstorming teams that traveled the country, often playing interracial games that would never have been allowed during the regular season. It was generally acknowledged by both players and fans that the Negro leagues as a whole performed at about the level of the AA white leagues, and the best black players could make it in the majors. Certainly Satchel Paige, Dan Bankhead, Monte Irvin, and Roy Campanella, all of whom played in the 1941 All Star Game, showed that potential.

For most people, football in 1941 meant college football. The National Football League, whose ten teams played an eleven-game season, was limited in geographic extent and fan support. The Western Division had the Bears and Cardinals in Chicago, the Packers in

Green Bay, the Lions in Detroit, and the Rams in Cleveland, all still familiar names if not all in the same cities. In the east New York had the Giants; and Brooklyn, still insisting on its separate identity, had the Dodgers. The Washington Redskins, Philadelphia Eagles, and Pittsburgh Steelers completed the Eastern Division. A rival five-team American Football League was struggling to complete its second season. There would not be a third. Professional football was certainly not as attractive to athletes as baseball or even nonathletic careers. Even Slingin' Sammy Baugh, the star quarterback of the Washington Redskins, had first tried to make it in baseball, playing the 1938 season at shortstop with the AA Rochester Red Wings. Of the six Heisman Trophy winners through 1941, only 1938 winner Davey O'Brien went straight into the N.F.L.; and even he quit after two seasons with the hapless Eagles to join the F.B.I.

The N.F.L., however, was slowly getting stronger. It had already started limited television broadcasts in the New York area in 1939. In March of 1941 it hired its first commissioner, Elmer Layden, and set up its headquarters in Chicago. Attendance in 1941 set a record with 1,108,615 paid admissions for the 55-regular season games and 55,870 more for the two post-season games. (These numbers, of course, were nothing like the 9,689,603 for Major League Baseball.) For fans in the league's limited geographic area, there was also some excitement on the field. The Bears and the Packers finished the regular season tied at 10-0-1, leading to the first divisional playoff game in N.F.L. history. Chicago won the playoff 33-14 (although end Don Hutson of the Packers won the M.V.P. award for the season) and then won the championship game 37-9 over the Giants. The latter game, played just two weeks after Pearl Harbor, drew only 13,341 fans.

At the college level, 1941 was a year of changes. The flexible T formation, which had helped Stanford to a perfect season in 1940 and a victory over Nebraska in the 1941 Rose Bowl, now spread widely across the college ranks. Already popular in the N.F.L. for several seasons, it supplanted the formerly widespread single wing set. A rule change in 1941 also introduced the possibility of more flexibility and coaching control. This season, for the first time, player substitutions were allowed whenever the clock was stopped. Now coaches could send in plays from the sidelines with greater frequency.

There were also important coaching changes in 1941. This was the final year for Illinois coach Bob Zuppke, who retired at the end of the season after twenty-nine years on the job. Zuppke is credited with designing the modern, streamlined football, which changed the nature of the forward pass. He also claimed credit for introducing the huddle, the onside kick, the flea-flicker, and the screen pass (although Pop Warner also claimed credit for this last). Unfortunately, Zuppke's last season turned out to be something of a disaster. The Illini went 2-6, beating only Miami (Ohio) 45-0 and Drake 40-0. They scored only 27 total points in all the rest of their games.

The year 1941 was also the first year in new jobs for two of the most famous coaches in college history. In 1940, after two seasons in which Army had won only four games, West Point Superintendent Brigadier General Robert Eichelberger persuaded Dartmouth coach and Army alumnus Red Blaik to return to his alma mater and turn things around. Blaik did so, beginning with the 1941 season, although most of his distinguished career is beyond the scope of this book. This was also the year that Frank Leahy went to Notre Dame from Boston College to revive the Fighting Irish program. He was so successful in his first season that he was named Coach of the Year for 1941 by the American Football Coaches Association.

The military draft had an unexpected impact on college football teams in '41. Before the season, analysts had ranked Alabama fifth in the nation and Georgia seventh, giving every prospect of a high-powered contest for the championship of the Southeastern Conference. But just before the start of the season, the entire right side of Georgia's line was drafted; and the Bulldogs dropped to eighteenth in the rankings, just ahead of Navy. Head Coach Wally Butts did some quick work with the remaining players and managed to finish 3-1-1 in the conference and 8-1-1 overall, ranking fourth in the SEC and earning a trip to the Orange Bowl. There Georgia tailback Frankie Sinkwich played with a special chin strap that protected the jaw he had broken early in the season. Despite his wired jaw, Sinkwich passed for three touchdowns and rushed for another as Georgia beat T.C.U. 40-26.

The draft was also responsible for one amusing incident in professional football. When Dan Topping, principal owner of the N.F.L.'s Brooklyn Dodgers, was called up for his draft physical in January, he announced to the press that he would not seek an exemption based on his need to support his family. The press got the joke. Topping's wife was the figure skating star Sonja Henie, whose touring show grossed over $1,000,000 a year.

Although professional baseball and college football were by far the most popular spectator sports in 1941, remarkable contests in other sports made the year memorable. In two striking cases, the whole nation followed events in sports that generally had more limited appeal.

Thoroughbred racing usually attracted little attention from the general public, but in 1941 a three-year-old named Whirlaway drew wide public notice as much for his quirks as for his speed. In 1940 Whirlaway had been a promising two-year-old, winning seven out of sixteen starts and earning over $77,000. But he ran in a highly idiosyncratic fashion. Jockeys had a hard time keeping him focused. He had a pronounced tendency to swing extremely wide on turns and then run like mad on the straightaways to make up for the lost time. If he swung too wide or the race was too short, there was not enough track left to catch up. Whirlaway also had an unusual personality in the stable. He was highly sensitive to flies, and they constantly distracted him. Finally his owner, Warren Wright, screened in Whirlaway's stall and even had a screened box built in the doorway so the horse could stick his head out of the stall and look around without being bothered by pesky insects. It was something like his own private screened porch.

Whirlaway's behavior on the track and off endeared him to the crowds, and his appearance added to the effect. Trainer Ben Jones left his tail and mane uncropped and unbraided, believing that the flicking of the tail might help to distract some of the other horses. But the colt's eccentric way of running led to problems as the 1941 season started. Other horses of his year had matured and were running well. Especially dangerous was Our Boots, who had been two-year-old Horse of the Year in 1940. So when Whirlaway finished a dismal fourth at Hialeah in February, the odds makers began to lower their expectations. Wright and Jones had always had their sights set on the Kentucky Derby. Since Wright was the owner of Calumet Farm near Lexington, Kentucky, the Derby was practically a home-town race for him; and a great deal of pride was involved. Jones spent the spring putting the horse though an intensive training program, hoping to get him into disciplined shape for the Derby. But Whirlaway continued his erratic ways and lost to Our Boots in the Blue Grass Stakes on April 24. The Derby seemed a lost cause.

Jones, however, had seen a few changes he could make. Realizing that Whirlaway was exceptionally strong and willful, he replaced jockey Wendell Eads, who simply did not have the physical strength to control his mount. Warren Wright called his old friend John Hay Whitney and arranged to borrow Eddie Arcaro, one of the strongest and most experienced jockeys in America, who was under contract to Whitney. That problem solved, Jones turned to the problem of riding wide on turns. Many horses wore masks with partial blinders that allowed them to see straight ahead without being distracted by happenings to either side. Jones created a new mask with just one partial blinder, on the right eye, so Whirlaway could look left and concentrate on staying close to the rail without being tempted to go explore the outside country to his right. Finally, Jones gave special instructions to his jockey. Knowing the horse was contrary and would try to do what you told him not to do, Jones told Arcaro to allow Whirlaway to hang back at the start of the race, survey the field, and then move through the field as close to the rail as possible.

The morning of the Derby, Ben Jones took Whirlaway for a private walk around the track. He talked to the colt, describing to him how he wanted him to run each part of the race. Whirlaway was not the only one who was regarded as eccentric, but the horse seemed to understand.

At post time the horses moved into the starting gate, and veteran announcer Clem McCarthy prepared to call the race over NBC. "And they're off!" Arcaro followed instructions exactly, keeping back at an easy pace. Dispose held the early lead and stayed in front into the far turn. Then, as he began to tire, Our Boots made his move and seemed ready to take the race, with Staretor just outside and behind him. Whirlaway was fourteen lengths back, seemingly out of the race. But Arcaro spotted the gap between Our Boots and Staretor and pushed his colt toward it. Whirlaway responded, shot through the gap, shot past the fading Porter's Cap and Blue Pair, shot past Dispose, and kept on going. Whirlaway set four track records that day, winning by eight lengths, setting a total time of 2:01.4, and running the last quarter mile in 23.6 seconds. His fourth record was perhaps the most remarkable. He covered the last eighth of a mile in eleven seconds, a race record that still stands. Altogether, from the far turn to the finish line, Whirlaway gained twenty-two lengths on the field. Staretor held on to place, but both Dispose and Our Boots faded badly, finishing sixth and eighth.

After the Derby came the Preakness, and the excitement of Whirlaway's performance increased the attention being paid to the middle race of the Triple Crown. It also intensified the pressure on Ben Jones. In 1941 the Preakness was run only one week after the Derby, and the horse had to travel to Baltimore and be rested and ready in that time. Since 1919, when Sir Barton became the first Triple Crown winner, twenty-one horses had won the Kentucky Derby. Only five had gone on to win the Preakness. Even worse, the Preakness is the shortest of the Triple Crown races at $1^3/_{16}$ miles (9½ furlongs), a sixteenth of a mile shorter than the Derby. A shorter race was less suited to Whirlaway's late-charging style.

Once again Ben Jones told Arcaro to start slowly, but this time Whirlaway took the instructions too literally. He came out of the gate last and seemed not to realize that a race was being run. At $5/_8$ of a mile the horse was twenty lengths behind the leader, King Cole. Arcaro got his attention, and the colt took off. In the space of just a quarter of a mile he moved from seventh place to first and won by five lengths, a performance even more remarkable than the twenty-two lengths he made up at Churchill Downs. Whirlaway was perhaps not the greatest racehorse in history, but he certainly could make a fair claim to being the most exciting.

There remained only the Belmont, the longest of the Triple Crown races and therefore the best suited to Whirlaway's style. Here it was Arcaro's racing instincts that won the day. Most other owners had decided that Whirlaway was too much to handle, and the Belmont field on June 7 consisted of just four horses: Whirlaway, Robert Morris, Yankee Chance, and Itabo. Knowing their horses had little chance against Whirlaway, the other three trainers hatched a plot to keep him out of the race. Out of the gate they would set a very slow pace, hoping to lull him into too relaxed a feeling so that, with a little luck, one of them would have enough strength left at the end to make a sprint for the finish. But almost as soon as they broke from the gate, Arcaro sensed what they were doing. Seizing the opportunity, he reversed strategy and took the lead at ½ mile, maintaining a steady pace for the remaining mile and finishing a comfortable 2½ lengths ahead of Robert Morris.

Boxing in 1941 had a somewhat wider appeal than thoroughbred racing, although it certainly was not in the same league as baseball or even college football. But in June a seemingly invincible champion, a challenger with a quick mouth and quicker fists, and a well-developed promotional campaign combined to capture the country's attention. Joe Louis, the Brown Bomber, was the heavyweight champion of the world and was seemingly unstoppable. His only professional loss had been to the German fighter Max Schmeling in 1936 when Louis was a contender on his way up. Louis had not taken the match seriously and had trained too lightly, while Schmeling trained intensely and studied films of Louis's fights to detect any weakness. Taking advantage of Louis's tendency to drop his left hand after jabbing, Schmeling scored a twelfth-round knockout that thrilled the Nazi leaders back in Germany, who took it as evidence of German racial superiority. For Louis it was a sign that his great physical gifts were not enough to win consistently. To reach the championship he would have to be much more serious, to work and train harder for every bout.

The training paid off, and in 1937 Louis won the World Championship with an eighth-round knockout of James J. Braddock. But Louis would not really think of himself as the champion until he had avenged his loss to Schmeling. The opportunity came in June of 1938, and Joe Louis was ready. The rematch with Schmeling lasted all of two minutes and four seconds. Schmeling threw only two punches and was knocked down three times before the referee stopped the fight. After a six-month breathing spell, Louis embarked on a rapid series of title defenses, fighting four times in 1939 and four more times in 1940. Then in January of '41, little more than a month after his latest title defense, Louis began fighting every month, causing the press to refer to his opponents as the Bum of the Month Club. He knocked out Red Burman and Gus Dorazio, then scored T.K.O.s over Abe Simon and Tony Musto. His victory over Buddy Baer in May was technically gained on a disqualification. Baer claimed he had been knocked down after the bell at the end of the seventh round, and he refused to answer the bell in the eighth. In fact, Baer had taken such a beating that he was in no shape to come out.

Louis's June fight against Billy Conn promised to be just one more easy victory over a Bum of the Month. Conn was a light-heavyweight who tipped the scale at 167 pounds. He was fighting over his head for the heavyweight championship against the 202-pound Louis. Only twice before had a light-heavyweight successfully challenged for the heavyweight crown, most recently in 1906. Conn was cocky, ambitious, and talented. He knew that the heavyweight division was the only one that carried real prestige, and also the only one that offered big paychecks. Although he happily projected the image of a free spender, Conn actually devoted most of his earnings to the care of his mother, who was dying of cancer. His boxing allowed him to buy her a house and provide the best medical care available. Billy came from a working-class Irish background. Boxing, like other sports, was a way upward for physically gifted young men from poor families.

Preparation for the Louis-Conn fight was a sportswriter's delight, with quotable remarks coming from the challenger almost daily. On the evening of June 18 more than 54,000 people crowded into the Polo

Grounds in New York to watch the fight. The Yankees were in town for a series with the White Sox, and Joe McCarthy, Joe DiMaggio, and Lefty Gomez were all at ringside for the fight. Bob Feller caught the train from Philadelphia, where the Indians had played the Athletics that afternoon. They kept company with such other notables as Al Jolson, Bob Hope, and even J. Edgar Hoover. The fight they saw was one of the most memorable ever, rated the Fight of the Year by *The Ring Magazine*.

The first two rounds were totally predictable. Conn landed a few punches that had little effect. Louis stayed with him and landed hammer blows that stunned the challenger. But in the third round Conn shifted to the tactics that almost won him the fight. He would land hard blows and then dodge quickly, denying Louis an easy target. Knocking out Joe Louis was out of the question for a boxer of Conn's size, but Conn's tactics put excitement in the fight. Billy won the third and fourth rounds, while Joe came back strong and won rounds five and six. Billy evened the score by taking the next two rounds, but he slipped on the canvas in the tenth and lost the round. In the eleventh and twelfth rounds the feeling of the fight suddenly shifted. Conn increased the pace of his attack, and Joe Louis suddenly seemed to be an old man, unable to keep up with his challenger. When the bell sounded at the end of the twelfth, Billy was clearly in control of the fight. Three more rounds of this pace would make him the world's heavyweight champion.

It was at this point that Billy Conn lost his head. Instead of sticking to his fight plan, he decided to try to close in and knock Louis out. It didn't matter that he had tired the champion but never really hurt him. Conn thought he could finish the fight in the thirteenth round. He went on the attack with increased vehemence, but this time he didn't duck and dodge. He kept hitting and hitting until, just for a split second, he let down his guard and exposed his jaw. That was all the opening Joe Louis needed. A powerful right to the jaw, a left to the ribs, and another right to the jaw sent Conn to the canvas for the count. Later there was some debate over whether Conn managed to get back on his feet before the count of ten, but none of that mattered.

Referee Eddie Joseph had counted him out, and Joe Louis was still World Heavyweight Champion. After the fight Billy was asked why he had changed his tactics in the thirteenth round. His reply, repeated for years afterwards, was simple. "What's the point in being Irish if you can't be thick?"

Few other sports attracted as much national attention as did baseball and football. Basketball was gaining in popularity and had even been included in the Berlin Olympic Games of 1936. In the United States it was mainly an amateur sport, and there was a substantial following for the college game. The real powerhouse of 1941 was Wisconsin, which won the Big 10 championship in a season that included a 14-game winning streak. The Badgers then swept through the N.C.A.A. Tournament, defeating Washington 39-34 in the first championship game to be broadcast over radio. For players not attending college, the A.A.U. provided opportunities to play on a local and regional level against other A.A.U. teams and against local colleges. As in other sports, many of the A.A.U. teams were sponsored by local industries, which regarded the sponsorships as good advertising.

At the professional and semi-professional levels there were teams throughout the country that attracted some local following; but schedules were irregular and there was no national organization to coordinate competition. On the East Coast a small league, the American Basketball League, attracted some regional attention. In the Midwest the National Basketball League was somewhat more stable, in part because of the corporate sponsorship that a number of teams enjoyed. The names of the Akron Firestone Non-Skids, the Akron Goodyear Wingfoots, the Fort Wayne Zollner Pistons (still in existence as the Detroit Pistons), and the Toledo Jim White Chevrolets reflect these corporate links. All of these teams were for white players only, but two notable black teams had considerable success in barnstorming tours, crossing the country and playing local white teams. The New York Renaissance, generally known as the Rens, and the Harlem Globetrotters (who had never even played in Harlem) were so powerful that when the invitational World Professional Basketball Tournament was established in Chicago in 1939, the Rens won the championship in the first year and the Globetrotters followed them as champions in the second year, in both cases playing against all-white teams.

Other sports attracted far less fan attention in 1941, and most were regarded as primarily amateur pastimes. Except for tennis, they were also principally male endeavors. In other sports, athletic prowess seemed somehow unladylike. Up until this year virtually the only intercollegiate sport open to women was fencing. In June, for the very first time, a national women's intercollegiate golf tournament was played. The tournament was held in Columbus, Ohio, and was won by Eleanor Dudley of the University of Alabama. Certainly the most famous woman athlete of all was Babe Didrikson Zaharias, who had shown her prowess in a number of sports, especially basketball, track, and golf. Her great passion was for golf, and as an amateur golfer she had won the Women's Texas Amateur Championship in 1935. But Didrikson was a coarse, uncultured young woman from a poor immigrant family. Her success (with its attendant publicity) was an embarrassment to the more genteel and socially prominent women who were accustomed to dominating the sport. After her Texas victory, she suddenly found herself barred by the U.S.G.A., purportedly for being in fact a professional, not an amateur. The decision was clearly a pretext, and in 1940 she applied to have her amateur standing reinstated. The appeal was approved, with the stipulation that she had to serve a three-year waiting period. In the meantime, professional golf was left to the men, whose top money winner in 1941 was Ben Hogan, with $18,358.

While Didrikson was sitting out her waiting period before resuming her golf career, she turned her competitive attention to tennis, taking lessons from Eleanor Tennant, one of the nation's top teaching professionals. In the autumn of 1941 Didrikson tried to enter the Pacific Southwest Championships. Once again the amateurs closed ranks against a woman who was just too good and too uncouth. The U.S. Lawn Tennis Association rejected her, holding that if she had been found to be a professional in any sport, she would have to be regarded as a professional in tennis also, even though she had never played the game before. With no tournaments available for her to win, Didrikson dropped the sport and never played again.

With tournaments open only to amateurs, and most players trying to exhibit socially proper behavior, tennis was regarded as acceptable for women. Professionals were generally teachers like Tennant or former amateur champions capitalizing on their fame by playing exhibition matches. To survive at the top of the game, players needed to be wealthy themselves or to find wealthy sponsors. The National Lawn Tennis Association would pay tournament expenses for top players, and sporting-goods companies like Spalding would provide free equipment. But players had to cover their basic living expenses from some outside source. It was a rare exception when a potential star like Alice Marble found a coach who would take her on as a protégée and support her financially. When Eleanor Tennant saw Marble play, she recognized her potential and started to oversee her development both on the court and in business affairs. Marble established a remarkable record during the late '30s before deciding in 1941 to turn professional. Only the few players at the very top of the game could turn professional and make good money playing exhibitions and giving clinics, and Marble found herself in that category. In January L. B. Icely, president of Wilson Sporting Goods, organized a professional tour with Marble, Don Budge (arguably the best player of the first half of the century), Bill Tilden, and Mary Hardwick Hare. Marble and Budge each received a salary of $75,000 plus a percentage of the gate, an arrangement that allowed each to earn over $100,000 during the year. Yet even then, Marble was able to match Budge's contract only through her determination and business acumen. She had originally agreed to a much lower salary. When she discovered what Budge was making, she threatened to quit the tour unless her contract was rewritten to give her the same terms as Budge. Icely recognized Marble's value and readily agreed. For the first time in professional sports, a woman had demanded and received salary parity with men.

CHAPTER 8

August: Leisure Time and Travel

By 1941 A combination of factors had brought about a striking change in working conditions for millions of Americans. Barely fifteen years earlier the typical work week for industrial workers had been forty-eight hours. By 1941 it was down to forty hours. Further, the two-week vacation, while far from universal, was becoming more common. Consequently, Americans in 1941 had more leisure time than ever before; and thanks to the defense buildup, they had more money to spend on recreation than ever before. This is not to say that spending on leisure time was lavish. The Depression was too recent a memory for that. But the American people now could devote some of their time and money to purely recreational activities.

While more people were able to enjoy paid vacations, that ability still varied enormously by social class. The wealthy, of course, could travel as they wished. Even middle-class vacations were accepted as normal. Most salaried employees could take one and often two weeks off with pay. Even hourly workers were beginning to receive vacation benefits. Vacations for industrial workers were only indirectly the result of union activity. Mostly they were granted at the initiative of employers, especially in large industries. Owners and management hoped to develop employee loyalty, increase productivity from a rested work force, and co-opt potential union demands.

Building employee loyalty was a major incentive for many business owners. Consequently a substantial waiting period, often as much as five years, was required before a man qualified for paid vacation. The requirement for female workers was often less, commonly three years of continuous employment. For industrial workers the most common vacation allowance was one week a year, although the two-week vacation was by no means rare. By 1941 over half of America's industrial workers were covered by some form of paid vacation plan. It is worth remembering, however, that almost a quarter of all Americans lived on farms. For them finding time to get away was extremely difficult. Crops and livestock could not be neglected for even a few days. Occasionally one or two family members might get away for a short trip, especially after the harvest; but farming made it all but impossible for an entire family to take a vacation together.

The range of vacation possibilities was broad. Those on tight budgets might spend a week visiting family or friends who lived within a reasonable driving distance. Camping, too, was a popular and inexpensive option for many people. Thanks largely to the work of the Civilian Conservation Corps over the last decade, there were numerous campsites and recreation areas within an easy drive of most workers, especially in the East. Pitching a tent near a stream offered an additional way to save money: Fishing was a good way to feed a family at little or no cost and had always been a favorite recreational activity. For those with a bit more money, there were options other than the tent. By 1940 there were perhaps 100,000 travel trailers on the road, and trailer camps were being developed to cater to the needs of their owners.

For those with just a bit more money to spend, the rapidly expanding network of motels, or mo-tels (motor hotels), offered reasonably attractive accommodations at moderate prices. The first hostelry to use the name was the Milestone Mo-tel, which opened in San Luis Obispo, California, in 1926. During the 1920s many municipalities had established auto camps to control the practice of pitching tents along the roadside. When cities started charging fees for the use of municipal camps, entrepreneurs moved in and established camp sites with improved amenities. Soon the camps were offering primitive cabins for those who wanted a bit more protection from the weather, and the cabin camps soon evolved into auto courts, perhaps the most common term for these nascent motels.

By 1941 there were thousands of auto courts all across the country. All featured rows of detached or semi-detached cottages, generally with small carports attached. Owners preferred to call these buildings cottages rather than cabins to distinguish them from the more primitive accommodations found at campgrounds. While auto courts varied widely, generally each cottage provided a single bedroom with attached bathroom, a closet or wardrobe, hot and cold running water, and a radiator or electric heater for the colder months. Furnishings were simple, usually one or two double beds, a writing table, and a lamp. Costs varied, but often a single room could be had for as little as a dollar a night. Many auto courts had an adjacent service station, often owned by the same family, where travelers could buy gasoline and have their cars repaired. A simple diner nearby would cover travelers' remaining needs.

Waitresses and cooks in diners had their own special language which, with certain regional variations, prevailed across the country. After a long day on the road, a traveler might enjoy a hearty dinner of Bessie with violets and Irish terriers (roast beef with cabbage and potatoes). Dessert might be sin pie with a glob (apple pie with vanilla ice cream) or perhaps a dish of fish eyes (tapioca pudding). For breakfast the next morning one could have Adam and Eve on a raft (two poached eggs on toast) or perhaps hog's hips and cackleberries (bacon and eggs) with a squeeze and tar (orange juice and black coffee). For lunch one might have choked beef and frog sticks with a hemorrhage plus a Georgia special (hamburger and French fries with catsup plus a Coca-Cola). Baked beans were variously known as artillery, belly busters, musical fruit, repeaters, whistle berries, or a variety of other more or less familiar terms. The jargon of the diner had also kept up with the times. If food was spoiled and had to go in the garbage, the order was to give it to Hitler.

The vast majority of auto courts were local mom-and-pop operations. Only a handful of chains had been established, the best known being the Alamo Plaza Hotel Courts. This chain had begun in Waco, Texas, and by 1941 had spread eastward as far as Louisiana, where the newest establishment opened on March 30 in Baton Rouge. The Alamo Plaza Courts were easily recognized from their architectural style: The façade of each unit was made to look like the façade of the Alamo in San Antonio. Generally a large central unit containing the offices and manager's lodging faced the highway, with a smaller unit, connected by an archway, on either side. Travelers could drive through the archway, check in, and find a cottage in a row on the back side of the courtyard, buffered from the highway by the main buildings in front.

The most architecturally distinctive auto court chain was Wigwam Villages, a small chain of three auto courts in Kentucky, Alabama, and Louisiana. Each cabin was built in the shape of an oversized Indian teepee. The cabins were arranged in a circle with an even larger teepee in the center, serving as an office and restaurant. Despite the odd external appearance, the interiors were fitted out much as in any other auto court.

Although auto court chains were rare and small, referral services had already become common. For an annual fee, each member auto court received a listing in the annual brochure that all members made available to their guests. Each member agreed to maintain certain minimum standards and to display the emblem of the service on its signs and advertising. These associations were generally regional, although the United Motor Courts, with over 280 members, covered most of the United States except the Northern Plains and the Northeast. DeLuxe Motor Courts were found largely on the West Coast and in the Southwest, although they reached as far as Virginia and the Carolinas along highway U.S. 70 and connecting roads. Drivers wanting to see new parts of the country could now take advantage of the American Guide series, begun as a W.P.A. project to offer a reliable guide book to each of the forty-eight states. By 1941 the series was substantially complete, with only the guides for Arkansas, Oklahoma, Washington, and West Virginia remaining to be published. Prices ranged from $1.25 for North Dakota to $3.50 for Idaho, with most guides costing $2.50 or $3.00.

Vacationers generally fell into one of two categories. One was the traditional family group, husband and wife, perhaps children, perhaps a grandparent. The other group consisted of pairs of younger people, most commonly young women, who could share expenses and therefore take vacations that might otherwise be out of reach. Camping, fishing, and canoeing were among the least expensive and most popular activities. In Grand Teton National Park a cabin for four people could be rented for $30 a week. In the Southeast, where the resort season was winter and early spring, bargains were available in the summer when the hot weather discouraged many travelers. Coastal resorts, where sea breezes moderated the summer heat, were pleasant and affordable. At the fashionable Cloisters on Sea Island, Georgia, a room for two could be had for $49 a week in the summer, meals included.

Vacationers with money had a wide range of travel possibilities. Long-distance vacation travel was mainly for the well-to-do, but it was still something everyone could dream about. Each summer the popular magazines were filled with vacation advertisements, especially from the railroads and from destinations in Florida and Arizona. Since traditional short holiday cruises were no longer available because of the war at sea, American Express Travel Service offered a two-week train cruise for $188 a person including meals. A special train with 150 passengers traveled from Chicago across country to Los Angeles, and thence to Lake Louise in Canada before returning to Chicago. Numerous stops along the 6,000-mile route allowed travelers to visit local attractions, just as they might in a cruise ship's ports of call.

For long-distance train travel, the United States functioned almost like two separate countries. Between East and West were major gateways in Chicago, St. Louis, and New Orleans. Eastern and western railroads met at these terminals, and passengers wanting to travel across country would have to change trains there. Sometimes travelers even had to find transportation across town from one railroad station to another. In the East there was more cooperation between North and South. Passengers could board a train in Chicago or New York and not leave it until their arrival in Atlanta or Miami. But there was still a delay in Washington, Louisville, or Cincinnati as passenger cars were transferred from one railroad to another.

During the Depression the railroads had seen a sharp decline in passenger traffic. As the country came out of the Depression, traffic picked up, but not as much as the railroads hoped. For shorter trips there was increasing competition from the automobile, while the rapidly expanding airlines were beginning to nibble at long-distance travel. To meet this competition the railroads adopted two different but related strategies. They spent large amounts of money upgrading the quality of the travel experience; and, especially on cross-country trips, they worked to cut travel time. The development of the diesel locomotive was central to both efforts.

In 1941 most people thought of railroad power in terms of the reciprocating steam locomotive. A fire, fueled with either coal or oil, heated water in a long horizontal boiler. The central principle had not changed for more than a hundred years. The big, black steam locomotive, with all its fascinating machinery exposed to view, held thousands of boys, young and old, enthralled. Many a grown man would spend his lunch hour with a packet of sandwiches and a thermos of coffee, sitting by the tracks and watching the engines at work. The life's dream of thousands of boys was to leave school as soon as possible and hire out on the railroad.

Yet the steam locomotive had certain substantial drawbacks from the point of view of railroad management. For one thing, the beasts were incredibly thirsty. Water tanks could seldom be located more than one hundred miles apart, where trains had to stop to replenish the water in the tenders. Even more important, the reciprocating parts of the locomotive needed constant maintenance. An engine could travel only a little over 100,000 miles before needing a major overhaul. Lesser repairs, taking a day or two, might be needed more frequently.

The 1930s saw the beginnings of the diesel takeover on American railroads. It took time for management to become convinced of the value of the diesel. After all, the machines cost three times as much as steamers for equivalent horsepower. But the savings in operating costs soon showed up. With no water to convert to steam for propulsion, diesels could easily run 500 miles before needing to stop for fuel. Most of all, diesels could and did run as much as a million miles before needing an overhaul. In many cases a specially trained mechanic could repair a diesel engine while the train was in motion. Diesels had first been used to switch freight cars in the railroad yards. Passenger trains came next. It was only in 1941 that the railroads began to buy diesel locomotives specifically designed to pull freight trains. Freight diesels were such a novelty that when the Santa Fe Railroad bought its third such engine, it thought enough of the event to publicize it in half-page advertisements in national magazines.

One of the most noticeable effects of dieselization was the acceleration of passenger train schedules. In the days of steam it was possible for a business traveler to get on the Baltimore and Ohio Train #1 in Washington, D. C., at 4:05 P.M. Eastern Time, spend the night and the next day on the train, and arrive in St. Louis at 6:00 P.M. Central Time, twenty-seven hours later. In 1941 diesel-powered Train #1, now known as the *National Limited*, left Washington at 6:30 in the evening and arrived in St. Louis at 1:00 the next afternoon, a saving of seven and a half hours. Improved roadbed, track, and signaling contributed to the saving. But much of it could be attributed to the General Motors E-6 passenger diesels that pulled the train. Even greater savings were achieved on the long runs from Chicago, St. Louis, and New Orleans to the West Coast. When the Santa Fe Railroad introduced the *Super Chief* between Chicago and Los Angeles, the 39¾-hour schedule cut ten hours off the previous record.

Despite all the improvement, the fastest schedules on the most expensive trains still required a 2½-day trip to get from New York to Los Angeles. The railroads were well aware that airlines had made tremendous advances in the last decade. While transcontinental air travel still required numerous stops to refuel and take on passengers, it was nevertheless possible to fly from New York to Los Angeles in thirteen hours and forty-five minutes. That was a great deal faster than the train—for those who could afford it. A one-way airline ticket from New York to Los Angeles cost $149.95, out of the reach of all but the most prosperous travelers. But time and cost were both coming down, and the railroads needed something more than just faster schedules to stay competitive. Their answer produced some of the most comfortable and luxurious trains ever created, trains of modernistic design matching the streamlined shape of the diesel locomotives.

The sleek-nosed diesel locomotives produced by General Motors readily lent themselves to colorful visual treatments that caught the public imagination. Some railroads took a dignified and refined approach to color schemes. The New York Central preferred a restrained gray and black, while the Southern Railway settled on apple green and white. The Baltimore and Ohio, traversing what had been the Border States during the Civil War, commemorated that conflict with a blue and grey paint scheme. Western lines were generally more colorful. The Union Pacific chose a vivid yellow set off with grey and red, while the Chicago, Burlington and Quincy took delivery of locomotives with bright stainless steel sides trimmed in red. Perhaps the most dramatic contest for color dominance was that between the Santa Fe and the Southern Pacific. The Santa Fe dressed its freight diesels in a restrained blue and yellow, but passenger engines were painted silver with a dramatic, bright red "war bonnet" covering the cab. The Southern Pacific not only decorated its diesels with a glorious red and orange scheme inspired by the names of its *Daylight* trains; it also applied these colors to some of its passenger steam engines as well, creating what many regarded as the most beautiful steam locomotives of all time.

In late 1941 there were already 140 diesel-powered passenger trains operating in the United States, but that left a great many trains, including many elite passenger trains, to be pulled by steam. Some railroads, especially in the Northeast, employed noted industrial designers like Henry Dreyfuss (who also designed the standard telephone set and John Deere tractors) and Raymond Loewy (the Studebaker and the Sears Coldspot refrigerator) to design streamlined shrouding for the steam locomotives assigned to their fastest trains. The dean of transportation designers, Otto Kuhler, designed streamlined steam and diesel locomotives as well as passenger cars and trolleys.

Inside the extra-fare name trains were appointments as luxurious as the railroads could make them. Whether the décor was traditional dark wood paneling or modernistic chrome plated steel, the railroads invested millions of dollars in improving the appearance of their top trains. In some cases their imagination ran away with them. When the Union Pacific introduced its new train, the *City of Denver*, running between Chicago and its namesake city, the bar car was named the Frontier Shack. It was decorated like an Old West saloon, with rough-hewn paneling and log beams across the ceiling. Wanted posters from Wells Fargo and pictures of boxer Jim Jeffries and actress Lillian Russell completed the impression. The concept was so successful that the railroad introduced a Gay Nineties bar theme on the *City of Los Angeles*. Complete with painted Victorian furniture and plush velvet, the bar was manned by a bartender with high collar, vest, horseshoe tie-pin, and button boots.

Even the less imaginative cars had been modernized as far as finances permitted. On the major roads all the name trains featured air conditioning and fluorescent lighting throughout. Coaches had individual lighting and adjustable seats with head and foot rests. Interestingly, these and other innovations that enhanced passenger comfort were pioneered by Olive Dennis, Design Engineer on the Baltimore and Ohio. The second woman to graduate from the School of Engineering at Cornell and the only woman in the country working as a service engineer for a major railroad, Dennis also contributed designs for the B&O's centennial dining car china, for passenger car interiors, and even for the shrouding on one of the railroad's stream-lined steam locomotives.

Dining cars received special attention from the railroads, and few lines were content with anything less than the finest gourmet food and service. Chefs and waiters were attracted away from hotels and restaurants, and menus created the impression that travelers were dining in the finest establishments on the continent. Most railroads were content to break even or take a small loss on their food service in order to provide the highest quality. The Santa Fe went even further and contracted with noted restaurateur Fred Harvey to manage its dining car service.

All these improvements in speed and design were intended to attract the traveling public, especially the more prosperous among them, and keep them away from airplanes. Even for shorter trips, by 1941 it was clear that the airplane was the vehicle of choice for people in a hurry who had the money to spend. The Douglas DC-3 and the Lockheed Super Electra were tremendous improvements in speed, safety, and capacity over commercial aircraft of just five years earlier. With room for only about twenty passengers, they also offered an air of exclusivity. Air travel was, of course, still a good deal more expensive than travel by train. A rail journey from Pittsburgh to Chicago, for example, would take eight hours and cost $9.40 in a coach car. The same trip by air would cost $23.95 but take only two and a half hours.

There was also a lingering concern with airline safety. There had been remarkably few crashes in the late '30s, but in January a TWA flight crashed near St. Louis killing the pilot and a mechanic and injuring twelve. Then in late February a notable crash spoiled Eastern Airlines' four-year-old perfect safety record. A new Eastern DC-3 coming from New York by way of Washington crashed on approach to Candler Field in Atlanta. Of the seventeen passengers and three crew, seven were killed in the crash and one died later. The survivors, all seriously injured, included Captain Eddie Rickenbacker, World War ace fighter pilot, Medal of Honor winner, and president of the airline. While Rickenbacker was recuperating in the hospital, he received word of still another Eastern Airlines crash. On the morning of April 3, the airline's Jacksonville Flyer took off from West Palm Beach for the one-hour flight to Daytona Beach. The plane soon ran into a heavy thunderstorm, was hit by an intense downdraft, and pancaked into a swamp. Fortunately, all sixteen people on board survived, though several had broken bones and other injuries.

Despite the safety concerns regarding air travel, in March the nation was reminded that even rail travel could be disrupted with deadly results. On March 16 the Pennsylvania Railroad's *Buckeye*, headed east toward Pittsburgh, derailed and plunged into the Ohio River. Five people were killed and 104 were injured. Investigators found that spikes had been removed and one rail had been moved out of alignment, a clear case of sabotage. The F.B.I. was called in to help investigate, and the railroad offered a large reward for information, but the perpetrators were never identified.

Safety was a special concern for flights to and from the Nation's Capital. For many years Washington had been served by Washington-Hoover Airport, a small field located at the Virginia end of the Highway Bridge (14th Street Bridge) over the Potomac River. Even by the lax standards of the 1930s, Hoover Field was a hazard. A public road, owned and controlled by the War Department, crossed the runway; and a guard had to stop traffic for takeoffs and landings. Nearby electric power lines made takeoffs and approaches dangerous. Rubbish was burned in the open at a garbage dump next to the airport, and the thick smoke often prevented pilots from seeing the field when they were trying to land. The sod runways were not paved until 1936, and then only with packed cinders. Aviation pioneer Wiley Post was quoted as saying that there were better landing grounds in the wilds of Siberia. Accidents were common, and a number were fatal. A new airport was clearly needed.

Late in 1938 President Roosevelt persuaded Congress to pass the Civil Aeronautics Act, establishing federal control of the growing aviation business and creating the Civil Aeronautics Administration to provide supervision. A few weeks later the president authorized the C.A.A. to oversee the construction of a new airport, to be built with federal money, at Gravelly Point, about a mile south of Hoover Field on the Virginia side of the Potomac. Construction began immediately and progressed rapidly. The president laid the cornerstone for the new terminal building in September of 1940, and by the following summer the airport was ready for use. Four concrete runways, up to 7,000 feet long, could accommodate the largest aircraft in existence with safe takeoffs and landings. On June 15 preparations were completed for the transition, and exactly at midnight Washington-Hoover Airport ceased operations. One minute later, at 12:01 A.M. on June 16, an Eastern Airlines DC-3 made the first scheduled landing at Washington National Airport. The nation's capital now had the largest, most modern, and most technologically advanced airport in the country. The old Hoover Field was purchased by the War Department and provided part of the land for the Army's new pentagon-shaped headquarters (Chapter 9).

Even those who could not take long vacations by rail or air had ample leisure time for activities close to home. The four most popular pastimes were going motoring, going to the movies (Chapter 2), attending sporting events (Chapter 7), and listening to the radio.

For those who had cars, a popular Sunday activity was a drive through the countryside. By 1941 it was clear that America had developed a love affair with the automobile. At the beginning of the year Americans had 27.5 million cars registered, and the states were steadily improving their road systems to handle the growing traffic. Some states even built four-lane highways to speed traffic from city to city. Connecticut had opened the Merritt Parkway just the previous year. While conceived as a parkway for leisurely driving, it also cut travel time from Connecticut communities into New York City. Even more ambitious was the Pennsylvania Turnpike, the first section of which had also opened in 1940. The Turnpike was planned to run all the way from Ohio to New Jersey, though the first section, 159 miles from Carlisle to Irwin, was all that was open. With four lanes along most of the distance, there were at first no speed limits, apparently under the inspiration of the German *Autobahnen*. Speed limits were introduced in April of 1941, although the 70-mph limit for automobiles would have strained most passenger cars then in use. Off the main highways the speed limits were substantially lower, as the Archduke Otto of Austria, head of the Imperial House of Habsburg, found to his chagrin late in the summer. The Archduke, in this country as a refugee from the Nazis, had his driving license suspended indefinitely when he was stopped for going 60 mph on the Concord Turnpike in Massachusetts.

For young men with a sense of adventure, a love of the outdoors, and a strong interest in gas powered machines, the motorcycle provided another form of motorized recreation and entertainment. Harley-Davidson and Indian produced most of the motorcycles sold in the United States, with some competition from the much smaller Crocker Company, which produced a small number of very high quality racing machines. Riding motorcycles was not quite acceptable socially, and many families forbade their daughters to go out with young men who rode them. Of course, police officers in the elite motorcycle squads were a different matter, and they held a somewhat elevated status with their skills and daring. As a result of the defense buildup, the Army was increasing its orders from both Harley and Indian; and courier and scout duties on cycles were coveted assignments for soldiers. In the civilian world, however, the motorcycle remained more a form of recreation than a means of transportation, and its social standing was not high.

Whatever the vehicle, Sunday drivers had to face the reality that paved roads were by no means universal outside the cities. Especially in the South and West, the prevalence of dirt or gravel roads in rural areas made it difficult to get about or drive to town. In bad weather the roads could become all but impassable, especially in late winter and early spring, before the state could send out plows to restore a reasonable driving surface for the summer. School buses, often driven by high school students, were especially prone to getting stuck in the mud; and the difficulty of getting to school on time (or at all) was one of the factors limiting the effectiveness of education for many rural children. If a family did own a car, it owned only one. In rural areas the man of the house needed it to get to work, and the rest of the family had to make do.

But highway conditions were improving quickly, and the cars themselves were changing even faster. The new streamlined body styles that had appeared a few years earlier were now evolving into even more "modern" shapes, and even more significant changes were occurring under the hood. In 1939 General Motors introduced HydraMatic Drive, the first fully automatic transmission, in its Oldsmobile line for the 1940 model year. HydraMatic Drive turned out to be so successful that GM was able both to expand it to the Cadillac line for the 1941 model year and to raise the price to $100 on the Olds and $125 on the Cadillac.

Chrysler, too, introduced a semiautomatic transmission in 1941. Called the Vacamatic on the Chrysler, Simplimatic on the DeSoto, the transmission required the driver to clutch once to put the transmission in gear. After that it would shift by itself with just a slight lightening of the accelerator. A fluid drive connection with the engine prevented stalling when the car came to a stop. Significantly, Chrysler also offered the semiautomatic option on its low-priced Plymouth, as well. Since the Plymouth was Chrysler's competitor with the GM Chevrolet, this inexpensive option gave Plymouth a competitive advantage to offset its slightly higher base price.

One innovation that did not quite work out was air conditioning. Packard introduced a clumsy and expensive ($274) air conditioning option for the 1940 model cars. The device had neither a thermostat nor an on-off switch, and it occupied half the trunk. When its belt drive was connected, it came on when the engine started and kept running until the engine was shut off. It could be turned off only by opening the trunk and disconnecting the belt. Although it was never very popular and disappeared after 1941, it did show potential for future refinements.

With a combination of attractive styling, modernized engineering, and a base price for some models under $800, the automobile had become an affordable convenience, no longer a luxury, for all but the poor. Even in the relatively impoverished South, a middle-class family was generally able to afford a car. The automobile also introduced a new flexibility in housing choice, allowing families to live farther away from established public transportation routes. The automobile was now the preferred form of transportation for those who chose to take a modest vacation not too far from home.

Long drives could be tiresome, but in most parts of the country the trip could be enlivened by the sights and scenery along the road. Architectural oddities like the Alamo Plaza Courts could be found all over the country. In Bedford, Pennsylvania, the Coffee Pot luncheonette was built in the shape of an eighteen-foot-tall coffee pot. A few miles west, on the side of Allegheny Mountain, the Grandview Ship Hotel offered dining and accommodations in a structure built in the shape of a huge steam ship. In Neelsville, Maryland, the Cider Barrel roadside stand sold apple cider from the local orchard through a window in the side of a twelve-foot-tall, red, white, and blue wooden barrel. But perhaps the most widely known roadside diversions were the advertising signs put up by the Burma-Vita company of Minneapolis advertising their brushless shaving cream, Burma-Shave.

Burma-Shave signs were uniform in appearance, each set consisting of six one-inch-thick pine boards, about three feet long and ten inches high, painted red with white lettering. The last sign in the set always had the Burma-Shave logo, while the first five contained a brief piece of doggerel. Many of the jingles promoted the virtues of being clean shaven: HE HAD THE RING / HE HAD THE FLAT / BUT SHE FELT HIS CHIN / AND THAT/ WAS THAT / **Burma-Shave**. Safe driving habits were a constant theme, especially at railroad crossings: REMEMBER THIS / IF YOU'D / BE SPARED / TRAINS DON'T WHISTLE / BECAUSE THEY'RE SCARED / **Burma-Shave**. By 1941 sets were starting to appear that recognized the increasing number of young men in uniform: SOLDIER / SAILOR / AND MARINE / NOW GET A SHAVE / THAT'S QUICK AND CLEAN / **Burma-Shave**. Most sign sets were placed ten to twenty yards apart in open country where cars traveling at a typical 35 mph would take almost twenty seconds to pass a complete set, a remarkably long span of attention for casual advertising. Near cities, where space was at a premium, sets of only two or three signs were more common: BEARD UNRULY / MEET YOURS TRULY / **Burma-Shave**. The company introduced twenty to thirty new jingles every year, twenty-three of them in 1941.

In some parts of the country the pastimes of motoring and going to the movies could be combined in an evening at the local drive-in theater. The first drive-in had opened in Camden, New Jersey, in 1933; and during the 1930s they had spread rather slowly. By the end of 1941 there were about ninety-eight of them located in urban areas in twenty-nine different states. Operating during the summer months, drive-ins were regarded with great hostility by the owners of indoor theaters, even in the South where the climate forced indoor theaters, which lacked air conditioning, to close during the hot, muggy summer. Drive-ins were most commonly referred to as ozoners, although they were also known as passion pits or even less respectable names. Theater owners employed staff to walk among the cars and make sure that heads were showing above the seat backs. They constantly proclaimed the purity of their establishments, but the need for such protestations left no doubt as to their reputation.

A typical ozoner had a capacity of about four hundred cars, spread over seven or eight acres. Admission prices ranged from 25¢ to 35¢. Older screens were around thirty by forty feet, while newer ones were usually about fifty by sixty feet. The great technological challenge was sound. At this point there were no in-car speakers. RCA developed one in 1941, but the war intervened before it could be put into regular production. The earliest ozoners had just a few speakers ranged along the front of the lot, broadcasting sound loud enough to elicit serious complaints from neighbors. The sound delay getting to the back row of cars also upset the synchronization with the picture on the screen. Newer theaters had a separate speaker in front of each parking space, a great improvement but still less than satisfactory if rain made it necessary to close the car windows.

Most ozoners ran two showings a night, one starting somewhere between 8:30 and 9:00, and one starting two hours later. The major Hollywood studios owned their own indoor theater chains (Chapter 2) and were unfriendly to the new outdoor enterprises, refusing to rent them first-run films. Audiences, however, tended to be somewhat different in the two types of theater. Patrons of drive-ins tended to be family groups or perhaps people whose physical conditions made it difficult for them to get to regular theater seats. By 1941 the overt hostility of the early years had abated somewhat, and ozoners now found it easier to get popular movies on their secondary release, increasing the variety on offer to their patrons.

Despite its recreational value, for most people the automobile was primarily a way to get around town and through the surrounding area. In this role it was rapidly replacing the mode of transportation that had prevailed for the better part of a century, steel wheel on steel rail. For decades street cars had carried people where they needed to go in cities large and small. Sometimes, as in New York and Chicago, the trains ran on elevated tracks above the streets. In New York and Boston many trains ran underground. In most cities lightweight steel rails carried passengers down the middle of the street, leaving room on either side for cars and trucks as well as for horse-drawn delivery wagons. In 1941 the streetcar was omnipresent in American cities. Usually the streetcar, or trolley car, drew its electric power from an overhead wire. A pole (trolley) from the roof of the car pressed upward against the wire with spring pressure. Current flowing through the pole to the motorman's controller box was passed on to electric motors that powered the wheels. In Washington, D. C., the streetcars drew their power from an underground conduit between the rails. A plow-shaped device suspended beneath the car provided the electrical contact. It also provided an exciting display of fireworks when it short-circuited the electrical conduit.

San Francisco operated one of the most fascinating systems of downtown travel, the cable car. Running on just five remaining routes in 1941 (a sixth was converted to buses in April), the cable car had been largely supplanted by electric streetcars and buses. From the street, the conduit between the rails looked very much like the conduit on Washington's streetcar line. But this conduit contained a cable moving at a constant 9½ miles an hour. The operator, or gripman, in the car would work a mechanical level that connected to a clamp suspended beneath the car. The clamp grabbed hold of the underground cable to move the car along. Stopping the car required releasing the cable and applying brakes, which were nothing more than wooden blocks pressed down hard against the rail. Municipal authorities wanted to get rid of the cable cars and replace them with more modern vehicles, but local traditionalists kept that from happening. Since the tourist industry was in its infancy, the value of the cars in attracting tourists was as yet scarcely apparent. To most San Franciscans they were just a quaint way to get around.

All across the country the downtown streetcar lines were still generally in good shape, and many cities were still ordering new, modern, attractive, and comfortable cars. Most of those being built in 1941 were constructed to designs that had been worked out by the Electric Railway Presidents' Conference Committee. With streamlined styling and redesigned electrical controls for smooth operation, the P.C.C. car dominated the market. Through the end of the year a total of 1,896 of these cars were placed in service on lines all across the country. With a top speed of 50 mph, as against the 30 mph for older trolleys, the cars were adaptable for use on some of the few remaining interurban lines. Although the P.C.C. cars, like their predecessors, were not air conditioned, their improved ventilation systems added markedly to passenger comfort.

To get from city to city, travelers also rode on steel rails. In a few parts of the country interurban electric railways still carried passengers quickly (usually) and safely (most of the time) from town to town. The interurbans had grown up in the early twentieth century as something of an extension of the urban trolley car. Interurbans were especially common in the Midwest, linking cities large and small with a network of light rail lines drawing their power from overhead trolley wires. In the 1920s and '30s the coming of the automobile started a period of decline for the interurban. The new, faster highways made it possible for the automobile, which had been around almost as long as the interurban, to travel from city to city at the convenience of the driver. Speeds were comparable; and if several passengers shared the trip, the cost was less. As state highway programs expanded, the interurban gradually became irrelevant.

By 1941 only the West Penn system, operating east and south of Pittsburgh, was still running interurban service based solely on passenger traffic. Electric railways in Southern Illinois, Iowa, and Utah all depended largely on freight shipments through connections with the major steam railroads. Perhaps the most interesting of all the remaining interurbans still in operation was the Pacific Electric, whose Big Red Cars linked the fast-growing communities in Southern California. The P.E. had been assembled in the early part of the century by Henry Huntington, nephew of Collis P. Huntington of Central Pacific Railroad fame. Built before the population boom, the P.E. evolved with the communities it served. Still running traditional interurban service as far east as San Bernardino and Redlands, it operated its routes closer to downtown Los Angeles much more like suburban commuter lines and city streetcars. Of the 1,000 trains each day operating out of Los Angeles, some within the city operated on schedules as frequent as seven and a half minutes. And partly because Pacific Electric was controlled by the Southern Pacific Railroad, it also provided extensive freight service for customers as diverse as fruit growers and the aircraft industry. By 1941 the original interurban routes were losing passengers, and in November all passenger service was discontinued east of Covina. But many of the other lines remained in operation to serve the rapidly growing population of the area.

As paved roads reached farther into sparsely populated areas, the automobile and bus also put an end to one of the quaintest forms of transportation, the daily mixed train. Running mostly on short-line railroads and sometimes on isolated branch lines of the larger roads, the mixed train provided daily service to out-of-the-way places where other contacts with the outside world were limited or unavailable. On most branches and short lines, the railroads ran a freight train every weekday to deliver and pick up loads at various businesses and industries along the route. By attaching a passenger car to the freight train, the railroads created mixed trains (mixes of freight and passengers) to provide otherwise unavailable transportation. Mixed trains were found all over the country, though they were most common in the South and in the southern Rockies. The equipment was generally old, what would have been considered obsolete on larger railroads. In areas of the South, where large stands of pine yielded lumber, tar, and turpentine, some steam locomotives still burned wood for fuel. Abandoned as locomotive fuel in the rest of the country seventy-five years earlier, the pine knots from the logging operations were plentiful, cheap, and rich in the resin that produced a good hot fire. They also produced plentiful sparks that could start wildfires along the way, so these charmingly quaint engines proudly carried the fancy, bulbous smokestacks (known as cabbage stacks) with spark arrestors to reduce the damage to the surrounding country. Passenger cars were often made of wood rather than steel, and they carried truss rods under their floors to keep them from sagging in the middle with age, at least when the railroads bothered to tighten them. The wooden cars on the Kelly's Creek and Northwestern in West Virginia were of a design dating to the Civil War. Sometimes the railroads would dispense with passenger cars altogether and provide travelers with seats in the caboose. The mixed train also provided recreation, not for riders, but for an increasing number of rail fans who spent their leisure time seeking out these relics of an earlier era.

For families that stayed at home during their leisure hours, evening entertainment centered on the radio. The 34,850,000 homes in the US had 29,300,000 radios, and there were an additional 8,000,000 radios in cars. Except for the very poorest, almost everyone had access to a radio. Newspapers were available in cities, but in small towns and rural areas the radio often provided the only source of national and international news. Even farm families still unreached by electricity would make periodic trips to the general store to buy a new wet-cell battery for the family radio.

In 1941 the local radio stations all across the country were commonly affiliates of the four great radio networks. The National Broadcasting Company had been organized in 1926 by the Radio Corporation of America and operated two separate networks, NBC Red and NBC Blue. The Red network had originally been the larger and more commercial network, with Blue doing more cultural and unsponsored broadcasting. The two at first shared many technical services, but by 1941 they were mostly operating as two distinct entities. By the end of the year, NBC was well advanced in the process of divesting itself of the Blue network; and references to NBC, without additional qualification, always meant Red. Second to NBC was the Columbia Broadcasting System under its president and majority stockholder William Paley. CBS had been the first network to establish its own news division and it had a talented staff that included Edward R. Murrow and his colleagues in Europe (Chapter 5). Although CBS was the acknowledged leader in prestige, especially for its news and public service programs, it had never been able to match NBC in the ratings contest. The newest of the networks was the Mutual Broadcasting System, a cooperative owned and operated by affiliate stations. Mutual had by far the largest number of affiliates, but most were low-powered stations in relatively small markets. As a result, Mutual was in the weakest financial position of the big four networks and relied largely on programming generated by its leading affiliate stations, WOR in New York, WGN in Chicago, and KHJ in Los Angeles.

For most of the country, AM radio was the only kind available. Since the beginning of the year a very few FM stations had been operating commercially. Although the quality of sound from an FM radio was clearly superior to AM, the effective range of the early FM transmitters was about one hundred miles. Only the Northeast had the population density to make FM commercially viable.

Besides music (Chapter 2), radio provided a wide range of entertainment for all ages. Morning programming started with news and commentary at 8:00 on all three networks. There followed the morning talk shows, of which the best known was probably Don McNeil's *Breakfast Club* at 9:00 (broadcast from Chicago at 8:00 local time) on the Blue Network. On weekends the breakfast shows were followed by children's programs, such as *Let's Pretend* on CBS. *Let's Pretend* presented dramatizations of classic stories, often nursery tales, adapted for a children's audience.

After lunch time the networks were all given over to the soap operas, a genre specifically aimed at the interests of housewives, who made up the vast majority of the audience. Program sponsors represented the kinds of companies and products for which housewives were the natural customers: Oxydol, Ivory Soap, Dr. Lyon's Tooth

Powder, Camay Soap ("The soap for beautiful women"), and others. Soap operas ran in fifteen-minute segments, just time enough to advance the plot (if such it can be called) a few inches. Nothing much ever happened on any given episode, as the shows moved slowly from segment to segment. The pattern was intentional. Producers knew listeners might have to miss an episode or two from time to time, so the writers made sure they would miss very little. The plot conflicts were formulaic, with a little bit of tension raised at the end of each segment (especially on Friday) to bring the devotee back for the next episode.

The real interest in a series was not in the plot but in the characters as they slowly developed over time. Listeners came to regard the characters as members of their own extended families, or at least as familiar friends and neighbors. The small-town setting of shows like *Just Plain Bill, Ma Perkins, Young Dr. Malone,* and *Pepper Young's Family* encouraged such feelings. The principal characters themselves were kept simple and unremarkable, as if they might be people who lived down the street. If they were notable for any special quality, it was a kind of simplicity and accessibility to which listeners might aspire. Male characters tended to be rather flat. Real interest centered on the female lead, to whom the housewife audience could more easily relate.

Late afternoon was a time for young people who had gotten home from school and done whatever chores were assigned before supper. Juvenile adventure shows like *Little Orphan Annie, Mandrake the Magician, Captain Midnight* (all on Mutual), the *Green Hornet* (Blue), and *Jack Armstrong, the All-American Boy* (Red until September, then Mutual) generally ran in fifteen-minute segments, one after another. *The Lone Ranger* was so popular with adults as well as youngsters that it escaped the late-afternoon juvenile lineup and was heard at 7:30 in the evening on Mutual. Indeed, it was so popular that General Mills (Cheerios) sponsored it for a full thirty minutes.

Evening news was an almost sacred time for many families. Children were cautioned to maintain strict silence while their parents listened to reports of world events. When a rural family limited radio listening time in order to extend the life of the wet-cell radio battery, the evening news was the one program that was never cut out. Network commentators developed their own loyal followings, and some attracted continuing commercial sponsorships. The generally acknowledged dean of the commentators was H. V. Kaltenborn, who back in 1936 had done the first live broadcast from a battlefield during the Spanish Civil War. Kaltenborn's thrice-weekly broadcasts on NBC Red were sponsored by Pure Oil. Lowell Thomas, also on NBC, was sponsored by Sun Oil, while Raymond Gram Swing on Mutual was supported by White Owl Cigars. Some commentators had developed special areas of expertise. John Daly of CBS affiliate WJSV in Washington served as White House correspondent for the network. While most news and commentary was broadcast nationwide, the West Coast had certain distinctive programs of its own. The highly respected *Richfield Reporter*, an excellent straight news program, was confined to NBC's West Coast affiliates because its sponsor, Richfield Oil, was a West Coast company.

The radio networks took seriously their obligation to provide cultural programming for the general public, and several excellent drama programs could be heard every week. Perhaps the lightest of these was the *First Nighter*, which aired Tuesday evenings at 8:30 (later Fridays at 9:30) on CBS. The 30-minute program, sponsored by Campana cosmetics, featured original scripts, generally upbeat and romantic, sometimes verging on melodrama. Much more substantial and of very high quality was the *Lux Radio Theater*, also on CBS, which occupied a full hour every Monday night at 9:00. The show was broadcast from Hollywood, and Cecil B. DeMille served as producer and host. Each program was a radio adaptation of a popular movie, often with much of the movie's script intact. Hollywood actors, often the same ones who had appeared in the movies, played the roles on the radio. As in most radio programs, the performers appeared on stage in front of a live audience. In this case the hall held 1,000 seats, and they were all filled every week.

To compete with CBS, NBC offered the *Cavalcade of America* on Wednesdays at 7:00 (later on Mondays at 8:00). The 30-minute program presented dramatizations of historical events or notable biographies from America's past. The *Cavalcade* was sponsored by E. I.

duPont de Nemours, in part as an attempt to dispel the company's reputation as a profiteering merchant of death during World War I. The sponsor kept an intentionally low profile and did not even use the customary commercial break in the middle of the program. Instead they reserved two minutes at the end of the show for an informative presentation on current work being done in duPont's laboratories. This was where duPont introduced their slogan, "Better things for better living through chemistry."

Probably the most extraordinary drama program on radio was the *Columbia Workshop*, which came on at 10:30 (later 2:30) Sunday on CBS. The network wanted a program that would explore the distinctive artistic possibilities of radio. Consequently they refused to accept sponsorships for the *Workshop*. Each week there was a new experimental drama, pushing the boundaries of the medium. From May 4 through November 9, the program was given over to *Twenty-six by Corwin*, a series of original dramas by Norman Corwin, one of the most creative and respected writers of the era. Corwin's writing walked the line between prose and poetry. The final program aired on November 9, and the whole series was very well received. Unfortunately for Corwin, William Lewis, the CBS vice president who had hired him and who had backed the *Columbia Workshop*, had recently left the network to go to Washington and head the radio division of the new government Office of Facts and Figures. His replacement at CBS, Douglas Coulter, was far more interested in programming that attracted sponsors. Coulter informed Corwin that the network was ending its experimental, noncommercial programming; and he hinted that Corwin's job was therefore becoming superfluous. Within a few days a new opportunity opened up when Corwin was asked to come to Washington and prepare an hour-long drama to mark the 150th anniversary of the ratification of the Bill of Rights on December 15 (Chapter 12).

Continuing dramatic programs on radio often crossed into the category of melodrama. Most were thirty minutes long and aired once a week. Crime stories were always popular: *Gang Busters* (Fridays at 9:00 on the Blue Network) was based on actual closed cases from the F. B. I. Far more imaginative, even fantastic, was the *Shadow* (Sundays at 5:30

on Mutual), based on the pulp fiction novels of Walter Gibson, who wrote under the pen name Maxwell Grant. Gibson's melodrama centered on the millionaire playboy Lamont Cranston, who, donning a slouch hat and cape, became the Shadow. "Who knows what evil lurks in the hearts of men? The Shadow knows." Somewhat different was *Inner Sanctum* (Sundays at 8:30 on the Blue Network), a horror show that began and ended with the loud creaking of a door. Some of the programs were based on classic Gothic tales such as Poe's "The Tell-Tale Heart" or "The Fall of the House of Usher," while others used original scripts. Sometimes parents complained of too much blood and gore, but the producers knew that the children listening wanted more, not less. Lest one think that all evening programs were crime and horror, one of the most enduringly popular of the evening dramas was *Dr. Christian* (Wednesday at 8:30 on CBS). Dr. Christian was a small-town family doctor who seemed to spend more time on the problems of the townsfolk than he did on his medical practice. It was a light drama that never took a summer vacation in all the years of its run.

Radio's situation comedies built up large armies of fans over the years. *The Aldrich Family,* airing on Thursdays at 8:30 on NBC, was consistently one of the ten most popular programs on radio. Every week teenage Henry Aldrich managed to turn some minor problem into a chaotic disaster. Most evening comedies ran for thirty minutes once a week. The *Easy Aces,* with Goodman and Jane Ace, was unusual in being a 15-minute program three times a week. Jane was famous for her malapropisms. Several, like "Congress is still in season" and "time wounds all heels," became common in everyday speech. One of the most beloved comedies was *Fibber McGee and Molly,* Tuesdays at 9:30 on NBC. Molly also contributed some familiar expressions to American English, including "'Tain't funny, McGee," and "Don't open that door, McGee!" The latter came just as Fibber opened the famous closet door, setting off a crashing and clattering of pots and pans and whatever else fell out. The sound effects were produced live on a small set of steps in the studio and became a regular gag on the program. Many a householder had a storage room that was referred to as Fibber McGee's closet.

Radio variety shows offered what was arguably the greatest array of brilliant entertainers ever presented at the same time. At the top in the rankings was Bob Hope on the *Pepsodent Show,* which came on at 10:00 on Tuesdays, right after *Fibber McGee and Molly*, on NBC. Hope's carefully crafted monologues delivered jokes at a timed rate of one every ten seconds. The show was totally predictable in format and totally unpredictable in content. Hope regularly had guests on the program, one of the most frequent being his friend Bing Crosby. Bing had his own show, the *Kraft Music Hall*, at 9:00 on Tuesdays, also on NBC. The *Kraft Music Hall* ran for a full hour and put more emphasis on music, with Bing as the lead vocalist. Humor was provided by Bob Burns as the Arkansas traveler, with wild tales of life back in the Ozarks. Burns was also noted for his bazooka, a musical (?) instrument he had invented and named back in 1905. The bazooka consisted of two pieces of telescoping pipe with a funnel at one end. It played and sounded somewhat like a bass trombone, albeit with a severely limited range. Burns was so popular that in the fall he got his own show, the *Arkansas Traveler*, Tuesday evenings at 8:30 on CBS.

Several of the variety shows were headed by husband-wife teams, though the fact of their marriage was not usually noted on the program. The *Jell-O Program with Jack Benny* came on Sunday evenings at 7:00 on NBC. Jack was joined by his real-life wife Mary Livingstone, who played an airhead whose crazy remarks often made a sort of nonsensical sense. One of the most popular regulars was Eddie Anderson who played Rochester, Benny's black valet and chauffeur. Anderson walked a fine line in a racially mixed environment, being neither obsequious nor uppity. His jibes always got the better of Benny, but they were delivered in a most respectful way. Jack was also known for his long-running feud with Fred Allen, whose show, the *Texaco Star Theater*, aired for sixty minutes on Wednesdays on CBS. Allen had taken a chance and initiated the feud back in 1936 when he lampooned the much more famous Benny and his violin playing. Jack heard the show and thought it was hilarious. The two carried on their verbal duel for years, with Benny generally getting the worse of it. Like Benny, Allen was accompanied on the show by his wife, Portland

Hoffa, whose scatterbrained comments often hit the mark. Benny and Allen were frequent guests on each other's programs, though they were carried on rival networks. The views of the sponsors were more important in 1941 than the opinions of network executives. If the feud brought Jell-O and Texaco more attention, nothing else mattered.

Yet another husband-and-wife team was George Burns and Gracie Allen, whose *Burns and Allen Show* aired at 7:30 on NBC. *Burns and Allen* was the last major program to preserve the old vaudeville format, having jokes and skits presented in series with no connection among them. The format was showing its age, and the program's rating dropped below 15 during the 1940-41 season. A change was clearly needed. In the fall *Burns and Allen* moved from Monday to Tuesday and introduced a number of changes. Bandleader Artie Shaw left to form his own orchestra, and Paul Whiteman took his place. More important, George and Gracie appeared for the first time as husband and wife; and the comedy was held together by a unified plot for each show. Gracie was still her scatterbrained self, and George played her straight man. The new formula worked, and the ratings again rose above 20.

The first notable radio quiz show was NBC's *Dr. I. Q., the Mental Banker.* The show offered silver dollars to contestants who could answer rapid-fire questions correctly. A children's version, *Dr. I. Q., Jr.* aired on Sundays at 6:30. CBS responded with its own quiz show, *Take It or Leave It*, which came on at 10:00 on Sundays. Contestants were offered a series of seven questions of progressive difficulty. The first was for $1, and subsequent questions were offered on a double-or-nothing basis, up to the final $64 question. At any point contestants could stop and take their money. The format led to high ratings and continuing sponsorship from Eversharp. Something of an inverted quiz show was *Information, Please*, Friday evenings at 8:30 on NBC Red. On this Lucky Strike program, a panel consisting of Clifton Fadiman, Franklin P. Adams, and John Kieran would be joined by a special guest to answer questions submitted by the audience. A listener who stumped the experts won a set of the *Encyclopædia Britannnica*, but the witty repartee among the panelists was what really held the program together. *Quiz Kids*, a children's version of *Information, Please*, could be heard on the Blue Network on Wednesday evenings.

Late-night radio had a more limited audience, but bigger numbers than the stations realized. One night a little-known announcer named Arthur Godfrey read a department-store advertisement for ladies' black lace panties on WJSV in Washington. After reading the copy, he told his listeners that his face was turning red from embarrassment. The next morning the store was mobbed with women wanting the panties that made Arthur Godfrey blush.

Apart from motoring, movies, sports, and radio, recreational activities in 1941 were socially stratified to a great degree. Golf, for example, was generally limited to the upper classes and to the upwardly mobile middle class. The most exclusive clubs had fee structures barring all but the well-to-do. They also often had bylaws that imposed ethnic exclusions. Jews were not welcome at the more exclusive country clubs, and a membership application from even a socially prominent Jew would be silently rejected. It was also a male sport. Despite the efforts of women like Babe Didrikson Zaharias to gain acceptance for women as athletes, many country clubs closed their golf courses to women. In smaller towns and cities, country club membership was less restricted, with middle-class men and women enjoying the sport.

Tennis was increasing its appeal as the game developed into something far different from the genteel sport of the turn of the century. An estimated four million Americans took part, with about a quarter of those playing for free on the municipal courts being built across the country. Tennis also had an impact on women's fashions, as the short skirts and strong bare legs of the professionals and top amateurs fostered a new image of the healthy female form.

Swimming was one sport enjoyed by members of all social classes. Municipal pools and beaches alone registered attendance levels of over 200,000,000 a year. Other beach-related activities included the highly popular bathing beauty contests.

Softball developed great popularity during the 1930s, and in 1941 it was a principal form of community recreation. In 1933 the Amateur

Softball Association had been formed, with a tournament held in Chicago. By 1941 the number of men and women playing softball was estimated at over ten million. Women's softball had a special appeal to working-class women as an inexpensive outlet and vehicle for social cohesion. By 1941 it had acquired an image, especially at the top amateur level, as a tough, "masculine" game.

Bowling was a popular pastime with even stronger working-class overtones. When the sport developed around the turn of the century, it had an ambiance much like that of pool halls. By the 1930s bowling had shaken off some of that image and become an attractive form of exercise for working-class women. Bowling also offered a distinctive job opportunity for boys. Although Gottfried Schmidt had developed the mechanical pinsetter for American Machine and Foundry in 1936, thousands of school boys still earned money as pinsetters in alleys across the country.

Roller skating was a recreational activity that appealed to adults as well as young people. There were some 3,500 roller rinks across the country that allowed both general skating and dancing on skates. An evening of skating often began with the Grand Promenade, with musical accompaniment. A rink's regular patrons would compete for the privilege of leading the promenade, an honor reserved for the most experienced and skilled.

For young people who had to watch their money, entertainment often meant an evening at the local soda fountain, where the juke box allowed patrons to hear the latest popular songs for a nickel. In January a variant of the jukebox appeared, the Phonette, manufactured by the Personal Music Corporation of Newark, New Jersey. Designed for lunch counters, the miniature Phonette cost just a penny to play. It was wired to a central record player in the store and offered no choice of music. Songs were played in a fixed order reflecting their popularity ratings. The volume on the Phonette was much lower than that on the usual jukebox, and it directed the music just to the couples sitting near it. Phonettes were generally installed in groups of ten at a drug store lunch counter, and they could be found mainly in the big-city drug chains like Cunningham's in Detroit, Skillern in Dallas, and Thrifty in

Los Angeles. They came to New York rather late, appearing in Whelan and Walgreen by the end of the year. Distributors bought them from the manufacturer for $20.00 each and handled the installation and servicing in return for 60 percent of the gross, the remaining 40 percent going to the drug store owner. They were such a success that by the end of the year the receipts were almost $10,000 a week, and the manufacturer was swamped with orders.

As has always been the case, young people had their own vocabulary to set themselves apart from their elders. "Scram" was just one of the currently hep words. A popular joke told of a newly hired secretary meeting her boss for the first time. "Young woman, there are two words that I do not want to hear in this office. One is 'lousy' and the other is 'swell.'" "That's fine by me," the secretary replied. "What are the two words?" A young man on a date looked forward to a hoytoytoy (good time), especially if he had squirrel fever (romantic urges). He hoped that his lamb pie (charming date) would be the yum-yum type (kissable). Otherwise the evening might turn out to be gestanko. Dig me? A girls' school was a dilly mill, where girls' club meetings were called harpie-huddles. A gentlemanly friend was a he-pal, and he probably worked in a cage (office). Most of the new expressions proved transient, but a few, like "chicken" (cowardly) and "off the beam," became regular parts of the language.

CHAPTER 9

September: Preparedness

ON SEPTEMBER 15, the United States Army launched the largest peacetime maneuvers ever undertaken in this country. Across 3,400 square miles of Louisiana and a bit of East Texas, two armies totaling some 460,000 men carried out a mock campaign that provided both training in large-scale operations and a chance to evaluate the Army's combat readiness. Along the line of the Red River from the Texas state line west of Shreveport down river to Alexandria, the Second Army, commanded by Lieutenant General Benjamin Lear, waited to defend against an invasion by the Third Army, commanded by Lieutenant General Walter Krueger, moving up from the Gulf Coast. Supervising and evaluating the maneuvers was Lieutenant General Leslie McNair, Chief of Staff of General Headquarters. Watching closely and making careful notes was the Chief of Staff, General George C. Marshall.

Ben Lear was a crusty old soldier who had started his career as a sergeant in the 1st Colorado Infantry during the Spanish-American War. He was a fine horseman and was a member of the American equestrian team that won the bronze medal at the 1912 Stockholm

Olympics. But on July 6 of this year, Lear acquired a nickname he could never shake. That Sunday afternoon Lear, in civilian clothes, was playing golf at a county club in Memphis when a convoy of soldiers from the 110th Quartermaster Company, 35th Infantry Division, drove by. The 35th was a National Guard Division with soldiers from Missouri, Kansas, and Nebraska. The men were returning from maneuvers in middle Tennessee. Lear, a strict disciplinarian, had already gained some notoriety by stating very publicly that the Army's field commanders had to improve and that eliminating unfit officers was more important than new equipment. Although he did not single anyone out, he probably had in mind Major General Ralph Truman, commander of the 35th, of whom Lear held a rather low opinion. Already two brigadier generals, one colonel, and several other officers from the 35th had been "reassigned" to other duties.

As the convoy drove past the country club, the soldiers began whistling and calling out, "Yoo-Hoo," and, "Hi, Baby!" to some attractive young women who were watching them. Lear, standing at the first tee, was appalled at what he heard. Even worse, as he was addressing the ball, some of the soldiers called out, "Fore!" and "Hey, buddy, do you need a caddy?" Lear put aside his club and ran over to the slow-moving convoy, stopping a command car and ordering the officers out. Despite his civilian clothes, the officers recognized him. Unfortunately, the enlisted men did not. Lear expressed his outrage in the kind of language he had learned as an old sergeant. The soldiers responded in kind, some even giving him the bird. Lear ordered the column to return to Camp Robinson, 145 miles away. When the troops arrived at sundown, they found orders awaiting them, directing them to turn around and drive back to the Memphis airport, where they bivouacked for the night. The next morning Lear assembled the whole company and gave them a thorough dressing down. He then told them to get a good night's rest and return to Camp Robinson the next day—on foot. He did not make them march the entire distance, just fifteen miles in five mile segments. But the day of the march was one of the hottest of the whole summer, with the heat reaching 97° and the humidity brutal. Not all the men made it. About a dozen passed out from the heat and stress, and many were upset that Lear had punished the innocent with the guilty. A letter-writing campaign was begun, demanding that Lear be sacked. There were fulminations on the floor of Congress, and there was even some worry that General Truman's cousin, Missouri Senator Harry S. Truman, might intervene. But the senator remained quiet, although his colleague, Senator Bennett C. Clark, called Lear a "superannuated old goat who ought to retire." The Army did ask Lear for an explanation, which was forthcoming. Lear's superiors regarded the incident as a simple case of enforcing discipline. The matter passed without further incident, but Lear was known ever after as General Yoo-Hoo Lear.

Ben Lear's assessment of the officers and men under his command was generally accurate, and Lear himself would not escape criticism. The United States Army in 1941 was totally unprepared for the task it would soon face. Low budget allocations during the '20s and '30s had helped ensure that few men of skill and ability found the Army an attractive career. For those who did stick it out during the lean years, funds for proper training were woefully inadequate. Congress and the American people had no clear idea of what they wanted the Army to accomplish, and consequently the Army had no clear sense of its own identity. Lack of integration of the combat arms reflected this uncertainty. Weapons systems, especially air and armor, had made great advances since the end of the World War; but no new combat doctrines had been developed to employ them effectively. Basic weapons like rifles and artillery were obsolete and in short supply. All these deficiencies would become painfully evident in the course of the General Headquarters maneuvers during the summer and autumn.

Lear's Second Army, based in Memphis, was the smaller force for the first stage of the Louisiana maneuvers, but Lear had most of the armor. His 130,000 men, designated the Red Army, were organized into a cavalry division (still on horseback), two regular infantry divisions, three National Guard divisions, and two armored divisions with 762 tanks. He was opposed by General Krueger's 330,000 troops, based in San Antonio. Designated the Blue Army, it consisted of a cavalry division and separate cavalry brigade, ten infantry divisions (mostly National Guardsmen, but with two divisions of regulars), and a tank group with 60 light tanks and attached anti-tank companies. Each army was also provided with 300 planes for reconnaissance and support.

A principal object of the Louisiana maneuvers was to evaluate the comparative effectiveness of a smaller but more mobile army (Red) against a larger but presumably slower army (Blue). Both forces were given similar offensive objectives: to move out aggressively, attack, and destroy the "enemy" force. At 5:30 A.M. on September 15, both armies started in motion, equally hampered by a tropical storm and torrential rain. Lear's Red Army crossed the Red River and moved south to meet the advancing Blue Army. Almost immediately it became clear that the principle of mobility would not be tested in the way the high command expected.

Lear, 62 years old, was a cautious leader who left his armor in reserve until he judged the time right for a decisive blow. Krueger, on the other hand, was much more aggressive and committed to a battle of movement. Two years younger than Lear and far tougher, Krueger, too, had worked his way up from the ranks, having enlisted as a private during the Spanish-American War. At the start of operations on the 15th, Krueger pushed his army forward toward the northeast, hoping to trap the Red Army with its back to the Red River where it could not take advantage of its mobility. Lear, as if reading Krueger's mind, concentrated his armor in the northwestern part of the maneuver area, hoping to get it in behind the left of Krueger's line and attack the Blue Army from the rear.

Despite the foul weather, Krueger made effective use of his air force for reconnaissance and interdiction. On the morning of the 15th Blue planes spotted Lear's armor to the northwest, and Krueger quickly divined Lear's intention. Instead of trying to close the line of the Red River, Krueger swung his forces to the northwest and seized high ground that Lear's tanks would need to maneuver. For two days the armies fought, with the Blue Army breaking through Lear's lines to reach the Red River at Colfax. On the 18th the Red Army finally launched its expected tank offensive, but the attack ground to a halt when a Blue Army cavalry raid captured all of the Red Army's gasoline supplies. Lear was thrown further off balance when a squad of Blue soldiers captured his headquarters staff in a nighttime raid. A staff officer told the men they had gone too far, but one of the soldiers reportedly replied, "Nuts to that, General. This is war." A maneuvers umpire agreed with the officer and disqualified the raid. The first phase of the exercise ended on the 19th with Lear's Red Army in full retreat.

The exercise resumed on September 24 after the 2nd Armored Division under Major General George S. Patton had been transferred to Krueger's Blue Army for further practice in offensive operations. Now the missions of the two armies were changed. The Blue Army objective was to capture Shreveport, while the Red Army was expected to defend the city by delaying the Blue Army's advance until (imaginary) reinforcements arrived on the 30th. Lear took his orders so literally that he decided not to fight at all if he could help it. He hoped simply to stall for time until his "reinforcements" could arrive. General McNair became so frustrated with Lear's unwillingness to fight that he finally sent him an order informing him that the "reinforcements" would not arrive and he should resist the Blue advance more aggressively. The order had little effect. McNair ended the maneuvers on September 28 with the Red Army just holding on to its positions.

A number of news correspondents accompanied the armies through the maneuvers, and their reports kept the country informed about what was happening. The Army's public relations radio staff assisted the reporters, and even got into the battle in its own way. The Red Army radio staff "captured" radio station KALB in Alexandria and held it for seven hours. During that time they kept the civilian broadcasts going normally, but they included false traffic reports that disrupted the movements of the Blue Army. Finally the Blue Army realized what was happening and "recaptured" the station.

The reporters were greatly assisted by Lieutenant Colonel Dwight D. Eisenhower, Third Army Chief of Staff, who answered their questions freely and urged them to let the country know the real state of Army preparedness. The newsmen were blunt in their assessments. Several were veteran European correspondents who had seen the

German armies in action. They rated the Germans superior in equipment, leadership, and battle technique. Problems with morale, leadership, and equipment were especially serious. Many soldiers had to carry dummy weapons. For those who had real weapons, there was not enough ammunition to give realistic live-fire experiences. Of equal concern was the shortage of motorized transport for the troops. General McNair's critique of the maneuvers was also generally negative, especially regarding combat leadership. Important lessons had been learned, but many officers were over age, slow, and unsuited to combat. Over the next few months review boards went through the officer corps and recommended many retirements and replacements. One of the first generals replaced was General Truman, 61, who was relieved of his command in October. A certain amount of political noise was heard in Washington, but Lear and Marshall stood firm.

In addition to weeding out unfit officers, the Army was looking for younger men with potential for service at a higher level. Several officers showed exceptional ability in the Louisiana maneuvers. For many years General Marshall had kept a little black notebook in which he recorded the names of officers who showed promise of future excellence. One he especially noted was Colonel Eisenhower. Krueger freely gave Eisenhower credit for the planning that had led to the Blue Army's success, and nine days later Eisenhower was promoted to brigadier general. Another notable but erratic officer marked for distinction was Major General Patton. Patton had been largely responsible for what success the Red Army achieved in the first phase, and he also contributed significantly to the Blue Army's success in the second phase. Others who performed exceptionally well were Brigadier General Mark Clark, deputy director of the maneuvers, and Colonel J. Lawton Collins, Chief of Staff of VII Corps.

Limits on available transportation precluded army-level exercises in the West, but corps-level maneuvers could be held. In California in June the III Corps (Red Force) under Major General Walter Wilson "attacked" northward from its base in Los Angeles against the IX Corps (Blue Force) under Major General Kenyon Joyce, which was "defending" San Francisco. These exercises were conducted at the Hunter Liggett military reservation south of Monterey. Major General Joseph Stilwell, commanding the 7th Division (Red) took the initiative by launching a surprise night attack, but he was driven back by a Blue force that outnumbered him two to one. Although the Blue Force "won the war," Stillwell's initiative and daring earned him promotion to command of III Corps when Wilson was transferred. In August the maneuvers were resumed at Ft. Lewis, Washington, in an exercise designed to test the command structure at corps level. Both Chief of Staff Marshall and Secretary of War Stimson were present as observers.

The final Army maneuvers of 1941 were conducted in November along the North Carolina-South Carolina border between the Catawba and Pee Dee Rivers. The first phase of the exercise was again staged to test the strength of a light but highly mobile force against a larger but much slower army. The Blue Army, with 195,000 men in three corps, was under the command of Lieutenant General Hugh Drum, an experienced but old-fashioned officer who held command of the First Army in New York. Opposing him was IV Corps, 100,000 men, under Major General Oscar Griswold, an able but inexperienced commander. Griswold had never held corps command before and had taken over IV Corps just the previous month. Both forces had orders to undertake offensive operations, and each commander devised plans to exploit the special strengths of his command. Griswold planned a rapid attack all the way to his enemy's starting point on the Pee Dee. Drum planned a slow, methodical advance intended to grind down his smaller opponent. In spite of the disparity in numbers, Drum was caught off guard by Griswold's rapid advance; but he recovered quickly. After initial successes, Griswold's inexperience began to show. His command structure unraveled and he lost effective control of many of his units. When the first phase ended, IV Corps was in full retreat and at risk of total "destruction."

After three days of rest and realignment, the two forces resumed the maneuvers but with new objectives. Drum's Blue Army was to attack southward and seize the town of Camden. Griswold's assignment was simply to hold the town as a bridgehead over the river.

Again Drum moved ponderously with his superior force, and again Griswold used his mobility to keep his opponent off balance. This time Griswold exercised much better control over his forces and might well have driven the Blue Army back into North Carolina had not a raiding force captured a copy of Griswold's battle plans and given them to Drum. The maneuver ended with Griswold in retreat, but still holding the Blue Army well away from its objective.

Once again the Army conducted extensive critiques of the exercise, and once again special attention was paid to the effectiveness of the officers in command. Although Griswold had made a number of mistakes, as might be expected of a new commander, he had nevertheless shown aggressiveness, imagination, and ability to learn quickly. Drum, on the other hand, had "won" the battle; but he was ponderously slow and unimaginative in employing his forces. At the end of the year he was offered a position as Chief of Staff to Chiang Kai-shek in China, but he turned it down. He remained at a desk job in New York until he reached mandatory retirement age two years later.

The army that engaged in the fall maneuvers was far different from the army that was needed to win a war, but it was also far different from the army that had existed just two years earlier. In 1939 the United States Army numbered only 188,565 of all ranks. It was rated 17th in the world, just behind Rumania. Adding the National Guard and Organized Reserves brought America's total strength to something over 400,000 men, but that number was deceiving. Many National Guard units were primarily social organizations rather than fighting forces. Their officers held rank by virtue of their political connections rather than any military ability, as the fall maneuvers so clearly revealed. Consequently, advancement opportunities for competent officers were severely limited. Almost one quarter of all first lieutenants in the National Guard were over 40 years old. In South Carolina the post of Adjutant General, the commander of the state's Guard, was an elective office; and all his staff officers were appointed by the governor. In Virginia, when the 176th Infantry was called up for its year of federal service, the 1st Battalion held a special ceremony. This battalion was the venerable Richmond Light Infantry Blues, first organized in 1789. In their dress blue uniforms with white facings, ornate shakos with white feather plumes, and heavy gold epaulets for the officers, the Blues held a final formal muster, marching to St. Paul's Church for a service before their closing dinner. The officers gathered around their punch bowl for a last toast and retired to the smoking room for pleasant social conversation. A few days later they were in Army khaki at Ft. Meade, Maryland, beginning what they thought would be just a year's service.

Nor should it be thought that only southern Guard units maintained the active social life. The 207th Infantry from New York (formerly the 7th New York Infantry of Civil War fame) was called into federal service during the year and was assigned to Camp Stewart outside Savannah, Georgia. Many of the soldiers brought formal letters of introduction to socially prominent residents of Savannah, and soon the New Yorkers were being hospitably integrated into Savannah society. Even the Regular Army had its share of officers who were more devoted to the traditions of the past than to the needs of modern warfare. Major General John Herr, Chief of Cavalry, was so enamored of the glorious image of the cavalry charge that early in the year he was able, with a completely straight face, to testify before a congressional committee that four mounted troopers spaced 100 yards apart could charge half a mile across an open field and destroy a machine gun emplacement without getting a scratch on them.

Many of the reserve officers called to active duty were graduates of the country's eight military colleges. (The eight were Texas A&M, Virginia Military Institute, Virginia Polytechnic Institute, Pennsylvania Military College, Norwich University, North Georgia College, Clemson University, and the Citadel.) With four years of formal military training behind them, these men generally made good officers once they had progressed through their branch schools. The R.O.T.C. cadets who graduated this year all expected to be called to active duty upon graduation, even those whose other career plans were well set. Notable among them was John Kimbrough of Texas A&M. Kimbrough was an All-American fullback who had just signed a $37,500 contract to play for the New York Yankees of the American

Professional Football League when he learned that the Army planned to exercise its first claim on his services.

One of the criticisms leveled at the Army in 1941 was the extent to which it remained segregated, underutilizing the talents of capable African Americans. Although the Army had traditionally maintained a recruiting goal of 10 percent African Americans, the rapid expansion of the service had failed to maintain that rate. Of over 600,000 men in uniform at the beginning of the year, only 19,000 were black. In the entire Regular Army there were only two black officers, Brigadier General Benjamin O. Davis and his son, Captain Benjamin O. Davis, Jr. The elder Davis had just become a general officer the previous fall, concurrent with his assignment to command the 4th Cavalry Brigade at Ft. Riley, Kansas. The decision to promote him to brigadier general just before the 1940 election was widely regarded as a political move to attract black votes; but there was also general recognition that he did, in fact, deserve the promotion. The younger Davis began 1941 as an aide to his father at Ft. Riley, but a few weeks later he was released from duty with the cavalry and was reassigned to Tuskegee Army Air Field for pilot training. Davis had applied for assignment to the Air Corps upon graduation from West Point in 1936, but the Army was fearful of the reaction of white ground crew having to take orders from a black officer. Instead he was assigned to the infantry and served there until his father requested his services as aide.

Typical of the waste of black talent was Master Sergeant Hansen Outley of the 349th Field Artillery Regiment. Outley enlisted in the 9th Cavalry in 1914 and served in France and the Philippines. In 1925, at the request of the State Department, he was released from active duty and sent to Liberia, where he served as Chief of Staff of the Liberian Frontier Force, as the small Liberian Army was known. After six years in command of the L.F.F., he returned to active duty with the U. S. Army at his old rank of sergeant. The Army had no place for him as a commissioned officer. Outley was still serving as a master sergeant at Ft. Sill, Oklahoma, when he died in an auto accident on June 20, 1941.

The need for trained manpower, combined with increasing political pressure from African Americans, resulted in some small changes. In January Robert Patterson, Under-Secretary of War, announced the formation of an all-black pursuit squadron with thirty-three pilots, a 400-man ground crew, and twenty-seven planes. The 99th Pursuit Squadron was activated at Chanute Field in Illinois in March and began training at Tuskegee Institute in Alabama in June. Reviving Captain Davis's earlier application for assignment to the Air Corps, the War Department relieved him of duty as aide to his father and sent him to Tuskegee for training as a fighter pilot. Upon completion of training, Captain Davis was placed in command of the squadron, the first of the famed Tuskegee Airmen.

Among ground troops there was a substantial increase in the number of black soldiers during the year, but only a small increase in the number of officers. By the time the Louisiana maneuvers began in September, over 74,000 African Americans were serving in the Army, but only 337 were officers. During those maneuvers there were numerous incidents of racial discrimination and even violence that the Army tried to keep quiet. The black press published the reports from the field, but white reporters took little notice. Nevertheless, the Army was beginning to take small, slow, halting steps to open up more opportunities for African Amercans. Not so the Navy and Marine Corps. Despite their manpower needs, at the time of Pearl Harbor the Navy was accepting African Americans only as mess stewards. The Marines were not accepting them at all.

By July the Army had increased its size to 1,460,998, but this increase brought a new set of problems. Equipment shortages plagued all parts of the Army. Congress had been appropriating funds to remedy the deficiencies, but repairing years of neglect took time. In 1940 the Army had received its new .30-caliber Garand rifles at the rate of 6,000 a month. By mid-1941 the delivery rate had increased to 22,500 a month, but even that was not enough to equip all of the soldiers entering the service. To improve soldiers' safety, the new M1 "steel pot" helmet was adopted for use in 1941. But soldiers went into action in the fall maneuvers still wearing the old 1917 "doughboy helmet," if, indeed, they had helmets at all. So embarrassing was the shortage of armored vehicles that the Army sometimes had to use trucks with the word "TANK" painted on the sides to represent that weapon in maneuvers. Wooden frames nailed together to look like machine guns had to stand in for the real things. Umpires would score their effectiveness based on how well their crews positioned and aimed them at their supposed targets. As for heavier weapons, the principal field piece was the 75-mm gun, which had been obsolete since the end of World War I. The Army did not have enough anti-aircraft guns to defend a single American city.

Yet another problem area was the availability of training facilities, where construction was proceeding at a frantic pace. At Ft. Bragg in North Carolina, the peak period of construction saw the completion of a new building every thirty-two minutes. The Army regarded these new structures as temporary expedients to meet the emergency. So in order to maintain the needed rate of construction, the Army planned to leave the buildings unpainted. That was the plan, at least, until Eleanor Roosevelt paid a visit. Always concerned with morale, the First Lady put enough pressure on the War Department to get a coat of paint added to the construction schedule.

The rapid pace of expansion placed huge strains on the communities nearest the new or enlarged bases. Housing shortages were common. Public sewer systems were pushed to the point of failure. Traffic overloaded the outdated road system. Even when the federal government tried to provide relief funds for impacted areas, bureaucratic complications got in the way. There were serious problems of waste and mismanagement. Contractors and suppliers were inflating prices, and government efforts to bring prices under control were only occasionally successful. In January Leon Henderson, Director of the Office of Production Management, released a letter suggesting that the president direct the Army to pay no more than $25 for a thousand board feet of number 2 southern pine and to enter lumber yards and seize the wood if the suppliers refused to accept the price. With the publication of the letter, prices for pine suddenly dropped. Such successful intervention was rare enough to be newsworthy.

Waste and profiteering at Ft. Leonard Wood in Missouri brought letters of complaint to the state's junior senator, Harry S. Truman. The building contractor had no experience in construction, costly supplies were being neglected and ruined, and men were being paid to stand around and do nothing. Truman decided to look into matters himself, and early in the year he embarked on an automobile tour of Army bases from Florida to Michigan, covering perhaps 10,000 miles. What he found appalled him. The complaints at Ft. Leonard Wood were all too valid, and they were repeated at bases throughout the country. On his return to Washington, Truman called the White House for an appointment to discuss the creation of a Senate Special Committee to investigate the National Defense Program. Roosevelt's reaction was typical of the president's style. He was cheerful and reacted positively to Truman's idea, but he never actually came out and endorsed it. Truman went ahead on his own, and on February 10 he introduced a resolution creating the committee. Roosevelt decided that an investigation would be safe in Truman's friendly hands, especially if the committee had a very small budget. The one thing the president wanted to avoid was having a congressional committee actively interfere with defense efforts, a concern that Truman fully shared.

On March 1 the Senate unanimously approved Truman's resolution, but it appropriated only $15,000 to support the investigation. Truman got to work immediately, knowing that if he produced results, more funding would follow. Hearings began on April 15, with testimony from senior officers and officials, including Chief of Staff Marshall and Secretary of War Stimson. The following week the committee toured Ft. Meade, Maryland, and other nearby bases to see the problems for themselves. Returning to Washington, the senators learned that after the First World War, the Army had made a special study of the problems and principles of camp construction. Asking to see the study, they learned that it had been lost. No one knew where it was.

From the start Truman made it clear that his object was not to seek publicity or to damage his opponents. All he wanted to do was improve defense production. In August the Committee issued its first report, a modest (by government standards) 98-page document detailing the waste and inefficiency in the Army's construction program. There were three principal findings. First, the Committee found that no adequate plans had been drawn up for the camps. As a consequence, waste and duplication of effort cost the government at least $100,000,000 out of the $828,000,000 spent. As Senator Truman put it, "We used that $100,000,000 figure because the Army admitted that much. It will run two and a half times that much, easily." In the second place, the Committee found numerous examples of poor judgment and outright misinformation. For example, Camp Davis, near Wilmington, North Carolina, was laid out without a proper site survey. As a result, contractors discovered that they were expected to build an Army base in a swamp. Third, the Committee found numerous examples of bad management, many of which seemed designed to increase contractors' profits. For example, instead of purchasing trucks and necessary machinery, the Army rented them at excessive cost.

The Committee's overall evaluation was scathing: "There were very few officers in the Quartermaster Corps or in the engineering corps who were at all fitted to cope with the problems involved in the camp-construction program." The committee recommended that construction be taken away from the Quartermasters and handed over to a totally new organization. The Army's first reaction was predictably defensive. Major General Edmund Gregory, Quartermaster General, responded testily, "It is axiomatic that you can't save time and money at the same time." He attributed the cost overruns to the Army's desire for speedy construction. But under Truman's intense scrutiny, Army practices began to improve; and even his enemies eventually conceded that the committee's suggested reforms saved the Army at least $250,000,000.

One officer especially annoyed at the committee's probing was Brigadier General Brehon B. Somervell, appointed in December 1940 to take over the floundering construction program. Somervell brought his administrative skills to bear on Army camp construction, removing officers who were not up to their jobs and driving his staff relentlessly. The improvement in the pace of construction during the first months of 1941 was largely due to his forceful leadership. Somervell also employed all of the charm and political skill for which he was famous. He cajoled Congress into increasing his inadequate budget, and he unhesitatingly used his friendship with Harry Hopkins to win White House support.

But Somervell soon found that the senator from Missouri was not susceptible to his charm. Truman's probing questions could not be swept aside, and Somervell began to reveal the other side of his personality, an explosive temper. One day early in the year, his aide Major Gar Davidson was shocked to hear the general conclude a telephone conversation with Truman by saying, "Mr. Senator, as far as I'm concerned you can go piss up a rope." Davidson was convinced that remark was what drove Truman to create his investigating committee.

Regardless of his relations with Truman, early in the summer Somervell was handed a project that would test all his skills as an engineer, an administrator, and a politician. When Henry Stimson was appointed secretary of war in 1940, the War Department's offices were scattered through twenty-three different buildings all over Washington. Most officials, including the secretary, were in the Munitions Building, one of a group of "temporary" office buildings erected quickly during World War I. A new War Department building had been constructed at 21st and C Streets, but Secretary Stimson inspected it in April and found it totally inadequate. Even with the new building, the Army would still be short of office space by about a million square feet. Meeting the Army's space needs with another building in downtown Washington would cause unimaginable traffic jams. The Army had a different solution in mind.

Across the Potomac River in Arlington was a site known as Arlington Farm, on the edge of Arlington National Cemetery. The War Department had recently acquired the site from the Agriculture Department, which had once run an experimental farm there. The Army asked Congress for $6,500,000 to build four temporary office buildings on the site. The request went to a subcommittee of the House Appropriations Committee, chaired by Representative Clifton Woodrum of Virginia. Woodrum was a fiscal conservative except when money could be directed to Virginia. At the initial hearing on Thursday, July 17, Woodrum objected to the Army's piecemeal approach to its space needs and asked Brigadier General Eugene Reybold to come up with a comprehensive solution. Reybold promised to have something ready the following Tuesday. Returning to his office, Reybold summoned Somervell and told him to have plans for a new building ready by Monday morning.

Somervell gathered his team of architects and engineers. It was clear that Arlington Farm was not just suitable; it was practically the only site in the Washington area that would work. Someone suggested that a pentagonal building would fit into an area bounded by five roads that crossed the property. Working through the weekend, Somervell's men delivered the preliminary plans and an aerial view of the proposed building right on schedule. They projected a building of 5,000,000 square feet and a construction cost of $7.00 a square foot, totaling $35,000,000, with an additional million to come later for the parking lot. On Monday Somervell presented the plans to Reybold, General Marshall, Asstant Secretary Patterson, and Secretary Stimson, securing approval all along the line. Tuesday morning, before the hearing, Somervell went over the plans with Woodrum and secured his support. The formal hearing went well, with Somervell promising to get started on the building within two weeks and to finish it within a year, with the first sections ready for occupancy within six months. The president approved the project at his Cabinet meeting on July 24th.

Then things began to come apart. Woodrum attached the $35,000,000 as a rider to an $8 billion military appropriations bill, a technical violation of House Rules. The sleight of hand was spotted by Representative Merlin Hull, Progressive of Wisconsin, who objected on a point of order. The entire appropriations bill was sent back to the Rules Committee for reconsideration. More important, the press got wind of the largest appropriation ever made for a single office building. Although the House Rules Committee quickly agreed to waive the rules and let the funds to be attached to the appropriations bill, the newspapers had a field day. Hull led a fight on the House floor, but he and his allies failed three times to delete the expenditure. The

House approved the whole bill with only eleven nays, and the bill went to the Senate.

In the Senate the project benefitted by being sent to the Appropriations Committee, chaired by the venerable Senator Carter Glass of Virginia. Glass was another fiscal conservative and implacable opponent of the New Deal—unless, of course, the Commonwealth of Virginia stood to benefit. Passage of the bill seemed assured until another storm arose, this time over the building's size and location. The Arlington Farm site lay at the foot of the hill on which stood the Custis-Lee Mansion, former home of Robert E. Lee and the visual heart of Arlington Cemetery. Placing a 5,000,000-square-foot building squarely in the sight line between the Mansion and the Capitol was unthinkable to many people. It was especially unthinkable to Gilmore Clarke, famous landscape architect and Chairman of the Commission of Fine Arts, which was supposed to guide architectural development in Washington. It was also unthinkable to Frederic Delano, Chairman of the National Capital Park and Planning Commission and, just incidentally, President Roosevelt's uncle. He is said to have muttered about his nephew, "My God, what will that boy do next?" Clarke and Delano had not been consulted, and both were vociferous in opposing the new building.

The Appropriations Committee hearings were heated, and the newspapers covered them gleefully. The president, having some second thoughts, even suggested that the size of the building be cut in half to reduce the impact. Glass, however, was having none of it. Virginia was going to get a $35,000,000 construction project, and the committee duly reported the bill favorably. The fight on the Senate floor was tougher, with several amendments beaten back by narrow votes. Finally, however, H.R. 5412 passed the Senate and went to the president for signature. Somervell already had his architects and contractors at work, awaiting only final approval. The War Department was going to get its new pentagonal headquarters on the Arlington Farm site.

Or so it seemed.

The Senate had debated the military appropriations bill while the president was at the Arcadia Conference in Newfoundland (Chapter 6). When he returned to Washington and saw the bill on his desk, he was horrified. It was bad enough that the Senate had ignored his suggestion to halve the size of the building. Even more, Uncle Fred Delano convinced his nephew that the Arlington Farm site would create a permanent ugly blight on the Washington landscape. Roosevelt was particularly sensitive to such a remark. During World War I, when he was Assistant Secretary of the Navy, F.D.R. had been responsible for construction of the "temporary" office buildings along the mall. He said his original intention was to make them so ugly (they truly were) that they would be torn down right after the war. Instead, they were so well built that they were still standing and badly needed by the services. Roosevelt called them "a crime for which I should be kept out of heaven." At his first press conference after his return, the president was asked about the new War Department building. He replied that he still thought the building was too big and he strongly opposed the location.

The next day Somervell met with Roosevelt to try to salvage his plan. Roosevelt seemed willing to bend on the size of the building, but not on the site. He told Somervell that he preferred that the building be placed on a site known as Hell's Bottom, about three quarters of a mile south of Arlington Farm. This site was next to the recently closed Washington-Hoover Airport. Somervell insisted that the ground at Hell's Bottom was unsuitable for the foundations for such a large building, but Roosevelt was unmoved. He directed Somervell to finish the plans so he could examine them. At a press conference on August 25, the president made it clear he thought a building of 2.25 million square feet would be suitable and it should be located at Hell's Bottom, even though the appropriations bill specified Arlington Farm. In Roosevelt's view, if any part of the project extended onto the Arlington Farm site, the language of the bill would be satisfied. The press, most of whom disliked the idea of putting a big office building next to Arlington Cemetery, supported the president's decision.

Roosevelt may have considered the matter settled, but Somervell kept fighting. Two days later he met at the White House to go over the plans with the president and Fred Delano. Somervell continued to insist on the full 5,000,000 square feet and on the Arlington Farm site. Roosevelt told the two men to work out their differences. After extended negotiations, they agreed on language each thought he could interpret to support his own view. After further intervention by the president, the matter was settled. The Army would get the building it wanted, but it would be located on the site chosen by the president.

Somervell's staff began site preparation immediately and told the architects to prepare of construction drawings. Construction finally began on September 11. There was no formal ground-breaking ceremony. The general contractor, John McShain, Inc., of Philadelphia, simply got to work. With the politics out of the way and with Brehon Somervell and Leslie Groves, his deputy, driving the project, progress was rapid. Men worked 48-hour weeks, happy for the overtime pay. McShain established a food service so the men would not have to leave the work site for meals. Construction went on seven days a week. At times the work was begun before even basic architectural decisions had been made. Foundation work was well under way before a decision was reached on whether the walls would be brick, concrete, or limestone. (The president again made the final decision, choosing concrete, but with the exterior walls faced with limestone.)

After persistent questioning by the press, Somervell issued a release giving the basics of the Pentagon. The five exterior walls were 921 feet on a side. There were five concentric rings, joined by corridors, surrounding a six-acre central courtyard. The whole building would be air conditioned, a remarkable achievement for the time. In addition to offices it would have shops, a cafeteria, and even an underground bus terminal. To mislead critics who thought the building too large, it was described as having three stories plus a basement. The deception was Somervell's idea. The so-called basement was in fact the first floor. There were also two more floors below ground, not mentioned in the press release. The price tag, $31.1 million for direct construction costs alone, shocked the reporters who received the information. When the price appeared in the papers, it became clear the building had not been reduced in size as Roosevelt had said. The Army was getting the headquarters building it wanted.

The excitement surrounding the construction of the Pentagon made for high morale among the officers, contractors, and civilian workers involved. Elsewhere, however, the Army was finding that keeping up morale in a rapidly expanding citizen army was very different from the task of sustaining a small, professional force. Reports surfaced of serious problems among National Guardsmen and draftees who had been called up for their year of training, possibly to be extended to eighteen months. In the summer *Life* magazine sent a reporter to interview National Guardsmen in an unidentified division at an unnamed Army base in the South. What he reported was worse than anyone had feared. The number one complaint among soldiers was uncertainty as to their future. With the War Department asking for an extension of their term of service and with strong opposition being voiced in Congress, the men could not make reasonable plans for their civilian lives. Graffiti on Army bases made the point clearly. Virtually every latrine had OHIO scrawled on its walls, an acronym for "Over the Hill In October." Going "over the hill" was traditional soldier slang for desertion. For draftees, the one-year term of military service would begin to expire in October. The graffiti were intended as a warning that the men had no intention of remaining in uniform, extension or no extension.

Uncertainty over the term of service was by no means the only complaint voiced by the soldiers. These men expected to be trained to defend their country, and they had nothing but contempt for the quality of training they received. They told the visiting reporters quite bluntly that their officers just did not know their jobs. Regular Army officers were widely respected; but 85 percent of the training officers were members of the Guard or reserves, and they themselves had never been trained properly. Neglect of the Army through the '20s and '30s had left too few professionals to do the training that now was needed. *Life* reported that the frustrated soldiers had contributed a new word to the English language, "snasu," an acronym for "Situation normal: all screwed up." The word was actually "snafu," but the magazine chose not to print this more obscene version, nor its companion "fubar" ("beyond all recognition"). These complaints of incompetence went far beyond the usual soldier gripes about Army routine, and many men were willing to speak their minds freely.

One complaint that echoed through all ranks was discrimination against men in uniform. This discrimination seemed stronger in the South than elsewhere. New York District Attorney Thomas Dewey, touring military bases in the South, reported seeing signs that said, "SOLDIERS AND DOGS KEEP OUT," and "COFFEE 5¢ SOLDIERS' COFFEE 10¢." While social life could be very pleasant for well-connected National Guardsmen, most soldiers had a strong sense that they were not welcome in the towns near Army bases. This rejection came partly from a feeling in many small towns that they were being overwhelmed by a flood of new soldiers. The feeling was also in part a holdover from the nation's turning its back on the Army and Navy after the World War. The latent hostility toward all things military still persisted, even as the country came to recognize the dangers posed by the European conflict and the need for improved defense. The attitude was so strong that even in Washington, military personnel at the War Department had long been instructed to wear civilian clothes rather than uniforms to work. The department did not want an appearance of militarism to offend civilian sensibilities. When the order was reversed immediately after Pearl Harbor, the variety of obsolete uniforms appearing in Washington was truly remarkable. Many portly officers found they no longer fitted into the uniforms of their slender youth.

As might be expected, the quality of Army food was a constant source of gripes, but here the Army encountered a surprising twist. America in 1941 was marked by a provincialism that astonished those whose perspective was national. The Quartermaster Corps, led by Regular Army officers, tried to provide the best food it could from all over the country. But Southern soldiers, who had no experience of the North, let alone of northern food, did not like Boston baked beans and found pure maple syrup a distasteful substitute for molasses. Northern soldiers, on the other hand, had trouble understanding why anyone would want to eat hominy grits or corn bread, let alone why Louisianans would complain about not having chicory in their coffee. Gradually small improvements appeared, though significant internal changes did not come until after Pearl Harbor.

One of the most important contributions to improved morale came from outside the military. In October of 1940, Frank Weil of the National Jewish Welfare Board called a meeting in New York with representatives of the major organizations that had worked together to support troop morale during World War I. Six organizations, the N.J.W.B., the Y.M.C.A., the Y.W.C.A., National Catholic Community Service, the Salvation Army, and the Traveler's Aid Association, organized the United Service Organizations for National Defense. The name was later shortened by dropping "for National Defense," but everyone knew it as simply the U.S.O. Walter Hoving, a director of the Salvation Army, agreed to serve as the U.S.O.'s first president. The organization was incorporated in New York on February 4 and immediately began a fundraising campaign headed by District Attorney Thomas E. Dewey. The drive brought in more than $16,000,000 in the first year. Almost at once the U.S.O. began opening local centers wherever it could. Many churches provided facilities, but barns, museums, and railroad sleeping cars were pressed into service when needed. The first government-built facility opened in November at Ft. Bragg in North Carolina, but by that time local U.S.O.s were operating near Army and Navy bases all across the country, with the largest concentration in Hawaii. Services included meals (better than the mess hall), coffee and doughnuts, recreation and entertainment, quiet spaces for reading and writing, and even such basics as sewing on buttons and insignia.

Very early in its existence, the U.S.O. began what would become one of its most famous services, traveling entertainment programs. The effort started in May, when Bob Hope broadcast his regular radio program from March Field in California, performing in front of a live audience of airmen. Programs expanded quickly, and the first overseas tour left for the Caribbean on October 30. From the very first the U.S.O. had great success in recruiting celebrities as volunteers. Besides Bob Hope, one of the best known early supporters was Rosemary LaPlanche of Los Angeles, Miss America of 1941. LaPlanche was a controversial Miss America. She had been First Runner-Up in 1940, and many participants thought the experience had given her an unfair advantage. As a result of the controversy, the contest rules were changed the following year to allow contestants to participate only once. Apparently lost in the controversy was the fact that LaPlanche was technically ineligible. She was still two months shy of eighteen when she went to Atlantic City. Nevertheless, she served well during her year, traveling widely for the U.S.O. and taking part in Defense Bond rallies, some of which sold $50,000 worth of bonds in a single day.

While the U.S.O. was working to improve morale, the Army and Navy were increasing their expansion efforts, including the development of new combat arms and tactics. Under the leadership of generals like Adna Chaffee (who died of cancer in August), Charles L. Scott, and George S. Patton, Jr., the Army was already learning to take full advantage of the armored corps. At the Infantry School at Ft. Benning, the Army was also expanding its fledgling airborne program. The success of the German paratroopers in capturing Crete had prompted the Army to create the First Provisional Parachute Group, which provided paratroopers in the Louisiana maneuvers. The publicity generated by the glamorous new program brought hundreds of volunteers streaming into Ft. Benning, putting a severe strain on the post's resources. Congress had been generous with appropriations as the war danger became more apparent. But the one thing Congress could not appropriate was time, time to design new weapons, time to manufacture and distribute equipment, time to train the soldiers.

Fortunately, the U.S. Navy had started on rearmament sooner than the Army. Shipbuilding is a slow process. The U.S.S. *North Carolina* was authorized in 1936, but its keel was not laid until October 1937. Because it was the Navy's first modern battleship and the first to use welded construction, the designers faced a number of special challenges. It was thirty-one months before it could be launched and an added ten months of fitting out before it could be commissioned. On April 9, 1941, the Navy finally received its first new battleship since

1923, with grand ceremonies in New York. Sea trials in the Caribbean followed, and the *North Carolina* was still in the Atlantic at the time of Pearl Harbor. With the design problems worked out, *North Carolina's* sister ship, the U.S.S. *Washington*, was built more quickly and was commissioned just a month later, on May 15. Three more battleships, the *South Dakota*, the *Indiana*, and the *Massachusetts*, had been laid down in 1939 and were launched during 1941.

Other ships were being added to the fleet as well. At the beginning of the year the Navy had 80 submarines under construction to add to the 105 already in service, more than any other country except Germany and Russia. The numbers were deceiving, however. Of those 105, only 37 were less than thirteen years old. The rest were already obsolete. The Navy also took delivery of four new aircraft carriers, the *Yorktown* (1937), *Enterprise* (1938), *Wasp* (1940), and *Hornet* (1941). These were all that the United States was allowed under the terms of the Washington Naval Treaty of 1922. But with the lapse of naval agreements after the outbreak of the war in 1939, Congress recognized the need for a rapid expansion of the Navy's capabilities. The Two-Ocean Navy Act of 1940 had included authorization for eighteen new aircraft carriers and seven new battleships, as well as numerous cruisers, destroyers, and other vessels, plus 15,000 aircraft.

In April Navy Secretary Frank Knox (assisted in the writing by Fletcher Pratt) published in the *Saturday Evening Post* an effective and remarkably prescient essay on the current state and future needs of the Navy. His analysis of the battleship fleet took note of "the increasing range and accuracy of the torpedo, [and] the fact that it may come in at any moment from an airplane." He noted that the new battleships being built were provided with heavy deck armor and effective anti-aircraft guns, and he correctly observed that "no armor as thick as that borne by our battleships and heavy cruisers has yet been penetrated by an airplane bomb." "But in the meantime," he continued, "there is the problem of the older ships, which need dive-bomber defense, too, at a time when all our production facilities on the new guns are wanted for the new ships."

With the number of new ships being launched under the Two-Ocean Navy Act, the Navy was also short of properly trained manpower.

Traditional training programs had produced a naval force second to none, but the old instructional methods took too much time and could not produce enough skilled sailors to man the ships being built. In addition to intensified recruitment, the Navy needed a way to speed up training without sacrificing quality. Finally, the Navy needed additional bases overseas in order to protect the country effectively. Knox asserted confidently that the Navy could defeat any attack on the Continental United States, but he conceded that it lacked the bases needed for a more extended reach. Subsequent events proved Knox to be substantially correct. The attack on Pearl Harbor in December especially validated his concerns about the vulnerability of older battleships.

The nation's maritime concerns were by no means limited to naval vessels. Back in 1936 the U.S. Maritime Commission had been created to help rebuild the American shipping industry. At that time more than 90 percent of American merchant ships were at least twenty years old. The Maritime Commission was empowered to make grants to shipping companies for the construction of new ships. It even had the authority to build ships on its own account and lease them to shipping firms. Its regulatory powers controlled the whole U.S. shipping industry. After the outbreak of the war in Europe, and especially after the fall of France, German submarines and surface raiders began to decimate British shipping, threatening to strangle Britain by cutting off its imports of food and other necessities. Britain was losing more tonnage than its shipyards could replace, and it became clear that Britain needed to look elsewhere for merchant vessels. Elsewhere meant the United States and, to a lesser extent, Canada.

In 1940, despite the tremendous pressures placed on American shipyards by naval rearmament and the rebuilding of the shipping industry, the Maritime Commission granted permission to the British Purchasing Commission to place orders with American companies for sixty merchant ships of a standardized design. The orders went to several shipbuilding consortia coordinated by industrialist Henry J. Kaiser. Kaiser already had experience assembling consortia to carry out large projects beyond the capabilities of any individual firm, projects like the Boulder Dam or the San Francisco-Oakland Bay Bridge.

Most of the shipbuilding work was to be done on the West Coast, where Kaiser's interests were concentrated.

The first ship in the British order, the *Ocean Vanguard*, was laid down at the Permanente Metals shipyard in Richmond, California, in April of 1941, less than four months after the contract was signed. By that time the Lend-Lease Act had been signed into law, and it had become clear that shipments to Britain would require a substantial and rapid expansion of the American merchant fleet. Heretofore the Maritime Commission had concentrated on building custom-designed, fast, strong, and long-lasting merchant ships. Now they would have to change over to mass production of standardized vessels that might not be as sturdy or as fast, but that could carry goods across the ocean in huge quantities. The result was the Liberty Ship, described thus in a Congressional report:

> It is slow and seaworthy and has the longevity of a modern steel ship, but for the demands of normal commerce in foreign trade it would not compete in speed, equipment and general serviceability with up-to-date cargo vessels. The design is the best that can be devised for an emergency product to be quickly, cheaply, and simply built. They will be constructed for the emergency and whether they have any utility afterward will have to be determined then.

Work on the Liberty Ships got under way very quickly. The greatest problem was constructing new shipyards. Existing facilities were already working at full capacity. Initial contracts were awarded to Oregon Shipbuilding Corporation, a Kaiser subsidiary in Portland, and to Bethlehem-Fairfield, a Bethlehem Steel subsidiary in Baltimore. Work progressed so speedily that Bethlehem-Fairfield was able to lay the first keel on April 30. On September 27, less than five months later and only six months after the signing of the contract, the first Liberty Ship, the *Patrick Henry*, slid down the ways in Baltimore. It was the first of 2,710 Liberty Ships that eventually would come down the ways, a huge tribute to the power of American mass production.

One bright spot in defense preparedness was the development of combat aircraft. Although gaps remained (the Army had completely neglected to develop dive bombers and had to borrow a Navy squadron for the Louisiana maneuvers), the Army Air Corps (reorganized in June and redesignated as the Army Air Forces) had spent much of its available money during the 1930s working out new designs for a variety of aircraft. As a result, almost all of the Army combat planes that would see service during the war already existed, at least in prototype, and had even had their first flights by the end of 1941. Even the great B-29 was in the advanced design and development stage. While the Army had to use its production funds to buy established designs, its development program allowed it to switch over to the more modern types of aircraft as soon as they were deemed ready.

Civilians, too, played their part in national preparedness, albeit sometimes reluctantly. Businesses especially wanted to take full advantage of government purchasing power, occasionally with' less than happy results. Alcoa had a virtual monopoly on aluminum production in the United States, a market position it tried to maintain. As aircraft production fell behind schedule, Alcoa was forced to admit that even working at full capacity, its plants could not meet both civilian and military demands. Over strong protests from Alcoa, the Reconstruction Finance Corporation, a government agency, extended a large loan to Reynolds Metals to build an aluminum processing plant (Chapter 10). But the plant could not be built overnight. So in June the Office of Production Management announced a scrap aluminum drive to collect pots and pans that could be turned into aircraft bodies. O.P.M. launched the drive with well-publicized kickoffs in Madison, Wisconsin, and Richmond, Virginia; and the public response far exceeded the expected results. Of course, few people knew enough metallurgy to realize that much of the metal contributed was of alloys not suitable for airframes. The civic spirit exhibited in the drive made the transition much easier a few months later when auto makers, faced with similar materials shortages, started replacing many metal components in automobiles with plastic.

With full employment and rising wages, the government sought new ways to fund the defense effort while also holding down inflation. In February the Treasury Department announced it would begin issuing Defense Savings Bonds in smaller denominations so individuals could buy them more readily. On April 30 the president bought the first of the new Series E Defense Bonds from Treasury Secretary Morgenthau. The next day the bonds were offered for sale to the general public. For those who could not afford the $18.75 needed to buy a basic $25 bond, the post office began selling defense savings stamps in denominations as low as 10¢. These stamps were pasted into savings books which, when filled, could be exchanged for a savings bond. In Union City, Tennessee, Johnny Vaughn, age 38, bought $650 worth of Defense Bonds, saying, "If I can't use the money, Uncle Sam can." Vaughn was serving a life term for murder.

CHAPTER 10

October: Labor and Business

WHEN THE DELEGATES to the sixty-first annual convention of the American Federation of Labor convened in Seattle on October 6, the Federation could look back on a year of tumult in labor relations. The previous year, 1940, had been a relatively quiet one for labor. It was the first full year in which defense production had a major effect on employment. Workers were happy to have jobs again; and the number of strikes, as well as the number of workers out on strike, was the lowest since 1932. But in 1941 things changed dramatically. The total number of strikes jumped from 2,508 in 1940 to 4,288, a number that had been exceeded only in 1937 and 1917. The year got off to a troubled start with 220 strikes in January alone. One worker in twelve went out on strike at some time during 1941, the highest level since 1919. Many of the strikes, 35 percent, were over wages and hours, a reflection of the desire of the workers to share more fully in the prosperity arising from defense production. An additional 50 percent of the strikes arose from attempts by unions to secure recognition from industry, and in this effort the A.F. of L.

was sometimes pitted against its rival, the Congress of Industrial Organizations.

The upsurge in strikes in 1941 was especially damaging to the rapidly expanding defense effort, and President Roosevelt had issued a plea shortly before the convention for an end to strikes in defense industries and especially for an end to jurisdictional strikes in competition with the C.I.O. Federation President William Green scorned Roosevelt's plea, observing piously that most A.F. of L. members refrained from defense strikes. Journalists noted, however, that even while the convention was in session, A.F. of L. unions were out on strike at two shipyards, one steel plant, one chemical plant, one ordnance depot, and three Army food storage plants. Green also told F.D.R. that if he wanted peace between the two labor associations, he should go talk to the C.I.O.

The A.F. of L. had been organized in 1881 as an association of guilds for skilled craftsmen, each trade having its own union. By the time of the First World War, this form of labor organization was becoming obsolete. Large, complex industries employing large numbers of skilled, semi-skilled, and unskilled workers dealt individually with the separate trade unions in the Federation. There was no way for labor to bring significant pressure on an entire industry, and there was no place in the unions for unskilled workers to organize and press their own demands. To many in the labor movement, it was becoming clear that progress would be achieved only by uniting all workers in a given industry, regardless of their trades. But this approach was strongly resisted by many of the older unions, which were highly protective of the privileged position they had won for their members. The few industry-wide unions, led by the United Mine Workers, made a number of attempts to move the Federation in the direction of industry-wide organization; but all were rebuffed. Finally in November of 1935, leaders of eight industrial unions met in Washington to discuss strategy for more aggressive organizing efforts. The leader of the group was U.M.W. President John L. Lewis, a man of great ability and even greater ego. The eight created a committee to work within the A.F. of L. to advance industrial unionism. Officially known as the Committee for Industrial Organization, the C.I.O. was from the outset at odds with the leadership of the A.F. of L. In November of 1938 the tensions between the two became so great that the C.I.O. withdrew from the A.F. of L. and constituted itself as an independent body, the Congress of Industrial Organizations. Since then the C.I.O., led by the irascible and unpredictable Lewis, had taken the lead in aggressive labor organizing drives targeting entire industries.

No one was neutral about John L. Lewis. His supporters, mainly union members in the U.M.W., followed him unhesitatingly. For them his ego, his manners, his bombast, and his obvious desire for power were of little consequence. The miners cared about results, and Lewis had delivered. To his detractors, however, Lewis was a dangerous demagogue. He was regarded as power hungry and unprincipled, with no vision for the future of the labor movement and no loyalty to any interest except John L. Lewis. Ironically, Lewis's principal opponent, William Green, President of the A.F. of L., was himself a member of the U.M.W. In earlier years Green had been a supporter of industrial unionism. But as he rose in the ranks of the Federation, he came to realize that the entrenched power structure was fiercely protective of the privileges of the craft unions. If Green was to advance politically within the Federation, he would have to back the interests of the conservative Federation leadership. By 1940 most informed observers knew that the struggle between the A.F. of L. and the C.I.O. was in the main a power struggle between John L. Lewis and William Green.

In the fall of 1940 the rivalry between Lewis and Green changed dramatically. Long the most powerful labor leader in America and far better known than his rival, John L. Lewis took on another rival more powerful yet, Franklin D. Roosevelt. During the 1920s Lewis had been a staunch Republican, even supporting Hoover in the 1932 election. But the advent of the New Deal caused Lewis to rethink his position, and he became a firm supporter of Roosevelt's policies. The alliance was strengthened with the passage of the Wagner Labor Relations Act in 1935. This law gave powerful support to unions, guaranteeing their right to collective bargaining and their freedom from employer control. It provided the crucial legal environment that enabled the C.I.O. to gain recognition from General Motors (for the United Auto Workers) in February of 1937 and from United States Steel (for the Steel Workers Organizing Committee) the next month. Lewis supported Roosevelt in the 1936 election and continued to support Democratic candidates in the 1938 mid-term election.

Nevertheless, the relationship between Lewis and Roosevelt was beginning to fray. As early as 1937, when the S.W.O.C. turned from its victory with U.S. Steel (commonly referred to as Big Steel) and tried to organize the workers in the companies collectively referred to as Little Steel, F.D.R. played the impartial national leader and denied Lewis the governmental backing the labor leader thought he deserved. Partly because of Roosevelt's refusal to intervene, the organizing drive and resulting strike failed to achieve recognition for the union. Two years later, with the outbreak of the war in Europe, the relationship between the two men deteriorated sharply. Lewis was an uncompromising isolationist who feared that American involvement in the conflict would turn back labor's gains, create an authoritarian presidency, and make the country into an imperialist power. In January of 1940 Lewis openly broke with Roosevelt in a speech castigating the president's economic record, especially his ineffectiveness in dealing with the recession of 1937. Then in the fall Lewis made a move that left labor leaders gasping. In a radio address on October 25, he endorsed Republican Wendell Willkie for the presidency. He asserted that Roosevelt could win only with labor support and asked C.I.O. members to vote for Willkie. Reinforcing this plea, he said that if Roosevelt won, he would take it as a personal repudiation by the rank and file of the C.I.O. and would resign the presidency of the organization that he founded. There was great speculation as to why Lewis had made such a pledge or what he would actually do if Roosevelt won. Those closest to the man believed he actually expected Roosevelt to be re-elected, and he welcomed a graceful way to retire from the C.I.O. presidency. In the event, that is exactly what happened. Lewis stepped aside (though he retained the presidency of the U.M.W.) and his protégé Philip Murray took over as C.I.O. president.

No one really expected that the replacement of Lewis with Murray would open the door to reconciliation with the A.F. of L. The entrenched craft union leaders in the latter organization had made it clear that any reunion of the two bodies would require nothing less than the total surrender and submission of the C.I.O. As a result the conflict continued as before. In the rivalry between the two labor organizations, sometimes two unions would be formed claiming the same jurisdiction. Both bodies, for example had member unions known as the United Auto Workers, but the U.A.W.-A.F. of L. and the U.A.W.-C.I.O. were rivals whose battles weakened the labor movement and complicated relations with industry.

The government itself was sometimes caught in the rivalry. Because of the defense buildup and the movement of workers to areas near defense plants, many parts of the country were experiencing an acute housing shortage. Detroit was one such area, and in the summer of 1940 the Federal Works Agency put out a call for bids for 300 new houses for workers. The low bidder, at $3,200 a house, was the Currier Lumber Company. Immediately the A.F. of L. Carpenters Union protested to Sidney Hillman, Associate Director of the Office of Production Management and himself a labor leader, though ironically in the Garment Workers Union of the C.I.O. The A.F. of L. objection to Currier was twofold. First, the company planned to use labor-saving prefabrication on many of the house components. Second, and probably more important, the company's workers belonged to a union affiliated with the C.I.O., a direct threat to the powerful building trades unions of the A.F. of L. Under the threat of strikes and disruption by the A.F. of L., Hillman withheld the contract from Currier, ultimately giving it to another company, unionized by the A.F. of L. carpenters, at a cost of $4,600 a house.

Both union groups regularly came in for heavy criticism over issues not directly related to union activities. The A.F. of L. had an unfortunately long list of union leaders who had close associates in organized crime or who were themselves engaged in criminal activity. George Browne of the International Alliance of Theatrical Stage Employees and 12th Vice President of the A.F. of L. was not able to attend the

October convention in Seattle. While that meeting was going on, Browne was on trial in New York on racketeering charges. The convention had to remove him from his vice presidency. The top leadership of the A.F. of L. seemed incapable of dealing with the criminal element in the organization, and their weakness stood in sharp contrast to the decisive leadership of Lewis and Murray in the C.I.O.

The A.F. of L. also received blows to its image from irresponsible wildcat strikes that the Federation did not endorse but over which it had no control. In September electrical workers in Kansas City, offended by an unfavorable ruling from the National Defense Mediation Board, showed their displeasure by staging an unannounced strike that shut down public power in the city. At midnight on September 17 the workers walked out and the city went dark. With no traffic lights, automobile accidents were common. A number of people were injured, some seriously, but the hospitals had trouble treating them. Without electricity, operations had to be carried out by candlelight. Without refrigeration, blood and plasma quickly spoiled. Doctors struggled to save one paralyzed baby who had been supported by a now inoperable iron lung. Most of the city faced a water shortage as the pumping stations shut down. At the Sheffield Steel plant, molten steel hardened in the molds. The plight of Kansas City received nationwide publicity, while union leader Albert Wright, who had called the strike, lamely explained, "I didn't realize the hazards."

Yet the C.I.O. had its own image problem to deal with. During the mid-30s the Communists had been an active force in union affairs, welcomed (though sometimes warily) as full partners by Lewis and most C.I.O. leaders. Communism at the time had much less of the negative reputation it later required. The excesses of Stalinism were not yet widely known in the West, and Communist support for the Republicans during the Spanish Civil War caused many observers to think of the party as a partner in the battle of democracy against fascism. In 1939, however, just prior to the outbreak of the war in Europe, Stalin signed the nonaggression pact with Hitler; and the Communist Party in the United States abruptly dropped its anti-fascist rhetoric.

The Communist presence in unions now became an embarrassment to the labor movement, and John L. Lewis in particular was criticized for his prior close association with Communist leaders. While the A.F. of L. had consistently maintained an anticommunist posture, the C.I.O. had welcomed any help it could get in its organizing drives. Lewis's tolerance of the Communists disturbed many C.I.O. leaders, including his successor Philip Murray. At the 1940 convention where he was elected president, Murray had pressed for a resolution excluding Communists from all leadership positions in the organization. Lewis, who still exercised powerful influence, had the resolution watered down; and the convention settled for a tepid blanket condemnation of all dictatorships.

In the spring of 1941 the role of Communists in labor unions was brought sharply to the attention of the American public when U.A.W. Local 683 went on strike against the North American Aviation plant in Inglewood, California. Labor unrest had already had an impact on defense production. During the first ten weeks of the year there had been 125 strikes in defense industries, seriously affecting the production of steel and aluminum. The off-and-on Allis-Chalmers strike began on January 22, was tentatively settled on March 28, restarted on April 1, and was finally settled on April 7. During this period it effectively shut down the production of critically needed turbine engines. In all these walkouts there was strong suspicion of Communist involvement. During the first week of June, strikes in defense industries took 52,800 workers off the job; but it was the North American strike that moved the issue of Communist involvement to the front pages of the papers.

The original strike issue was a simple matter of wages. The United Auto Workers local was demanding an across-the-board wage increase of 10¢ an hour plus an increase in the beginning wage from 50¢ an hour to 75¢ an hour. The workers had a just complaint, for wages at Inglewood were well below national norms for the industry. The matter had been referred to the National Defense Mediation Board, and the U.A.W. had agreed not to strike until the Board handed down its decision. Local officials, however, had different ideas. Local president Elmer Freitag, an admitted Communist, saw an opportunity to extend party control over the whole U.A.W. on the West Coast. In this he was supported by Wyndham Mortimer, the West Coast head of the U.A.W.'s aviation division. Using as a pretext the slowness of the Mediation Board in reaching a decision, Freitag called a strike on June 5 that took 11,400 men out of work at the Inglewood plant, stopped work on $200,000,000 in defense contracts, and—most important from the government's point of view—halted the production line that was turning out ten combat planes a day.

Sensing a crisis that could severely damage the labor movement, the C.I.O. reacted swiftly. President Philip Murray called for the strikers to return to work. So did U.A.W. President R. J. Thomas. The Executive Board of the U.A.W. instructed Mortimer to use all his influence to end the strike. Mortimer refused. Richard Frankensteen, national aviation director for the U.A.W., flew to Inglewood to try to end the walkout. But when Frankensteen got up on a platform to address the strikers, he was booed by Freitag's supporters. When he asked the local president to allow the men to vote on whether to continue the strike, he met a peremptory refusal. When he suspended Freitag and Mortimer, they ignored him. Clearly Freitag felt he was in total command, but he had not reckoned on the intervention of another president.

Franklin Roosevelt, long known as a friend of labor, was quickly losing patience with strikes in defense industries. On June 7 he gave the strikers until the morning of June 9 to return to work. They ignored him as they had ignored the others. So at 8:35 on the morning of the deadline day, Lieutenant Colonel Charles E. Branshaw of the Army Air Corps arrived on the scene with the first of 3,500 Regular Army troops. When the strikers refused to obey Branshaw's order to disperse, the soldiers fixed their 16-inch-long bayonets and cleared a path so anyone willing to return to work could do so safely. About 100 men did. When the strikers failed to move out of the way promptly, the soldiers used their weapons to speed the process. Fortunately, only one person, strike leader Carl Clements, moved too slowly and was rewarded with a small bayonet wound in his hip. With the path cleared, Branshaw marched into the plant and announced that he was taking change of the plant and it was open for work under government control. In a matter of hours, production had resumed; and within three days almost all the men were back at work.

Government action did not end with armed intervention. The House promptly attached an amendment to the Defense Appropriations Bill that mandated binding arbitration for strikes in defense industries. Brigadier General Lewis B. Hershey, the Selective Service Director, instructed local draft boards to reclassify and induct any strikers in defense work who had received draft deferments because of the critical nature of their jobs.

The aircraft industry was a particularly sensitive area, one in which the government seemed inclined to react swiftly in order to maintain production. The response was not limited to actions against unions. Recalcitrant business owners could feel the pressure, too. The next time the government sent in troops to secure labor peace was also in an aircraft plant, this time the Air Associates Incorporated factory in Bendix, New Jersey. After a protracted walkout that was starting to turn violent, the government sent in 2,100 soldiers on October 31. Arriving early in the morning, the men secured the plant and maintained order all through the day. The Army also gathered the owners and the union leaders and forced them to sit down and resume negotiations. Under such pressure, a settlement was reached in less than one day of negotiations, and production resumed the next day. But an investigation into the root causes of the strike put the blame squarely on company president F. Leroy Hill. Late in November the Army announced that the plant would not be returned to the owners until they found a replacement for Hill.

Certainly the most dramatic labor victory of the year came out of the battle to organize the Ford Motor Company. Ford was the last major automaker to remain nonunionized, and the resistance of the family-owned company came from Henry Ford's unwillingness to believe anything except what he wanted to be true, supported by the repressive tactics of his deputy, Harry Bennett. It appears that Henry Ford really did believe his company was one big happy family, and his employees were content. Ford made all major decisions himself. He gave production head Charles Sorensen some freedom to find ways to increase productivity and profits; and he gave a great deal of freedom to Bennett, head of the Service Division, to suppress employee discontent. Most of all, Bennett was charged with preventing any kind of union activity.

Sorensen's tactics for increasing profits were brutal. Paying wages 5-10 percent below the rest of the industry was only the start. Every year, when production of the current year's models was ended, there would be a slack period to permit retooling for the next production year. During this time the production workers, especially the most highly paid, were laid off. When they were brought back to resume production, they were treated like new workers and rehired at beginner's wages. Workers were given no rest periods, and the company could speed up the production line at any time, driving the workers until they collapsed. Lawyers handling workman's compensation cases had a special category, the "Ford client," a man who was 50 but looked 65.

But brutal as Sorensen's methods were, Bennett's were even worse. Bennett's Service Department employed as many as 3,000 men, all physically tough, many with underworld connections, who had full authority over the production workers. Servicemen had authority to discipline and even fire any worker. Beatings were not uncommon. Servicemen would even patrol the surrounding community to see whether any Ford workers were committing the unpardonable sin of owning a Chevrolet. In May of 1937 they pushed their tactics to the limit when they surrounded and brutally beat five U.A.W. organizers who were waiting to hand out union literature to workers at the time of the shift change. The servicemen then turned on women who were passing out handbills and even attacked reporters and photographers. The attack made it clear to the U.A.W. that government assistance would be needed. And given the company's dominance of local officials, government assistance meant the federal government.

Following the beatings at the River Rouge plant, the U.A.W. filed a comprehensive set of unfair labor practice complaints with the

National Labor Relations Board. In December of 1937, the Board handed down its decisions, all, with minor exceptions, in favor of the union. Ford immediately hired a powerful legal team and appealed to the courts. The case wound through the federal judicial system for three years, with the company losing at every stage. Finally, in February of 1941, the Supreme Court declined to hear the appeal, effectively ending the process and dealing Ford a severe blow. While the main case was working its way through the courts, the U.A.W. was filing and winning N.L.R.B. complaints against Ford in company plants across the country, from Somerville, Massachusetts, to Long Beach, California. Bolstered by these victories, the union stepped up its organizing efforts. Workers began to lose their fear of Bennett and his toughs and signed up in large numbers.

In the summer of 1940 the U.A.W. decided the time had come to launch a major campaign to organize Ford. The C.I.O. contributed $50,000 and the services of Michael Widman, one of their most experienced organizers. Widman arrived in Detroit on October 1 and opened his office. Bennett was ready for the battle. He had organized his army of servicemen and launched a political counterattack. Ford's River Rouge plant is in the city of Dearborn, and Bennett was firmly in control of the city council. He had that body pass an ordinance prohibiting the distribution of literature in congested areas. Several U.A.W. leaders promptly allowed themselves to be arrested in order to force a constitutional test of the ordinance. The courts quickly found the ordnance in violation of the First Amendment, and the union secured an injunction against any interference with their literature distribution.

As the organizing effort continued into 1941, more and more workers joined the U.A.W. During one week in March more than 6,000 men signed up, and the union offices had to stay open 24 hours a day. Bennett responded with mass firings of union members, prompting yet another N.L.R.B. complaint. Finally the union members, feeling their growing strength and losing patience with the treatment they were getting from Ford, took matters into their own hands. On the night of April 1, they sat down on the job, catching both Bennett and the U.A.W. by surprise. The union responded quickly, issuing an official strike call, and the battle was on. Bennett, anticipating the usual picket lines, assembled his army of toughs and prepared for a fight. But this time the union tricked him. Instead of setting up picket lines at the gates, they established roadblocks a few blocks away, completely shutting off traffic to and from the plant.

For a short time on April 2, the strike threatened to turn seriously violent. At one gate the union did set up a conventional picket line. Inside the plant were several hundred black workers, many only recently arrived from the South in search of better jobs. Race relations were already tense in Detroit, and Bennett had no trouble preying on their fears. He convinced them that the pickets meant to harm them and their families and the only way to protect themselves was to launch a pre-emptive attack against the pickets. The African Americans responded with several attacks on the picket line, and the violence was suppressed only with the prompt intervention of N.A.A.C.P. Secretary Walter White and other black community leaders.

Bennett next turned to Michigan Governor Murray Van Wagoner and to President Roosevelt for help in ending the strike. But Ford had little political influence with these men. Henry Ford was a noted isolationist and member of the America First Committee. More, his labor policies had become so notorious that Sidney Hillman of the O.P.M. had been withholding government contracts from the automaker. With little defense work going on at Ford, the company simply did not have the importance of a North American Aviation. The government declined to get involved. Further, a union-inspired boycott was cutting into Ford's market share. The company was losing money, shut down, and friendless. It was at this point that Edsel Ford finally decided to confront and defy his domineering father. He faced down both Henry Ford and Harry Bennett and forced the company to enter negotiations with the union. With Governor Van Wagoner acting as mediator, the two sides quickly came to an agreement for N.L.R.B. elections to be held on May 21.

But Harry Bennett still had one more ploy to try. He had already been in contact with William Green of the A.F. of L. concerning the establishment of another rival union to compete with the U.A.W.–C.I.O. Green quickly chartered a new U.A.W.–A.F. of L. local in Dearborn to take part in the election. It was Bennett's hope that the two unions would split the union vote and allow the "No union" option to gain a plurality in the voting. Bennett's plan was a total failure. The A.F. of L. affiliate managed only 27 percent of the vote at River Rouge against almost 70 percent for the U.A.W.–C.I.O. Most important, the "No union" option gained less than 3 percent. It was this last number that was so devastating to Henry Ford.

Ford, occupying his own fictitious world, seemed truly to believe that his happy employees would vote to reject unionization. The shocking realization of their true attitude made it all the more difficult for him to cope with declining business, pressure from the government, and increasingly bad national publicity. Under additional pressure from his son, Edsel, Ford instructed Bennett to enter negotiations and do whatever it took to get a settlement. Bennett took him at his word, and by June 18 the two sides had concluded an agreement granting all of the union's demands. The company simply caved in on every point, creating the most favorable agreement in the entire industry from the union's point of view.

Although the federal government managed to stay out of the dispute at Ford, that fall it got dragged reluctantly into the captive mine strikes. Government involvement in this conflict was inevitable, but it was not well handled and left a sense of bitterness in much of the country. Captive mines were those coal mines owned by steel companies rather than by independent operators. The coal they produced was used exclusively in steel-making, and a strike would have no direct effect on the general public. Nor, indeed, would it have an immediate effect on the steel mills themselves, since the steel companies maintained a stockpile of coal that would sustain full production for about a month. The cause of the captive mine strike was simple. The U.M.W. already represented about 95 percent of the mine workers. All mine workers benefited from the contracts negotiated by the union, and John L. Lewis felt it was only fair that the remaining 5 percent should be required to join the union. So the U.M.W.'s demand in the contract negotiations was simple: Establish a closed shop in the captive mines. On all other issues the parties were able to reach agreement with little trouble.

Lewis's reason for insisting on facing this issue in the current negotiations was quite simple. Staunch isolationist that he was, Lewis nevertheless saw that war was probably coming, and at no distant time. He also expected that, as in the last war, once the United States was involved, the government would freeze all labor contracts and practices as they were for the duration of the conflict. If he did not get a closed shop agreement now, it would probably be a number of years before he could try again.

Lewis's opposite numbers in the steel industry had no serious objection to the closed shop in the mines. They saw the logic of Lewis's position and were willing to accept it. But the mine operators were afraid that if they accepted the closed shop voluntarily, the steel workers' unions would cite that agreement as a precedent for the whole industry. The owners therefore wanted the National Defense Mediation Board to intervene and order implementation of the closed shop. Then the industry could characterize this agreement as a special case that, because of exceptional government interference, could not be used as a precedent.

For these reasons, both Lewis and the mine owners saw the advantages of a short strike that would get the issue referred to the N.D.M.B. A resolution would be dictated to the parties, and everyone would be reasonably content. Accordingly, on September 15 the U.M.W. struck the captive mines. Two days later, his point made, Lewis proposed that the miners go back to work for thirty days while the N.D.M.B. considered the dispute. The owners readily agreed, the matter was formally submitted to the Board, and the miners went back to work. Unfortunately, the executive order that had created the N.D.M.B. had given it mediation powers only. It did not have the authority to impose an involuntary settlement. The Board appointed a three-member panel to mediate the dispute, but the panel members quickly realized that the parties were deadlocked on the key issue and could settle it only if the resolution were imposed on them. The panel delayed submitting a report that it knew no one wanted; and as the thirty-day limit approached, Lewis ordered the miners to walk out again, setting the strike time as midnight on October 25.

When the report finally came out the day before the strike deadline, the three-member panel passed the buck. They recommended that the disputants choose one of two paths forward. On the one hand they could refer the case to the full Board, with the parties agreeing in advance to accept the Board's ruling as final. Alternatively, they could return to collective bargaining and agree to binding arbitration if the bargaining failed. U.S. Steel, speaking as the industry leader, announced that they would have no response until their Board met on Tuesday, October 28. The president, worried that the miners would walk out again at Lewis's direction, sent Lewis a letter asking him to keep the miners at work while negotiations continued.

Hoping to increase pressure on Lewis, Roosevelt made the letter public. The tactic backfired. Lewis viewed the dispute as one between labor and management. Now the president was turning it into a dispute between the government and John L. Lewis. Lewis responded with a fiery letter rejecting Roosevelt's appeal and challenging any imputations of a lack of patriotism on the part of the miners. The workers walked out as scheduled on October 27. The next day the U.S. Steel Board agreed to send the dispute to the full N.D.M.B. Lewis agreed, but neither side would agree in advance to accept the Board's decision as final. As a gesture of good faith, Lewis sent the miners back to work on the 30th, but only for fifteen days, time enough for the Board to render a decision.

The N.D.M.B. consisted of eleven members: four from labor, four from business, and three representing the public. Of the labor members, two, Philip Murray and Thomas Kennedy, represented the C.I.O., and two, George Meany and George Harrison, represented the A.F. of L. Lewis assumed that when the case went to the Board, the four labor members would vote for him and the four business members would vote against him. But he counted on getting two of the three votes from the public members. Consequently he was stunned when, on November 10, the Board voted 9-2 against the mine workers. Possibly reflecting the old animosity between the two labor organizations, both A.F. of L. representatives voted in favor of the owners. Lewis also failed to gain the support of any of the public members. Murray and Kennedy immediately resigned from the Board, which then ceased to function.

Now Roosevelt was in a serious bind. He was determined that the government would not force unwilling miners to join the union. The owners would accept the closed shop, but only upon government orders. Lewis would keep the miners out until he got the closed shop; and he almost certainly had a secondary goal of humiliating Franklin D. Roosevelt, whom he detested. In a last attempt to get a voluntary agreement, Roosevelt called all the parties to the White House on November 14. He insisted that they resume negotiations, that they come to an agreement by the 17th, and that the mines stay open in the meantime. Nothing worked. The 17th came, the negotiations broke down again, and the miners walked out again. Two days later, the president again asked Lewis to send the miners back to work. He asked that the U.M.W. either accept the *status quo* for the duration of the national emergency or agree to binding arbitration.

Lewis's reply hinted broadly that he would accept binding arbitration if he could be assured of the outcome. Roosevelt seized the opportunity. He appointed a three-member arbitration panel consisting of Lewis, President Benjamin Fairless of U.S. Steel, and federal mediator Dr. John Steelman as an impartial public member. Since Steelman was known to favor the union position, Lewis agreed. The owners, willing to accept the closed shop as long as it was forced upon them, also agreed. The predictable result was a decision in favor of the union. Lewis had his victory over the mine owners, and also over Roosevelt. But he had no opportunity to enjoy any publicity from this victory. The arbitration panel announced its decision on December 7, and the end of the captive mine strike was swallowed up in other news.

Despite all the labor troubles, business in general enjoyed a highly profitable year in 1941. Plants were running at full capacity and new factories were being built, often with government money. On September 27, at the height of the captive mines crisis, the Board of

U.S. Steel met not only to decide how to deal with the union, but also to receive reports on the performance of the company up to that point in the year. They learned that their profits for the first three quarters of 1941 were up by almost a third from the corresponding period in 1940. Other firms were showing similar increases in profitability.

On occasion, however, the tremendous increase in government business gave companies more work than they were capable of handling. For most of its fifty-three years, the Aluminum Company of America had enjoyed a virtually impregnable monopoly in the production of primary aluminum in the United States. Over the years the company had maintained production capacity that was just ahead of demand while keeping its profit margins very moderate. The technical expertise required to produce aluminum, the high initial capital investment, and the low projected rate of return had discouraged potential competitors from entering the field, even when Alcoa's initial patent protection had long since expired. Alcoa had not abused its monopoly by charging excessive prices, and it had freely sold its aluminum ingots to other firms that were in competition with Alcoa in the manufacture of finished products. By the late '30s, while Alcoa controlled 100 percent of the American market in raw bauxite ore, basic alumina (aluminum oxide), and primary aluminum, its market share in finished aluminum products ranged from around 60 percent for sheet and wire down to about 22 percent for engine pistons. Despite another round of antitrust litigation that began in 1937 and would drag on long past 1941, Alcoa's market dominance remained secure.

The first signs of trouble appeared in 1939. For some years Reynolds Metals had been an important Alcoa customer, buying primary aluminum to make foil for packaging and other products. But in 1939 demand for aluminum had increased to the point that Alcoa could no longer provide the metal that Reynolds needed. Richard S. Reynolds traveled to Europe to find other sources, and there he saw the tremendous expansion of the German Luftwaffe and the early but still significant British moves to expand the size of the R.A.F. Driven by the production of military aircraft, the German aluminum industry had become the largest in the world, producing almost 200,000 metric tons a year and still hard put to meet the need. Reynolds promptly got in touch with Alcoa president Arthur Vining Davis and urged him to treble his output immediately. But Davis, like most industrialists, still had in his mind the memory of excess manufacturing capacity during the Depression. That was an experience he did not want to see repeated. The company had begun 1940 with 215 million pounds of aluminum in inventory, and that amount seemed adequate for the country's needs. Government officials, too, thought that Alcoa's output of aluminum would be ample. Even as late as November of 1940 the National Defense Advisory Committee claimed that America had a surplus of aluminum.

That attitude lasted barely into 1941. With unprecedented increases in aircraft production, Alcoa quickly ran into difficulties producing enough metal to meet both military and civilian needs. As complaints mounted, both the company and the Office of Production Management came under fire for grossly underestimating the need for aluminum. Help was sought from Aluminium Limited, a Canadian company that had been spun off from Alcoa but was still owned by Alcoa's principal stockholders. But Limited was unable to provide any assistance. Canada, as a part of the British Empire, was already in the war; and the British aircraft industry needed all the metal they could get. It soon became apparent that government intervention would be needed. Alcoa was increasing its capacity as quickly as it could, but the company simply did not have the capital to build all the plants that were needed. Finally, under prodding from the Truman Committee, O.P.M. created a subsidiary, the Defense Plant Corporation, through which it could fund the construction of essential facilities. Although other companies saw an opportunity to break Alcoa's monopoly with government financing, few had the expertise to take advantage of the opportunity. Reynolds had already begun work on a plant in Alabama, and the Olin Corporation received a contract for a smelter in Washington. But Alcoa had the technical knowledge and the management resources to take on the job. In August the company signed government contracts to build 23 smelters, refineries, and other plants. Alcoa would operate them under contract, but final control and ultimate disposition would rest with the government.

As the pressures mounted for increased defense production, big corporations found themselves trapped between the needs of the government in the emergency and the antitrust sentiments held over from the New Deal. More than one company had, simply by its efficient operations, achieved a monopoly or near monopoly position in a certain area. Some of the more liberal New Dealers, including Thurman Arnold, head of the Anti-trust Division at the Justice Department, regarded any monopoly as contrary to the public interest and were quick to perceive conspiracies in any complex business contract. Several years earlier, the German chemical giant I. G. Farben had entered into an agreement with Alcoa to create the Magnesium Development Corporation. Farben had transferred to this company its patents covering its method for producing magnesium and its patents for fabricating products from the magnesium. The fabrication patents were then licensed to Dow Chemical, which at the time held a monopoly position in the production of the raw metal in the United States. At that time Magnesium Development was buying about one third of Dow's annual output of raw magnesium. Arnold saw the monopoly, failed to distinguish between production and fabrication, and concluded that Dow was in collusion with Farben in order to hold down production of a vital war material. In fact, Dow had been trying to increase its production of magnesium and to convince the Navy and Air Corps of its importance in the manufacture of planes. These facts did not matter. At the end of January Arnold got a federal grand jury in New York to hand down an indictment of Dow for establishing a monopoly in the production of magnesium and conspiring with a foreign company (and a German one, at that) to hold down production. Dow admitted it held a monopoly in the United States, although it claimed its position had evolved naturally in the course of business and not as a result of any illegal attempt to corner the market. But the big scandal in the indictment was the claim of the conspiracy with Farben, which at the time was producing 75,000 tons a year, much of which was going into the manufacture of explosives and military aircraft. The company vigorously denied the allegations, claiming that their limited production of the metal was a response to the limited demand, and pointing out that Dow was not a party to the contract between Alcoa and Farben. In an attempt to shore up the company's position, President Willard Dow called Washington and offered to increase production to 100,000 tons a year. He would build the necessary plants at the company's expense if the government would agree to buy the metal. There was no response.

Arnold insisted on taking the case to trial, and President Willard Dow insisted that the company could not waste time and money defending the suit while at the same time raising production levels, which the O.P.M. was now beginning to see as a necessity. Arnold would not budge; so to save time and money on litigation, Dow agreed to plead no contest and pay a fine on the monopoly charge. Unfortunately, the conspiracy allegations would continue to tarnish Dow's reputation for several more years. Worse, the production issue did not go away. As reports came in from the Battle of Britain, and as British orders for more magnesium started increasing, the government realized that, just as with aluminum, it had grossly underestimated the need for magnesium in the defense effort. The War Department reviewed their calculations and found that instead of the 40.8 pounds of magnesium they thought would be needed for each airplane, the true figure was more like 1,000 pounds. In March, the Reconstruction Finance Corporation asked Dow to enlarge its plant in Texas so it could produce an additional 9,000 tons a year. Immediately the Office of Production Management, which managed Lend-Lease aid, allocated 200 of those extra tons for British military production. In June O.P.M. asked Dow to increase production to 200,000 tons. Monopoly concerns were forgotten. Conspiracy concerns were shoved aside. All that counted was production. In November the Defense Plant Corporation entered into a contract with Dow for yet another magnesium plant, this one with a capacity of an additional 36,000 tons.

For all his qualities as a national leader, Franklin Roosevelt was a singularly inept manager of the machinery of government. When presented with a large-scale problem, his instinct was to create another agency, often with ill-defined scope that overlapped with the areas of authority of other agencies. These agencies, even at their best, were fumbling with massive problems of a magnitude previously unknown to government bureaucrats. The result could be tremendous uncertainty and tremendous headaches for business leaders. The uncertainties of government policy also led to unproductive jockeying for position among various competing industrial interests. The threatened oil crisis of late 1941 was a classic example.

The Battle of the Atlantic was not going well for Britain early in the year, as shipping losses to German submarines and surface raiders exceeded Britain's shipbuilding capacity. Especially serious were the losses in oil tankers. Britain produced only 5 percent of the oil it needed; the rest had to be imported. The Middle East, especially Iraq, was able to supply about 4 percent of Britain's imported oil, but that 4 percent went to fuel the Mediterranean Fleet. Oil for home consumption and military and other naval purposes had to come from other sources, principally in the United States and the Caribbean. The U.S. produced about 63 percent of the world's oil, more than enough for its own needs with plenty left for export. But oil from the Americas had to cross the Atlantic to reach the United Kingdom, and the Germans were sinking large numbers of the tankers that carried the fuel.

To help replace the British losses, the U.S. Maritime Commission announced in May that 50 tankers out of a total fleet of 345 ships would be withdrawn from the U.S. coastal trade and transferred to the English route. The announcement elicited howls of pain from American oil companies. The majority of American oil came from wells in Texas and Oklahoma, but most of the refining capacity was on the East Coast, where almost half the gasoline used in the country was consumed. The problem was to get the crude oil from the Texas Gulf ports to the refineries in the Northeast. Ninety percent of this oil went by ship, primarily because of cost. Tankers could transport oil at a cost of 21¢ a barrel. Small amounts went by pipeline, at a cost of 60¢ a barrel, and by rail at about $1.80 a barrel. Cutting back on the tanker fleet would have serious repercussions in the form of higher gasoline prices, this at the very time the government was trying to fight the inflationary pressures of the defense economy.

Maritime interests wanted to retain the oil trade and avoid the risks of trans-Atlantic shipment. They argued that tanker transfers should be minimal until additional ships could be built. The oil companies, on the other hand, argued for the construction of additional oil pipelines across the country. The additional shipment costs would benefit the oil companies since they owned the pipelines. But pipeline construction had been blocked by railroad interests, which argued that additional tank cars were already available for immediate use. Arguments among these competing interests and the prospects for fuel shortages and higher prices in the coming winter led to a series of congressional investigations.

While Congress was investigating, the American Petroleum Institute made its own study. Its conclusions, presented to Congress, predicted that without intervention oil supplies would be down by 8.8 percent over the summer and 15 percent by the winter. The report suggested a variety of measures to ease the situation. No more tankers should be taken out of service. Some twenty European-owned tankers were sitting idle in Latin American ports, trapped there because their home countries had been overrun in the war. These could be pressed into service. About 19,000 railroad tank cars were currently sitting idle. These, too, could be used. Plans for the construction of additional oil pipelines should be speeded up, with federal intervention if necessary. With these measures, the Northeast could avoid a fuel shortage until additional tanker capacity could be provided. It was noted that 139 new oil tankers were currently under construction. Eleven would be in service by the end of the year, and fourteen more by April 1942. They would provide the long-term relief the industry needed. All that was required now was a series of temporary interventions to tide the country over. Then, one by one, the proposed interventions fell apart.

Early in June the irascible Interior Secretary Harold Ickes was named Petroleum Coordinator for National Defense. Within six weeks he ordered that in addition to the fifty tankers already transferred to British service, a hundred more should be handed over, with twenty-five of those being transferred immediately. This move would have reduced transport capacity by about 40 percent and led to shortages of gasoline and heating oil. Ickes tried to address the potential shortage by asking for an immediate reduction of one third in gasoline consumption, the reduction to be assisted by a curfew requiring all gas stations to close from 7:00 P.M. to 7:00 A.M. He also announced that a failure of voluntary reductions would lead to gasoline rationing in the fall. It is not at all surprising that the press began to refer to him as Horrible Harold. Gas station operators welcomed the curfew since it gave them their evenings at home with their families. They counted on selling as much gas as ever in spite of the curfew. In this they were proved entirely correct. During the curfew period gasoline consumption in the Northeast actually rose 8 percent. As a result Leon Henderson of the Office of Price Administration and Civilian Supply took direct action in August, ordering oil suppliers to cut deliveries to gasoline stations by 10 percent. The result was rough and uneven rationing, with the station owners being left to determine how they allocated their limited supplies.

Other measures also failed. It turned out that almost all of the idle tankers in Latin American ports either were unfit for use or had already been pressed into service. Most of the idle railroad tank cars were needed for seasonal peak shipments or were designed to transport liquids other than crude oil. And in September Donald Nelson of the Supply Priorities and Allocations Board announced that no new steel would be allocated for pipeline construction. Nelson ruled that the material could be better used for the construction of ships and tank cars. By this time the congressional investigations were coming to a close, with the congressmen just as befogged about the true situation as everyone else. Gradually, however, it dawned on people that the situation just was not as serious as had been predicted. Gasoline was available. Home heating oil was available. Supplies were holding steady. No more than eighty tankers had ever been transferred to the British, yet Britain seemed to be holding on, too. Then in November it was announced that the Battle of the Atlantic had turned in favor of Britain. Losses were down, replacement ships were becoming available, and the British were returning forty of the eighty tankers to American use. Ickes quietly lifted the curfew, and life returned to something like normal.

Not all major businesses had trouble adapting to new government policies and organization. As far back as the beginnings of the New Deal, Thomas J. Watson, President of International Business Machines, had seen that the proliferation of new government agencies offered prime targets for his salesmen. Watson had already systematized the art of selling and was teaching his system to all his new salesmen through an extensive educational program at the corporate head-quarters in Endicott, New York. Watson had adjusted his curriculum slightly, the better to appeal to government administrators. Now with the introduction of the draft and the increased procurement needs of the defense buildup in 1940 and 1941, the government desperately needed even more of the kind of massive data processing capabilities that I.B.M. offered. Here Watson's sales strategy paid big dividends. He had always taught his salesmen to present themselves first of all as helpful consultants to their prospective clients. They were to take time in the cultivation process to understand their clients' needs, to structure their product offerings to meet those needs, and to maintain a continuing relationship with the client throughout the training and implementation process. This approach was a godsend to government bureaucrats who could not even imagine how they would otherwise be able to cope with mountains of new data. Watson's forces went to work with a will, and I.B.M. profited handsomely.

The boom times created by the defense buildup were beneficial primarily to big industries that had the knowledge and resources to take advantage of the opportunities. By contrast, small businesses often had trouble staying afloat. Higher wages at large defense plants drew away workers, and shortages of critical materials idled production as the larger firms claimed higher priority. When key employees were called away by the draft, small businesses had neither the influence to secure deferments for them nor the flexibility to hire qualified temporary replacements. The smaller companies were also at a disadvantage in securing government contracts. Many small business owners simply did not have the financial resources to go to Washington and find the manufacturing opportunities that were available. Complaints grew loud enough that in the fall the Office of Production Management decided that if the country could not come to Washington for information, the government would take the information to the country. O.P.M. chartered three five-car railroad trains, each car loaded with displays of the kinds of things the armed forces needed that small businesses might be able to manufacture. Each train also carried O.P.M. representatives who could help businessmen understand the contracting process. Over the next several months the trains covered the country, helping businessmen understand the kinds of opportunities that were available to meet government needs. Although contracts could not be signed on the spot, the information helped ensure that smaller operations could continue to function profitably and make their own contribution to the defense effort. A second, but very important purpose was to prevent a string of small business failures from throwing large numbers of employees out of work.

Increased production often put extraordinary pressure on communities near defense plants. In addition to the housing shortage that was felt nationwide, local roads and streets proved totally inadequate for the load that was placed on them. Illustrative were the problems encountered by the Glenn L. Martin Company at its aircraft plant on the east side of Baltimore, Maryland. The Martin Company did all they could to ease the problems of the 30,000 workers in the factory and attached offices. They maintained a parking lot with a capacity of over 10,000 cars. They brought in 300 travel trailers to be used as temporary on-site housing, and they ordered 2,000 more low cost housing units for immediate construction. But every morning there was a twelve-mile backup of cars traveling out two-lane Eastern Avenue to the plant gates, and the congested traffic flow was reversed in the evening. Everyone who could reach a trolley line rode the streetcar to and from work, but the overworked transit system was able to relieve very little of the pressure. The transportation nightmare was repeated in so many communities across the country that Congress appropriated $578,000,000 for urgently needed road construction near defense plants. Construction took time, however; and in this as in so many areas, time was one thing the country did not have.

CHAPTER 11

November: Home Life

ON NOVEMBER 20, the third Thursday in November, most Americans gathered in their homes for a traditional Thanksgiving dinner. It was, of course, not the traditional date. Two years earlier the president, casting about for yet another way to stimulate the economy, had concluded that consumer spending might increase if the Christmas shopping season were lengthened. Then as now, the season customarily began on the day after Thanksgiving. Roosevelt reasoned that he might be able to stretch out the spending season by moving Thanksgiving from the traditional last Thursday in the month to the next-to-last. And since Lincoln had established the modern Thanksgiving Day by presidential proclamation, Roosevelt decided he could do the same. In 1939 November had five Thursdays, and Roosevelt's proclamation designated the next-to-last Thursday, November 23, as Thanksgiving Day. In 1940 and 1941 it would fall on the third Thursday. But a presidential proclamation is not the same as a law, and 16 states refused to go along with the change. Republicans especially decried the gesture as dishonoring the memory of Lincoln. The next-to-last Thursday was commonly referred to as the Democratic Thanksgiving, and the last Thursday was called the Republican Thanksgiving.

Whatever the effect of the backlash, Roosevelt's move did not work. In 1939 and 1940 retailers reported no significant increase in Christmas sales that could be attributed to the change of date. Clearly the early Thanksgiving was causing turmoil with minimal benefit. So in June Roosevelt announced that Thanksgiving would revert to its traditional date on the last Thursday in November. Since five months was deemed too short a time to make the necessary calendar changes and reset the traditional date, the change would take effect in 1942. But Congress was not going to let the president get off so easily. To stabilize matters and make the date permanent, Congress in December passed a law setting the fourth Thursday in November as Thanksgiving Day, beginning in 1942. Roosevelt the pragmatist signed the law and let the controversy fade.

Regardless of the date of the celebration, Americans had much to be thankful for in 1941. Defense production brought a boom in employment. Despite labor troubles that continued to afflict the country, Americans could look forward to steady jobs and adequate pay. The typical family income was about $2,500 a year; and with taxes fairly low, most of that money was available to the family. In fact, taxes were one of the few concrete worries that families had for the future. In 1941 only 20 percent of Americans owed any federal income tax. Among the 80 percent who had not heretofore paid any federal taxes there was widespread support for broadening the tax base to support national defense. But the increases announced for 1942 were heavier than most people had expected. A married couple making $2,500 in 1941 paid just $11 in federal income tax. For 1942 their tax bill was going up to $90, and many were worried where they would find the money. A similar family making just $2,000 would face a 1942 tax bill of $42; in 1941 they had owed nothing. The well-to-do were also being hit hard, though their income could absorb the blow. A couple making $50,000 in 1941 owed $14,128.40 in federal taxes. In 1942 that bill was going to jump to $20,439. Only relatively poor couples making $1,500 or less could escape 1942 taxes altogether. Among singles, just about everyone would have to pay something.

Average Americans could take some small comfort in the tax increase awaiting the wealthy. The Tax Foundation carried out an analysis to see how much a millionaire would have to make in order to take home a true net income of $1 million. For a California resident with no dependents, the answer was $5.7 million. Of the $4.7 million in taxes, almost $3.8 million would go to the federal government, with the rest going mostly to the State of California. One innovation in tax collection was designed to make the new taxes a little less painful. In 1941 the federal government was still operating on a delayed collection basis. At the start of the calendar year the taxpayer would file a tax return and pay tax on the previous year's income in one lump sum. Now the government announced plans to move to the pay-as-you-go system, with taxes being paid all through the year as the income was earned.

Food prices were rising, too, though not as steeply as the income tax. With unemployment down and wages rising, natural inflationary pressures started showing up in price increases. Since 1939 the average price of a one-pound loaf of white bread had gone up from 8¢ to 9¢. Chuck roast was up from 24¢ a pound to 27¢ and a pound of bacon from 32¢ to 37¢. Bananas from Central America had become quite popular and were relatively inexpensive at 7¢ a pound, up from 6¢ two years earlier. Dairy prices were mixed. A quart of milk was up only a penny, from 13¢ to 14¢, but butter had jumped from 34¢ a pound to 44¢, while cheese was up by 8¢ to 33¢ a pound.

Those who could do so planted gardens and canned their own vegetables to cushion the 25 percent increase for green beans (up to 10¢ a pound) and the 33 percent increase in the cost of onions (up to 4¢). While cost was a concern, families also savored the better taste of fresh produce. People also paid attention to nutritional value. In February the National Research Council announced that across the country millers and bakers would start immediately to add B-vitamins, iron, and nicotinic acid (niacin) to flour, with no additional cost to the consumer.

In cities the American housewife would probably buy most of her groceries at a supermarket. In the East she might shop at one of the 11,000 stores of the Great Atlantic and Pacific Tea Company, known to everyone as A&P, the largest grocery chain in the country. In the Midwest it was more likely to be one of the 3,600 stores of Cincinnati-based Kroger, the second largest chain. In the West it was Safeway, headquartered in Oakland. Safeway was in third place with 2,500 stores, including a strong eastern presence around Washington, D. C. In May Safeway announced a merger with Daniel Reeves, Inc., a New York area grocery chain with almost 500 stores.

In small towns the big chain stores were not available. The housewife would most likely buy her groceries at a small, privately owned store, often managed by a local family she would know well. By 1941 there were thousands of these small stores that belonged to the Independent Grocers Alliance, I.G.A., which gave the small store the cost benefits of high-volume purchasing. I.G.A. also emulated the big chains by offering a wide variety of products under its own store-brand name. With the return of jobs and prosperity, and with the ready availability of good food, America was by far the best fed country in the world.

When it came to buying clothes, families were cutting back a bit. Most basic items were going up modestly in price. A woman could get a pair of panties for 57¢, up only 3¢ in two years, although a slip was now up to $2.77 from an average price of $1.91 in 1939. But as *Life* observed, a man could still get a "good business shirt" for $1.50. Other prices were also pushing upward. A woman's cloth coat now averaged $47.59, up from $39.90 two years earlier, and a man's overcoat would run about $32.10 as against an earlier average of $27.18. Clothes shopping was generally done locally, and virtually every town in the country had one or more locally owned clothing stores. In the larger cities there were the big department stores or specialty shops whose names were widely known: Filene's in Boston, R. H. Macy in New York, Marshall Field in Chicago, Wanamaker's in Philadelphia, Rich's in Atlanta, Neiman-Marcus in Dallas, Goldwater's in Phoenix, Gump's in San Francisco. The May Department Store Company, founded in Colorado but now headquartered in St. Louis, had branch stores in Los Angeles that were especially well known. Their fame was spread by Jack Benny's radio program, where Jack's girlfriend (and real-life wife) Mary Livingstone appeared in her skits as a saleswoman in the May Company store.

An important feature of retailing was how the industry advertised its products. Most American newspapers received the bulk of their income from advertising by local businesses. The stores looked on this advertising in a purely commercial light and seldom used it as leverage to influence the editorial content of the papers. For this reason American newspapers enjoyed a freedom in their editorial stances that was far less common elsewhere in the world. In contrast to party-owned papers in Europe, newspapers like the Detroit *Free Press* and the St. Louis *Post-Dispatch* could and did change their editorial positions on major issues like intervention and preparedness without being answerable to any higher authority.

For families that did not live near a town with a suitable store, and for those who wanted greater variety in available merchandise, mail-order giants Sears, Roebuck; J. C. Penney; and Montgomery Ward covered the country with their catalogues. People living near medium-sized or larger cities could often drive to the stores owned by these chains, especially J. C. Penny, which had some 1,600 retail locations covering all forty-eight states. Mail-order sales still were the economic backbone of these companies, although Sears was no longer selling houses by mail order as it once had. This year also brought an end to its mail-order grocery business.

Mail-order sales were also good for smaller businesses and sometimes put a strain on local postal facilities. L. L. Bean was sending out so many catalogues (300,000 twice a year) and so many packages (up to 500 mail sacks a day) that the local Freeport, Maine, post office, which occupied the ground floor of the L. L. Bean building, was swamped by the volume. The postmaster, who happened to be Bean's brother Guy, submitted a proposal to Washington for a new $85,000 post office building. Brother Leon had different ideas. He spent $25,000 of his own money to build an extension on his building for the post office to use, rent free. He felt the convenience of keeping the post office in the same building as his shipping department was worth the money.

Transportation costs for families were reasonably well under control in 1941. Gasoline averaged 20¢ a gallon, up only a penny in two years, and the average streetcar fare in the country had held steady at 8¢. Many other items had increased by only a penny in two years: a bar of toilet soap from 6¢ to 7¢, a box of soap flakes from 31¢ to 32¢, a tube of toothpaste from 32¢ to 33¢, and shaving cream from 31¢ to 32¢. The average cost for admission to a movie had climbed two cents to 35¢.

Using data from the Bureau of Labor Statistics, *Life* presented the following chart showing how a family with a $2,500 annual income spent its money in 1939 and in 1941.

	1939	1941
Food	$630	$733
Clothing	$242	$267
Rent	$450	$461
Fuel, light	$128	$134
Home Furnishings	$88	$97
Miscellaneous	$797	$808
Savings	$165	$0

The true figures were adjusted slightly to stay within the projected income. The actual price increases in the Miscellaneous category would have brought that amount up to $829, putting total expenditures above the family income of $2,500. So families were cutting back to stay within their means. In this context, the looming tax increases for 1942 were viewed with considerable anxiety.

One area that seemed immune to cutbacks was tobacco consumption. Though the cost of a pack of cigarettes had risen from 14¢ to 15¢ in the past year (a uniform increase across the major brands that drew the attention of the Justice Department's Anti-Trust Division), sales were up 12 percent. The tobacco industry spent more on advertising than any other business except perhaps the auto industry. Annual cigarette consumption in 1941 was over 2,200 smokes for every adult, and tobacco advertising was amazingly creative. When American Tobacco Company, makers of Lucky Strike, decided in 1941 that it needed to update the well-known green packaging so familiar to consumers, executives knew they were running a risk in changing something familiar. So the company hired famed industrial designer Raymond Loewy, designer of the Studebaker, the Shell Oil logo, and the Coca-Cola bottle, to redesign their pack. Loewy designed the plain white package with the bright red Lucky Strike logo on both front and back. The company claimed the green dye previously used was needed for the defense effort; and it launched an advertising campaign with the slogan, "Lucky Strike Green Has Gone to War." In November R. J. Reynolds Tobacco, maker of Camels, introduced the huge billboard on Times Square in New York where the face of a smoker, holding a Camel, puffed smoke rings (actually steam) fifteen times a minute. Raleighs included a coupon on every pack. Smokers could collect the coupons and redeem them for gifts.

Very little was said about the health effects of smoking. Many doctors had known for a decade that cigarette smoke contained chemicals that could induce carcinoma in rats. It was also known that nicotine caused a contraction of the blood vessels and contributed to various cardiovascular diseases. But such early findings were lost in the mass of cigarette advertising that flooded the public media. Tobacco companies even touted purported health benefits, saying that cigarettes soothed the nerves, aided digestion, and provided a lift.

Two decades of intensive advertising had made cigarette smoking universally accepted among men. And despite two decades of intensive advertising, smoking was still not totally acceptable for women. Various promotional devices, including movie scenes showing women smoking, still left many Americans feeling that smoking was the habit of young, chic, and probably fast women. While many older women smoked in the privacy of their homes, they hesitated to light up in public. And many of the young women who did smoke were at great pains to conceal that fact from their parents. Nevertheless, the tobacco smell that pervaded most homes and offices went generally unnoticed because of its ubiquity. Occasionally the industry tried a proactive approach by advertising the fresh aroma of cigarettes, as if cigarette smoke were comparable to fresh air. So despite the price increase, Americans still found a way to afford their increased use of cigarettes.

With some products, however, the concern was not cost but availability. Since the fall of France in 1940, French wines had virtually disappeared from American stores. Americans had always identified good wine with France, and the cutoff of supplies left wine drinkers wondering how they were going to provide for their dinner tables. American wine producers were not slow to respond, and magazines and grocery stores soon were filled with advertisements extolling American vineyards and their products. American wine production jumped by almost 20 percent in 1941, and over forty new farm wineries were established.

Brewers, too, saw an opportunity in the reduced competition and promoted beer as the natural beverage to serve, even at dinner parties. Their efforts had little effect in 1941, as beer consumption for the year fell slightly from 12.5 to 12.3 gallons a person. One alcoholic import, however, was unaffected by the war. British distillers had been sharply reducing the production of whiskey for home consumption. In March they announced another 15 percent reduction, to just 65 percent of prewar levels. But distillation for export was unaffected. Whiskey was an important source of export revenue for Britain, and good Scotch remained readily available in the United States.

Similarly, although most women paid little attention to the shipping news, they took note when the *Tatuta Maru* docked in San Francisco with what was expected to be the last load of raw silk from Japan. Since 81 percent of all women's hosiery sold was made of silk, and since the Office of Production Management was moving to reserve all stocks of raw silk for the Army to use in parachutes, the arrival of a shipload from Japan was news indeed. The preferred alternative to silk was nylon, but manufacturers could supply only about 18 percent of the demand. Even worse, the Army, faced with its own silk shortage, also was looking at nylon for parachutes. Other choices, like fine cotton mesh or sheer lisle, were regarded as far less glamorous. Rayon sagged badly. The prospects for hosiery fashion were not bright.

For women's intimate apparel, the Blue Swan Mills in Pennsylvania produced more panties than any other manufacturer, over 26 million a year. Yet industry analysts estimated that half of the women in America did not even wear such undergarments, and Blue Swan conducted regular promotional campaigns to encourage women to wear them. For the fashionably patriotic woman they produced red, white, and blue panties; and in 1941 they introduced their Panty-of-the-Month, with styles and colors suited to the various seasons and holidays. Their December Panty of the Month was the Yoo-Hooikin, an olive drab panty with "Yoo-Hoo" lettered on the side in honor of General Ben "Yoo-Hoo" Lear (Chapter 9).

For those who could afford the latest fashions, the war news from Europe did nothing to suppress sartorial expression. For young men, the zoot suit made a fashion statement of a very particular kind. Originating in the black community in New York during the 1930s, the zoot suit, with its long coat, wide, heavily padded shoulders, wide lapels, baggy trousers with high waist and tight cuffs, and accompanying long watch chain, had become an object of fascination for young men of all races by 1941. The amount of cloth required to produce a zoot suit made it a likely casualty if rationing had to be introduced, but few of its wearers worried about such things at this time.

In the vast majority of America's 34.9 million homes, the family pattern was a highly traditional one. The husband was employed and the wife stayed home and took care of the house and family. A young bride or older wife might occasionally seek a job to help with the family income, but such cases were rare. When children were at home, their mother was expected to be at home to care for them. In any event, few occupations apart from teaching, nursing, and secretarial work were easily open to women. While it was possible for a woman to become a doctor or a lawyer, it was understood that women who made those career choices were giving up any prospect of marriage. A woman who wanted a medical career but who also wanted a family life would choose to become a nurse. In some places a woman could not even continue to be a teacher after she married. A married teacher who became pregnant was required to resign as soon as her condition became apparent, lest the innocent minds of her pupils wonder how she got that way. It was assumed that the husband's salary would provide what the family needed, and the wife would manage the household accounts within that figure.

During the latter part of 1941, however, this traditional pattern began to break down. The large number of men being drafted into the Army meant that industries, especially defense industries, were hard pressed to find enough workers. Increasingly women were being hired for defense-related jobs, and they were expanding their presence from the secretarial desk to the production floor. Aircraft manufacturers might still think of women as not strong enough to move large aluminum plates and rivet planes together, but there were many jobs in areas like electronics and light mechanical assembly where women performed excellent work.

When a family faced health problems, medical care in the United States was as good as it was anywhere. There were, of course, wide regional and social variations, but basic medical services were available to anyone within reach of a doctor. Sulfa drugs, the first widely available antibiotics, had been in general use since the mid-'30s; and infections no longer carried the deadly fear they once had. People were still cautious since the sulfanilamide scare of 1937, in which about a hundred people died from a sulfa elixir made with a poisonous solvent. The Food and Drug Administration had been formed in response to the tragedy, and the agency proved its worth in April of 1941 when it ordered the recall of a contaminated batch of sulfathiazole. In the summer doctors at Johns Hopkins announced a new use of sulfadiazine in spray form to treat patients with severe burns. Doctors also were encouraged by promising reports on the new wonder drug penicillin, although it was not yet widely available. But there were some persistent diseases that even the new wonder drugs could not touch. In the summer the annual polio outbreak recurred in the eastern part of the country, with 350 new cases reported.

For patients requiring surgery, April brought promising news from Beth Israel Hospital in New York. While all surgery had its risks, patients needing blood transfusions faced special dangers. In a small number of cases, there were fatal reactions even though patients were given the correct blood type. Now Dr. Philip Levine announced the discovery of a new blood antigen, which he called the Rh factor, which seemed to account for these fatal reactions. Screening for this antigen held the promise of much safer surgical procedures.

One kind of medical care remained highly controversial. Contraception, euphemistically referred to as family planning, was strongly opposed by many conservative forces, especially the Catholic Church. In August the New York State Federation for Planned Parenthood received permission to set up an educational display at the State Fair in Syracuse. When word of the plan leaked out, conservative groups raised such objections that the issue was referred to the governor for a decision. Acting Governor Charles Poletti said he believed the display would violate state law, and he asked the Fair authorities to ban it.

To present a general picture of ordinary family life in America, *Life* magazine prepared a feature article that ran in the September 28 issue. The editors selected what they regarded as a typical American family, the Ambergs of Kankakee, Illinois. While the Ambergs' lifestyle and income were clearly a bit above the mean, they were close enough to be considered exemplars of America's middle class. Mr. Amberg and his brothers ran the family business. Of Mrs. Amberg and those like her, *Life* said, "In the movies, in fiction and advertising in women's magazines, the modern U.S. housewife is portrayed as the sort of woman who keeps her figure, her husband, her make-up and her humor no matter how tough the going. One effect of this constant propaganda is that millions of U.S. women are doing just that." The family's monthly rent of $45 was slightly above the national average of $37.50, but it provided a nice two-story frame house for the couple and their three children. The couple had carried out a few renovations and improvements on the house, and Mr. Amberg cared for the lawn, the gardens, and the furnace. Mrs. Amberg cared for everything else.

The family had one car, and Mrs. Amberg drove her husband to work so she could take the children to school and run errands. But she did her grocery shopping by phone and had the groceries delivered to the house to save wear and tear on the car. Mr. Amberg had been able to provide a number of modern conveniences for his wife, such as a front-loading washing machine and a pop-up toaster. Recreation generally meant evenings at home with the radio or a book or magazine. Once a week the Ambergs would go out, often to movies, but they tried to keep early hours. A baby sitter cost 35¢ from 8:00 P.M. to midnight, and after midnight the rate was 10¢ an hour. For leisure reading they took several magazines (it was understood that *Life* was one), and they also subscribed to Book-of-the-Month Club.

Entertaining friends for dinner, often with cards or games afterwards, was a common social activity. For the middle and upper classes, the Saturday night dinner party was a routine way of maintaining one's place in society. For a young family on a careful budget, like the Ambergs, the wife would prepare the supper and decorate the house. Dressing for dinner was important—dark business suits for the men and nice dresses for the women, such as they would wear to church the next morning. As a family progressed economically, the dinner party was a chance to exhibit small signs of growing prosperity. The men might wear dinner jackets—only those who did not know better would call them tuxes. Women might even wear modest evening gowns. Servants were still inexpensive in 1941, especially in the South, where customs were usually more formal. There was some difficulty in getting good help: War industries offered much better pay than domestic service. But it was usually possible to find a good cook, even if she worked only part time. A sign of real prosperity was having a servant, even a part-time housekeeper, to open the door and greet guests. But even for those anxious to exhibit their increasing prosperity, small economies were still observed. It was a rule always to use a good deal of ice in the drinks. It saved on the cost of liquor.

Magazines gave families an important link to the world, especially if they did not live near urban centers. Those who wanted to keep up with the news on a weekly basis might subscribe to *Time* or *Newsweek*.

Those who wanted more picture coverage might subscribe to *Life* or *Look*. *The Saturday Evening Post* provided short stories, serialized novels, and occasional nonfiction pieces, together with humorous cartoons and (generally weak) jokes.

The most popular monthly magazines were all aimed at women, with *Good Housekeeping* leading the list, followed by *Ladies' Home Journal, McCall's, Better Homes & Gardens, Cosmopolitan, Woman's Home Companion,* and *American Home.* Although it had a smaller circulation, just under 1.3 million, *National Geographic* was highly influential, appearing in school libraries, being passed around among families, and usually being saved and reread long after other magazines had been discarded. With rather few people able to travel much within the country and very few able to travel abroad, *National Geographic* offered the principal link to the outside world.

Children often amused themselves in the evenings with comic books chronicling the adventures of Superman and other heroes. Around 75 different comic books were being published, with monthly sales of about 11,000,000 copies and annual revenue of around $15,000,000. The content of most comics was aptly described as murder, mayhem, and death rays; and many parents were concerned about the steady exposure of their children to such material. In January Parents' Institute, Inc., launched a new series of comic books, called *True Comics.* These featured historical material, especially stories from American history intended to inspire patriotic feelings among school children.

For many families evening entertainment centered on the piano. A piano was considered essential in most middle-class homes, and families that could afford it would see that their children received piano lessons. Increased employment and prosperity brought this form of entertainment within the reach of more and more people. Piano manufacturers were happy to report that sales in 1941 were up by 16 percent over the previous year.

Throughout the country radio was the dominant, almost sole medium for mass communication (Chapter 8). A few families, mostly in New York City, were able to watch news and entertainment on the country's twenty-two television stations. Television was generally regarded as experimental rather than an established commercial enterprise, but July 1 in New York was a memorable date, for better or worse. At 2:30 P.M. that day, operating under the first FCC commercial license, WNBT (NBC) broadcast an advertisement for the Bulova Watch Company, the very first television commercial. Nineteen other stations, from New York to San Francisco, had announced their intention to follow suit; but the coming of war in December put off most of those plans for several more years.

All the foregoing applied to middle- and upper-class families, those with steady jobs and good income. But America in 1941 was a land of great inequality, and a great part of this inequality was regional. In many ways the United States of 1941 was four different countries. While the boundaries were somewhat fuzzy, the regional differences were real and pronounced. The North was essentially the area north of the Potomac and Ohio Rivers and east of the 98th meridian. It was the cultural, economic, and political center of the country. It had the best schools, the highest *per capita* income, the best health care, and the best cultural and entertainment resources. The Pacific Coast was in many ways a detached portion of the North, sharing its characteristics, but separated by great distance and slow communication. In between the two lay the West, a great, arid, underpopulated land of ranches and farms, few notable cities, and magnificent natural wonders. Last of all, in just about every sense, was the South, the region south of the Ohio and the Potomac and east of the 98th meridian. It was last in education, last in *per capita* income, last in health care, and last in cultural resources.

A few quick facts will help illustrate how different the South was in 1941. It was a poor region. The *per capita* income in the wealthiest Southern state was lower than the *per capita* income in the poorest state outside the South. Average personal income was only half of that in the rest of the country. The South had one third of the nation's school-age children, but only one sixth of the nation's total outlay for public education. Even this limited amount was diluted because of segregation and the need to maintain two separate (and very unequal) school systems. The rate of illiteracy was 8.8 percent, more than twice as high as in the rest of the country. In South Carolina 15 percent of the population could neither read nor write. Many Southerners never traveled far from where they were born, and their isolation and ignorance of the rest of the country were extreme.

Health services and sanitation in the South were poor. There were few four-year medical schools. Most aspiring doctors had to go elsewhere to complete their medical education. When Selective Service doctors examined draftees, they found that 11.4 percent of the men in Georgia, Louisiana, Mississippi, and Florida were suffering from venereal disease, a rate four times that in the rest of the country. Two million cases of malaria were reported every year. Pneumonia and tuberculosis were rampant. Hookworm and typhoid were common in rural areas because of contaminated soil and water. Because Southern agriculture concentrated on cash crops, the region produced only one fifth of the food it needed. Year after year, 60 percent of the land was planted in tobacco, cotton, and corn, which wore out the soil. These cash crops were produced in quantities larger than the market could absorb, and even these did not bring in enough money for farmers to feed their families. The South had to import 80 percent of its food and clothing from other areas but lacked the money to pay for it. Consequently malnutrition was widespread, even among farm families.

The South's agricultural woes became even worse in 1941 as the region experienced one of the worst droughts in memory. The entire eastern part of the country was affected, and dry weather fueled major wildfires in the Northeast. But the South was hit the hardest, with rainfall as much as 15" below normal in parts of Tennessee and North Carolina. Kentucky was worst hit, receiving only 33" for the whole year, less than three quarters of its annual average. Farmers in Maryland noted in their diaries that the weather was the driest in memory, and they worried that most of their crops would be lost if rain did not come soon. Good rains in June and July helped alleviate the worst of the drought, but they came too late to save the early crops. By late summer the drought had returned, and southern famers suffered badly. At the same time, all the rain that was missing from the South was falling west of the Mississippi. New Mexico received nearly twice the usual amount of rain. There were floods in normally arid West Texas, and news photographs showed locomotives splashing along tracks that were completely hidden by the water.

Even without the drought, living standards in general were low in the South. Nationwide there were still over 700,000 rural homes that did not have a toilet or even a privy, and 70 percent of those were in the South. Even in the cities over a third of all homes lacked a flush toilet. The Nation's Capital, an essentially Southern city, still had 15,000 outhouses. In the United States as a whole, 30 percent of all homes had no running water. In the South the figure was 54 percent. Among Southern blacks it was 77 percent, and for rural farm homes the absence of running water rose to the astonishing levels of 88 percent for whites and 99 percent for blacks. By the most conservative estimate, half of all Southern families were living in substandard housing. It is little wonder that President Roosevelt in 1938 had told the National Emergency Council, "It is my conviction that the South presents right now the Nation's No. 1 economic problem—the Nation's problem, not merely the South's. For we have an economic unbalance in the Nation as a whole, due to this very condition of the South."

Even outside the South, there were many barriers for African Americans, whose problems often remained invisible to the majority whites. One great inequity was segregation in housing, with many landlords unwilling to rent apartments in established middle-class neighborhoods to African Americans. Occasionally private initiative was able to address the problem just a little. In 1939 a black couple, Mr. and Mrs. Benjamin Mason, won $150,000 in the Irish Sweepstakes. After buying a new car and a modest new home, they used the rest of the money, with help from the Reconstruction Finance Corporation, to build a new apartment building in South Philadelphia. The building opened in April of 1941, providing 50 apartments for white-collar black families. All units were air conditioned, a great innovation even in housing for whites; and the building provided a basement playroom, a gymnasium, a chapel, and a bowling alley. An outdoor playground and a lawn and fountain completed the complex. Rent for the three- to five-room apartments was $30-39 a month, and the Masons fully expected to make a profit as well as provide a new level of housing comfort for people of their race. But the fact that this initiative was so newsworthy was a good indication of just how rare such opportunities were.

Still there was one area of life in which the regions of the country were more unified: religious participation. On Sundays a great many Americans got up and went to church, or at least acknowledged that they ought to do so. America was a religious country, with widespread involvement in organized religion and an even broader feeling that religion was vital to national life. One might almost say that most Americans went to church on Sunday, but the numbers do not quite justify that. The various Protestant denominations counted over 40 million members, while the Roman Catholic Church claimed over 21 million. The 4.6 million Jews made up the third large group, with the rest ranging from the Eastern Orthodox churches (754,227 members) to the Vedanta Society (628 adherents). Those who were assertively none of the above were viewed as somehow not quite good Americans.

The view in many quarters was that the best Americans were Protestants, specifically what historian Martin Marty calls old-stock Protestants. These were the white Anglo-Saxon Protestants descended from the nation's founders, people who, in their own view, were the guardians of America's religious and cultural life as it had been established by their ancestors. Roman Catholics and Jews, even though they were citizens, were not seen as real, true, pure Americans. This was a time when even Franklin Roosevelt could remark to Leo Crowley, an economist and a Roman Catholic, "Leo, you know this is a Protestant country, and the Catholics and the Jews are here on sufferance. It is up to both of you to go along with anything that I want at this time." Crowley professed to be shocked by the remark, but he probably was shocked less that Roosevelt harbored such views than that he had dared to voice them. Roosevelt embodied the subdued prejudices typical of his class and prevalent in the country as a whole.

Protestantism's influence in America was limited, however, by the vigor with which Protestants fought one another. These fights did not always follow denominational lines, but often split denominations into quarreling factions. In the '20s and early '30s many denominations endured battles between fundamentalists, who insisted on a literal interpretation of the Bible, and liberals, who allowed more figurative and metaphorical interpretation of certain passages. Some denominations escaped these battles, mainly because their members and pastors were almost unanimously committed to one side or the other.

Generalizations about the state of religion in America during this period are difficult and fraught with exceptions. But for the most part conservatives and liberals were also divided by their stance on involvement in social issues. Typically conservatives focused their attention on the salvation of individuals, leaving it then to those individuals to pursue social issues or not. Most often they did not. Conservatives tended to accept the social order as they found it and seldom were seen campaigning for reform.

Liberals, on the other hand, tended to take a positive view of the possibilities of human progress and involve themselves in social causes. They were also more willing to make common cause in such matters with other, non-Protestant organizations. In these areas liberal Protestants had to tread warily. Protestant pastors who took too strong a line on issues of social justice often found that wealthy businessmen among their parishioners were only too ready to withdraw financial support as a sign of their displeasure. As a result, the voice of Protestantism in civic affairs was decidedly muted. Liberal Protestantism was regarded as something of a national religion, and its leaders found it difficult to move far from socially and politically acceptable positions.

Despite their differences, most Protestants felt that their dominant position entitled them to see their views reflected in the legal system of the country. While most Americans paid lip service to the First Amendment, many Protestants, especially conservatives, gave it a rather narrow interpretation and were quite willing to have the government give legislative sanction to religious practices—that is, to *their* religious practices. This viewpoint gained national publicity when the Delaware legislature attempted to modernize its statute books by eliminating many obsolete laws that had been unenforced for generations. One such law, dating to 1740, prohibited "any worldly employment, labor, or business on the Sabbath Day." A bill was introduced repealing this law, but in early March the Republican-controlled House defeated the repeal bill by three votes. Much of the pressure against repeal came from the conservative Lord's Day Alliance of Maryland-Delaware. In answer to this rebuff, the State Senate passed a resolution calling on the Delaware State Police to begin enforcing the law "to the strictest letter." The police responded with gusto. Hundreds were arrested for violating the law. One who just barely escaped was the Rev. Dr. Albert H. Kleferman, pastor of West Presbyterian Church in Wilmington and President of the Lord's Day Alliance. Dr. Kleferman's offense was that he employed a sound technician at his church for the Sunday morning service. He escaped on a technicality, and a week later the embarrassed House passed the repeal bill.

In religion as in other areas of life, African Americans were a largely invisible presence. The greatest number of them were Baptist (about four million in the churches of the National Baptist Convention, the largest black denomination) or Methodist (a million and a half altogether in the African Methodist Episcopal Church, the African Methodist Episcopal Zion Church, and the Colored Methodist Episcopal Church). A proliferation of smaller groups included denominations like the Kodesh Church of Immanuel, with nine churches and 562 members. At a time when African Americans had practically no political voice and little influence in national affairs, these denominations focused their message on individual salvation, community solidarity, and support for members in coping with a segregated society. With most social organizations closed to African Americans, the church was the organizational center of black community life.

During the '10s and '20s a variety of small sects had appeared, many having only a transient existence, most remaining small, local bodies. Three, however, had continued to thrive to the point that the names of their leaders were familiar across the country, even to people unaffiliated with their churches. One of the most striking was the International Peace Movement, led by the Reverend Major Jealous

Divine, as he called himself. His followers knew him simply as Father
Divine. Born George Baker in Maryland, Father Divine had traveled
the country as an itinerant evangelist, developing a distinctive the-
ology in the New Thought tradition. He taught that Christ existed
in everyone, and that some people more than others had realized the
divine spirit and transcended the material world. Father Divine himself, of course, had perfectly realized the divine spirit, just as Jesus had
fully embodied the divine spirit 1,900 years earlier. To most of his followers this simply meant that Father Divine was God. He did not try
to elucidate a theological distinction.

By 1941 Father Divine's Peace Movement had its primary base in
New York. The central religious service was the Communion Banquet,
a sumptuous meal at which Father Divine or some other leader pre-
sided and delivered a sermon. The Peace Mission was interracial.
Although Father Divine was black, most of the senior leadership was
white. The Movement was strongly and consistently opposed to racial
discrimination; but rather than advocating empowerment for African
Americans, it simply rejected the validity of racial categories altogether. The Movement also demanded celibacy of its members, and
the conspicuous failure of some of them to abide by this rule was the
cause of no little embarrassment.

In 1938 the Peace Movement had suffered a setback when
another religious movement bought the building that Father Divine
was renting as the Movement's headquarters in Harlem. The Peace
Movement was summarily evicted by the new owner, the United
House of Prayer for All People, led by the flamboyant Daddy Grace.
Born Marcelino Manuel da Graca in the Cape Verde Islands, Charles
M. Grace, "Sweet Daddy" to his followers, was an evangelist within
the Christian Pentecostal tradition. He objected strongly to claims
that Father Divine was God. The United House of Prayer for All
People had been founded in Charlotte, North Carolina, in 1926. By
1941 there were branches flourishing all along the East Coast. Grace
decried "long-faced" religion and encouraged joyful expressions of
faith. Though firmly committed to an interracial outreach, the church
was not as successful as the Peace Movement in attracting whites.

Grace himself rejected racial categories, refusing to say whether he was white or black (perhaps a reflection of his Cape Verdean background). A notable practice in the United House of Prayer was the frequent, often annual rebaptism of members. Conducted by the elders of the church in Grace's presence, the ritual lasted several hours and attracted as many spectators as participants. In some cities the baptismal crowd was so great that Grace would arrange with the local fire department to provide fire hoses, which would direct their spray over the white-clad members.

Southern California was home to one of the best known Pentecostal churches of all, the International Church of the Foursquare Gospel, based at the Angelus Temple in Los Angeles. The denomination had been founded in 1927 by the evangelist Aimee Semple McPherson, who had gained nationwide celebrity through the '20s and early '30s with her charismatic personality and well-publicized faith healings. Even in her early days as an itinerant evangelist she had managed to keep her ministry interracial. When she settled in Los Angeles and built the Angelus Temple, she made provision for extensive and inclusive social ministries. During the Depression the Temple was the earliest, largest, and most effective relief agency in the city, providing help without regard to race. By 1941 her itinerant evangelizing was restricted by increasingly poor health. But thanks to the radio and her writings, her nationwide influence was still strong. She was one of the earliest and most vocal critics of Hitler and Mussolini and was an early advocate of a Palestinian homeland for Jews.

Although most Protestants viewed the Roman Catholic Church with suspicion, regarding it as a monolithic and authoritarian foreign influence, the Catholic Church itself was in fact no more unified a force than the Protestant denominations. Many Catholics were working-class immigrants or children of immigrants with a strong interest in social justice and economic and labor issues. Yet because of nativist suspicions held by old-stock Protestants, many in the Catholic hierarchy placed emphasis on showing that Catholics were 100 percent Americans, just like anyone else. They tended to avoid controversial causes and so were often somewhat out of tune with their parishioners. Indeed, the few activist priests like Father Charles Coughlin were a decided embarrassment to the hierarchy. Nevertheless, American Catholics represented a large part of the isolationist sentiment in the country. This was especially true after Hitler's invasion of Russia in June. Because of the Soviet Union's harsh atheist rhetoric and its suppression of Orthodox Catholic churches, the Roman Catholic hierarchy strongly opposed sending any Lend-Lease aid to "Godless Russia." To counter this sentiment, President Roosevelt asked Myron C. Taylor, at that time Chairman of the Board of U.S. Steel, to go to the Vatican as his personal emissary to try to convince Pope Pius XII that the aid would help the Russian people and not support Communist ideology. Taylor was successful; but Protestant suspicions of Catholicism still compelled Roosevelt to stress that Taylor was his personal emissary, not an ambassador.

Despite their efforts to prove themselves good Americans, Catholics remained to some degree a people apart. Having their own schools and social organizations, and being concentrated heavily in larger cities, ordinary Catholics had little opportunity to socialize with Protestants. Sometimes the Catholic hierarchy itself enforced the separation. With the opening of the new school year in the fall, Bishop T. J. Toolen of Mobile, Alabama, threatened to withhold the sacrament from Catholic parents who did not send their children to Catholic schools. Such limits on personal contacts tended to preserve mutual uncertainties and suspicions.

Even more than Catholics, American Jews were a people apart. Likewise clustered in urban areas, Jews remained a mystery to most Americans. Discrimination was subtle, yet no less strict. Many country clubs systematically excluded Jews, even if their bylaws contained no overt exclusionary clauses. In Southern California the exclusive Los Angeles Country Club was closed to even the rich and powerful Jewish leadership of the Hollywood film industry. The result was the formation of the Hillcrest Country Club, itself exclusive, but established by and for Jews. Likewise, Santa Anita racetrack was located in Arcadia, California, a town where Jews were not welcome. So Jewish racing enthusiasts established Hollywood Park, which would be open to their thoroughbreds.

Yet the Jews, too, were divided by internal tensions not apparent to outsiders. Reform Judaism had originated as an effort to adapt Jewish practice to the surrounding culture without losing its Jewish identity. By the start of the 20th Century, a reaction was setting in among Jews who thought that the adaptation had gone too far, and conservation of Jewish essentials rather than cultural adaptation should be their aim, hence the name Conservative Judaism. By the '20s and '30s this division had become strongly affected by Zionism, the movement that sought to establish a national home for the Jewish people. With few exceptions, Reform Jews, seeking like many Catholics to be viewed as 100 percent Americans, rejected Zionist aims. Conservative and (to some extent) Orthodox Jews were more receptive to the Zionist message. The result was confusion among Gentiles as to just who Jews were and where their primary allegiance lay. Such confusion helped perpetuate the anti-Semitism that was a part of the heritage of many Americans.

Regardless of their formal religious affiliation, many Americans had one passion they pursued with an almost religious zeal, a passion for the cult of celebrity. It was this passion that Father Divine, Daddy Grace, and Aimee Semple McPherson has tapped so effectively. Throughout the Depression ordinary people found diversion from their own troubles by following the lives and loves of the rich and famous. Hollywood was already a prime target for star-gazers, and magazines like *Photoplay* brought carefully crafted Hollywood images to readers across the country. *Life* magazine offered a regular "Movie of the Week" feature, which included production shots that gave readers a sense of having a part in making the movie. Gossip columnists chronicled the lives of celebrities for millions of newspaper readers, and no gossip columnist was more widely read than Walter Winchell.

Winchell had started out as a moderately successful vaudeville performer. When his career stalled, he turned to journalism and became one of the most widely read and widely feared reporters of his time. He knew how to trade favors (mainly endorsements in his column) for news tips, and he was sometimes able to break stories before the principals even knew about them. Winchell hardly ever admitted being wrong in what he published. On the rare occasions when he had to back down, he claimed his sources had misled him. Most celebrities feared Winchell's power, and few had the nerve to defy him openly.

Through the years Winchell made a gradual transition from Broadway reviews to celebrity gossip to more serious news. By 1941 he had become an outspoken interventionist and journalistic mouthpiece for the Roosevelt administration. His hatred of the Nazis (Ratzis in Winchellese) was of long standing, caused principally by their anti-Semitism. Yet as he made this transition, he did not adopt a more serious style of presentation. Whatever topic he discussed, his aim was to capture and hold his audience, using all the theatrical techniques he had learned in his youth. The result was a blending of news, celebrity gossip, and entertainment that marked a new direction in American journalism.

Winchell was especially noted for the way he handled (or mishandled) the English language. Poorly educated, he hid his lack of polish under some remarkably creative coinages and an almost telegraphic way of writing in short, memorable phrases. Always an outsider, he scorned high society, referring to young women of that class as debutramps. When a couple were dating, they were described as closerthanthat. His numerous terms for marriage included being welded or lohengrinned. If a couple were expecting a baby, they were infanticipating. If their marriage went bad, the couple might be Reno-vated. If he liked a person's work, he would award that person an orchid, the earliest such use of the word. Sometimes Winchell used the ambiguities of his neologisms to stay out of legal trouble. When he described a couple as making whoopee, he could always claim that he meant only that they were having fun, not necessarily having sex. Such colorful language contributed significantly to the popularity of his syndicated column, which reached almost nine million households daily and six and a half million on Sundays.

Winchell's prose style was also well suited to broadcasting. In addition to his column, he had a radio program every Sunday evening at 9:00 P.M. Eastern time on the NBC Red network. Winchell began every broadcast with the clacking of a telegraph key to suggest the urgency of the latest news (the signals were meaningless) and with the catch phrase, "Good evening, Mr. and Mrs. America," often expanded by such phrases as "Cuba and Canada," or "from Coast to coast," or "and all the ships at sea." He read his news and gossip items at a rapid-fire pace that left his listeners (but not him) breathless. In the middle of the program there would be a short advertising break, introduced with, "I'll be back in a flash with a flash." (His critics parodied him with the phrase, "I'll be back in a flash with more trash.") After catching his breath, he would repeat the entire program at 11:00 P.M. for broadcast to the West Coast, giving him a truly nationwide audience.

Winchell's radio program was followed immediately by that of another Hearst columnist, Louella Parsons. Just as Winchell's beat was officially Broadway, so Parsons officially covered Hollywood. But there was little similarity between the two. Hollywood was a one-industry town; and the major studios, for all their rivalry, joined ranks to protect and manage the image of the industry. Parsons was constrained to publish what the studios fed her. Scandal-mongering in the style of Walter Winchell would have cut off all her news sources. Even more, Hearst himself was personally involved with the movie industry. His mistress was the actress Marion Davies (who had retired from the screen in 1938), and he maintained a friendship (and sometimes business partnership) with movie giant Louis B. Mayer. Consequently, Parson's column purveyed to the country exactly the image of Hollywood that the studios wanted.

By 1941, however, the smooth image occasionally showed flaws. In 1938 the former actress Hedda Hopper began her own gossip column in the *Los Angeles Times*. Beholden to neither Hearst nor the studios, Hopper cultivated her own sources and created a certain amount of schizophrenic fear in Hollywood. In fact, Hopper was quietly promoted by none other than Louis B. Mayer, himself. His support was intended to provide competition that would keep Parsons from becoming too powerful. In return, Hopper could be counted on to be supportive of MGM. It was not a good thing to be on Hopper's bad side; but cooperating with her too openly could bring down the wrath of the other studios and their mouthpiece, Louella Parsons. By 1939 Hopper had achieved parity with Parsons as a gossip columnist, and the two women were on anything but friendly terms.

New York and Hollywood were not the only social centers whose residents drew the wondering attention of the public. Even Washington, D.C., then a sleepy Southern town, provided its full share of social excitement and gossip; and the main source of that gossip was the society section of the *Washington Times-Herald*. The publisher of the *Times-Herald* was Eleanor Medill Patterson, known to everyone as Cissy. Cissy Patterson was the adoring younger sister of Joe Patterson, publisher of the *New York Daily News*, America's first successful tabloid. She was also first cousin of Colonel Robert R. McCormick, the staunchly Republican and staunchly isolationist publisher of the *Chicago Tribune*. She was trained in the Hearst tradition of yellow journalism and actually acquired the *Times* and the *Herald*, which she merged into the *Times-Herald* in 1939, from W. R. Hearst. The *Daily News, Tribune,* and *Times-Herald*, controlled by the grandchildren of Chicago publisher Joseph Medill, presented a united front of conservative Republicanism, colorful writing, and abiding hatred of Franklin D. Roosevelt. Cissy Patterson built the *Times-Herald's* circulation into Washington's largest. Much of the paper's strength came from its society pages, which chronicled the doings of the rich and powerful in the Nation's Capital. Celebrities in Washington were not the movie stars, who seldom ventured there, but senators, congressmen, Supreme Court justices, ambassadors, visiting potentates, and above all the socialite hostesses who gave the parties and dinners for them. In this society Cissy, who hosted few parties herself, was the great power broker. Her social columns let people know who should be regarded as the most prominent hostesses and as the most interesting and desirable guests.

The doyenne of Washington society was Evalyn Walsh McLean, close friend of Cissy Patterson and the only surviving child of Thomas Walsh, a prospector who struck it rich. Evalyn Walsh was already well known in the Washington social world when she married

Ned McLean, grandson and heir to Washington McLean, owner of the *Cincinnati Enquirer* and the *Washington Post*. Evalyn and Ned had both grown up excessively spoiled, and both were accustomed to having whatever they wanted. One of the young couple's early purchases was the Hope Diamond, which Evalyn wore as if it were everyday jewelry. After her highly publicized 1932 divorce, she remained in Washington at the center of capital society. Invitations to her salons were eagerly sought, partly for the exceptional quality of the food and drink, partly for the diversity of the guest list. Evalyn loved to amuse herself by inviting political adversaries to dinners at her home, "Friendship." She would seat them at the same table, then sit back to watch the fireworks. More than once a guest stormed out of her house in a fury, but they were always eager to accept an invitation for another visit.

Evalyn McLean's guest list included such figures as Martin Dies, the oft-married actress Constance Bennett, Cissy Patterson, Drew Pearson, Isaiah Berlin, and Vice President Henry Wallace. The vice president was a special favorite since the guests loved to gossip about his supposed attendance at séances. Since 1939 one of her regular guests had been Robert R. Reynolds, junior senator from North Carolina. As the acquaintance progressed to friendship, Reynolds became more and more interested in Evalyn's daughter, Evalyn Washington McLean, or Evie as she was called. Evie was an independent sort who had refused to make her social debut and instead announced that she intended to pursue a career in music or radio. But in August of 1941, the twenty-year-old Evie informed her mother that she was engaged to be married to the fifty-seven-year-old Reynolds, who had already been to the altar four times. Evalyn's delight was matched only by the senator's surprise. Apparently Evie had neglected to inform him. But when Evalyn told him she wanted him to marry Evie in order to "take care of her money," Reynolds accepted the assignment with pleasure. Naturally, the newspapers had a field day. The Asheville *Citizen*, Reynolds's home-town paper and no supporter, suggested that he celebrate by taking some time off, indeed, all the time from then until 1944, when the paper hoped to see him voted out of office.

Fascination with the doings of the upper classes extended especially to the British. Their highly effective ambassador, Viscount Halifax, provided celebrity watchers with a special brand of amusement. Halifax was a dedicated fox hunter, and he did not propose to give up riding to hounds just because he now lived in Washington. Friends and acquaintances in Virginia and Pennsylvania provided ample opportunity, and Halifax soon acquired the nickname Lord Holy Fox. Carl Sandburg excoriated him for his pastime, saying of his fox hunting that "It's not un-American or subversive. It is merely indicative of the fraction of the British embassy which lives in the past and hopes the future will be the same." Despite Sandburg's criticism, most of Washington society saw the ambassador's fox hunting as just another amusing British trait.

Gossip about public figures—the more salacious, the better—perfectly fitted Cissy Patterson's *Times-Herald* and her leading scandal monger, Drew Pearson, whose daily column, "Washington Merry-Go-Round," targeted the prominent politicians and corporate leaders who wielded influence over national affairs. His newsgathering methods included eavesdropping, bribery, intimidation, even breaking and entering. Once he identified a subject for an exposé, he would sacrifice standards of accuracy in order to make a good story. But he was right often enough that he was one of the most feared (and hated) reporters in Washington; and United Features Syndicate distributed his column to more than six hundred papers across the country, a reach exceeded only by Walter Winchell.

Like Winchell and Parsons, Pearson and his partner Robert Allen had their own radio program, *Listen America*, on the Mutual network. The partnership ended in 1941 and Pearson moved to NBC with his own program, *Drew Pearson Comments*. The year 1941 also marked the start of another change of direction for Pearson. At first he had tended to be an isolationist like Cissy Patterson and her brother and cousin. But as he studied the development of the war in Europe, he became convinced that America had to support the Allies. His changing views put additional strain on his relations with Patterson, and by November, when he gave his annual (and last) birthday party for Cissy, the tension had grown almost to an outright breach. Surface civility was preserved (an achievement for Cissy), but the parting of ways was inevitable. Before the next year was out, "Washington Merry-Go-Round" would be dropped by the *Times-Herald* and picked up by the rival *Washington Post*.

CHAPTER 12

December: The End of Peace

DECEMBER 7, 1941, was one of those dates forever burned into the memory of everyone who lived through it. People retained vivid impressions of exactly where they were and what they were doing when they first heard reports of the bombing of Pearl Harbor. At Ft. Sam Houston, Texas, Brigadier General Dwight Eisenhower was taking a nap at his quarters when his aide called with the news. Cleveland pitcher Bob Feller was driving across the Mississippi River at Moline, Illinois, on his way to the baseball winter meetings in Chicago, listening to his car radio. Dr. Willard Dow was on a train from Detroit to Washington to discuss magnesium production with the Secretary of War. Edward R. Murrow was playing golf at the Burning Tree Country Club in Bethesda, Maryland. They all remembered.

That afternoon NBC newscaster H. R. Baukhage was taking a walk in Rock Creek Park in Washington. On his way home he stopped by his father's house for a visit. While he was there, the telephone rang.

It was the network calling with the news of the Pearl Harbor attack. Baukhage was to go to the White House immediately. He arrived there at the same time as presidential Press Secretary Steve Early, an old friend. Early quickly filled him in on what was known at that time about the attack, and Baukhage asked permission to set up a news desk in the White House press room. Early agreed, and Baukhage began reporting for the NBC Blue Network from one of the first on-the-spot news centers.

In Pittsburgh that afternoon, the America First Committee was preparing to hold one of its largest rallies. By 3:00 P.M. some 1,500 people had gathered in Soldiers and Sailors Memorial Hall to hear Senator Gerald Nye speak against Roosevelt's warmongering. Few had heard the news of Pearl Harbor, but one who had was Robert Hagy, a local reporter who was covering the rally. Hagy located Nye shortly before the senator was scheduled to speak and asked him if he had heard the news. Nye said the report sounded fishy to him and hinted that he thought it was just another Roosevelt deception. He then went on stage and launched into his usual tirade against F.D.R. After Nye had been speaking for about forty-five minutes, Hagy got a call from his editor, informing him that Japan had declared war on the United States. He wrote out the news on a note, marched onstage, and handed the note to Nye. The senator looked at it and then kept speaking for another half an hour. Finally, when he had exhausted his criticisms of the president, Nye said, "I have before me the worst news that I have encountered in the last twenty years." He then read the note aloud, said, "I can't somehow believe this," and left the podium. The next morning Senator Bennett C. Clark announced that the congressional investigation of Hollywood, in which Nye had been the first witness, was being abandoned.

Two days later the America First National Committee met in Chicago to discuss the future of the organization. A few members favored simply adjourning the meetings until after the war. But the majority, including General Wood, realized that America First's time had passed. They had fought the fight against intervention, and events had overtaken them. Now it was time to dissolve the organization.

After approving a final statement asserting the rightness of their original principles and the present need to pursue victory in the war, the Committee dispersed. The next morning readers of the *Chicago Tribune* could read about both the dissolution of America First and Hitler's declaration of war on America.

That Sunday afternoon Woody Guthrie and the Almanac Singers were performing at a hootenanny in New York. Woody had picked up the term hootenanny during the group's West Coast tour the previous summer. At the hootenanny on December 7, song sheets were distributed to the audience with six of the group's most popular songs, "Union Maid," "Reuben James," "The Ballad of Harry Bridges," "High Cost of Living," "Jim Crow," and a new piece, "Mister Lindbergh." This last was a vicious attack on Charles Lindbergh and the America First organization. The hootenanny was interrupted by a small commotion in the back, and Arthur Stern, a member of the Almanac Singers, took the microphone to announce that the Japanese had just attacked Pearl Harbor.

Over the next few days hard information about the Japanese attack was difficult to come by. The government knew that it could not permit news reporting that compromised national security, but it had little experience in balancing necessary censorship with honest reporting. The situation was even more difficult since many of the official reports from the field, especially those from Lieutenant General Douglas MacArthur in the Philippines, were so overblown with optimism that they lacked any connection with reality. Philippine and American troops were said to be throwing the Japanese invaders back into the sea when in fact the defenses against the Japanese attack were breaking down quite rapidly. MacArthur had been caught unprepared, and the ineffectiveness of his response to the attacks was covered up with rhetoric.

The Army and Navy felt an obligation to get some news out as quickly as they could. Families of those who died in combat were notified as soon as the information was processed in Washington. Even then, the families were asked not to reveal where their sons had been stationed. It was much later in the month before the first photographs from Pearl Harbor could be published. At this stage an inexperienced government simply had no idea what information might or might not be useful to the enemy.

In the absence of hard news, rumors became the rapidly spreading substitute. Japanese planes were said to be seen at many locations on the West Coast. Japanese ships were reported to have shelled places in California. A German bomber was thought to have been spotted over New York. Uncertainty also characterized the response of Americans to Japanese and people of Japanese ancestry who happened to be in this country. Acts of vandalism and physical aggression were not uncommon. Chinese were mistaken for Japanese often enough that *Life* published an article purporting to show how to tell from racial characteristics the difference between Japanese and Chinese. By the end of the month more systematic information was being released, and the early emotional reactions began to quiet down.

The attack on Pearl Harbor caused significant changes in the way the federal government viewed issues of civil rights. If African Americans were to be asked to share in the sacrifices that all citizens would have to make in order to restore freedom overseas, it would no longer be possible to deny them those same freedoms at home. One change in the government's attitude became apparent immediately.

For many years there had been attempts in the Deep South to restore some form of servitude to replace the slavery that had been abolished by the Thirteenth Amendment. A common device had the local sheriff jail able-bodied African Americans on various misdemeanor charges, often trumped up. A farmer or industrialist, in need of labor, would then pay the prisoner's fine, technically regarding the payment as a loan to the prisoner. Paperwork was seldom kept of the financial record, so evidence of the transaction was hard to find. The released African American would be taken to a farm, mine, or factory, where he would be imprisoned under armed guard and required to work off the loan. Since the employer could set the wages and impose a charge against them for food and housing, the prisoners found that instead of working off their loans, they were in fact sinking deeper into debt. They had effectively been returned to a condition of slavery from which there was no escape. Runaways were regularly recaptured and sometimes killed as a warning to the others. The federal government had for many years ignored the problem, leaving the matter to local officials. State laws were seldom enforced against the perpetrators, who had the full support of the local courts. On the rare occasion when a prosecution was brought, the white employer would plead guilty, trusting in the court to impose only a token punishment. As recently as October, in Alabama one Charles Bledsoe had pleaded guilty to holding an African American in peonage and had been given a fine of $100 and a six-month suspended sentence.

In the aftermath of Pearl Harbor, Attorney General Francis Biddle recognized that this situation could not be allowed to continue. On December 12 he issued Circular No. 3591, a directive to all United States attorneys. Biddle observed that very few prosecutions had been brought in cases of involuntary servitude, the excuse being that evidence of debt was hard to find. Biddle reminded the attorneys that servitude for debt (peonage) was only one form of involuntary servitude and that several sections of the U.S. Code prohibited involuntary servitude even when there was no debt involved. Citing the relevant sections of the code, he directed the U.S. attorneys to pursue prosecutions vigorously. His views were expressed bluntly and directly:

> In the United States one cannot sell himself as a peon or slave—the law is fixed and established to protect the weak-minded, the poor, the miserable. Men will sometimes sell themselves for a meal of victuals or contract with another who acts as surety on his bond to work out the amount of the bond upon his release from jail. Any such contract is positively null and void and the procuring and causing of such contract to be made violates these statutes.

There was, perhaps inevitably, a certain amount of foot-dragging among the attorneys. There was also reluctance at the F. B. I., where J. Edgar Hoover had little interest in pursuing such cases. But Biddle reinforced his order, prodding reluctant attorneys and the Bureau, and gradually progress was made.

As America prepared itself for full engagement in the war, the interest in the British war effort intensified. That December the news was not good. In the Mediterranean the introduction of a German submarine force to help the floundering Italian navy had already had an effect. On the night of November 13, a German submarine torpedoed the aircraft carrier *Ark Royal*. Despite efforts to save it, the ship capsized and sank the next day. Less than two weeks later the battleship *Barham* blew up when it was hit by three torpedoes from another submarine. Then in December the Italians were themselves finally able to exact some revenge for their humiliation at Taranto. Specially trained Italian frogmen penetrated the British defenses at the naval base at Alexandria, Egypt, and attached mines to the battleships *Queen Elizabeth* and *Valiant* and the oiler *Sagona*. When the mines went off, all three ships settled quickly to the bottom of the harbor. The water was so shallow that the British were able for a few days to maintain the fiction that the ships were still afloat and in service. Eventually, however, they had to admit the sinkings when the ships were patched, refloated, and sailed off for repairs. At least for the time being, there were no British battleships left in service in the eastern Mediterranean.

In the Far East, however, the news for the British was even worse. Japan had already demanded and received substantial concessions in French Indo-China from the helpless Vichy government. Japanese troops and planes were now based in Southern Indo-China, within striking distance of the great British naval and military base at Singapore. For Japan the issue was oil. The country had few oil reserves of its own, only 10 percent of its needs. Without fuel for her industry, waging modern war would be impossible. Historically Japan had gotten 80 percent of its oil from the United States and 10 percent from the Dutch East Indies. When these sources were cut off by the American oil embargo (in which the Dutch followed suit), war became practically inevitable.

Britain responded to the Japanese threat by reinforcing the garrison at Singapore. A fleet was dispatched under the command of

Admiral Sir Thomas Philips, who would take command of the China Station. The fleet was to consist of the new battleship H.M.S. *Prince of Wales* (which had fought *Bismarck* in the Denmark Strait and brought Churchill to Newfoundland), the battle cruiser H.M.S. *Repulse*, and the aircraft carrier H.M.S. *Indomitable,* plus escorts. Unfortunately, *Indomitable* ran aground at Jamaica, where it was to pick up its aircraft, and had to put in at the U.S. base at Norfolk for repairs. Philips (whose small stature earned him the nickname Tom Thumb) was not unduly concerned. He was one of the many naval officers who believed that a well handled ship at sea could never be sunk by aircraft.

Philips may also have counted on support from the R.A.F. in Southeast Asia. Unfortunately, that expectation was hampered by two problems. First, the R.A.F. was equipped with American Brewster Buffaloes, planes so obsolete that the U.S. Navy was removing them from combat service as quickly as modern replacements became available. Even worse, Philips would command only the naval forces in the region. Air and land forces were under the command of Air Chief Marshal Sir Robert Brooke-Popham. Once Philips arrived in Singapore, he and Brooke-Popham had very little time to coordinate their divided commands before the Japanese launched bombing raids on Singapore and began the invasion of Malaya and Thailand in the early hours of December 8 (December 7 on the eastern side of the international date line).

Sensing a need to move quickly to disrupt the Japanese landings on the Malay coast, Philips proposed to take his fleet north from Singapore at once and attack the enemy transports and support vessels. But it was already too late to disrupt the landings. Airfields in Malaya were falling to the Japanese, and the R.A.F. could not guarantee any air support for the mission. Despite the risks, on that very afternoon, December 8, Philips took *Prince of Wales, Repulse,* and their supporting destroyers out of Singapore Harbor and steamed north to attack. Proceeding up the east coast of the Malay Peninsula, Philips maintained radio silence in an attempt to achieve surprise. But during the second night a Japanese search plane dropped a flare that seemed to indicate that the Japanese had discovered the British ships. With the element of surprise gone, Philips reluctantly abandoned the mission and turned south for Singapore. On the way south the fleet was spotted by a Japanese submarine, and in the early morning hours of December 10, Japanese air patrols covered the area, searching for the British ships.

They found them not long after dawn, and the first attacks by bombers and torpedo planes began just after 11:00. With no air cover, the British ships had to rely on their anti-aircraft guns. It quickly became evident that anti-aircraft fire was totally ineffective against a determined air attack. Torpedoes dropped from airplanes were the main weapon. Six hit *Prince of Wales* and four hit *Repulse*. Neither ship could sustain such damage. A belated call went out for aircraft support from the RAF, but it was too late. *Repulse* sank at 12:33, just as the first British planes were arriving. *Prince of Wales* went down forty minutes later, taking Admiral Philips with her. Altogether 840 officers and men lost their lives, out of the 2,921 on board. The three escorting destroyers were undamaged and picked up the survivors. Americans were later to get an especially vivid account of the battle since one of the survivors of *Repulse* was CBS news reporter Cecil Brown.

Although the loss of *Prince of Wales* and *Repulse* sent shock waves through the British Empire and made newspaper headlines in America, news from the British battlefronts was not entirely bad. Especially in North Africa there were encouraging signs as Major General Neil Ritchie and the 8th Army continued to press *Generalleutnant* Erwin Rommel and his retreating German army. At Gazala Rommel stopped retreating and challenged the advancing British. Ritchie made a frontal attack with the 4th Indian Division and turned the German right flank with the 4th Armoured Brigade. The German retreat resumed, and on Christmas Eve the 8th Army entered Benghazi. Just after the first of the year Rommel reached a fortified base at El Agheila. The British were too exhausted, their tanks too worn out, for the attack to continue. But eastern Cyrenaica had been cleared of the enemy.

On the Russian front, also, the first good news began to trickle in. On the morning of December 5, the Russians surprised everyone by launching a major counter-offensive around Moscow. For weeks the new Moscow front commander, General Georgi Zhukov, had been preparing his assault, bringing in fresh Siberian troops from the Far East, arming and deploying new tanks that were properly insulated for the winter weather, and setting out artillery pieces that were lubricated with special low-temperature grease. Now he opened the assault with screaming Katyusha rockets followed by waves of warmly clad infantrymen carrying well lubricated weapons. The shocked Germans tried to react, but many of their weapons were as frozen as they were. Some German mechanics were able to get their tanks going by building fires under them to thaw the oil; and where they could bring tanks and artillery into play, the Germans put up a stiff resistance. But in just a few days the invaders were pushed back more than fifty miles. It was mid-January before the front finally stabilized for the winter. The pressure was off Moscow, and now the initiative in the center of the front lay with the Russians.

After Pearl Harbor it took Americans some time to adapt their peacetime habits to wartime practice, but the war's immediate impact on scheduled sporting events could not be avoided. Following the attack there was deep concern about the possibility of Japanese raids on the West Coast. Organizers of the Rose Bowl considered the 90,000 people expected for the game to be a prime target for enemy attack, and Lieutenant General John DeWitt, Commanding General of the 4th Army, issued orders for the parade and game to be canceled. But Percy Locey, Athletic Director at Oregon State, host team for the game, was not easily deterred. He put in a call to his opponent's coach, Wallace Wade at Duke, to see whether the game might be moved to Durham, North Carolina.

Wade immediately agreed to Locey's request and made arrangements for North Carolina Governor J. Melville Broughton to issue a formal invitation. The Rose Bowl Committee gladly accepted, and General De Witt concurred. Duke fans anticipated a victory, and the game was reported as sold out. A small *contretemps* was avoided when Duke departed from its usual ticketing policy and failed to set aside a section of seats for blacks in the segregated stadium. A vigorous blast from the local black press resulted in the "discovery" of 140 extra tickets, and black fans were able to attend. The evening before the game, Glenn Miller caught the spirit of the occasion on his radio program. Miller was sponsored by Chesterfield cigarettes, a product of American Tobacco Company, whose headquarters were in Durham. Always alert to an advertising opportunity for his sponsor, Miller introduced one of his signature tunes by saying, "Tomorrow's the Rose Bowl, and you Blue Devils had better be *In the Mood*!"

Duke was undefeated and went into the game as a two-touchdown favorite. But undisciplined play and missed opportunities cost them heavily. The weather certainly did not help the high-powered Blue Devil offense. Cold rain mixed with fog and temperatures in the forties affected fans and players alike. Oregon State played inspired football, stifled several late Duke drives, and came away with a 20-16 upset.

For America's Pastime, the beginning of the war raised questions as to whether the 1942 baseball season would even be played. The winter meetings began on Tuesday, December 9, just two days after the Japanese attack. Before they ended, both Hank Greenberg and Bob Feller had enlisted. While some trades were made and ordinary business transacted at the meetings, the attention of the owners was focused on the war and the impact it might have on the game. For some weeks owners Clark Griffith of the Washington Senators and Don Barnes of the St. Louis Browns had been lobbying other owners to allow more night baseball games. Each team was limited to seven night games, most of which were played in the American League. Griffith and Barnes wanted the number raised to twenty-eight. Commissioner Kenesaw Mountain Landis was generally opposed to night baseball, and most of the National League owners agreed with him. Now Landis argued that the coming of the war meant there should be no substantial changes to the way baseball did business. The number stayed at seven. But Griffith was not called the Old Fox for nothing. Working on the owners' uncertainty as to whether baseball should even continue during the war, Griffith and others asked Landis to write to the president for guidance.

Writing to Roosevelt was just about the last thing Landis wanted to do. The commissioner and the president cordially despised each other, and Landis blamed Roosevelt and Navy Secretary Frank Knox for the Navy's lack of preparedness at Pearl Harbor. Nevertheless, Griffith kept up the pressure; and on January 14 Landis finally wrote to Roosevelt asking whether the president thought baseball should continue during the war. Roosevelt replied immediately with the so-called green-light letter, in which he gave his opinion that the game ought to continue in order to provide entertainment to the people who would now be working harder than ever to win the war. In the drafting of this letter it appears that Old Fox Griffith, who enjoyed warm relations with the White House, exercised some subtle influence over one sentence that the president included in the middle: "And, incidentally, I hope that night baseball can be extended because it gives an excellent opportunity to the day shift to see a game occasionally." Landis swallowed his opposition, reconvened the owners, and raised the number of night games to fourteen, with a special allowance of twenty-one for Griffith's Senators.

The radio now took on added importance as a source of news and also as a unifying force for the country. Some weeks earlier William Lewis, head of radio at the U.S. Office Facts and Figures, had approached CBS writer Norman Corwin and asked him to prepare an hour-long program entitled *We hold these truths*. The program was to be broadcast on December 15, the 150th anniversary of the ratification of the Bill of Rights by the Commonwealth of Virginia, the ratification that brought the Bill of Rights into effect. The government would ask all of the major networks to carry the program simultaneously, the first time such an agreement had been made. Although he was exhausted from his recent series *26 by Corwin*, the writer accepted the challenge and began working on the script, with his deadline just over three weeks away. At the end of the first week in December, Corwin left for California, whence the narrative part of the program would be broadcast. The script was only three-quarters finished, and Corwin shut himself up in his Pullman compartment so he could work undisturbed. On Sunday afternoon he rang for a porter and asked to rent an on-train radio set, an amenity on the top name trains. The porter replied that all the radios were taken because the Japanese had bombed Pearl Harbor.

During the train's stop in Kansas City, a worried Corwin sent Lewis a telegram asking whether the program would still be aired. Lewis immediately contacted President Roosevelt, who was scheduled to participate in the show. When Corwin's train stopped in Albuquerque, a reply was waiting for him. The president believed it was now more important than ever that the broadcast should go ahead.

On the evening of December 15, an estimated 63,000,000 listeners gathered around their radios to hear these words, spoken as the orchestra played "America the Beautiful" softly in the background:

> This is a program about the making of a promise and the keeping of a promise.
> This is a program about the rights of people.
> This is a program coming to you over the combined radio networks of the United States,
> Bringing you the voices of Americans,
> Bringing you the voice of the President of the United States.
> This is a program for listeners in all zones of continental time,
> For listeners on ships away from home,
> For listeners in uniform,
> For listeners on the American islands in the two great oceans.
> This is a program about the guarantee made to the people of America 150 years ago,
> A guarantee that has been kept through peace and war and peace and war,
> A guarantee we call the Bill of Rights.

The program was a mix of narrative and dramatization portraying the drafting, ratification, and effects of the first ten amendments to the Constitution. The writing was typical of Corwin, a text that walked the line between poetry and prose:

> One hundred, fifty years is not long in the reckoning of a hill,
> But to a man it's long enough.
> One hundred, fifty years is a weekend to the redwood tree,

But to a man it's two full lifetimes.
One hundred, fifty years is a twinkle to a star,
But to a man it's time enough to teach six generations what the meaning is of liberty,
How to use it, when to fight for it.

Corwin had gathered Edward Arnold, Lionel Barrymore, Walter Brennan, Bob Burns, Walter Huston, Marjorie Main, Edward G. Robinson, James Stewart, Rudy Vallee, and Orson Welles to perform his script. Bernard Herrmann conducted a studio orchestra performing the background music that he had written and arranged. The narrative included the text of the Bill of Rights, interspersed with dramatizations depicting the protections it afforded. The spoken program concluded with a brief address by President Roosevelt, who took the opportunity to fix in the minds of his listeners, perhaps half the population of the country, a clear and precise understanding of why we were at war. The attack on the United States, the president said, represented a direct attack on the Bill of Rights. Focusing his attention on Germany, President Roosevelt portrayed the war that had just broken over the country as an attempt by totalitarian states to wipe out the protections embodied in the Bill of Rights, protections that were the dream of peoples in all the rest of the world. The president's talk was followed by the playing of the National Anthem by the New York Philharmonic under Leopold Stokowski.

Popular response to the program was slow to develop. With all three networks broadcasting it, people did not know exactly where to write to express their feelings. But over the next few days the reactions began to come in, and the response was overwhelming. It was a personal triumph for Corwin, a triumph made all the sweeter because it set off a bidding war between MGM, anxious to obtain his services, and CBS, now anxious to retain him (Chapter 8).

Precious as the Bill of Rights was, the original document, kept on display in the Library of Congress, could not be exposed to the risk of damage during wartime. Shortly after Pearl Harbor, Archibald MacLeish, the Librarian of Congress, called Treasury

Secretary Morgenthau to ask whether there would be space for the Declaration of Independence, the Constitution, and other founding documents to be stored in the nation's bullion depository at Ft. Knox, Kentucky. Morgenthau allocated sixty cubic feet of space; and the day after Christmas a heavily armed convoy took the carefully packaged documents to Union Station, where they were placed in a special Pullman car guarded by Secret Service agents for transportation to Ft. Knox.

In August Roosevelt and Churchill had felt the time was right for them to meet face to face so they and their staffs could discuss, among other things, a joint course of action if America should become involved as a combatant. Now that the Japanese had brought this country into the fighting, a second meeting was desirable, almost imperative. Once again Churchill was the one to make the journey across the Atlantic, and once again that journey had to be shrouded in complete secrecy. On December 12 the Prime Minister and his staff took an overnight train bound from London to Greenock, Scotland, on the Firth of Clyde. There they boarded Britain's newest battleship, H.M.S. *Duke of York*, which had just been placed in commission on November 4. The trip across the Atlantic must have stirred complex emotions in Churchill. *Duke of York* was almost identical to her sister ship, H.M.S. *Prince of Wales*, which had carried Churchill to Argentia Bay in August and which had just been sunk by the Japanese off the coast of Malaya.

The journey was slowed by weather so heavy and seas so rough that the escorting destroyers had to turn back, but the battleship finally drew into American waters on Monday, December 22. Churchill, anxious to arrive at the White House for dinner that evening, asked that the ship dock at Hampton Roads so he could debark and fly from there to Washington. An airliner was provided for the prime minister and his senior staff, while the others followed by special train. When Churchill's plane landed at Anacostia Naval Air Station, he was surprised and pleased that the president had broken protocol to come meet him in person. The next morning Press Secretary Stephen Early handed reporters a short announcement that the prime minister had arrived for consultations with the president. The day was occupied with preparations for the conferences to follow, the arrival of the rest of the British entourage from the Navy base at Norfolk, and a formal welcoming dinner. On Tuesday the meetings began in earnest, and at his 4:00 P.M. press conference the president introduced his guest to American reporters for the first time. Churchill had long experience in talking in generalities without really giving out any information, but the reporters seemed content with a number of usable quotations as they went away to write their stories.

Christmas Eve was filled with more meetings, and in the evening Churchill shared in the traditional lighting of the National Christmas Tree on the White House lawn. The Secret Service had wanted to move the location of the tree across the street to Lafayette Park, but the president insisted that the traditional location be maintained. A compromise of sorts was worked out. All packages had to be left outside the White House fence, and only specially invited guests were allowed to get close to the South Portico. At 4:30 the Marine Band began its concert of Christmas music, and at 5:00 they began "Hail to the Chief" as Roosevelt and his party emerged from the White House onto the South Balcony. Following the usual preliminaries, the president addressed the crowd gathered there and, by radio, the entire country. After speaking of the war preparations that clouded the celebration of Christmas this year, he continued,

> There is another preparation demanded of this Nation beyond and beside the preparation of weapons and materials of war. There is demanded also of us the preparation of our hearts; the arming of our hearts. And when we make ready our hearts for the labor and the suffering and the ultimate victory which lie ahead, then we observe Christmas Day—with all of its memories and all of its meanings—as we should.

At the end of his prepared remarks, Roosevelt invited the prime minister, standing beside him, "my associate, my old and good friend, to say a word to the people of America, old and young, tonight Winston

Churchill, Prime Minister of Great Britain." Churchill's brief but moving remarks struck just the right note with his American listeners.

I spend this anniversary and festival far from my country, far from my family, yet I cannot truthfully say that I feel far from home. Whether it be the ties of blood on my mother's side, or the friendships I have developed here over many years of active life, or the commanding sentiment of comradeship in the common cause of great peoples who speak the same language, who kneel at the same altars and, to a very large extent, pursue the same ideals, I cannot feel myself a stranger here in the centre and at the summit of the United States. I feel a sense of unity and fraternal association which, added to the kindliness of your welcome, convinces me that I have a right to sit at your fireside and share your Christmas joys.

This is a strange Christmas Eve. Almost the whole world is locked in deadly struggle, and, with the most terrible weapons which science can devise, the nations advance upon each other. Ill would it be for us this Christmastide if we were not sure that no greed for the land or wealth of any other people, no vulgar ambition, no morbid lust for material gain at the expense of others, had led us to the field. Here, in the midst of war, raging and roaring over all the lands and seas, creeping nearer to our hearts and homes, here, amid all the tumult, we have tonight the peace of the spirit in each cottage home and in every generous heart. Therefore we may cast aside for this night at least the cares and dangers which beset us, and make for the children an evening of happiness in a world of storm. Here, then, for one night only, each home throughout the English-speaking world should be a brightly-lighted island of happiness and peace.

Let the children have their night of fun and laughter. Let the gifts of Father Christmas delight their play. Let us grown-ups share to the full in their unstinted pleasures before we turn again to the stern task and the formidable years that lie before us, resolved that, by our sacrifice and daring, these same children shall not be robbed of their inheritance or denied their right to live in a free and decent world.

And so, in God's mercy, a happy Christmas to you all.

On Christmas morning Roosevelt and Churchill, both Anglican but neither especially religious or a regular church-goer, set off for the Christmas service at Foundry Methodist Church on 16th Street. When asked why he, an Episcopalian, chose a Methodist service for Christmas Day, Roosevelt answered, "What's the matter? I like to sing hymns with the Methodys." They returned to the White House for more conferences over the latest war news. The most disquieting report was that Hong Kong had surrendered to the Japanese early that morning. The fall of the British Crown Colony had been inevitable, but it was no less embarrassing and painful for all that.

Meeting followed meeting; and on the day after Christmas, Churchill journeyed to Capitol Hill to address a joint session of Congress. Playing on his ancestry, Churchill began his address by noting that through his American mother he was descended from a lieutenant in George Washington's Continental Army. That fact, he said, made this opportunity to address Congress "one of the most moving and thrilling of my life, which is already long and has not been entirely uneventful. I wish indeed that my mother, whose memory I cherish across the vale of years, could be here to see me. By the way, I can't help reflecting that if my father had been American and my mother British, instead of the other way round, I might have got here on my own." His audience loved it. Warming to his theme, Churchill leveled not-too-veiled criticism at America's reluctance to prepare for war. Then he turned to the common enemies: "What kind of a people do they think we are? Is it possible that they do not realize that we shall never cease to persevere against them until they have been taught a lesson which they and the world will never forget?" By the end of the speech, Churchill had Congress thoroughly on his side, convinced as they had not been before that, whatever reverses it might suffer, Britain would never give in. Even isolationist Senator Burton Wheeler grudgingly conceded that it had been a clever speech.

Canadian Prime Minister Mackenzie King arrived in Washington that afternoon, just too late to hear Churchill's speech. King was deeply concerned by a small but important diplomatic *contretemps* that had offended the Canadian government. Saint-Pierre and Miquelon are two small and largely insignificant islands off the south coast of Newfoundland, less than fifteen miles from the Burin Peninsula. They are the last remnant of France's once extensive North American Empire and are inhabited by a few thousand fishermen. In 1941 the islands were held by the Vichy French government, and a powerful radio transmitter regularly broadcast Marshal Pétain's propaganda to French-speaking Quebec. There was a strong suspicion that the same transmitter was broadcasting coded information to German submarines at sea. Canada and England were in favor of a Canadian operation to win over the islands to the allied cause. The United States, trying to maintain its already delicate relations with Vichy France, was opposed. Into this mix stepped the proud and testy leader of the Free French, General Charles de Gaulle. The Free French Admiral Émile Muselier was on his way to Canada to inspect French warships impounded there. On de Gaulle's instructions, Muselier diverted his ship to Saint-Pierre, landed on Christmas Eve to an enthusiastic welcome, and quickly organized a plebiscite that resulted in an overwhelming victory for the Free French. The Vichy governor was held captive, and a new governor was appointed by Muselier. While the British and Canadians were somewhat upset by de Gaulle's coup, Secretary of State Cordell Hull was furious. He wanted to mollify Vichy by forcing the Free French to pull out, but cooler heads prevailed. No action was taken, but the strong American hostility impaired relations between de Gaulle and Roosevelt.

On December 28 Churchill and King departed Washington on an overnight train for Ottawa, where Churchill was to address the Canadian Parliament on the 30th. The speech was a masterpiece, in which Churchill defused the issue of Saint-Pierre and Miquelon by launching into a criticism of France for not fighting on from her overseas empire. "When I warned them [the French] that Britain would fight alone whatever they did, their generals told their Prime Minister and his divided Cabinet, 'In three weeks England will have her neck wrung like a chicken.' Some chicken! Some neck!"

After his triumphant speech, Churchill walked out into an ante-room where a young Ottawa photographer, Yosuf Karsh, had been given two minutes to take Churchill's portrait. Karsh himself describes their encounter best:

> Mr. Churchill, as he was then, had been addressing the Canadian Parliament in Ottawa on December 30; he was in no mood for portraiture and two minutes were all he would allow me as he passed from the House of Commons Chamber to an ante-room—two niggardly minutes in which I must try to put on film a man who had already written or inspired a library of books, baffled all his biographers, filled the world with his fame, and me, on this occasion, with dread. He marched in scowling, and regarded my camera as he might regard the German enemy. His expression suited me perfectly, if only I could capture it, but the cigar thrust between his teeth seemed somehow incompatible with such a solemn and formal occasion. Instinctively I removed the cigar. At this the Churchillian scowl deepened, his head was thrust forward belligerently, and the hand placed on his hip in an attitude of anger. So he stands in my portrait in what has always seemed to me the image of England in those years, defiant and unconquerable.

The result was probably the most famous wartime portrait taken of Churchill and is one of the most widely reproduced portrait photographs of all time.

America could not transform overnight from a peacetime economy, even one so heavily dependent on defense spending, into a full war economy. As Christmas approached, the seasonal advertisements tempted shoppers with holiday gifts of all kinds. Luxury items were still readily available. Fine men's and ladies' watches from manufacturers like Hamilton and Elgin ranged in price from about $44.00 up to ten times that much, while Longines offered their men's watches for as little as $27.50. Coty and Max Factor offered gifts starting as low as $1.00 for face powder and going up to $9.75 for their elegant gift sets. Yardley's English Lavender gift sets ran as high as $15.00. Yardley toiletries were still being produced in England and, like Scotch whiskey, provided much needed export income for Britain.

Gifts for the home were already showing the first signs of wartime restrictions. While Community Plate, "the bride's favorite silverware," was still available, Rogers Silver had to warn customers that the priorities of defense production had led to some shortages in their line. Sterling, on the other hand, seemed to be in good supply for those who could afford it. International offered services for four from $74.00. Radios and phonographs were often substantial pieces of furniture and were usually sold in furniture stores or in department stores with furniture departments. Lane advertised a Christmas special on one of its simpler hope chest designs in walnut veneer with a quarter-matched walnut veneer panel on the front. The price was just $29.75 in the East, but it would be slightly more in the West and Canada "due to freight costs." The new G.E. automatic blanket with a built-in thermostat, "the blanket with a brain," was $34.50.

Even highly practical products were being advertised as thoughtful and romantic gifts. Men were encouraged to buy a Hoover vacuum cleaner "because it saves the strength, beauty and time of that woman." A Silex 8-cup electric coffee maker ($8.95) was easy to clean. Women were encouraged to "Give him the BEST," as Interwoven Socks were still available with toes reinforced with DuPont nylon. Botany Ties, "Wrinkle-proof," were available for as little as a dollar, as was Old Spice after-shave in the ceramic bottle. B.V.D. robe and pajama sets started at $5.00. For wrapping gifts, Texcel Tape returned with their Christmas line of tapes decorated with colorful seasonal images.

As might be expected, cigarette manufacturers offered cartons with Christmas decorations as appropriate gifts for family and friends. P. Lorillard took the occasion to advertise the addition of

Latakia tobacco to its Old Gold blend. Camels and Prince Albert pipe tobacco (in a can, of course) were "Gifts that are sure to please in beautiful Christmas wrappers." Perhaps surprisingly, distillers and liquor importers were among the heaviest advertisers. Seagram's, Johnnie Walker, I. W. Harper, Canadian Club, Calvert, Continental, and Martin's were just some of the brands taking out full-page color advertisements in national magazines. Four Roses thoughtfully printed their own eggnog recipe: Take 6 eggs, ¾ cup sugar, 1 pint cream, 1 pint milk, 1 oz. Jamaican rum, 1 pint Four Roses. Separate eggs. Beat ½ cup sugar into yolks. Beat whites very stiff and beat in ¼ cup sugar. Mix whites and yolks. Stir in milk and cream. Add whiskey and rum. Stir thoroughly. Serve very cold with grated nutmeg. Makes 5 pints. Wine producers, especially those in New York, Ohio, and California, promoted their beverage as the perfect drink for the holidays.

Those who could afford them were still buying new cars this holiday season, aware that it might be a long time before new models would be available again. Detroit kept the assembly lines moving, turning out new 1942 model cars until the factories were fully converted to war production. To encourage buyers, General Motors was promoting the GM Installment Plan that would allow would-be purchasers to own a new car with affordable monthly payments. The cars were being shipped all across the country. Indeed, this very month a new shipping route was opened up for then. A load of new cars moved by rail from Detroit to Evansville, Indiana, where they were loaded onto a specially constructed barge for transport down the Ohio River and up the Tennessee River to Guntersville, Alabama. From Guntersville the cars were transported to dealerships across the Middle South. This load was the first of many that would take advantage of the work of the T.V.A. From the confluence of the Ohio and the Mississippi all the way to Northern Alabama, the Tennessee River was now fully open to commercial navigation.

Material shortage that had already hit the automobile industry changed many of the technical characteristics of the new 1942 models. Ford replaced the aluminum heads in its engines with cast iron, and all makers introduced plastic instead of metal wherever possible. Nevertheless there were quality improvements in many models. Hudson announced its new Drive-Master automatic. Crosley introduced its first all-steel body. Lincoln introduced a new optional 130-hp. engine. General Motors restyled most of their line with cars becoming lower and wider. Best of all, prices were not significantly higher. A low-end Ford was still available for $665.

As 1941 came to an end, Americans could not yet see that their world had changed irretrievably. As far as possible they tried to follow their old habits, regarding this new war as just another job to be done. The country's characteristic optimism, which though sorely tested had carried it through the Depression, remained intact. As he closed his Chesterfield radio program on December 31, Glenn Miller signed off in this way, with his whole ensemble shouting out the last three words:

It'll soon be 1942, and so this is Glenn Miller speaking for the makers of Chesterfield, all the boys in the band, everybody, let's all get together and make it a **HAPPY NEW YEAR!**

Notes

INTRODUCTION

v. The dinner is described in Seib, pp. 147ff.

vii. The comparison of tax policies is taken from Kaiser, pp. 213–4.

CHAPTER 1

6. "the Congress is not a body . . ." Laski, p. 19.

7. "no democracy in the modern world . . ." Laski, p. 163.

7. He was an ambitious man whom . . . *New Republic,* June 15, 1938, p. 158.

8. The inclusion of 12-year-old Shirley Temple . . . Ogden, p. 64.

8. The Texas senatorial election is discussed in Goodman, p. 120.

12. For a good description of the Byrd machine see Heinemann *passim.*

14. "Governors of Virginia are appointed . . ." Heinemann, p. 266.

14. Darden easily defeated . . . Heinemann, p. 267.

14. Virginia regularly ranked . . . Heinemann, p. 272.

15. The story of the Shelby Dynasty is told in Christensen, Chapter 2, and in Morrison *passim.*

16. In cases of dire necessity . . . Christensen, p. 98.

16. "Well, Mr. President, she's not so fat. . . ." Pleasants, pp. 65–6.

17. The story of the Crump machine is told in Genther, pp. 749–758.

18. As John Gunther pointed out . . . Gunther p. 752.

18. It was said that a statewide election . . .Gunther, p. 749.

19. Since Anaconda owned . . . Howard, p. 334.

19. One lobbyist was heard to boast . . . Gunther, p. 169.

20. A worker who caused trouble . . . Gunther, p. 170.

20. So did the city of Burlington . . .Gunther, p. 497.

20. The justification offered . . . Gunther, p. 502.

22. LaGuardia's career is covered in Elliott *passim*.

22. "I don't know. . . ." Elliott, p. 194; Cerf, p. 268.

23. Chicago politics during this era is covered in Biles; in Smith, Richard; and in Green and Holli.

23. "To hell with the public. . . ." Smith, Richard, p. 185.

24. For reasons unreported . . . . Biles 10.

25. The story of the sewer demonstration is told in Morgan, p. 529 and Biles, p. 86.

26. Hague's multiple ways . . . Fleming, p. 33.

26. His message to potential opponents . . . Fleming, p. 41.

27. Instead of being indicted . . . Fleming, p. 42.

28. The story of the relationship between McDaniel and Donnell was told in an article in *Time*, March 3, p. 16.

29. The last act of the drama . . . *Newsweek*, April 14, pp. 22–23.

CHAPTER 2

33. The Academy Awards did produce . . . *Newsweek*, March 10, p. 65.

34. The review disappeared . . . . *Newsweek*, January 20, p. 62.

34. One critic, Joshua O'Hara . . . . *Newsweek*, March 17, p. 60.

34. Just after the edict came out . . . . *Newsweek*, August 11, p. 60.

35. Hollywood self-censorship is covered in Black and in Koppes and Black.

35. Even United Artists had to conform . . . . Koppes and Black, pp. 13–24.

36. With foreign markets . . . . Eyman, p. 277.

36. Every sweater was rejected . . . . *Life*, April 14, p. 32; *Newsweek* August 11, p. 12.

37. In April he resigned . . . . Black, p. 292.

37. The story of Stewart's efforts to join the Army is told at the Jimmy Stewart Museum web site, www.jimmy.org.

37. For some in Hollywood . . . Kurlansky, p. 80.

39. Woody Herman was . . . . Clancy, p. 40.

40. Popular opinion was also . . . . *Newsweek,* March 3, p. 57.

40. Early in May the Mutual network . . . . Gronow and Saunio, p. 90.

41. While their 1940 radio revenues . . . . *Newsweek,* May 12, p. 70; August 11, p. 58.

42. It was therefore important . . . . Wald, pp. 97–98.

42. The next time the band played . . . . Wald, p. 127.

44. Some critics believe . . . . Shaw, p. 160.

44. Similarly Sy Oliver . . . . Wald, p. 106.

44. Ellington, especially, was creating . . . . Hamm, p. 524

44. On another occasion, Krupa . . . . *Cleveland Gazette,* January 3, 1942, p 2.

44. Duke Ellington performed at Loew's . . . . Manchester, p. 296.

44. The Benny Goodman Sextet . . . . Hamm, p. 531.

45. Woody described their first record . . . . Clancy, p. 41.

45. Stylistic boundaries were constantly shifting . . . . Nicholson, pp. 122–3; Wald, p. 105.

46. Finally the struggling young band . . . . Easton, pp. 64–5.

48. Christian has been described . . . . Davis, p. 156.

48. Back in 1938 he had performed there . . . . Simon, p. 214.

49. A little more than a third of these . . . . Smith p. 285.

49. A recording of a longer work. . . . The use of the term "album" to refer to music recordings dates from this period when records were stored in paper sleeves bound in book-like albums.

50. Certainly few families could afford . . . . *Life,* September 22, p. 16.

51. Over six days in the Cleveland . . . . *Life,* May 5, p. 34.

51. In 1941 they offered 261 . . . . *Newsweek,* February 17.59.

52. Far more familiar . . . . Mantle (1942), p. 458.

53. *Blithe Spirit,* such a success . . . . Mantle (1944), p. 15.

54. He also produced a revival . . . . Mantle (1944), pp. 22, 27.

54. Others like Faye Wray . . . . *Life,* September 1, p. 53.

CHAPTER 3

60. Education data are drawn from the *Statistical Abstract of the United States.*

61. Because of the pressure on facilities . . . Frederickson, p. 89.

62. A typical one-room school in Montana is described in *Life*, May 12, pp. 65–68.

62. Swedish sociologist Gunnar Myrdal. . . Myrdal, pp. 902–3.

62. Although only one adult in seven . . . Spring, p. 194.

63. The debate over progressivism is covered in Cremin *passim*.

64. Students from progressive schools . . . Bromley, pp. 407–416; Cremin, p. 255.

65. One professional writer in New York . . . *Newsweek*, January 27, p. 49.

66. The University of Georgia story is told in Anderson, William, Chapter 16.

68. "Georgia is one of the poorest . . ." *Life*, December 8, p. 40.

69. The story of Highlander is told in Glen *passim*.

70. In the spring and summer of 1941 . . . . Glen, p. 66.

70. By 1941 over 50 percent . . . . Glen, p. 69.

70. Literary critic Douglas Bush . . .Bush, p. 499.

72. There is one final question . . . . Shirer, pp. 591–592.

75. In February Gertrude Stein published . . . *Newsweek*, Feb. 17, p.68; Cerf, p. 131.

CHAPTER 4

78. At the Tri-State Negro Fair . . . . *Life*, November 10, p. 46.

79. But Southern leaders . . . . Waldrep, p. 148.

80. In Philadelphia the Sun Oil . . . . *Newsweek*, September 8, p. 50.

80. Mrs. John L. Whitehurst of Baltimore . . . *New York Times*, July 31. Sec. 10, p. 4.

81. The story of the proposed march on Washington is best told from Randolph's point of view in Anderson, J., Chapter 16.

85. Virtually all of them paid . . . . Murray, pp. 233–4.

85. The case wound through the courts . . . . *Newsweek*, April 14, p. 74.

85. The story of rural electrification is told in Pence *passim*.

86. For farmers who could afford a tractor . . . *Statistical Abstract of the United States 1941*, Sections 25 and 27.

CHAPTER 5

91. The most comprehensive account of the Hess story is found in Douglas-Hamilton.

93. German leaders believed . . . . Van der Vat, p. 81.

93. Of the many retellings of the *Bismarck* story, the most thorough is that in Zetterling and Tamelander.

95. Speculation was rife. Sherwood, p. 295.

99. For the North African campaigns see Barnett *passim* and Collier *passim*.

99. Mockler provides the best overall treatment of the East African Campaigns.

100. Barnett provides a good overall account of the early fighting in North Africa.

109. The conquerors tried to enter . . . . Collier, p. 110.

112. By late in 1938 . . . . Hsiung, pp. 151–3.

114. This organization was founded . . . . *New York Times*, March 3, pp. 1, 6; June 8, p. 19.

114. In January of 1940, Mrs. Natalie Wales Latham . . . . *New York Times*, February 2, 2013; *New Yorker,* April 19, 1941, pp. 21–6.

CHAPTER 6

116. The story of Robert Sherwood's experience is told in Sherwood, p. 303.

120. "I stand aghast," . . . . Langer and Gleason (1952), p. 487.

121. The selection of Willkie . . . . Langer and Gleason (1952), p. 670.

122. Nevertheless, the exchange agreement . . . . Langer and Gleason (1952), Chapter XXII.

125. The quotation from Roosevelt is found in Roosevelt, p. 605.

126. The full text of the "Arsenal of Democracy" speech is found in Zevin, pp. 248–258.

128. Congressman Hamilton Fish . . . . Kimball, p. 163.

129. Give us the tools . . . . Churchill (1941), pp. 453–62.

129. the polls showed a small but perceptible shift . . . . Kimball, pp. 191–2.

130. It is the declared policy of the United States . . . . Kimball, pp. 205–6.

122. The text of the "Unlimited National Emergency" address is found in Zevin.

135. The entry of Communist Russia . . . . Quoted in Cole, p. 85.

136. Bennett C. Clark asked if anyone . . . . *ibid.*

136. On July 2 Charles Lindbergh was quoted . . . . Berg, p. 447.

136. A photographic article on *Sergeant York* was published in *Life*, July 14, pp. 30, 63ff.

137. The Senate hearings are described in Koppes and Black, pp. 39–45.

139. The close vote thus had . . . . Langer and Gleason (1953), pp. 571ff.

142. The Iowa speech and its aftermath are described in Berg, pp. 450–455.

145. Although General Wood had a policy . . . . *Newsweek,* October 6, p. 9.

145. The character of America First was changing . . . . *Life,* October 20, p. 40.

146. "asking Congress to issue an engraved . . . . Cole, p. 163.

147. The story of the Rainbow 5 leak is told in Smith, Amanda, pp. 392–392, and Smith, Richard, pp. 415–419.

CHAPTER 7

153. At the All Star break . . . . Creamer, p. 233.

155. . . . his big mattress of a chest protector. Home plate umpires in the two leagues wore different styles of chest protectors in 1941. American League umps, led by their supervisor Tommy Connolly, were encouraged to wear the large, thick padding that looked like a mattress. National League umpires, following the lead of supervisor Bill Klem, wore a lighter, more flexible protector under their coats, which allowed them to crouch lower. Many fans attribute the slightly different strike zones in the two leagues to this difference in chest protectors.

159. The story of Greenberg and the draft is told in Vaccaro, Chapter 1, and Kurlansky, Chapter 5.

160. At 24 Boudreau was the youngest . . . . Gilbert, p. 60.

161. For years the hapless St. Louis Browns . . . . Mead, pp. 33–35.

163. During the Depression . . . . Obojski, pp. 46f.

165. Their attitude encouraged contract jumping . . . . Peterson, pp. 92f.

166. Of the six Heisman Trophy winners . . . . Newhouse, p. 289.

166. The latter game, played just two . . . . Noverr and Ziewacz, p. 145.

167. He was so successful in his first season . . . . Whittingham, pp. 68ff.

168. Whirlaway's achievements are described in Vaccaro, Chapters 2 and 3.

171. For the Louis-Conn match see Vaccaro, Chapters 5 and 6, and Louis, pp. 134–138.

174. The Badgers then swept . . . . Noverr and Ziewacz, p. 148.

175. The tournament was held in Columbus . . . . *Newsweek,* July 14, p. 48.

175. The appeal was approved, with the stipulation . . . . Van Natta, pp. 163ff.

175. With no tournaments available . . . . Van Natta, pp. 205f.

176. For the first time in professional sports . . . . Marble, p. 173.

CHAPTER 8

177. By 1941 a combination of factors . . . . Dulles, p. 366.

178. Vacations for industrial workers were only indirectly . . . . Aron, pp. 248–9.

178. By 1940 there were perhaps . . . . Dulles, p. 317.

179. The development of the auto court is described in Jackle *et al.*, Chapter 3.

184. In late 1941 there were already 140 . . . . Beebe (1941), p. 133.

185. When the Union Pacific introduced its new train . . . . Beebe and Clegg, pp. 856, 863.

185. The second woman to graduate . . . . *Current Biography,* 1940.

187. The story of National Airport is told in Goode.

187. On March 16 the Pennsylvania Railroad's . . . . Pittsburgh *Post-Gazette*, March 17, pp. 1f.

188. The four most popular pastimes . . . . Dulles, *loc. cit.*

188. At the beginning of the year Americans . . . . Reutter, p. 393.

188. The Archduke, in this country . . . . *Newsweek,* September 8, p. 19.

191. The Burma-Shave story is well told in Rowsome.

192. The early history of drive-in theaters is covered in Segrave.

195. Perhaps the most interesting of all the remaining . . . . Hilton and Due, pp. 409–412.

195 For the story of the mixed train see Beebe (1947).

197. For most of the country, AM radio . . . . *Scientific American*, February 1941, pp. 96f.

197. Morning programming started. . . . It is conventional with radio programs to list the time of broadcast in the Eastern Time Zone unless otherwise noted. Since virtually all broadcasts were live, some shows were broadcast for the Eastern and Central Time Zones and then rebroadcast three hours later, again live, for the West Coast. After one broadcasting season ended in the spring, shows would sometimes change their time slots for the new season that began in the fall.

197. Coulter informed Corwin that the network . . . . Bannerman, pp. 60–72.

200. Far more imaginative, even fantastic . . . . The introduction to Gibson provides an enjoyable view of the pulp fiction industry.

202. Burns was also noted for his bazooka . . . . In 1942 soldiers began referring to the M1A1 rocket launcher as a bazooka because of its resemblance to Burns's instrument.

204. One night a little-known . . . . Dunning, p. 44.

204. Municipal pools and beaches alone . . . . Dulles, p. 367.

204. Softball developed great popularity . . . . Rader, p. 233; Dulles, p. 360.

205. Although Gottfried Schmidt had developed . . . . Rader, p. 330.

206. Distributors bought them from the manufacturer . . . . *Newsweek,* September 1, p.45.

206. A popular joke . . . . Cerf, p. 166.

CHAPTER 9

207. The best general treatment of the GHQ maneuvers is found in Gabel.

209. The matter passed without further incident . . . . *Time,* July 21, pp. 30ff; *Newsweek,* July 21, p. 30.

212. The California maneuvers were extensively covered by the *New York Times* on June 1 and 26. Stillwell's performance is discussed in Tuchman, pp. 225f.

214. In 1939 the United States Army . . . . Gabel, p. 8; Watson, p. 16.

214. In Virginia, when the 176th Infantry . . . . *Life,* April 21, pp. 112ff.

215. The 207th Infantry from New York . . . . *Life,* September 22, pp. 100ff.

215. Major General John Herr, Chief of Cavalry . . . . Brinkley, p. 59.

215. Kimbrough was an All-American . . . . *St. Petersburg Times,* January 6, p. 9; Newsweek, February 24, p. 40.

216. Of over 600,000 men in uniform . . . . *Newsweek,* February 3, p. 31.

216. The decision to promote him . . . . Fletcher, pp. 80–87.

216. Davis had applied for assignment . . . . B. Davis, pp. 63–69.

216. Typical of the waste of talent . . . . *The Message Magazine,* Vol. VII, No. 9, October 1941, p. 2; Baltimore *Afro-American,* August 30, p. 5.

217. By the time the Louisiana maneuvers began . . . . *Afro-American,* August 30, p. 1.

218. The Army regarded these new structures . . . . Goodwin, pp. 217f.

218. In January Leon Henderson . . . . *Newsweek,* January 27, p. 10.

219. In August the Truman Committee issued . . . . McCullough (1992), pp. 257ff.

220. The Army's first reaction was predictably defensive . . . . *Time,* August 18, p. 36.

221. One day early in the year . . . . Vogel, p. 24.

221. The story of the building of the Pentagon is comprehensively told in Vogel, especially in the first nine chapters.

223. "My God, what will that boy do next?" Vogel, p. 68.

226. What he reported was worse . . . . *Life*, August 18, pp. 16ff.

227. When the order was reversed . . . . Brinkley, p. 91.

227. But Southern soldiers, who had no experience . . . . *Newsweek*, March 17, p. 37.

230. Of those 105, only 37 were less than thirteen years old . . . . *Newsweek*, January 6, p. 32.

232. It is slow and seaworthy . . . . Elphick, p. 65.

233. It was the first of 2,710 Liberty ships . . . . Elphick, p. 67.

233. So in June the Office of Production Management announced . . . . Goodwin, p. 260; *Life*, June 16, p. 23.

234. In Union City, Tennessee . . . . *Newsweek*, July 28, p. 16.

CHAPTER 10

235. The previous year, 1940 . . . . Swafford, p. 3.

235. The year got off to a troubled . . . . *Newsweek*, March 24, p. 36.

236. Green also told F.D.R. . . . . *Life*, October 27, p. 38.

239. Under the threat of strikes . . . . *Life*, October 27, p. 38.

240. In September electrical workers . . . . *Life*, September 29, p. 34.

241. The story of the North American Aviation strike was reported in *Life*, June 23, pp. 32ff.

243. The story of the campaign to organize Ford is well told in Bernstein, pp. 734–751.

244. Lawyers handling workman's compensation . . . . Bernstein, p. 739.

251. Alcoa's production problems are described in Smith, George, pp. 214–217.

251. Despite another round of anti-trust . . . . Smith, George, pp. 199–201.

252. Even as late as November . . . . Smith, George, pp. 215–6.

253. The Dow Chemical story is told in Brandt, pp. 247–250.

258. Not all major businesses . . . . *Saturday Evening Post*, May 24, pp. 10–11, 38–42.

259. A second, but very important purpose . . . . *Life*, November 24, pp. 47ff.

CHAPTER 11

260. But a presidential proclamation is not the same as a law . . . . *Newsweek*, June 2, p. 17.

262. The Tax Foundation carried out an analysis . . . . *Newsweek*, October 6, p. 39.

262. In February the National Research Council . . . . *Newsweek*, February 10, p. 40.

262. *Life* published an extensive article on rising prices in its November 17 issue, pp. 102–109.

264. In contrast to party-owned papers in Europe . . . . Harris, p. xiv.

264. Brother Leon had different ideas. *Life*, October 13, p. 122; Mahoney & Sloane, p. 322.

266. In November R. J. Reynolds Tobacco . . . . Brandt, pp. 88ff.

266. Very little was said about the health effects . . . . Brandt, p. 117.

267. American wine production jumped . . . . Swaminathan, pp. 655ff.

267. Their efforts had little effect seemed to have . . . . Stack.

267. Whiskey for export was an important source . . . . *Newsweek*, March 10, p. 31.

268. For the fashionably patriotic woman . . . . *Newsweek*, July 28, p. 39.

269. In the summer doctors at Johns Hopkins . . . . *Newsweek*, September 1, p. 51.

270. Now Dr. Philip Levine announced . . . . *Newsweek*, April 14, p. 73.

270. In August the New York State Federation. . . . *Newsweek*, September 8, p. 63.

270. To present a general picture of ordinary family life . . . . *Life*, September 22, pp. 78ff.

271. Entertaining friends for dinner . . . . Gurney *passim*.

272. In January Parents' Institute, Inc., launched . . . . *Newsweek*, February 24, p. 64.

272. Piano manufacturers were happy to report . . . . *Newsweek*, March 3, p. 45.

273. Nineteen other stations, from New York . . . . *Newsweek*, July 14, p. 56.

274. When Selective Service doctors examined draftees . . . . *Newsweek*, February 17, p. 70.

275. The Nation's Capital, an essentially Southern city . . . . Brinkley, p. 26.

275. In 1939 a black couple. . . . *Newsweek*, April 28, p. 17.

276. This was a time when even Franklin Roosevelt could remark . . . . Morgan, p. 553.

277. Generalizations about the state of religion in America . . . . Marty *passim*, especially Chapter 9.

278. The police responded with gusto. *Newsweek*, March 10, p. 19.

278. A good treatment of Father Divine's Peace Movement is found in Watts.

279. The life of Daddy Grace is well told in Dallam.

280. A well-balanced account of the life of Aimee Semple McPherson is found in Epstein.

281. With the opening of the new school year in the fall . . . . *Newsweek*, September 22, p. 54.

281. In Southern California the exclusive Los Angeles Country Club . . . . Eyman, p. 268.

282. For the life and career of Walter Winchell see Gabler.

284. In 1938 the former actress Hedda Hopper . . . . Eyman, p. 188.

286. Evalyn loved to amuse herself . . . . Brinkley, p. 160.

286. The Asheville *Citizen*, Reynolds's home-town paper . . . . Pleasants, pp. 217ff.

287. Halifax soon acquired the nickname Lord Holy Fox . . . . Brinkley, p. 49.

287. It's not un-American or subversive. . . . Sandburg, pp. 499f.

287. His newsgathering methods included eavesdropping . . . Smith, Amanda, pp. 336–345.

CHAPTER 12

289. That afternoon NBC newscaster H. R. . . . . Rumer, p. 241.

290. In Pittsburgh that afternoon, the America First Committee . . . . Gillon, pp. 119ff.

291. That Sunday afternoon Woody Guthrie . . . . Klein, p. 216.

292. Chinese were mistaken for Japanese . . . *Life*, December 22, pp. 81–82.

293. On the rare occasion when a prosecution was brought . . . . Blackmon, pp. 376f; see also Daniel for a notorious 1921 case.

293. There was, perhaps inevitably, a certain amount . . . . Blackmon, pp. 377–382.

299. Landis swallowed his opposition . . . . Pietrusza, pp. 432ff.

299. The story of *We hold these truths* is told in Bannerman, Chapter 6.

301. Precious as the Bill of Rights was . . . Weintraub, p. 59.

305. "What's the matter?" Roosevelt's comment was recorded differently by different observers. See, for example, Weintraub, p. 93, and Bercuson and Herwig, p. 158.

305. The contretemps over St. Pierre and Miquelon is described in Lacouture, pp. 315–317 and Bercuson and Herwig, pp. 145–147.

309. Indeed, this very month a new shipping route . . . . Callahan, p. 84.

Bibliography

BOOKS

Abramson, Rudy. *Spanning the Century: The Life of W. Averell Harriman 1891–1986*. New York: William Morrow and Company (1992)

Acheson, Dean. *Present at the Creation: My Years in the State Department*. New York: W. W. Norton & Company (1969)

Adams, Frank, with Myles Horton. *Unearthing Seeds of Fire: The Idea of Highlander*. Winston-Salem: John F. Blair, Publisher (1975)

Adamson, Hans Christian. *Eddie Rickenbacker*. New York: The Macmillan Company (1946)

Allen, Frederick Lewis. *Since Yesterday: The 1930s in America: September 3, 1929—September 3, 1939*. New York: Harper & Row (1940)

Ambrose, Stephen E. *Eisenhower*. New York: Simon and Schuster (1983)

Anderson, Jervis. *A. Philip Randolph: A Biographical Portrait*. New York: Harcourt Brace Jovanovich, Inc. (1972)

Anderson, William. *The Wild Man from Sugar Creek: The Political Career of Eugene Talmadge*. Baton Rouge: Louisiana State University Press (1975)

Andrews, Maxene, and Bill Gilbert. *Over Here, Over There: The Andrews Sisters and the USO Stars in World War II*. New York: Kensington Publishing Corp. (1993)

Aron, Cindy S. *Working at Play: A History of Vacations in the United States*. New York: Oxford University Press (1999)

Ashby, Warren. *Frank Porter Graham: A Southern Liberal*. Winston-Salem: John F. Blair (1980)

Bannerman, R. Leroy. *Norman Corwin and the Golden Age of Radio*. University: The University of Alabama Press (1986)

Barnett, Correlli. *The Desert Generals*. London: George Allen & Unwin (1960)

Baruch, Bernard M. *Baruch: The Public Years*. New York: Holt, Rinehart and Winston (1960)

Beard, Charles A., and Mary R. Beard. *History of the United States*. New York: The Macmillan Company (1921)

———. *America in Midpassage*. New York: The Macmillan Company (1939)

Beauchamp, Cari. *Joseph P. Kennedy Presents: His Hollywood Years*. New York: Alfred A. Knopf (2009)

Bednarek, Janet R. Daly. *America's Airports: Airfield Development, 1918–1947*. College Station: Texas A&M University Press (2001)

Beebe, Lucius. *Trains in Transition*. New York: D. Appleton-Century Company (1941)

———. *Mixed Train Daily: A Book of Short-line Railroads*. New York: E. P. Dutton & Company (1947)

Beebe, Lucius, and Charles Clegg. *The Trains We Rode*. New York: Howell-North Books (1965)

Bell, Quentin. *Virginia Woolf: A Biography*. New York: Harcourt Brace Jovanovich, Inc. (1972)

Bercuson, David, and Holger Herwig. *One Christmas in Washington*. Woodstock: The Overlook Press (2005)

Berg, A. Scott. *Lindbergh*. New York: G. P. Putnam's Sons (1998)

Bernstein, Irving. *A History of the American Worker: Turbulent Years 1933–1941*. Boston: Houghton Mifflin Company (1970)

Biles, Roger. *Big City Boss in Depression and War: Mayor Edward J. Kelly of Chicago*. DeKalb: Northern Illinois University Press (1984)

Black, Gregory D. *Hollywood Censored: Morality Codes, Catholics, and the Movies*. Cambridge: Cambridge University Press (1994)

Blackmon, Douglas. *Slavery by Another Name: The Re-enslavement of Black Americans from the Civil War to World War II*. New York: Doubleday (2008)

Block, Maxine (ed.). *Current Biography: Who's News and Why 1940*. New York: H. W. Wilson Co. (1940)

———. *Current Biography: Who's News and Why 1941*. New York: H. W. Wilson Co. (1941)

Bohlen, Charles E. *Witness to History: 1929–1969*. New York: W. W. Norton & Company, Inc. (1973)

Boothe, Clare. *Europe in the Spring*. New York: Alfred A. Knopf (1940)

Boswell, Peyton, Jr. *Modern American Painting*. New York: Dodd, Mead & Company (1940)

Bradley, Omar N. (and Clay Blair). *A General's Life*. New York: Simon and Schuster (1983)

Brandt, Allan M. *The Cigarette Century: The Rise, Fall, and Deadly Persistence of the Product That Defined America*. New York: Basic Books (2007)

Brandt, E. N. *Growth Company: Dow Chemical's First Century*. East Lansing: Michigan State University Press (1997)

Brashler, William. *Josh Gibson: A Life in the Negro Leagues*. Chicago: Ivan R. Dee (1978)

Briggs, Thomas H., Max J. Herzberg, and Lucile Prim Jackson, eds. *American Literature*. Boston: Houghton Mifflin Company (1941)

Brinkley, David. *Washington Goes to War*. New York: Alfred A. Knopf (1988)

Brown, Cecil. *Suez to Singapore*. New York: Random House (1942)

Bryan, William Jennings. *The Speeches of William Jennings Bryan*. New York: Funk & Wagnalls Company (1909)

Bureau of the Census. *Sixteenth Census of the United States: 1940*. Washington: United States Government Printing Office (1943)

———. *Statistical Abstract of the United States 1941*. Washington: United States Government Printing Office (1942)

———. *Statistical Abstract of the United States 1942*. Washington: United States Government Printing Office (1943)

Butts, R. Freeman, and Lawrence A. Cremin. *A History of Education in American Culture*. New York: Holt, Rinehart and Winston (1953)

Callahan, North. *T.V.A.: Bridge over Troubled Waters*. South Brunswick: A. S. Barnes and Company (1980)

Campbell, Don G. *Master Teacher: Nadia Boulanger*. Washington: The Pastoral Press (1984)

Carlson, Stephen F., and Fred W. Schneider III. *P.C.C.: The Car that Fought Back.* Glendale: Interurban Press (1980)

Cash, W. J. *The Mind of the South.* New York: Alfred A. Knopf, Inc. (1941)

Chennault, Claire Lee. *Way of a Fighter: The Memoirs of Claire Lee Chennault, Major General, U.S. Army (Ret.).* New York: G. P. Putnam's Sons (1949)

Chotzinoff, Samuel. *Toscanini: An Intimate Portrait.* New York: Alfred A. Knopf (1956)

Christensen, Rob. *The Paradox of Tarheel Politics: The Personalities, Elections, and Events that Shaped Modern North Carolina.* Chapel Hill: The University of North Carolina Press (2008)

Churchill, Winston S. *Blood Sweat and Tears.* New York: G. P. Putnam's Sons (1941)
———. *The Second World War: The Grand Alliance (Vol. III).* Boston: Houghton Mifflin Company (1950)

Cerf, Bennett. *Try and Stop Me.* New York: Simon and Schuster (1945)

Clancy, William D. *Woody Herman: Chronicles of the Herd.* New York: Schirmer Books (1995)

Clay, Steven E. *U.S. Army Order of Battle 1919–1941.* Fort Leavenworth: Combat Studies Institute Press (2010)

Cleland, Robert Glass. *California in Our Time (1900–1940).* New York: Alfred A. Knopf (1947)

Coffey, Frank. *Always Home: 50 Years of the USO.* Washington: Brassey's (US), Inc. (1991)

Coit, Margaret L. *Mr. Baruch.* Cambridge: The Riverside Press (1957)

Cole, Wayne S. *America First: The Battle Against Intervention 1940–1941.* Madison: The University of Wisconsin Press (1953)

Collier, Richard. *The Road to Pearl Harbor 1941.* New York: Charles Scribner's Sons (1981)

Conant, Jennet. *The Irregulars: Roald Dahl and the British Spy Ring in Wartime Washington.* New York: Simon & Schuster (2008)

Cramer, Richard Ben. *Joe DiMaggio: The Hero's Life.* New York: Simon & Schuster (2000)

Crawford, Richard. *America's Musical Life: A History.* New York: W. W. Norton & Company (2001)

Creamer, Robert W. *Baseball in 41: A Celebration of the "Best Baseball Season Ever"—in the Year America Went to War.* New York: Viking Penguin (1991)

Cremin, Lawrence A. *The Transformation of the School: Progressivism in American Education, 1876–1957*. New York: Alfred A. Knopf (1961)

Crise, Steve, Michael A. Patris, and the Pacific Railway Historical Society. *Pacific Electric Railway*. Charleston: Arcadia Publishing (2011)

Cronin, A. J. *The Keys of the Kingdom*. Boston: Little, Brown and Company (1941)

Culver, John C., and John Hyde. *American Dreamer: The Life and Times of Henry A. Wallace*. New York: W. W. Norton & Company (2000)

Cummings, Troy Augustus. *"Mood-Stuff" and "Metaphoric Utterance:" Norman Corwin's Radio Art*. Master's Thesis in Musicology, University of Missouri-Kansas City (2013)

Dallam, Marie W. *Daddy Grace: A Celebrity Preacher and His House of Prayer*. New York: New York University Press (2007)

Danzig, Allison. *The History of American Football: Its Great Teams, Players, and Coaches*. Englewood Cliffs: Prentice Hall, Inc. (1956)

Davis, Benjamin O., Jr. *Benjamin O. Davis, Jr., American: An Autobiography*. Washington: Smithsonian University Press (1991)

Davis, Francis. *The History of the Blues: The Roots, the Music, the People: From Charley Patton to Robert Cray*. New York: Hyperion (1995)

de Seversky, Alexander P. *Victory through Air Power*. New York: Simon and Schuster, Inc. (1942)

D'Este, Carlo. *Eisenhower: A Soldier's Life*. New York: Henry Holt and Company (2002)

———. *Patton: A Genius for War*. New York: HarperCollins (1995)

Douglas, Kirk. *The Ragman's Son: An Autobiography*. New York: Simon and Schuster (1988)

Douglas-Hamilton, James. *Motive for a Mission: The Story Behind Hess's Flight to Britain*. London: Macmillan and Co (1971)

Dray, Philip. *At the Hands of Persons Unknown: The Lynching of Black America*. New York: Random House (2002)

Dubofsky, Melvyn, and Warren Van Tine. *John L. Lewis: A Biography*. New York: Quadrangle/The New York Times Book Co., Inc. (1977)

Dulles, Foster Rhea. *Labor in America: A History*. New York: Thomas Y. Crowell Company (1947)

———. *America Learns to Play: A History of Popular Recreation, 1607–1940*. New York: D. Appleton-Century Company (1940)

Dunning, John. *On the Air: The Encyclopedia of Old-Time Radio*. New York: Oxford University Press (1998)

Easton, Carol. *Straight Ahead: The Story of Stan Kenton*. New York: William Morrow & Company (1973)

Eisenhower, Dwight D. *At Ease: Stories I Tell to Friends*. Garden City: Doubleday (1967)

Elliott, Lawrence. *Little Flower: The Life and Times of Fiorello La Guardia*. New York: William Morrow and Company (1983)

Elphick, Peter. *Liberty: The Ships That Won the War*. Annapolis: Naval Institute Press (2001)

Epstein, Daniel Mark. *Sister Aimee: The Life of Aimee Semple McPherson*. New York: Harcourt Brace & Company (1993)

Erickson, John. *The Road to Stalingrad*. London: Cassell (1975)

Eyman, Scott. *Lion of Hollywood: The Life and Legend of Louis B. Mayer*. New York: Simon & Schuster (2005)

Fairbank, John K., and Albert Feuerwerker. *The Cambridge History of China: Volume 13: Republican China 1912–1949, Part 2*. Cambridge: Cambridge University Press (1986)

Feis, Herbert. *The Road to Pearl Harbor: The Coming of the War Between the United States and Japan*. Princeton: Princeton University Press (1950)

Finley, Keith M. *Delaying the Dream: Southern Senators and the Fight against Civil Rights, 1938–1965*. Baton Rouge: Louisiana State University Press (2008)

Fischer, Bernd J. *Albania at War, 1939–1945*. West Lafayette: Purdue University Press (1999)

Fletcher, Marvin E. *America's First Black General: Benjamin O. Davis, Sr.: 1880–1970*. Lawrence: University Press of Kansas (1989)

Forrester, C. S. *The Last Nine Days of the* Bismarck. Boston: Little, Brown and Company (1958)

Fraser, David. *Knight's Cross: A Life of Field Marshal Erwin Rommel*. London: HarperCollins Publishers (1993)

Frederickson, Earle (ed.). *State of Washington: "The Evergreen Empire."* Seattle: Convention Committee, Sixty-first Annual Convention, American Federation of Labor (1941)

Fugate, Bryan I. *Operation Barbarossa: Strategy and Tactics on the Eastern Front, 1941*. Novato: Presidio Press (1984)

Gabel, Christopher R. *The U.S. Army GHQ Maneuvers of 1941*. Washington: Center of Military History United States Army (1991)

Gabler, Neal. *Winchell: Gossip, Power and the Culture of Celebrity*. New York: Alfred A. Knopf (1994)

German Foreign Office. *Documents on Events Preceding the Outbreak of the War*. New York: German Library of Information (1940)

Gibson, Walter. *The Weird Adventures of the Shadow*. New York: Grosset & Dunlap (1966)

Gilbert, Bill. *They Also Served: Baseball and the Home Front, 1941–1945*. New York: Crown Publishers, Inc. (1992)

Gillon, Steven M. *Pearl Harbor: F.D.R. Leads the Nation into War*. New York: Basic Books (2011)

Glen, John M. *Highlander: No Ordinary School: 1932–1962*. Lexington: The University Press of Kentucky (1988)

Goldberg, Vicki. *Margaret Bourke-White: A Biography*. New York: Harper & Row, Publishers (1986)

Goodman, Walter. *The Committee: The Extraordinary Career of the House Committee on Un-American Activities*. New York: Farrar, Straus and Giroux (1968)

Goodwin, Doris Kearns. *No Ordinary Time: Franklin & Eleanor Roosevelt: The Home Front in World War II*. New York: Simon & Schuster (1994)

Green, Paul M., and Melvin G. Holli. *The Mayors: The Chicago Political Tradition*. Carbondale: Southern Illinois University Press (1987)

Greene, Jack, and Alessandro Massignani. *The Naval War in the Mediterranean 1940–1943*. London: Chatham Publishing (1998)

Gronow, Pekka, and Ilpo Saunio. *An International History of the Recording Industry*. London: Cassell (1998)

Gunther, John. *Inside Asia*. New York: Harper & Brothers (1939)

———. *Inside Europe*. New York: Harper & Brothers (1940)

———. *Inside Latin America*. New York: Harper & Brothers (1941)

———. *Inside U.S.A.* New York: Harper & Brothers (1947)

Guthrie, Woody. *Bound for Glory*. New York: E. P. Dutton & Company (1943)

Hamm, Charles. *Music in the New World*. New York: W. W. Norton and Company (1983)

Harris, Leon. *Merchant Princes: An Intimate History of Jewish Families Who Built Great Department Stores*. New York: Harper & Row (1979)

Hart, Scott. *Washington at War: 1941–1945*. Englewood Cliffs: Prentice-Hall, Inc. (1970)

Hearden, Patrick J. *Roosevelt Confronts Hitler: America's Entry into World War II*. DeKalb: Northern Illinois University Press (1987)

Heinemann, Ronald L. *Harry Byrd of Virginia*. Charlottesville: University of Virginia Press (1996)

Hemingway, Ernest. *For Whom the Bell Tolls*. New York: Charles Scribner's Sons (1940)

Hilton, George W., and John F. Due. *The Electric Interurban Railways in America* (Second Printing). Stanford: Stanford University Press (1964)

Hilton, James. *Random Harvest*. Boston: Little, Brown and Company (1941)

Holiday, Billie (with William Dufty). *Lady Sings the Blues*. Garden City: Doubleday & Company (1956)

Holway, John B. *The Last .400 Hitter: The Anatomy of a .400 Season*. Dubuque: Wm. C. Brown Publishers (1992)

Hsiung, James C., and Steven I. Levine (eds.). *China's Bitter Victory: The War with Japan 1937–1945*. Armonk: M. E. Sharpe, Inc. (1992)

Ickes, Harold L. *The Secret Diaries of Harold L. Ickes. Volume III: The Lowering Clouds 1939–1941*. New York: Simon and Schuster (1954)

Jakle, John A., Keith A. Sculle, and Jefferson S. Rogers. *The Motel in America*. Baltimore: The Johns Hopkins University Press (1996)

Kaiser, David. *No End Save Victory: How F.D.R. Led the Nation into War*. New York: Basic Books (2014)

Kaptur, Marcy. *Women of Congress: A Twentieth-Century Odyssey*. Washington: Congressional Quarterly Inc. (1996)

Karsh, Yosuf. *Karsh Portfolio*. Toronto: University of Toronto Press (1967)

Keats, John. *You Might As Well Live: The Life and Times of Dorothy Parker*. New York: Simon and Schuster (1970)

Keegan, John. *The Second World War*. New York: Viking Penguin (1990)

——— (ed.). *Churchill's Generals*. London: George Weidenfeld & Nicolson Limited (1991)

Kennedy, John F. *Why England Slept*. New York: Wilfred Funk, Inc. (1940)

Kennedy, Kostya. *56: Joe DiMaggio and the Last Magic Number in Sports*. New York: Sports Illustrated Books (2011)

Kershaw, Ian. *Fateful Choices: Ten Decisions that Changed the World, 1940–1941*. New York: The Penguin Press (2007)

Ketchum, Richard M. *The Borrowed Years: 1938–1941: America on the Way to War*. New York: Random House (1989)

Kimball, Warren F. *The Most Unsordid Act: Lend-Lease 1939–1941*. Baltimore: The Johns Hopkins Press (1969)

Klein, Joe. *Woody Guthrie: A Life*. New York: Alfred A. Knopf (1980)

Klingaman, William K. *1941: Our Lives in a World on the Edge*. New York: Harper & Row, Publishers (1988)

Knight, Eric. *This Above All*. New York and London: Harper and Brothers (1941)

Koestler, Arthur. *Darkness at Noon*. New York: The Macmillan Company (1941)

Koppes, Clayton R., and Gregory D. Black. *Hollywood Goes to War: How Politics, Profits, and Propaganda Shaped World War II Movies*. New York: The Free Press (1987)

Koskoff, David E. *Joseph P. Kennedy: A Life and Times*. Englewood Cliffs: Prentice-Hall, Inc. (1974)

Kurlansky, Mark. *Hank Greenberg: The Hero Who Didn't Want to Be One*. New Haven: Yale University Press (2011)

Lacouture, Jean. *De Gaulle: The Rebel, 1890–1944*. (Translated from the French by Patrick O'Brian) New York: W. W. Norton & Company (1990)

Landis, Benson Y., ed. *Yearbook of American Churches 1941 Edition*. Jackson Heights, New York: Yearbook of American Churches Press (1941)

Langer, William L., and S. Everett Gleason. *The Challenge to Isolation 1937–1940*. New York: Harper & Brothers Publishers (1952)

————. *The Undeclared War, 1940–1941*. New York: Harper & Brothers Publishers (1953)

Laski, Harold J. *The American Presidency: An Interpretation*. New York: Harper & Brothers (1940)

Lindbergh, Charles A. *The Wartime Journals of Charles A. Lindbergh*. New York: Harcourt Brace Jovanovich, Inc. (1970)

Lord, Walter. *Day of Infamy*. New York: Henry Holt and Company (1957)

Louis, Joe. *My Life Story*. New York: Duell, Sloan and Pearce (1947)

McCullough, David. *Truman*. New York: Simon & Schuster (1992)

————. *In the Dark Streets Shineth: A 1941 Christmas Eve Story*. Salt Lake City: Shadow Mountain (2010)

MacCambridge, Michael. *ESPN Sportscentury*. New York: Hyperion (1999)

MacVane, John. *On the Air in World War II*. New York: William Morrow and Company, Inc. (1979)

Mahoney, Tom, and Leonard Sloane. *The Great Merchants: America's Foremost Retail Institutions and the People Who Made them Great*. New York: Harper & Row (1974)

Manchester, William. *The Glory and the Dream: A Narrative History of America 1932–1972*. Boston: Little, Brown and Company (1974)

Mantle, Burns (ed.). *The Best Plays of 1940–41 and the Year Book of the Drama in America*. New York: Dodd, Mead and Company (1942)

————. *The Best Plays of 1941–42 and the Year Book of the Drama in America*. New York: Dodd, Mead and Company (1944)

Marble, Alice (with Dale Leatherman). *Courting Danger: My Adventures in World-Class Tennis, Golden Age Hollywood, and High-Stakes Spying*. New York: St. Martin's Press (1991)

Marquand, John P. *H. M. Pulham, Esquire*. Boston: Little, Brown and Company (1941)

Martin, Ralph G. *Henry & Clare: An Intimate Portrait of the Luces*. New York: G. P. Putnam's Sons (1991)

Marty, Martin E. *Modern American Religion: Volume 2: The Noise of Conflict. 1919–1941*. Chicago: The University of Chicago Press (1991)

Mead, William B. *Even the Browns: Baseball During World War II*. Chicago: Contemporary Books (1978)

Middlebrook, Martin, and Patrick Mahoney. *Battleship: The Loss of the* Prince of Wales *and the* Repulse. London: Allen Lane (1977)

Middleton, William D. *The Interurban Era*. Milwaukee: Kalmbach Publishing Company (1961)

Milner, Clyde A., II, Carol A. O'Connor, and Martha A. Sandweiss, eds. *The Oxford History of the American West*. New York: Oxford University Press (1994)

Mockler, Anthony. *Haile Selassie's War*. London: Oxford University Press (1984)

Moran, Charles McMoran Wilson, 1st Baron. *Churchill: The Struggle for Survival, 1940–1965*. Boston: Houghton Mifflin Company (1966)

Morgan, Ted. *F.D.R.: A Biography*. New York: Simon and Schuster (1985)

Morris, Sylvia Jukes. *Rage for Fame: The Ascent of Clare Boothe Luce*. New York: Random House (1997)

Morrison, Joseph L. *Governor O. Max Gardner: A Power in North Carolina and New Deal Washington*. Chapel Hill: University of North Carolina Press (1971)

Mosley, Leonard. *Marshall: Hero for Our Times*. New York: Hearst Books (1982)

Murray, John E. *Origins of American Health Insurance: A History of Industrial Sickness Funds*. New Haven: Yale University Press (2007)

Myrdal, Gunnar. *An American Dilemma: The Negro Problem and Modern Democracy*. New York: Harper and Brothers (1944)

Nachman, Gerald. *Raised on Radio*. New York: Pantheon Books (1998)

Nagorski, Andrew. *The Greatest Battle: Stalin, Hitler, and the Desperate Struggle for Moscow that Changed the Course of World War II*. New York: Simon & Schuster (2007)

National Emergency Council. *Report to the President on the Economic Conditions of the South*. Washington (1938)

Newhouse, Dave. *After the Glory: Heisman*. St. Louis: The Sporting News Publishing Co. (1985)

Nicholson, Stuart. *Billie Holiday*. Boston: Northeastern University Press (1995)

Noverr, Douglas A., and Lawrence E. Ziewacz. *The Games They Played: Sports in American History 1865–1980*. Chicago: Nelson-Hall (1983)

Obojski, Robert. *Bush League: A History of Minor League Baseball*. New York: Macmillan Publishing Co., Inc. (1975)

Ogden, August R. *The Dies Committee: A Study of the Special House Committee for the Investigation of Un-American Activities 1938–1944*. Washington: Catholic University of America Press (1965)

Olson, Lynne. *Those Angry Days: Roosevelt, Lindbergh, and America's Fight Over World War II, 1939–1941*. New York: Random House (2013)

Osborne, Robert. *80 Years of the Oscar: The Official History of the Academy Awards*. New York: Abbeville Press (2008)

Paige, Leroy (Satchel) (with David Lipman). *Maybe I'll Pitch Forever*. Lincoln: University of Nebraska Press (1993)

Patterson, James T. *Mr. Republican: A Biography of Robert A. Taft*. Boston: Houghton Mifflin Company (1972)

Pence, Richard A., ed. *The Next Greatest Thing*. Washington: The National Rural Electric Cooperative Association (1984)

Perrett, Geoffrey. *Days of Sadness, Years of Triumph: The American People 1939–1945*. New York: Coward, McCann & Geohegan Inc. (1973)

Peterson, Robert. *Only the Ball Was White: A History of Legendary Black Players and All-Black Professional Teams*. New York: Oxford University Press (1970)

Pietrusza, David. *Judge and Jury: The Life and Times of Judge Kenesaw Mountain Landis*. South Bend: Diamond Communications, Inc. (1998)

Pinney, Thomas. *A History of Wine in America from Prohibition to the Present*. Berkeley: University of California Press (2005)

Pleasants, Julian M. *Buncombe Bob: The Life and Times of Robert Rice Reynolds*. Chapel Hill: University of North Carolina Press (2000)

Pogue, Forrest C. *George C. Marshall: Ordeal and Hope: 1939–1942*. New York: The Viking Press (1966)

Price, Alfred. *Blitz on Britain 1939–45*. London: Ian Allen (1977)

Rader, Benjamin G. *American Sports: From the Age of Folk Games to the Age of Televised Sports*. Upper Saddle River: Prentice Hall (2004)

Rauch, Basil. *Roosevelt from Munich to Pearl Harbor: A Study in the Creation of a Foreign Policy*. New York: Creative Age Press (1950)

Reidenbaugh, Lowell. *Baseball's Hall of Fame: Cooperstown, Where the Legends Live Forever*. New York: Crescent Books (1993)

Reutter, Michael. *Sparrows Point: Making Steel*. New York: Summit Books (1988)

Roosevelt, Franklin D. *The Public Papers and Addresses of Franklin D. Roosevelt: Compiled with Special Material and Explanatory Notes by Samuel I. Rosenman: 1941 Volume: The Call to Battle Stations*. New York: Harper & Brothers Publishers (1950)

Rowsome, Frank, Jr. *The Verse by the Side of the Road: The Story of the* Burma Shave *Signs and Jingles*. Brattleboro: Stephen Greene Press (1965)

Rumer, Thomas A. *The American Legion: An Official History, 1919–1989*. New York: M. Evans and Company, Inc. (1990)

Salisbury, Harrison E. *The 900 Days: The Siege of Leningrad*. New York: Harper & Row (1969)

Schlesinger, Arthur M., Jr., and Roger Bruns (eds.). *Congress Investigates: A Documented History 1792–1974*. New York: Chelsea House Publishers (1975)

Schwarz, Jordan A. *Liberal: Adolph A. Berle and the Vision of an American Era*. New York: The Free Press (1987)

Segrave, Kerry. *Drive-In Theaters: A History from Their Inception in 1933*. Jefferson: McFarland & Company, Inc. (1992)

Seib, Philip. *Broadcasts from the Blitz: How Edward R. Murrow Helped Lead America into War*. Washington: Potomac Books, Inc. (2006)

Seidel, Michael. *Streak: Joe DiMaggio and the Summer of '41*. New York: McGraw Hill Book Company (1988)

Seidler, Hans. *Operation Barbarossa: Hitler's Invasion of Russia*. Barnsley: Pen and Sword (2010)

Shaw, Arnold. *Black Popular Music in America: From the Spiritual, Minstrels, and Ragtime to Soul, Disco, and Hip-Hop*. New York: Schirmer Books (1986)

Sheean, Vincent. *Dorothy and Red*. Boston: Houghton Mifflin Company (1963)

Sheed, Wilfrid. *Clare Boothe Luce*. New York: E. P. Dutton (1982)

Sherwood, Robert E. *Roosevelt and Hopkins: An Intimate History*. New York: Harper & Brothers (1948)

Shirer, William L. *Berlin Diary*. New York: Alfred A. Knopf (1941)

Simon, George T. *The Big Bands*. New York: Macmillan (1967)

Smiley, Jack. *Hash House Lingo*. Mineola: Dover Publications, Inc. (2012)

Smith, Amanda. *Newspaper Titan: The Infamous Life and Monumental Times of Cissy Patterson*. New York: Alfred A. Knopf (2011)

Smith, Denis Mack. *Mussolini*. New York: Alfred A. Knopf (1982)

Smith, George David. *From Monopoly to Competition: The Transformation of Alcoa, 1888–1986*. Cambridge: Cambridge University Press (1988)

Smith, Moses. *Koussevitzky*. New York: Allen, Towne, & Heath (1947)

Smith, Richard Norton. *The Colonel: The Life and Legend of Robert R. McCormick, 1880–1955*. New York: Houghton Mifflin Company (1997)

Snyder, Brad. *Beyond the Shadow of the Senators: The Untold Story of the Homestead Grays and the Integration of Baseball*. Chicago: Contemporary Books (2003)

Spring, Joel. *The American School, 1642–1985: Varieties of Historical Interpretation of the Foundation and Development of American Education*. New York: Longman (1986)

Stambler, Irwin, and Grelun Landon. *The Encyclopedia of Folk, Country and Western Music*. New York: St. Martin's Press (1983)

Swafford, Rosa Lee. *Wartime Record of Strikes and Lockouts 1940–1945: Study of the Number, Causes and Effects of Strikes During the Period of 1940–1945*. Washington: United States Government Printing Office (1946)

Swanberg, W. A. *Luce and His Empire*. New York: Charles Scribner's Sons (1972)

Swing, Raymond Gram. *Forerunners of American Fascism*. New York: Julian Messner, Inc. (1935)

Tuchman, Barbara W. *Stilwell and the American Experience in China, 1911–45*. New York: Macmillan (1971)

Turner, Lorenzo Dow. *Africanisms in the Gullah Dialect*. Chicago: University of Chicago Press (1949)

Urban, Wayne J., and Jennings L. Wagoner, Jr. *American Education: A History*. Boston: McGraw-Hill (2000)

Vaccaro, Mike. *1941: The Greatest Year in Sports*. New York: Doubleday (2007)

Valtin, Jan (Richard J. H. Krebs). *Out of the Night*. New York: Alliance Book Corporation (1941)

van der Vat, Dan. *The Atlantic Campaign: World War II's Great Struggle at Sea*. New York: Harper & Row (1988)

Van Natta, Don, Jr. *Wonder Girl: The Magnificent Sporting Life of Babe Didrikson Zaharias*. New York: Little, Brown and Company (2011)

Vogel, Stephen. *The Pentagon: A History*. New York: Random House (2007)

Voigt, David Quentin. *Baseball: An Illustrated History*. University Park: Pennsylvania State University Press (1987)

Wald, Elijah. *How the Beatles Destroyed Rock 'n' Roll: An Alternative History of American Popular Music*. New York: Oxford University Press (2009)

Waldrep, Christopher. *Lynching in America: A History in Documents*. New York: New York University Press (2006)

Walker, John. *National Gallery of Art, Washington, D. C.* New York: Harry N. Abrams (1975)

Waters, Ethel. *His Eye Is on the Sparrow*, Garden City: Doubleday & Company (1951)

Watson, Mark Skinner. *United States Army in World War II: The War Department: Chief of Staff: Prewar Plans and Preparations*. Washington: Historical Division, Department of the Army (1950)

Watts, Jill. *God, Harlem U.S. A.: The Father Divine Story*. Berkeley: University of California Press (1992)

Weintraub, Stanley. *Pearl Harbor Christmas: A World at War, December 1941*. Cambridge: Da Capo Press (2011)

Whitehead, Don. *The Dow Story: The History of the Dow Chemical Company*. New York: McGraw-Hill Book Company (1968)

Whittingham, Richard. *Rites of Autumn: The Story of College Football*. New York: The Free Press (2001)

Zetterling, Nicholas, and Michael Tamelander. *Bismarck: The Final Days of Germany's Greatest Battleship*. Philadelphia: Casemate (2009)

Zevin, B. D. (ed.). *Nothing to Fear: The Selected Addresses of Franklin Delano Roosevelt 1932–1945*. New York: Houghton Mifflin Company (1946)

JOURNAL ARTICLES

Anon. "... And the Migrants Kept Coming." *Fortune* XXIV, November 1941, pp. 102ff.

Armstrong, O. K. "Treason in the Textbooks." *The American Legion Magazine*, September, 1940, pp. 8–9, 51, 70–72

Bolles, Blair. "The Great Defense Migration." *Harpers Magazine* 183, October 1941, pp. 460–467

Breckinridge, Gerald. "Salesman No. 1." *The Saturday Evening Post*, May 24, 1941, pp. 10–11, 38–42

———. "Market Maker." *The Saturday Evening Post*, May 31, 1941, pp. 22–23, 116–118

Bromley, Dorothy Dunbar. "Education for College or for Life?" *Harpers Magazine* 182, March 1941, pp. 407–416

Bush, Douglas. "Scholars, Poor and Simple." *The Atlantic Monthly* 166.4, October 1940, pp. 498–503

Christensen, C. Lincoln. "The 1941 Carolina Maneuvers Found America Unprepared for a World Conflict." *World War II* 16.6, February 2002, pp. 18–21

Crockett, Ann L. "Lollipops vs. Learning" *The Saturday Evening Post*, March 16, 1940, pp. 29, 105–106

Daniel, Pete. "We are going to do away with these boys . . . .' *American Heritage* XXIII.3, April 1972, pp. 42–47, 100–101

Filene, Benjamin. "'Our Singing Country': John and Alan Lomax, Leadbelly, and the Construction of an American Past." *American Quarterly* 43, December 1991, pp. 602–624

Fleming, Thomas J. "The Political Machine II: A Case History: "I Am the Law." *American Heritage* XX.4, June 1969, pp. 32–48

Goode, James M. "Flying High: The Origin and Design of Washington National Airport." *Washington History* Vol. 1, No. 2, Fall 1989, pp. 4–25

Gurney, A. R., Jr. "The Dinner Party." *American Heritage* XXXIX.6, September/ October 1988, pp. 69–71

Harwood, Sharon Beischer. "'That Lady Engineer': B&O's Olive Dennis Set a Standard." *The Sentinel* Vol. 36, No. 3, Third Quarter 2014, pp. 17–26

Hellman, Geoffrey T. "Active Sparker." *The New Yorker*, April 19, 1941, pp. 21–6

Hollenbeck, Scott, and Maureen Keenan Kahr. "Ninety Years of Individual Income and Tax Statistics, 1916–2005." *Statistics of Income Bulletin*, Winter 2008, pp. 136–147

Howard, Joseph K. "The Montana Twins in Trouble?" *Harpers Magazine* 189, September 1944, pp. 334–342

Jenkins, Jeffrey A., and Justin Peck. "Building Toward Major Policy Change: Congressional Action on Civil Rights, 1941–1950." *Law and History Review*, Vol. 31, No. 1, February 2013

Knox, Frank, with Fletcher Pratt. "Ships, Men—and Bases: Secretary Knox Reports on the Navy." *The Saturday Evening Post*, April 5, 1941, pp. 16–17, 76–82

McBride, Ruth Q. "Old Masters in a New National Gallery." *The National Geographic Magazine* LXXVIII.1, July 1940, pp. 1–50

Marquis, Alice Goldfarb. "Written on the Wind: The Impact of Radio During the 1930s." *Journal of Contemporary History* 19.3, July 1984, pp. 385–415

Mattice, W. A. "The Weather of 1941 in the United States." *Monthly Weather Review* December 1941 [published February 1942], pp. 360–362

Obermeyer, Jeff. "War Games: The Business of Major League Baseball during World War II." *NINE: A Journal of Baseball History and Culture* 19.1, Fall 2010, pp. 1–27

Sandburg, Carl. "Lord Halifax on a Horse." *The Nation* 152.17, April 26, 1941, pp. 499–500

Sumner, Jim. "The Grandest Day in Duke Sports History: January 1, 1942: When the Rose Bowl Came to Duke." *Duke Sports Weekly*, January 1, 2007

Swaminathan, Anand. "The Proliferation of Specialist Organizations in the American Wine Industry, 1941–1990." *Administrative Science Quarterly* Vol. 40, No. 4, December 1995, pp. 653–680

ONLINE SOURCES

Anon. "1941: Rosemary LaPlanche, Los Angeles." missamerica.org (Miss America Organization) n.d. http://www.missamerica.org/our-miss-americas/1940/1941.aspx

Anon. "Hometown Boy." jimmy.org (The Jimmy Stewart Museum) 2006 http://www.jimmy.org/biography

Orlik, Peter B. "Music Licensing." museum.tv (Museum of Broadcast Communictions) n.d. http://www.museum.tv/eotvsection.php?entrycode=musiclicensi

Stack, Martin H. "A Concise History of Beer in America." EH.net (Economic History Association) 2010.02.01 http://eh.net/encyclopedia/article/stack.brewing.industry.history.us

Acknowledgments

A BOOK LIKE this is never a solo project, and I am pleased to thank the people who have provided assistance all along the way. My research could not have been completed without the help of the superb librarians at the Corriher-Linn-Black Library at Catawba College, the Transylvania County Public Library, and the Library of Congress. I also owe a special debt of gratitude to Robert E. Barton, whose editorial skills and acuity of judgment are matched only by his ability to spot my factual errors. Such errors as remain are all my responsibility.

The quotation from Yosuf Karsh (p. 307), taken from *Karsh Portfolio* (University of Toronto Press), is used by gracious permission of the Estate of Yosuf Karsh.

Of the photographs in the center section, most come from the Farm Security Administration and Office of War Information collections in the Library of Congress. The photograph of the P-40 Warhawk is by Tony Hisgett, licensed through Creative Commons. The photograph of the *Enterprise* is from the U. S. Navy and is now in the National Archives. The photograph of the *North Carolina* is from the U. S. Navy, Naval History and Heritage Command. The

Chevy Club Coupe is from RM Auctions, licensed through Creative Commons. The Southern Pacific train is from Audio-Visual Designs, licensed through Creative Commons. The Lockheed Super Electra is from William Zuk (public domain).

Index

Abbott, Bud, 38
Abbott, Charles, 57
Academic freedom and tenure, 66ff.
Academy Awards, viii, 31ff.
Ace, Goodman and Jane, 201
Acuff, Roy, 46
Adams, Franklin P., 203
Adams, William, 90
Agar, Herbert, 116
Air travel, x
Aircraft production, 233, 242f., 269
Allen, Fred, 202f.
Allen, Gracie, 203
Almanac Singers, 47, 291
Aluminum production, 233f., 251ff.
Amberg family, 270f.
America First Committee, 123f., 128ff.,
    135f., 141ff., 146f.
American Federation of Labor,
    8, 235ff.
American Medical Association, 26, 85
American Society of Composers,
    Authors, and Publishers, 39ff., 42,
    46, 51

Anaconda Copper Mining Company,
    19ff.
Anderson, Eddie, 202
Anderson, Judith, 53
Andrews Sisters, 38
Aosta, Duke of, 100
Arcaro, Eddie, 169f.
Argentia conference, 139ff., 224, 302
Ark Royal aircraft carrier, 96, 294
Arnall, Ellis, 69
Arnold, Edward, 301
Arnold, H. H., 140
Arnold, Thurman, 253f.
Astaire, Fred, 38
Atlantic Charter, 140f.
Auchinleck, Claude, 107
Augusta cruiser, 139
Autry, Gene, 38

Baer, Buddy, 172
Baer, Bugs, 154
Bagnold, Enid, 54
Bailey, Josiah, 15f.
Baker, George, 279, 282

Bankhead, Dan, 165
Bankhead, Tallulah, 54
Barbirolli, John, 48
Barham battleship, 294
Barker, Horton, 47
Barkley, Alben, 25, 126
Barnes, Donald , 161, 298
Barrymore, Lionel, 301
Baseball, x, 150ff.
Bases-for-destroyers, 122
Basie, Count, 44
Bates, Fred, 97
Baugh, Sammy, 166
Baukhage, H. R., 289f.
Bean, Guy, 264
Bean, Leon L., 264
Becker, William D., 29
Bellamy, Francis, 112
Benét, Stephen Vincent, 71, 90
Bennett, Constance, 286
Bennett, Harry, 243ff.
Benny, Jack, 146, 202f., 264
Bergman, Ingrid, 54
Berkshire Symphonic Festival, 49
Berle, Adolf A., 134
Berle, Milton, 38
Berlin, Irving, 43
Berlin, Isaiah, 286
Biddle, Francis, 78, 293f.
Bill of Rights, 299ff.
Billings, Henry, 59
Birmingham cruiser, 94
Bismarck battleship, vi, 93ff., 140, 295
Blaik, Red, 167
Bledsoe, Charles, 293
Blitz, 97f.
Block, Martin, 39
Bock, Fedor von, 110
Boothe, Clare, 113f.
Boudreau, Lou, 152, 160
Boyle, Joseph, 19
Braddock, James, 172
Branshaw, Charles E., 242f.

Breadon, Sam, 161
Breen, Joseph I., 35ff.
Brennan, Walter, 301
Brewster, Kingman, Jr., 123
Briggs, Dennis, 96
Broadcast Music, Inc., 39ff., 46
Brooke-Popham, Robert , 295
Broughton, J. Melville, 297
Brown, Cecil, 296
Browne, George, 239
Bruce, David K. E., 57
Budge, Don, 176
Bundles for Britain, 98, 114f.
Burman, Red, 172
Burma-Shave, 191
Burns, Bob, 202, 301
Burns, George, 203
Bush, Douglas, 70
Butts, Wally, 167
Byrd, Harry F., 12ff., 17

Caldwell, Harmon, 67
Calloway, Cab, 44
Campanella, Roy, 165
Cantor, Eddie, 52
Carle, Frankie, 43
Carreño, Mario, 58
Casey, Hugh, 158
Catroux, Georges, 108
Cerf, Bennett, 75
Cermak, Anton, 23
Chaffee, Adna, 229
Chamberlain, Neville, 73
Chandler, Walter, 18f.
Chaplin, Charles, 32
Chennault, Claire, 112f.
Chest protectors, 155, 316
Chiang Kai-shek, 112, 214
Christian, Charlie, 48
Christie, Agatha, 71
Churchill, Clementine, 114f.
Churchill, Winston, 72f., 92f., 101, 103, 108, 128, 140, 295, 302ff.

Civil rights, 11, 76ff., 216f., 292ff., 297f.
Civil Works Administration, 25
Civilian Conservation Corps, 16, 178
Clark, Bennett C., 123, 136, 209, 290
Clark, D. Worth, 137
Clark, Mark, 212
Clarke, Gilmore, 223
Clements, Carl, 242
Clinton, Larry, 43
Cocking, Walter D., 67f.
Collins, J. Lawton, 212
Committee to Defend America
    by Aiding the Allies (White
    Committee), 120, 129
Congress of Industrial Organizations,
    8, 236ff.
Conn, Billy, vi, 172ff.
Connolly, Tommy, 316
Cooper, Gary, 136
Copper collar, 20
Corwin, Norman, 200, 299f.
Costello, Lou, 38
Coughlin, Charles, 281
Coulter, Douglas, 200
Courthouse Ring, 13f.
Coward, Noël, 53
Cronin, A. J., 74
Cronin, Joe, 155
Crosby, Bing, 50, 202
Crosby, Bob, 41, 43
Cross, Milton, 51
Crowley, Leo, 276
Crump, Edward H., 12, 17ff.
Cunningham, Alan, 107
Cunningham, Sis, 47

da Graca, Marcelino, 279f., 282
Dali, Salvador, 59
Daly, John, 199
Danielovitch, Issur, 37
Darden, Colgate, 14
Darlan, François, 108
Davidson, Gar, 221
Davies, Marion, 284
Davis, Arthur Vining, 252

Davis, Benjamin O., 216
Davis, Benjamin O., Jr., 216f.
Davis, Bette, 36
Davis, Lawrence "Crash," 155
de Gaulle, Charles, 108, 306
Delano, Frederic, 223ff.
DeLoach, R. J. H., 67
DeMille, Cecil B., 199
Democratic National Convention,
    Chicago, 25f.
Dennis, Olive, 185
Depression, 6, 16, 177
Derringer, Paul, 157
Derwent, Clarence, 54
Deschler, Lewis, 127
Dewey, Thomas E., 5, 121, 227f.
DeWitt, John, 297
Dickey, Bill, 158
Dickman, Bernard F., 28f.
Dies, Martin, 7f., 69f., 286
DiMaggio, Joe 78, 150ff., 158, 173
Disney, Walter, 33
Donnell, Forrest C., 28f.
Dorazio, Gus, 172
Dorsetshire cruiser, 97
Dorsey Brothers, 41
Dorsey, Tommy, 43, 44
Douglas, Kirk, 37
Dow, Willard, 254, 289
Draft extension bill, 138f.
Drake, Alfred, 54
Dreyfuss, Henry 185
Drive-in theaters, 192f.
Drum, Hugh, 213f.
DuBois, W. E. B., 62
Dudley, Eleanor, 175
Duke of York battleship, 302
Durocher, Leo, 156, 164

Eads, Wendell, 169
Early, Steve, 145, 290, 302
Eberle, Ray, 43
Eden, Anthony, 101, 103
Eichelberger, Robert , 167
Eight-Year Study, 64

Eisenhower, Dwight D., vii, 211f., 289
Eldridge, Roy, 44
Ellington, Duke, 41, 44, 52
Emergency Committee to Defend
    America First, 123, 128ff., 135f.,
    141ff., 146f.
Enterprise aircraft carrier, 230
Erwin, Marcus, 16
Evans, Maurice, 53
Executive Order 8802, 83f.

Fadiman, Clifton, 203
Fairless, Benjamin, 250
Father Divine, 278f., 282
Federal Emergency Relief
    Administration , 25
Feller, Bob, 157f., 173, 289, 298
Finley, David, 57
Firestone, Idabelle (Mrs. Harvey), 51
Fish, Hamilton, 122, 128
Fitzgerald, Ella, 45
Fitzgerald, Geraldine , 54
Flatt, Lester, 47
Fontanne, Lynne, 32
Football, 165ff.
Ford, Edsel , 247
Ford, Henry, 243ff.
Ford, John, 32
Forester, C. S., 71
Foster, Rube, 164
Four Freedoms speech, 9f.
Frankensteen, Richard, 242
Freitag, Elmar, 242
Freyberg, Bernard, 106
Furtwängler, Wilhelm, 50

Gardner, Erle Stanley, 71
Gardner, O. Max, 12, 15ff., 17
Gariboldi, Italo, 98f., 102
Garner, John Nance, 2
Gehrig, Lou, 153, 154
George of Greece, 101
Geyer, Lee, 84
Gibson, Walter, 201
Gill, Brendan, 71

Glass, Carter, 223
Goddard, Paulette, 37
Godfrey, Arthur, 204
Goebbels, Josef, 92
Goldwyn, Samuel, 36, 37
Gomez, Lefty, 152, 173
Goodman, Benny, 41, 43, 44, 48
Gordon, Joe, 158
Grace, Charles M., (Daddy Grace)
    279f., 282
Grant, Maxwell, 201
Gray, Glen, 41
Graziani, Rodolfo, 98f., 102
Green, Paul, 53, 55
Green, William, 236f., 246f.
Greenberg, Hank, 158, 159f., 298
Greenberg, Joe, 159
Greenlee, Gus, 164
Greer destroyer, 142, 147
Gregory, Edmund, 220
Griffith, Clark, 298f.
Grimes, Burleigh, 156
Grimes, Oscar, 152
Griswold, Oscar, 213f.
Group Health Organization, 85
Grove, Lefty, 154
Groves, Leslie, 225
Gunther, John, 18, 73
Guthrie, Woody, 47f., 70, 291

Hague, Frank, 26
Hagy, Robert, 290
Haile Selassie, 100
Halifax, Viscount, 287
Hall, Edmond, 48
Hall, Vera, 47
Hamilton, Duke of, 91f.
Hamilton, Sylla, 67
Hampton, Lionel, 44
Hardwicke, Cedric, 54
Hare, Mary Hardwick, 176
Harridge, Will, 161
Harrison, George, 249
Hart, Moss, 53
Harvey, Fred, 185

Hayes, Frankie, 155
Hayes, Helen, 53
Hays, Lee, 47
Hays, William H., 34f.
Hearst, William Randolph, 33f., 284, 285
Henderson, Fletcher, 44
Henderson, Leon, 218, 257
Henie, Sonja, 38, 168
Henrich, Tommy, 158, 163
Herbert, Victor, 39
Herman, Woody, 38, 39, 43, 45
Herr, John, 215
Herrmann, Bernard, 301
Hershey, Lewis B., 243
Hess, Rudolf, 91f.
Highlander Folk School, 48, 69
Hill, F. Leroy, 243
Hillman, Sidney, 81, 83, 239
Hines, Earl, 44
Hitchcock, Alfred, 32
Hitler, Adolf, 32, 72, 92, 101, 104ff.,
    108, 109f., 119, 121, 128, 145, 148,
    180, 240, 280, 281, 291
Hoffa, Portland, 202f.
Hogan, Ben, 175
Hogue, Alexander, 59
Holiday, Billie, 45
Holland, Lancelot, 95
Holt, Homer, 11f.
Hood battle cruiser, 94f., 140
Hoover, J. Edgar, 173, 293
Hope, Bob, 32, 173, 202, 228f.
Hopkins, Harry, 25, 128, 221
Hopper, Hedda, 284f.
Horne, Lena, 44
Hornet aircraft carrier, 230
Horton, Myles, 69f.
Horton, Zilphia, 70
House Committee for the Investigation
    of Un-American Activities, 7f., 69
House, Son, 47
Hoving, Walter, 228
Huggins, Miller, 152f.
Hughes, Charles Evans, 2

Hull, Cordell, 127, 306
Hull, Merlin, 222
Huntington, Collis P., 195
Huntington, Henry, 195
Hurd, Peter, 59
Hurok, Sol, 48
Hurt, Mississippi John, 47
Huston, Walter, 301
Hutson, Don, 166

Icely, L. B., 176
Ickes, Harold, 256ff.
Illustrious aircraft carrier, 99
Indiana battleship, 230
Indomitable aircraft carrier, 295
Ingram, Rex, 52
Ink Spots, 45
Irvin, Monte, 165

James, Harry, 43
Jessel, George, 52
Johnson, Lyndon, 8
Jolson, Al, 38, 173
Jones, Ben, 168f.
Joseph, Eddie, 174
Joyce, Kenyon, 212
Jukebox, 42f., 205

Kaiser, Henry J., 231f.
Kaltenborn, H. V., 199
Kantor, MacKinlay, 71
Karsh, Yosuf, 306f.
Kauffman, Henrik de, 134
Kearney destroyer, 146f.
Keeler, Wee Willie, 151
Keller, Charlie, 158
Kelly, Edward J., 23ff.
Keltner, Ken, 152
Kennedy, John, 73
Kennedy, Joseph, 127
Kennedy, Thomas, 249f.
Kenton, Stan , 45f.
Kesselring, Joseph, 53
Keyser, Kay, 41

Kieran, John, 203
Kiesler, Hedwig, 35, 37
Kimbrough, John, 215
Kindler, Hans, 51
King George V battleship, 97
King, Mackenzie, 305
Kleferman, Albert H., 278
Klem, Bill , 316
Knight, Eric, 73f.
Knox, Frank, 83, 127, 131, 230f., 299
Knudsen, William, 83, 127
Koestler, Arthur, 74
Koryzis, Alexandros, 101, 105
Kress, Samuel H., 57f.
Krueger, Walter, 207, 209ff.
Krupa, Gene, 44
Kuhler, Otto, 185
Kuhn, Fritz, 7

La Guardia, Fiorello, 22f., 82f., 153
LaFollette, Robert, 123
Lamarr, Hedy, 35, 37
Lampell, Millard, 47
Landis, Kenesaw Mountain, 156, 162, 164, 298f.
LaPlanche, Rosemary, 229
Laski, Harold, 6f., 71
Lawrence, Jacob, 59
Layden, Elmer, 166
Leahy, Frank, 167
Lear, Benjamin, 207ff., 268
Ledbetter, Huddie, 47f., 70
Lee, Robert E., 223
Leeb, Wilhelm Ritter von, 110
LeGentilhomme, Paul, 108
Lend-Lease, 8, 18f., 124ff., 232
Leseur, Larry, 97
Levine, Philip, 270
Levinson, Nathan, 32
Levy, Marion Pauline, 37
Lewis, John L., 8, 236ff., 247ff.
Lewis, Meade Lux, 48
Lewis, William, 200, 299
Liberty ships, 232f.

Lincoln, Abraham, 260
Lindbergh, Charles, 127, 136, 141ff., 291
Livingstone, Mary, 202, 264
Locey, Percy, 297
Loewy, Raymond, 185
Lomax, Alan, 47
Lomax, Bess, 47
Lomax, John, 47
Lombardo, Guy, 39, 41
Longworth, Alice Roosevelt , 57, 123
Louis, Joe, vi, 171ff.
Luce, Clare Boothe, 113f.
Luce, Henry, 58f., 113f., 137, 146
Lunceford, Jimmie, 44
Lunt, Alfred, 32
Lütjens, Günther, 95ff.

MacArthur, Douglas, 291
Mack, Connie, 155
Mack, Ray, 152
MacLeish, Archibald, 301f.
MacPhail, Larry, 156
MacVane, John, 97
Magnesium production, 253f.
Mahoney, J. J., 142
Main, Marjorie, 301
Manchester cruiser, 94
Manella, Petassi, 102
Mann, Arthur, 97
Mannerheim, Carl, 110f.
Marble, Alice, 175
Marcantonio, Vito, 130
Marquand, John P., 74
Marshall, George C., 138, 140, 207, 212f., 219, 222
Marshall, Thurgood, vii, 11
Martin, Clarence E., 11f.
Martins, Maria, 59
Marty, Martin, 276
Marx, Harpo, 54
Mason, Benjamin, 275
Massachusetts battleship, 230
Matthews, J. B., 8

Maugham, W. Somerset, 59f.
Mayer, Louis B., 37, 284
McCarthy, Clem, 169
McCarthy, Joe, 173
McCormack, John, 126
McCormick, Robert R., 24, 124, 146, 148, 285
McDaniel, Lawrence, 28f.
McFarland, Ernest, 137f.
McGee, Fibber, 201
McGowan, Bill, 155
McKeever, Stephen, 156
McKellar, Kenneth, 19
McKinley, William, 1
McLean, Edward, 17
McLean, Evalyn Walsh, 17, 285f.
McLean, Evalyn Washington, 17, 285f.
McLean, Ned, 286
McLean, Washington, 286
McNair, Leslie, 207, 211f.
McNeil, Don, 197
McPherson, Aimee Semple, 280, 282
McShain, John, 225
Meany, George, 249
Medill, Joseph, 285
Mellon, Andrew W., 56ff.
Mellon, Paul, 57
Merman, Ethel, 146
Metaxas, Ioannis, 101
Metzler, Jost, 133
Meusel, Bob, 154
Miller, Glenn, 38, 39, 43, 298, 310
Milligan, Maurice, 27f.
Miranda, Carmen, 146
Mitchell, Arthur W., 76
Monroe, Bill, 46f.
Montana Power Company, 19ff.
Morgenthau, Henry, 127, 234, 301f.
Morris, Jimmy, 47
Morrison, Cameron, 15f.
Morshead, Leslie, 107
Mortimer, Wyndham, 242
Motels, 178ff.

Motion Picture Producers and Distributors of America (Hays Office), 34f.
Mulcahy, Hugh, 159
Muni, Paul, 37
Murphy, Frank, 79
Murphy, Johnny, 159
Murray, Philip, 238ff., 242, 249f.
Murrow, Edward R., v, 97f., 197, 289
Murrow, Janet, v, 98
Muse, Benjamin, 14
Muselier, Émile, 306
Mussolini, Benito, 32, 98ff., 280
Musto, Tony, 172
Myrdal, Gunnar, 62, 79f.

Nash, Patrick, 23f.
Nasi, Guglielmo, 100
National Association for the Advancement of Colored People, 11, 62, 82, 246
National Gallery of Art, 56ff.
National Guard, 122, 138, 208ff., 214, 226f.
Neame, Philip, 103, 107
Neely, Matthew, 11f.
Nelson, Donald, 257
Neutrality Acts, 117, 119, 145f.
New Deal, 5, 8, 85, 253, 258
Newsome, Dick, 151
Niemöller, Martin, 36
Norfolk cruiser, 94
North Carolina battleship, 229
Nye, Gerald, 122, 137 f., 290

O'Brien, Davey, 166
O'Brien, John P., 22, 27
O'Connor, Richard, 99, 102f., 107
O'Daniel, Lee, 8
O'Hara, Joshua, 34
O'Neill, Eugene, 54
Ocean Vanguard merchant ship, 232
Office of Civilian Defense, 23
Oil crisis, 255ff.

Oliver, Sy, 44
Ormandy, Eugene, 51
Otto of Austria, 188
Our Boots, 169
Outley, Hansen, 216
Overman, Lee, 15
Owen, Mickey, 158, 163

Page, O. T. "Hot Lips," 44
Paige, Satchel, 165
Paley, William, 197
Parker, Dorothy, 116
Parsons, Louella, 33, 284f., 287
Passeau, Claude, 153f.
Patrick Henry Liberty ship, 232f.
Patterson, Eleanor Medill (Cissy),
    148f., 285ff.
Patterson, Joseph, 148f., 285
Patterson, Robert, 83, 217, 222
Patton, George S., 211f., 229
Paul, Prince of Yugoslavia, 101, 104
Pearl Harbor, v, viii, 6, 23, 54, 100, 113,
    160, 161, 166, 217, 227f., 230f.,
    289ff., 293, 297, 299
Pearson, Drew, 286ff.
Peckinpaugh, Roger, 151
Pendergast, James, 28
Pendergast, Thomas, 27
Pershing, John J., 137
Pétain, Philippe, 306
Peter II of Yugoslavia, 101, 104
Philips, Thomas, 295f.
Phillips, Z. T., 57
Pipp, Wally, 152f.
Pittman, Marvin, 67f.
Pledge of Allegiance, 112
Poletti, Charles, 270
Poll tax, 84
Post, Wiley, 187
Potomac presidential yacht , 139
Pratt, Fletcher, 230
Price, James, 14
Prince of Wales battleship, 94f., 140,
    295f., 302

Prinz Eugen cruiser, 93, 140
Production Code Authority, 35ff.
Proust, Marcel, 71

Queen Elizabeth battleship, 294

Rainbow Five plans, 148f.
Randolph, A. Philip, 81ff.
Rauh, Joseph, 83
Reese, Pee Wee, 156
Regional differences, ix, 273ff.
Reiser, Pete, 156
Repulse battle cruiser, 295f.
Reuben James destroyer, 147
Reybold, Eugene, 222
Reynolds, Richard S., 251
Reynolds, Robert R., 4, 16f., 131, 286
Richelieu battleship, 94
Rickenbacker, Eddie, 186
Ritchie, Neil, 296
Rivera, Diego, 58
Rizzuto, Phil, 151f., 158f.
Robeson, Paul, 48
Robin Moor merchant ship, 133
Robinson, Bill "Bojangles," 146
Robinson, Edward G., 301
Rodney battleship, 97
Rogers, Billie, 45
Rogers, Ginger, 32
Rogers, Roy, 38
Rolfe, Red, 158
Rommel, Erwin, 107, 296
Roosevelt, Eleanor, 23, 36, 57, 82, 137, 218
Roosevelt, Franklin D., viii, 1ff., 5ff.,
    9f., 23ff., 31, 57, 71, 79, 82f., 87, 92,
    113, 118ff., 123, 124ff., 127ff., 131ff.,
    139ff., 146ff., 187, 219, 222ff., 234,
    236ff., 242, 246, 249f., 254f., 260f.,
    275, 276, 285, 290, 298ff., 302ff.
Roosevelt, James, 2, 36
Roosevelt, Theodore, 123
Rose Bowl, 166, 297f.
Rosenberg, Anna, 83
Rosier, Joseph, 12

Ross, Leonard Q., 69
Rundstedt, Gerd von, 110
Rural Electrification Administration, 88ff.
Ruth, Babe, 154

Saarinen, Eliel, 49
Sagone oiler, 294
Sandburg, Carl , 287
Sarnoff, David, 50
Saroyan, William, 52, 54
Schmeling, Max, 106, 171f.
Schmidt, Gottfried, 205
Schubert, Franz, 34
Scott, Charles L., 229
Seeger, Pete, 47f., 70
Selznick, David O., 31, 32, 35, 37, 54
Shaughnessy Plan, 162f.
Shaughnessy, Frank, 162
Shaw, Artie, 43, 44, 203
Shaw, George Bernard, 54
Sheffield cruiser, 96
Shelby Dynasty, 12, 15ff.
Sheppard, Morris, 8, 17
Sherwood, Robert, 116
Shirer, William L., 72
Simmons, Furnifold, 15
Simon, Abe, 172
Simović, Dušan, 104
Sinkwich, Frankie, 167
Sisler, George, 151
Slye, Leonard, 38
Smith, Al, 152
Smith, Kate, 43
Smith, Lonnie, 11
Smith, Tuck, 96
Somervell, Brehon, 220ff.
Sorensen, Charles, 244ff.
South Dakota battleship, 230
Spence, Stan, 151
Stalin, Joseph, 74, 109, 135f., 240
Stark, Harold, 140
Stark, Lloyd, 27ff.
Steel Seafarer merchant ship, 142

Steele, John, 97f.
Steelman, John, 250
Stein, Gertrude, 74f.
Stern, Arthur, 291
Stewart, James, 32 37, 301
Still, William Grant, 44
Stilwell, Joseph, 213
Stimson, Henry, 83, 127, 213, 219, 221f.
Stokowski, Leopold, 50, 301
Straw hat theater, 54
Stuart, R. Douglas, Jr., 122f.
Sturm, Johnny, 158
Suffolk cruiser, 94
Sugar Bowl, 19
Swing, Raymond Gram , 199

Tabor, Jim, 151
Taft, Robert, 121, 123, 138
Talmadge, Eugene, 66ff.
Tarkington, Booth, 71
Tatuta Maru merchant ship, 267
Taxes, vii, 261f., 266
Taylor, Myron C., 281
Tellera, Giuseppi, 103
Temple, Shirley, 8
Tennant, Eleanor, 175f.
Tennessee Valley Authority, 87f., 309
Thomas, Lowell, 199
Thomas, Norman, 127
Thompson, William H., 23
Thurber, James, 71
Tilden, Bill, 176
Tinkham, George, 148
Toolen, T. J., 281
Topping, Dan, 168
Toscanini, Arturo, 50
Tovey, John, 93ff.
Train travel, x, 181ff.
Triple Crown, 169ff.
Truman, Harry S., vii, 27, 209, 219ff., 252
Truman, Ralph, 208, 212
Tubb, Ernest, 46

Tuck, William, 14
Tucker, Sophie, 52
Two-Ocean Navy Act, 121, 230f.

United Confederate Veterans, 10
United Service Organizations for
    National Defense (U.S.O.), 228f.
Unlimited national emergency, 132f.

Valiant battleship, 294
Vallee, Rudy, 38, 301
Valtin, Jan, 73
Van Wagoner, Murray, 246
Vandenberg, Arthur, 121
Vaughn, Johnny, 234
Vittorio Veneto battleship, 103

Wade, Wallace, 297
Wales Latham, Natalie, 114f.
Walker, Dixie, 156
Walker, James J., 22
Wallace, Henry A., 2, 57, 286
Walsh, Thomas, 285
Walters, Bucky, 157
Wanger, Walter, 32
Waring, Fred, 42
Warner, Harry, 138
Warner, Pop, 167
Warnow, Mark, 43
Washington battleship, 230
Washington, Booker T., 62
Washington, George, 5, 305
Wasp aircraft carrier, 230
Waters, Ethel, 52
Watson, Thomas J., 258
Wavell, Archibald, 102f., 107
Webb, Chick, 45
Weil, Frank, 228
Weisenfreund, Meshilem Meier, 37
Welk, Lawrence, 41
Welles, Orson, 33f., 301
Welles, Sumner , 140

Wheeler, Burton, 19, 123, 128, 133,
    137, 146, 148, 306
Whirlaway, 168ff.
White, Josh, 47
White, Walter, 82, 246
White, William Allen, 120
Whitehurst, Sara A. (Mrs. John L.), 80f.
Whiteman, Paul, 42, 43, 203
Whitney, John Hay, 169
Widener, Joseph, 57
Williams, Aubrey, 83
Williams, Ben Ames, 71
Williams, Cootie, 44
Williams, Ted, 78, 151, 153ff., 158
Willkie, Wendell, 5, 121f., 137f., 238
Wilson, Henry, 105
Wilson, Teddy, 44
Wilson, Walter, 212f.
Wilson, Woodrow, 2
Winchell, Walter, 282ff., 287
Windsor, Duchess of, 74f.
Wood, Robert E., 123, 127, 141ff., 146,
    290
Woodrum, Clifton 221f.
Woollcott, Alex, 54
Works Progress Administration, 16, 25
Wray, Fay, 35, 54
Wright, Albert, 240
Wright, Richard, 53
Wright, Warren, 168f.
Wrigley, Phil, 161
Wyatt, Whitlow, 156, 159

York, Alvin, 136

Yorktown aircraft carrier, 230

Zaharias, Babe Didrikson, 175, 204
Zhukov, Georgi, 297
Zuppke, Bob, 167